Critical Web Design

Critical Web Design

xtine burrough and Owen Mundy

The MIT Press
Cambridge, Massachusetts
London, England

The MIT Press
Massachusetts Institute of Technology
77 Massachusetts Avenue
Cambridge, MA 02139
mitpress.mit.edu

The MIT Press would like to thank the anonymous peer reviewers who provided comments on drafts of this book. The generous work of academic experts is essential for establishing the authority and quality of our publications. We acknowledge with gratitude the contributions of these otherwise uncredited readers.

This book was set in Stone Serif and Stone Sans by Westchester Publishing Services. Printed and bound in the United States of America.

Cover image: Playables (Mario von Rickenbach and Michael Frei), Pointer, 2017, see pointer.playables.net

Library of Congress Cataloging-in-Publication Data
Names: burrough, xtine author | Mundy, Owen author
Title: Critical web design / xtine burrough and Owen Mundy.
Description: Cambridge, Massachusetts : The MIT Press, [2026] | Includes bibliographical references and index.
Identifiers: LCCN 2025044126 (print) | LCCN 2025044127 (ebook) | ISBN 9780262053167 paperback | ISBN 9780262053174 pdf | ISBN 9780262053181 epub
Subjects: LCSH: Web sites—Design | Critical theory
Classification: LCC TK5105.888 .B8557 2026 (print) | LCC TK5105.888 (ebook)
LC record available at https://lccn.loc.gov/2025044126
LC ebook record available at https://lccn.loc.gov/2025044127

EU Authorised Representative: Easy Access System Europe, Mustamäe tee 50, 10621 Tallinn, Estonia | Email: gpsr.requests@easproject.com

Contents

Acknowledgments

xtine burrough: When Owen asked me if I wanted to collaborate on this book, I really tried to convince him that he should go ahead and write it without me. I offered to write a preface. I offered to be a reviewer. In the end, I'm so happy he convinced me to be a coauthor. It has been a pleasure to collaborate, and I think this book conveys the spirit of collaboration. It is the work of two educators, artists, and thinkers. Thanks, Owen. I had a blast writing this with you. To my sons, Parker and Martin, thank you for always understanding when I'm on a deadline. And yes, we can order in tonight. The unwavering support of friends during these last few years, including Anne Balsamo, Amy Gurley, Sam Martin, Ashley + Stephen Plant, Kelly + Raj Rao, Sabrina Starnaman, Lucy H. G. Solomon, and Rachel Warner: "Thank you" barely captures the essence of my gratitude. I hold in my heart my teachers (artists and yogis) and try to pay forward lessons I have learned from you (Christopher James, Steve Kurtz, Sasha Patterson, Barbara Bannerman, and Paula Weithman). Finally, Avi Carmoega, you truly are filled with light, and I hope one day you might even follow those exercises in chapter 6. Tony Carmoega, I pass my light to you for always. Thank you for keeping me afloat.

Owen Mundy: xtine, thank you for joining me on this project. I've appreciated your collaboration. I am grateful to my partner, Joelle Dietrick, and our daughter, Sophia Mundy. Thank you for your inspiration, humor, and patience every day. Thank you to colleagues from whom I've learned so much about writing and teaching: Grant Kester, Mark Sample, Amy Alexander, Barbara Kruger, Jennifer Lynde Barker, Arthur Liou, Carol Henne, Phil Steinberg, and Shana Berger. I appreciate the insights of fellow artists and designers: Tim Schwartz, Ian Sienicki, Justin Rhoades, Rob Duarte, Chris Csíkszentmihályi, and Ryan Nole. Thank you to Kristen Eshleman, Suzanne Churchill, Fuji Lozada, Shireen Campbell, and other colleagues at Davidson College who worked on the Liberal Arts in Silicon Valley program. Thank you to: Lillian Milano, Lena NW,

Jesse Jackson, Rachel Rossin, Miguel Donado, Sarah Suttner, Tom Roff, David Yoder, and other students who provided valuable feedback and inspiration over the years I've been teaching this course. Finally, I send my love and appreciation to Joyce Mundy, for always believing in me and supporting my weird projects.

Owen and xtine would both like to thank Noah Springer, the MIT Press team, and reviewers for their help making this book a reality.

Introduction

> Designers . . . hack the present to create the conditions of the future.
> —Anne Balsamo

Context

"Critical design" is a phrase introduced by Anthony Dunne and Fiona Raby that seeks to challenge assumptions about the role that products play in everyday life. Similar to the form of social critique and questioning that scholars such as Karl Marx, members of the Frankfurt School, Michel Foucault, and others have put forward, critical design questions prevailing social values and asks how the privileged creative space of conceptual design can serve a utilitarian purpose.

Web design is a process that involves much more than the creation of graphics and "pictures under glass."[1] Ellen Lupton discusses the evolution of design considerations artists publishing on the internet face when she asks (in 1985), "How many ways will a document be output? How is the information organized and accessed? How is the user oriented within the document? Does the interface imitate a familiar environment . . . or does it try to develop a new 'vernacular' for an electronica culture?"[2]

Critical web design is our response to Lupton's last question. In turn, our classroom experiences motivated this book and the "vernacular," as Lupton calls it, that we use to encapsulate the information we include. Following the diversity we have witnessed across skills, interests, and outcomes in our classrooms, we are presenting critical web design (CWD) as a bridge across Dunne and Raby's design philosophies, subversive media and internet art, and hybrid practices such as critical making.

Critical Web Design, like critical design, employs a social usefulness to question, critique, and challenge the ways technology enters our lives. It reclaims the mechanisms, tools, and practices used to produce immeasurable coercive and commercial interfaces, harnessing the power of design and networked information to engage participants, provoke dialogue, and question preconceptions about the medium itself. This book focuses on a critical approach to the design and programming of responsive interfaces for the World Wide Web (WWW) that are functional, free to access, collaborative, and thought-provoking. However, since web interfaces react to more than devices, screen sizes, preferences, and actions, critical web design as a genre can include other forms such as mobile apps,[3] full-stack application development, software design, human-computer interaction, usability, and accessibility, to name a few.

The website **clickclickclick.click** is exemplary of this type of work (figure 0.1). It engages the user with a self-reflective and quantified narration of their mouse movements on the web page. The site tallies the untold and revealing information that can be gathered as a user hovers over a button, clicks, or drags their cursor across the page. Rather than feeling in command, the user begins to feel watched and controlled as their every action is documented and fed back to them in an ongoing text. This critique of gamification employed across web and application design relies on our knowledge of the increasing manipulation and remarketing of human attention. Yet it presents an

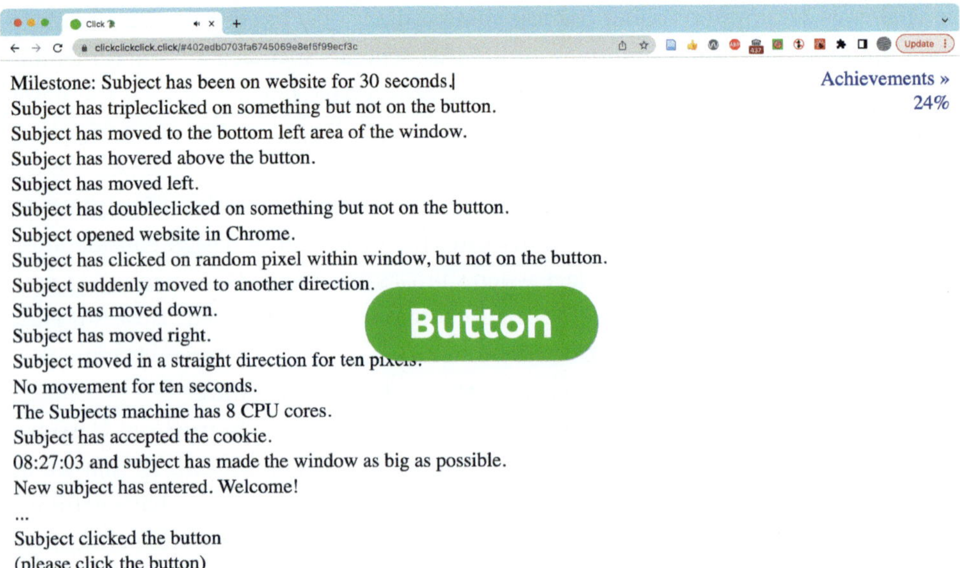

Figure 0.1
The website **clickclickclick.click** presents a simple button when it loads. Then a recorded voice and text in the interface slowly informs the user that their actions are not only being recorded but measured, scored, and represented as achievements.

alternative that is not only clever, enjoyable, and educational, but public, immediate, and free to use and appreciate by anyone with a networked device.

Author Note: Links

We are hosting links to important resources, references, and inspirational websites, organized by chapter, in the *Critical Web Design* wiki. Bookmark **criticalwebdesign.github.io#wiki** as a reference you can consult while reading and completing exercises in each chapter.

Critical Web Design Includes Diverse Creative Practices

We have been creating projects for audiences on the web since the early 2000s. There was a time when we introduced ourselves as internet artists—xtine's subversive coffeeshop finder project shows up as a case study in chapter 3 and Owen's worldwide cat catalog is a case study you can read about in chapter 9. However, as we mentioned, our students are hardly ever interested in learning only about "internet art." As it exists, "Art" is often not relatable to students who walk into our classrooms. Not all of our students aspire to become artists. And even if they did, the scope for "internet art," as defined by the art world's gatekeepers, is unusually narrow and exclusive. Rachel Greene explains in *Internet Art* that the presentation of online works alongside commercial websites, as well as their technicality, generally "does not reconcile with 'art' experiences like browsing in quiet galleries."[4] Likewise, the experiences students have had with "Art" prior to our classes don't encompass all the potential ways that creativity can be unleashed and appreciated on the internet as games, memes, live performances, and more. Or it could be, as Julian Stallabrass describes, that the art world places such high value on sales and "one-of-a-kind" works that it is impossible for physical art spaces to embrace online work that is infinitely reproducible, uses open-source code, and is free for everyone anytime.[5] Even agreeing on a definition of "Art" can be difficult, since subjectivity is so often emphasized in art programs, while works that incorporate utility are usually misunderstood and dismissed as commercial design.

But we'll let you in on a secret: Our students make art for the internet all the time. We hope they describe their work (and its contexts) however they like, and we prompt them to draw from as many sources as possible, incorporating an array of creative practices, perspectives, and methodologies to craft functional, thoughtful, and intentional web-based works. Thus, the material presented in this book is for artists, designers, makers, and anyone interested in communicating in text, media, and interactivity on the internet.

Perhaps unrelated to internet art, but tangential to critical design, is critical making. In *The Critical Makers Reader: (Un)learning Technology*, the editors Loes Bogers and Letizia

Chiappini explain that critical making "and related approaches like Critical Technical Practice [instead] seek to produce objects that uncover injustice, highlight discrimination, and point to issues of power such as gender inequality, surveillance, racism, and human rights."[6] They amend this with the directive that makers also "assess how one's own disciplinary framework and professional habitus might be contributing to such inequalities," which, in turn, "have consequences for the way we imagine, position, and organize physical spaces for making and whose agendas they should serve."[7] As critical web designers, we foster a creative practice that doesn't have to be shoehorned into a single academic field, art genre, or label and instead encompasses a way of thinking about designing and making experiences for the web. Maybe you are an internet artist or a critical maker or a graphic designer or an activist. Maybe you will be an entrepreneur or a journalist or a marketing whiz. Maybe you will incorporate methods from all of these roles into whatever unique trajectory you discover and this book is just one of the many stars in the constellation that forms your path to success in networked society.

Dunne and Raby note that there is more power when critical design is embedded in the everyday. They write about critical design,

> If it is too weird, it will be dismissed as art, and if too normal, it will be effortlessly assimilated. If it is labeled as art it is easier to deal with but if it remains design, it is more disturbing; it suggests that the everyday life as we know it could be different, that things could change.[8]

We encourage readers to answer the challenge set forth by Dunne and Raby to design works that "take on a social and possibly political role, combining the poetic, critical, and progressive by applying excessively imaginative thinking to seriously large-scale issues."[9] To do this, they suggest approaching design not from the angle of trying to fix or solve a problem, but instead as a speculative activity that expresses a dream of the future that could be possible—even in the face of problematic histories. In this way, they argue that speculative design is a "catalyst for . . . inspir[ing] imagination and a feeling that, if not exactly anything, more is definitely possible."[10] We, too, believe that more is possible, and our offering is to equip anyone who wants to engage in this practice with the methods, understanding, and tools required for critical web design. In summary, critical web design:

- can be found online and publicly accessible, to load, view, or install;
- is functional, usable, even utilitarian;
- may include things categorized as internet art, software activism, cultural production; and
- involves designed, not necessarily beautiful, but intentional interfaces, experiences, and thinking.

Who Is This Book For?

More than any other design or software development field, designing, coding, and publishing websites involves a diverse list of concepts, technologies, and practices. This book provides both a survey of and depth in these areas to give readers a solid and engaging introduction to creative production on the web.

You may have knowledge in some of the subjects we present in this book. For example, if you are an adept programmer in a non-web-based language or a computer science student with some knowledge of programming, you will find important perspectives and challenges in interface design. Or perhaps you are an artist with experience creating type and image relationships, but you are new to writing code. Regardless of your background, know that design is a process that requires time for thinking, feeling, and iterating. Anyone willing to follow our suggestions can be a designer if they slow down, create multiple versions of their layouts, and leave time between those versions to appreciate and incorporate new perspectives.

Design, on its own, is a large field of study—there are many resources we suggest in our bibliography (see the wiki) for readers who want to learn more. To create a cohesive reading and learning experience, we focus on a selection of core ideas and principles that relate to the objectives in each chapter. You might already have a strong background in design, and this book acknowledges that coding might seem mystical and complex. It is not. Computers seem smart, but they are far from sentient. They do what you tell them to, but it is up to you to find the best way to give them instructions. If you are a designer who wants to learn to code by connecting what you already know to the world of responsive mobile layouts, interactive JavaScript, and website production, this book will serve you well.

Finally, if you are an artist, or creative person not willing to take on that label, welcome. You will find the critical perspectives and experimental practices of this book to be familiar and helpful in preparing you to dive into making engaging, functional, and thoughtful works to publish on the internet.

Who Are We?

We are both artists who first came to interactive media design with industry experience that included commercial, institutional, and nonprofit clients as well as other experiences directing artistic, experimental, and educational projects. We are also educators who regularly teach a variety of students with different skill levels and backgrounds in interactive media design classes. We have taught at a liberal arts college, a STEM university, state universities, community colleges, and for-profit design institutions. We have taught thousands of students over the past twenty years. This book is an opportunity for us to organize and distribute our ideas for students we teach, and to share them with readers outside of the classroom.

The courses we teach have titles like "Critical Web Design," "Interactive Media Design," "Internet Studio," "Net Art," "Multimedia," and more. All of these course descriptions would include techniques for the creative production of projects that could be experienced in a web browser. Many of the course descriptions would also include an art-historical overview or an introduction to the history of science and technology as it relates to the WWW. These courses attract students with varying backgrounds and interests: Some became professional designers, others became professional artists, some are entrepreneurs, and many of them now work in other related industries such as marketing or journalism. Sometimes we felt like we were "sneaking" art education into a classroom that was designed (by someone else, usually an administrator) to address a bulleted list of techniques for creative decision-making across a variety of outcomes. The accumulation of these experiences has led us to balance our method for delivering the course that inspired this book with information across several disciplines: the history of the internet; examples of artworks made for viewing or interacting on the internet; foundations of design as they may apply to the production of visual projects for interaction online; issues central to designing media for online audiences, such as accessibility and inclusion; techniques for creating responsive interactive designs; design methods that encourage empathizing with users and prevent deceptive design; and design concepts that inspire contemporary projects, such as speculative design.

Module 0.1 How This Book Is Organized

Chapters are consistently organized so you can plan for how you work with sections and exercises in this book at home or in the classroom.

0.1.1 Context

Each chapter begins with a section called **Context**, in which we introduce the chapter's guiding ideas. In this section, we describe historical, political, and cultural information that expands an understanding of why to use the applied knowledge provided in the modules. We provide this for several reasons:

- First, creativity doesn't happen in a vacuum; it's often a messy business that benefits from knowing the world in multiple dimensions and perspectives.
- Second, history, ideas, culture, and politics may inspire the work that comes after; readers can implement skills from the technical modules that follow.

- Third, the more you know about the world can lead to empathy for others' situations, provide perspective on one's own good fortune, and ultimately, promote ethical use of the power contained in this book to create, design, code, and publish information for the world to see.

In *79 Short Essays on Design*, the commercial designer Michael Bierut explains how as a young designer, one of his first important lessons was a realization that he had failed on a project with his "empty-headed graphic design."[11] His perception of the layouts he created for a catalog of the work of visionary theater designer Robert Wilson changed drastically *after* he saw his first Wilson production. Bierut says his layouts failed to capture the epic and transcendent work of Wilson because he hadn't done his research; he wasn't aware of the contexts of the subject he was portraying. He concludes with this statement that we often relay to our students: "The more things you're interested in, the better your work will be."[12] The Context section ends with a case study in which we introduce the reader to someone who has influenced our thinking about the ideas presented within the section.

0.1.2 Modules

Modules follow the Context to guide readers through the diverse practices required for designing and coding web pages. These generally build on one another, and on knowledge presented in previous chapters, but can be referenced at any time as single components. Modules include section introductions, activities, callouts, and exercises, which are tutorials that readers or students may complete on their own or in groups.

The **technology** in the book is focused on making professional front-end development tools accessible to all. Readers will learn to write HTML, CSS, and JavaScript code; use common frameworks and libraries like Google Fonts, Bootstrap, and Faker.js; and publish content on the web with Git and GitHub. In later chapters, readers will use Node.js (a JavaScript runtime) to edit two introductory full-stack web projects: a web interface and API (application program interface) for fetching remote data and a dynamic website that uses a database and Leaflet to show user input on an interactive map.

0.1.3 Active Learning

In our classrooms and in this book, we use active learning wherever possible to keep students and readers engaged and involved in the learning process. As experienced educators, we know the benefits of "learning by doing" (instead of passively listening to a lecture) and see how it improves knowledge of the subject, critical thinking skills, problem-solving, and, perhaps most importantly, enthusiasm for the material. Thus, we employ learning activities throughout the modules for students/readers to reflect on material through writing and group discussion, provide analysis and evaluation through peer review, brainstorm and ideate to solve design problems, and apply their knowledge with hands-on technology instruction.

Prompts

Spanning all three modules are **prompts** that guide the reader in the making of interactive media informed by the Context presented in the introduction. These act as a connective tissue among the various parts of the text. While you can complete just one part, combining all prompts together encapsulates the learning objectives for the chapter. These prompts incorporate active learning methods for readers to learn by doing as they practice new skills and techniques in each chapter. We imagine them as in-class activities that may be continued at home as practice-based work with individual, student-/reader-driven outcomes. The first prompt serves as a place to see what you'll make as you work through the chapter exercises; and the last one, at the end of module 3, prompts the reader to extend the exercise and make the project their own.

We have included our own responses to the chapter prompts to demonstrate a range of outcomes that are accessible and exciting. The chapter prompts weave together the chapters' content, exercises, and learning objectives to ensure the flow and scaffolding of new ideas to accommodate various types of learners. You can see our outcomes in the *Critical Web Design* Git repository **github.com/criticalwebdesign/book**, which we recommend bookmarking as you read/work through this book.

Exercises

Exercises appear in the modules following the chapter prompt "What You'll Make." These include step-by-step instructions with code snippets and images documenting our process. We made these exercises as short and deliberate as possible so that they could easily be bookmarked and revisited as you are learning the essential methods for writing and publishing code for online audiences.

Activities

We intend this book to be an excellent classroom companion, and have already tested it in our own courses, though you will find that it works equally well for individual learners outside the classroom. In callouts throughout the chapters, you will find activities that benefit readers working alone, or in groups, in or outside the class environment, as well as through remote instruction, even asynchronously. These activities aid in the understanding of the materials but are not necessary for the construction of the chapter exercises.

Author Note: Activities and Exercises in the Classroom

If you are teaching a course, and you are short on time, you might consider assigning activities or exercises in class, and one or the other as homework assignments.

Callouts

Readers will find callouts throughout the book with the following headings: "Author Note," "Best Practices," "Inspiration," "Pro Tip," "Check Your Work," and "Watch Out!" At the start of each chapter, a callout encourages readers to explore the book's wiki for additional resources and content, and in the "What You'll Make" chapter prompt, readers are directed to the book's GitHub repo to find important chapter files and assets.

We tested selections of our exercises using artificial intelligence to showcase best practices, specifically with GitHub Copilot. You will find callouts regarding our successes and failures with AI in chapters 2 and 8. Other than these callouts, we did not use AI in the writing of this book. While it can be an enticing tool, we recommend learning the fundamentals before requesting AI for help so that you can make informed decisions about how you will use it.

0.1.4 Teaching Guide

We limited the content in this book to a focused set of chapters, but often we have students with diverse skill levels entering our classrooms whom we are accustomed to offering additional materials and activities. Some of the content we intended to include was pushed to **criticalwebdesign.github.io#wiki** and/or published in the teaching guide, which also contains examples of in-class demos and activities we have used in our own classes, hosted on the wiki and the MIT Press website. Some exercises are demonstrated in a series of videos also linked from the wiki.

0.1.5 Chapter Summaries

In *Design Writing Research*, Ellen Lupton and Abbot Miller explore the discipline of design in conversation with Michel Foucault's *The Archaeology of Knowledge*. In particular, they call forth Foucault's philosophical deconstruction of the book. Foucault writes,

> The frontiers of a book are never clear-cut: beyond the title, the first lines, and the last full stop, beyond its internal configuration, and its autonomous form, it is caught up in a system of references to other books, other texts, other sentences; it is a node within a network. . . . The book is not simply an object that one holds in one's hands; . . . it's unity is variable and relative. As soon as one questions that unity, it loses its self evidence; it indicates itself, constructs itself, only on the basis of a complex field of discourse.[13]

We are especially drawn to this way of thinking that relates books to critical web design as systems of references. To study the WWW and to learn how to design projects that can be seen and used in the browser is to get "caught up in a system of references" as you will understand the network as a distributed set of nodes that you will learn to reference, for instance, using absolute and relative paths to images and other resources from your pages. But more importantly, you will understand that across all chapters of this book and beyond the book's scope, we are presenting readers with a way to enter critical web design as a praxis—a philosophy put into action—that is variable and relative. Beyond these chapters, designed for delivery in a single course, we offer resources for further exploration and development.

This book balances descriptions of the practices of web design and development with the historical, theoretical, and political contexts around such tools and methods.

Chapter 1 begins with the origins of the internet, factors in the rise of the information age, and how the various impacts of networked computers can be understood by looking at other media revolutions. Likewise, we introduce foundational HTML elements for making web pages; Git version control, a workflow for editing, staging, and committing pages via GitHub Codespaces; and publishing a web page hosted by GitHub Pages.

In chapter 2 readers will learn about copyleft practices while reimagining a quote from a design manifesto as a work of concrete poetry in the browser using HTML, CSS, and JavaScript. Following the prompts in chapter 2, readers will choose a license for their manifesto/concrete poem and cite their source in the console.

Chapter 3 includes a contextual discussion of critical design and culture jamming to initiate a prompt for readers to create their own interactive subvertisement. The resulting web page allows viewers to hover over an image in the page and watch the message it makes change as an act of subversive interaction. Modules show how to use custom fonts via Google Fonts and incorporate additional styling through CSS.

Chapter 4 introduces readers to grid-based design, starting with a historical overview of the use of layout grids in printing with moveable type and concluding with grids for responsive design. The modules put this into practice, introducing frames and layout grids for desktop, tablet, and mobile devices in Figma; discussing content hierarchy using display and body type; and coding a simple responsive layout with the Bootstrap framework using lorem ipsum placeholder text to work across all devices.

In chapter 5 we introduce foundational design principles for usability, including focus, contrast, and negative space. We demonstrate how to create a usability test for a website, deliver the test, and reflect on the outcomes. The prompt for this chapter has students create their own usability test using professional standards and methods, implement this test with a friend or colleague, and design and code a responsive webpage showcasing a form that contains their reflections on the outcomes with recommendations for the site owner.

Chapter 6 takes the reader "off the grid," introducing them to historical experimental and expressive print-based layouts spearheaded by designers such as April Greiman and David Carson, as well as artists who collage, deconstruct, and use other methods both off- and online. The modules provide technical underpinnings for such experiments in web pages, explaining CSS transform and animation, and how to use JavaScript to change content and affect user experiences in the browser with loops.

In chapter 7 we turn to accessibility and inclusion as goals of ethical design. We explore and offer examples of "deceptive design" (formerly dark patterns), such as hidden costs, confirm shaming, and disguised ads, and discuss alternatives to such practices. Readers will learn how to identify and test for accessibility using the WAVE web accessibility evaluation tools, as well as best practices for coding with accessibility in mind.

In chapter 8 we explore generative design, looking at the loop as a computational construct that evades the human condition. That is, the loop allows a viewer a never-ending and no-way-out experience. Works by Amy Alexander, Allison Parrish, and Lauren Lee McCarthy influence exercises in the modules as readers create a playful *Generative Arp* website, riffing on a series of paintings by the Dada artist Jean Arp.

Chapter 9 focuses on data as part of the networked landscape that is surveilled, bought, and sold, including a discussion of cookies, browser fingerprinting, and advertising business models. The modules guide readers to create a *Bad Password API* front end. Readers can continue to create a full stack project using Node.js and Express using instructions on the wiki.

Chapter 10 discusses the power designers have to evoke participation and collective experiences. The modules show readers how to use tools to create a participatory experience combining interactive maps with a database. The printed book includes the front-end tutorials for creating *Big Feelings*, while, again, readers can head to the wiki to learn how to implement the full stack project.

Chapter 11 is the coda to this text. We offer readers places where they might exhibit or showcase works made using the skills they have learned throughout the book, as well as resources and advice for the labor market.

Module 0.2 Technical Requirements

You can use a Mac, Windows, or Linux desktop or laptop computer while working on prompts and exercises throughout this book. You will need reliable internet access, and you should be comfortable navigating your hard drive as you will save and refer to many new files you will create.

0.2.1 What Software Do I Need?

Most of the coding you will do in this book will be in HTML, CSS, and JavaScript. These are the three essential languages that work together to control (respectively) the structure, presentation, and behavior of web pages. While we recommend and will demonstrate how to use a source code editor to build and manage files for freestanding websites throughout the book, you should be familiar with using online code playgrounds to write and test HTML, CSS, and JavaScript.

We point to free or open-source software where possible throughout each chapter in this book. While our exercises will work with any source code editor, we demonstrate the exercises using **GitHub's Codespaces**. We have found that it greatly simplifies file management, version control, and publishing workflows for all types of new learners, including large undergraduate sections of the class.

For designing layouts and making and exporting images, we have included exercises that use the free (at the time of this writing) online software **Figma**. You will need an account to save your work, whether you use Figma primarily in the browser or download their desktop application. If you already know how to use Adobe products or their open-source counterparts, you are welcome to use them.

In addition to a code and image editor, you will need a **web browser** to preview and test your work. A browser is more than the software we use to access data on the internet. Browsers manage requests for hundreds of remote files on web servers, combine and render data from the responses as media-rich "web pages," and make these documents interactive to provide the essential hyperlink function that "connects" information on the internet.

Since the browser is the primary vehicle through which users will encounter your web pages, it follows that it is essential to test in the same environment. It would be overwhelming to check every page you build in all the different browsers, operating systems, and display sizes that are available to your users. Looking at the **user agent** (how browsers and other software that make internet requests identify themselves) market share graphs provided by Wikimedia[14] (figure 0.2), we can see that some browsers are more popular than others and should thus be prioritized when you test the pages you build. In the graph on the left, you can see that the most popular desktop browsers in order are Chrome, Other, Edge, Firefox, and Safari, while the mobile graph (right) shows that Chrome Mobile is the dominant browser, followed by Mobile Safari, Other, and Chrome Mobile OS. Note that the Other categories represent a large number of

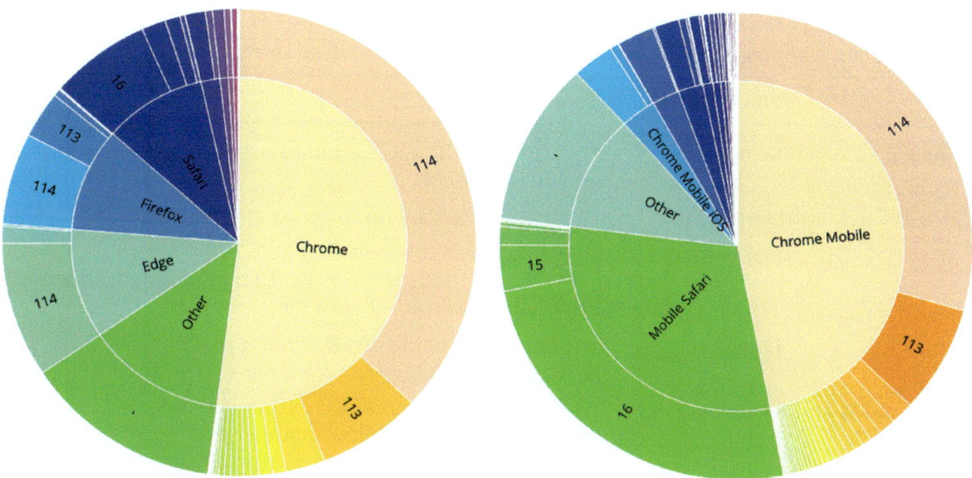

Figure 0.2
Wikimedia Foundation user agent breakdown **(analytics.wikimedia.org/dashboards/browsers)** by desktop (left) and mobile (right).

niche browsers, echoing what Chris Anderson referred to as "the long tail of the internet," encompassing all that exists beyond the most popular choices in mass culture.[15]

Other analytics tools like Statcounter[16] offer line charts showing how this statistic has changed over time, with clear losers like Internet Explorer (IE) and winners like Chrome. The ongoing competition for this usage share, or **browser wars**, is influenced by factors like how well the browser adheres to web standards, if the code used to create the software is open source, and whether the software is already installed on a user's computer.[17] So, the action item here is to install Chrome, Edge, and Firefox on your computer and Chrome on your phone. But perhaps just as important, especially given Chrome's dominance (for example, Edge for desktop and mobile are actually just restyled versions of Chromium, on which Chrome is based), is that you should test all your pages first in Chrome browser, and the others, before you publish the site. This is our recommendation and what we practice throughout the book.

0.2.2 Differences Between Mac and Windows Platforms

Anyone working on a computer can perform tasks much faster if they apply all five digits of their nondominant hand to the work in front of them. This is why we always show students how to use **key commands** in the classroom from the outset of the term. Also known as "keyboard shortcuts," or "keystrokes," every software you will encounter shows these more efficient methods next to the name of the command in

Table 0.1
Common key commands for Mac, Windows, and Linux operating systems

Mac	Windows/Linux	Description
Finder	Explorer	The name for the application to navigate files and folders on your filesystem.
Dock	Start menu	The main system menu to access apps, settings, and files.
Ctl+click	Right+click	Open a **contextual menu**. Right-clicking a mouse works on both, but we thought it was worth mentioning for users of Apple laptops, which do not have two buttons.
Return key	Enter key	The key to add a line break or run a command in the terminal or console.
Command ⌘ key	Control key	These keys, when combined with other keys on your keyboard (e.g., Ctl+s) allow quick access to common tasks.
Option key	ALT key	Additional keys used to combine with others to perform common tasks.
Command +Shift+4	Windows key + Print Screen key	Create a screenshot.

the menu. We encourage you to always look for and use key commands to make completing the exercises in this book easier.

As we discussed above, one can use any computer for creating websites. We will write for the Mac operating system (MacOS), but we want to keep instructions from overwhelming the content of the book, so we're including table 0.1 to help readers map all Mac terms, key commands, and so on, to their equivalent on Windows and Linux machines. You will find that most common key commands, for example saving a file, can be performed on Mac (Command+S) or Windows and Linux (Control+S) by simply swapping the Command key for the Control key.

0.2.3 Why Not React, Angular, or Taco?

We haven't mentioned any (currently) popular front-end frameworks. Many tutorials on YouTube and Google focus on using tools like React, Angular, and Taco. These projects are built by big tech companies to maintain complex websites, packed with bells and whistles, and appear to make creating websites almost effortless, even magical. But you should know:

- We advise you to be suspicious any time you see people flocking to the "next big thing." Why? By definition, **trends come and go**. The recent billionaire-ego-inspired Twitter disaster is proof that these tools are only as stable as the companies that support them. For example, ever heard of an NFT (non-fungible token)? How about

Beanie Babies? The fanciful names of today's fashionable framework (like the "Taco" framework we fabricated in the section title) will eventually fade.

- The open technologies that power the web are intended to let you choose how you want to create websites. Projects like Facebook's React create **vendor lock-in**, confining you to a proprietary ecosystem that requires you to do everything their way. This teaches you not to code using the *best* tool, but to create using *their* tool. And this dependency ultimately manifests loyalty to companies that you may or may not want to support. Throughout the book we show when there are good alternatives to help readers internalize this consideration.
- These tools are **complex to use**—they are built to power enormous applications (e.g., Google Docs), involve a lengthy setup, and have a complicated build process—even though many output plain HTML/CSS/JS. Referencing documentation is confusing because they can be vastly different across releases. Publishing is also murky, often costly, and can cause your entire project to fail because of a single misplaced comma.
- React, Angular, Shiny, and other **frameworks hide and abstract the underlying code** so much that when you get stuck, you are seriously stuck unless you know the fundamentals of HTML/CSS/JS.
- We do introduce several technologies on which the so-called modern web is built. The command line, DevTools, ES6, Node/NPM, JavaScript object notation (JSON), Leaflet, APIs, and databases are just some of the tools that we discuss.
- Perhaps the most important reason this book is **focused on the foundations** of designing and coding for the web is because we want readers to come away with a solid understanding of how the web works. A firm grounding in the lasting technologies and principles can be applied to nearly any tool, computer language, or technology field. For example, e-books are coded in HTML/CSS, most cross platform desktop and mobile apps use HTML/CSS/JS, and the principles of responsive design and usability apply to interfaces across the web, game development, and screens in cars, household appliances, and electronic billboards.

Exercise 0.2.1 Get Free Software and Accounts

Install the following free software on your computer.

1. Download the Chrome web browser: **google.com/chrome**.
2. Create a GitHub account: **github.com**.
3. Create a Figma account and install the desktop app: **figma.com**.

Module 0.3 Conventions and Resources

This final module addresses essential information about conventions we are using and where to find additional resources you will use in concert with this text. We employ typographic styles to alert readers to important words and code examples throughout the book using the following rules:

1. New terms are set in bold the first time they are used throughout the book, such as: A **website** is simply a collection of text files and images that are stored on a computer and available to download and view by users.
2. When we refer to code examples throughout the book, like HTML, CSS, or JavaScript, we use a monospace font. For example, you will create a basic web page in chapter 1, and it looks like:

```
<html>
<head>
  <title>Hello, World!</title>
</head>
<body>
Hello, World!
</body>
</html>
```

3. When you update a code sample, the previously written code will be gray so that you know what is new content. For example, wrap "Hello, World!" in an `<h1>` tag:

```
<body>
  <h1>Hello, World!</h1>
</body>
```

4. The text you enter into the command line and browser console exercises will also be shown using a monospace font, such as:

```
alert("Hello, World!");
```

0.3.1 CWD Resources

Here are the primary links referred to in chapter exercises throughout the book:

- Starting in chapter 1 you will use GitHub.com to set up your own repository and host your live web page and GitHub Codespaces to edit your code. You can find all our examples and exercise assets in the *Critical Web Design* book repository **github.com/criticalwebdesign/book** on GitHub.

- The repo also includes a discussions section where you can share your work and see what other readers have created. If you find an issue with the code in the book, you can find a fix on the errata page or submit an issue to let us know about a new problem.
- The book's wiki **criticalwebdesign.github.io#wiki** hosts additional exercises, images, and resources for each chapter. You should bookmark it!
- In chapters 3–10 we provide Figma templates you can use, as well as finished files.
- We often refer to online documentation. Our favorite is the Mozilla Developer site (see the wiki), but there are other resources like StackOverflow, **stackoverflow.com**, which are good for locating examples and discussions on coding.

Author Note: AI

As we acknowledge several times throughout this text, the technology and practices used to build websites are in constant flux. At present, in addition to the myriad technologies used to build front and backends, the emergence of code-enabled Large Language Models (LLMs) like ChatGPT, Gemini, and Claude adds new questions and challenges.

We can't stress enough how important it is that you read this book before you dive into AI tools. The more you let an AI write code for you, especially code you don't understand, the more you will become dependent upon those tools. Not only are you financially liable, unless you have an understanding of the foundational web technologies we present you will spend much more time attempting to guide and modify generated code past AI-slop and into something that matches your vision. See our guide for more information about possibilities and best practices around the use of AI **criticalwebdesign.github.io#ai**

1 Networks

> Cyberspace. A consensual hallucination experienced daily by billions of legitimate operators, in every nation, by children being taught mathematical concepts. . . . A graphic representation of data abstracted from the banks of every computer in the human system. Unthinkable complexity. Lines of light ranged in the nonspace of the mind, clusters and constellation of data. Like city lights, receding.
>
> —William Gibson

Context

The origin story of the internet reveals much about the medium you are about to explore. Often used interchangeably, the terms "**internet**" and "**World Wide Web**" (WWW) are not synonymous. Instead, imagine the internet as the plumbing—the series of physical connections and protocols that make possible the transmission of data (water in our metaphor). If the internet is the network of pipes, the WWW is the faucet, or the interface to the data that is transmitted. This includes your web browser and the text, media, and hyperlinks the browser renders as a clickable interface. You can technically use a web browser without being connected to the internet, and alternatively you could transmit data across a network without using a browser. However, together they are a powerful combination—with the "pipes" of the internet, including routers, undersea cables, and functionality being essential to the WWW—to be able to offer instantaneous access to seemingly unlimited information with the click of a button.

Keywords: Common Terms

A **website** is simply a collection of text files and images stored on a computer and available to download and view by users. The web browser is a **client** that **requests** and downloads these files from a **server** (another computer on the internet) and then renders the **response** as a clickable web page. An app on your phone is another example of a client that can download and display information. A client displays the website **front end**, or the aspects that users see and interact with. While live websites are stored on servers, many also have a **back end**, which includes server-side scripts, databases, and other resources needed to create dynamic web pages that can store and display user input and other data. For example, YouTube.com has a front end where you watch videos and a back end that stores user comments and encodes videos, among other functions.

The technology of the internet is essential to understanding its history. Consider the ability to connect and transmit data by each node (the circles) in the three networks represented in figure 1.1. Which nodes have more power than others to include or exclude information?

There are many different versions of the internet's history and the underlying technologies that make it possible. Bruce Sterling and others suggest that the internet exists today because of contributions from pioneers of science and technology made toward the security of American interests.[1] This popular account centers the role played by the US government and the RAND corporation, a research and development think tank created at the beginning of the Cold War. RAND identified issues with the centralized networks of the day, especially the potential for disruptions to occur if one of the

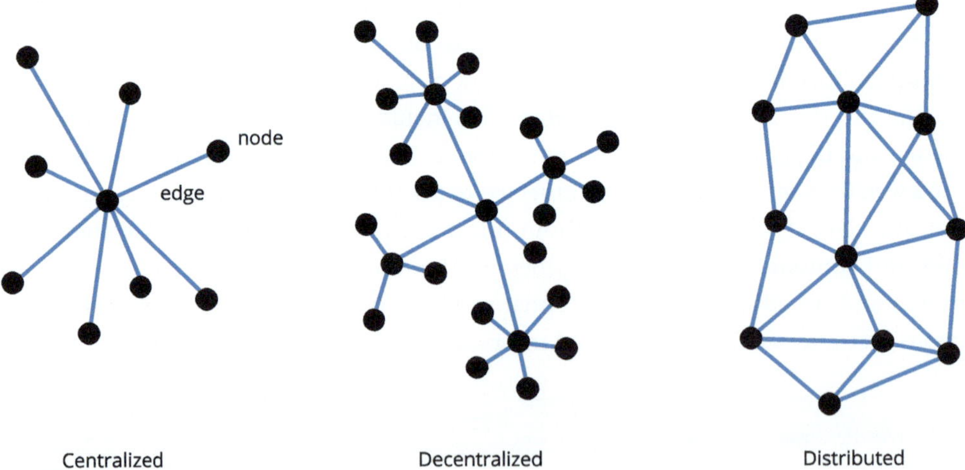

Figure 1.1
Visual representations of centralized, decentralized, and distributed networks.

Additional Materials and Resources

Explore links and other content related to this chapter:
criticalwebdesign.github.io#wiki-01

important nodes was destroyed. A centralized network creates a hierarchy among the locations in the network by routing all communication through pipes (or "edges") that depend on a single node. The more connections a node has, the more power it has over how information flows in the network.

RAND envisioned a new network structure to ensure connections between important nodes on a communications network in the event of a nuclear strike. Unlike centralized networks, where a disabled central node disrupts all communication, RAND imagined a network with no central authority. ARPANET, a distributed network, was a new framework for communication technologies first conceived in 1960 (figure 1.2).

Author Note: Network Structures

We encounter a mix of both decentralized and distributed network structures today. If you are reading this in a computer lab, you are connected to a smaller network of other computers in a lab or building. Similar to a decentralized model, your connection to the **subnet** sends and receives data via a "switch" that transmits information out to the internet. You may also have considered that websites create networks through hyperlinks to other sites. While the internet is generally distributed, and the ideas you code into websites throughout this book have an equal chance of being seen as Amazon.com, search engines like Google often prioritize and direct users to the most popular (usually commercial) sites. Additionally, a separate **dark web** exists with content that can be accessed only using special web browsers and protocols.

The internet as we know it is made possible through several key technologies that enable the transmission of data through its nodes. In **packet switching**, files are broken into small chunks of data, called packets, sent using the fastest route through the network, and reassembled into the original files at their destination. Depending on the anticipated speed of connections at the moment, parts of a file might even take separate routes.

While proving to be a more durable method for communication, there were other unplanned effects of the "flattening" caused by the removal of the hierarchy of nodes of the centralized network. Almost immediately after the internet started to function,

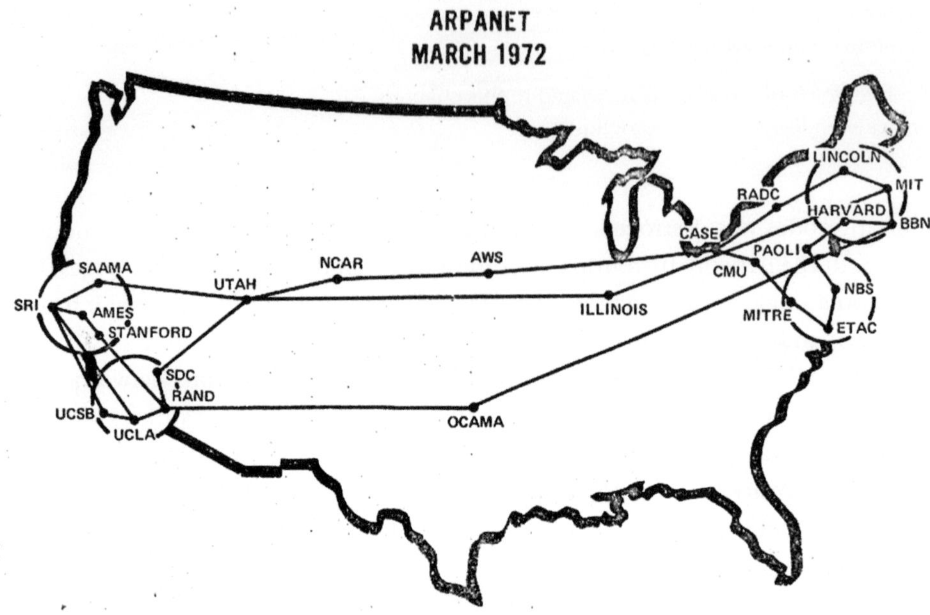

Figure 1.2
"Arpanet 1972 Map" by UCLA and BBN is licensed under CC BY-SA 4.0.

people began to use it for non-work purposes such as mailing lists and sharing knowledge. In 1993 Bruce Sterling wrote, "The internet is a rare example of a true, modern, functional anarchy." To his point, there is still no single company that governs or controls the internet. Sterling went on to point out, "There are no official censors, no bosses, no board of directors, no stockholders."[2] While this remains true, we have also seen the rise of capital and the power that comes with it centrally located in Silicon Valley over the past twenty years.

However, for every story, there are counternarratives, resistance movements, and alternatives. To be engaged in critical web design is to understand the history of the internet as one that has multiple stories, actors, and possible outcomes. In the early 1970s, the People's Computer Company held an ethos of what we would refer to now as "hacking." The founders Dennis Allison, Bob Albrecht, and George Firedrake published a newsletter, then a journal, that advocated learning through play, teaching others to manage, tinker, and open technology as a mode of forward progression. In their first (1972) introduction, they wrote, "Computers are mostly used against people instead of for people; used to control people instead of to free them; Time to change all that—we need a . . . People's Computer Company."[3]

Media Revolutions

The move from a centralized system to a distributed system of information flow echoes other important shifts in media history. For example, in the fifteenth century Johannes Gutenberg introduced his moveable type printing system. This new technology made it affordable to reproduce and access literature, causing literacy rates to explode across Europe.[4] Like the days before the printing press, even in the 1980s, unless you worked for the military or a large research institution, access to the internet was economically and technically prohibitive since computers at the time were expensive and still required knowledge of command line programming.

Hypertext is text displayed with clickable references, known as **hyperlinks**, to other resources (pages, files, or images, for example) that readers can access. The first hypertext project was conceived by Ted Nelson in the 1960s for Project Xanadu, though it never took hold. In a 1995 *Wired* magazine story, Gary Wolf writes, "Xanadu, a global hypertext publishing system, is the longest-running vaporware story in the history of the computer industry. It has been in development for more than 30 years."[5] Nelson's hypertext enabled text documents to be displayed on a computer and accessed via links from other texts. Hypertext is an essential aspect of the modern internet and WWW. A variety of similar systems have been proposed and influence what we use today, such as the Memex system to index, search, and link content using microfilm, proposed by Vannevar Bush in 1945. It was in 1989 that Tim Berners-Lee's system of hypertext, including an HTTP server and WWW browser, created the resources that enabled the entire world to quickly access information at any time.

While hypertext is often used to navigate from page to page or resource to resource, early internet artworks transformed the didactic nature of the "link" into a poetic interaction. "Hypertext poetry" is seen in works that date back to Olia Lialina's *My Boyfriend Came Back from the War* (1996). This work of early "net.art" made such a splash in the context of art on the web that more than a decade later remixes of the original project can be viewed on *The Last Real Net Art Museum* (hosted by Lialina). Contemporary artists create games with hypertext, such as Mark Sample's interactive fiction *Content Moderator*. This game was made with Twine, an open-source software tool used to create hypertext games and interactive fiction.

Power and Networks

Written well after Ted Nelson's ideas for hypertext as a two-way contextualized form of communication, Manuel Castells's influential 2009 publication *Communication Power* outlines four types of power evidenced in the network that has become common experience on the WWW. With an understanding that power is relational, asymmetric, and mutable (because resistance is possible), Castells offers these four types of power in networks:

1. Networking power (who/what is included)
2. Network power (a structural understanding of the power inherent to the protocols and standards)
3. Networked power (certain nodes have more power than others in the network)
4. Network-making power (the power those who set up the networks have over those who use the network)

While you are learning to create markup language and transfer data to a public web page throughout this chapter, you should be aware that doing the basic activities outlined here—the fundamentals of creating usable interfaces to information on the web—puts you in a position of power.

Safiya Umoja Noble is a contemporary internet studies scholar whose research clarifies how technologies, software, and hardware reflect the values that are enmeshed in society. Her 2018 book *Algorithms of Oppression: How Search Engines Reinforce Racism* unpacks the many ways that the structure of the internet and the code developed for our most common usages, such as Google's search engine, carry forward the agenda of white supremacy. While we encourage you to use the Chrome browser in the making and viewing of your work, we also encourage you to rethink networking, network, networked, and network-making power in the projects and designs you create. Who are they for? Who is included or excluded? How does your work amplify, criticize, or acknowledge its role in the matrix of nodes on the internet? What network-making power do you (or don't you) have as the creator and publisher of your work?

Case Study: Josh On, TheyRule.net

JO: My name is Josh On (he/him). I live in San Francisco, California, where I work as a designer. I also call my personal work "design"; it covers a wide range of things from kids' apps to political sites. I like to go back and forth between design tools—mostly Figma today, and code—mostly JavaScript (removing for redundancy). My favorite designs online right now are the React Three Fiber demos, **r3f.docs.pmnd.rs/getting-started/examples**, which are ostensibly utilitarian but are some of the most beautiful interactive experiences on the web. I love that you can open them and fork them—truly in the spirit of sharing and everything good about web 1.0.

Describe *They Rule* in your own words.

JO: *They Rule* is an interactive visualization of the interlocking directories of the largest US companies. It shows that eighty-seven of the top one hundred US companies in 2021 were connected through shared directors on their boards. It allows visitors to browse through the boardroom connections and create maps that they can share with others.

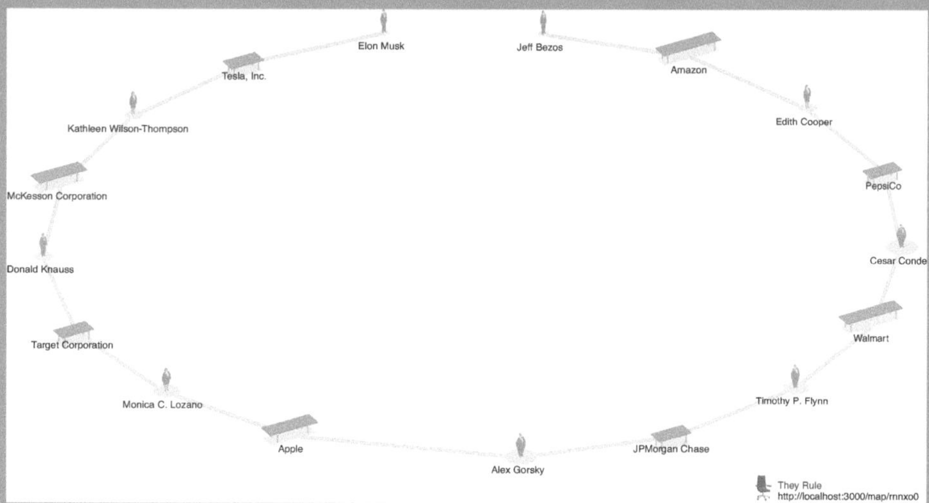

Figure 1.3

Josh On, *They Rule* (2023). The connections between Elon Musk and Jeff Bezos on TheyRule.net.

How does this project speak to the way that networks enable power structures?

JO: That is a little on the nose for this project! By browsing through these boardroom connections, it opens many questions about how power is distributed in society. I originally made the site to assert the idea that there is a ruling class in the United States, even if this just presents a glimpse of it. I explain my thinking more here: **theyrule.net/so_what**.

Could you explain the choices regarding the technology you used in the different versions of this project?

JO: I originally made this in Flash—because at the time (2001) that is what I was familiar with, and it would have been difficult to make an SVG version of the site that worked well across all browsers. This time (2022) I made it using React Three Fiber—a JavaScript framework that helps produce 3D graphics on a canvas. I store the data locally and on Wikidata, which is a wonderful project.

Prompt 1 What You'll Make
Create and Publish Your First Web Page

In this chapter you will create and publish your first web page using GitHub Codespaces. In addition to "Hello, World," you will search the *Critical Web Design* index, **criticalwebdesign.github.io/index**, then display links to works that inspire you (figure 1.4).

View the results of our webpage showing works that inspire us at **criticalwebdesign.github.io#1-3**. You can see the final code for every chapter on the CWD repo, **criticalwebdesign.github.io#repo**.

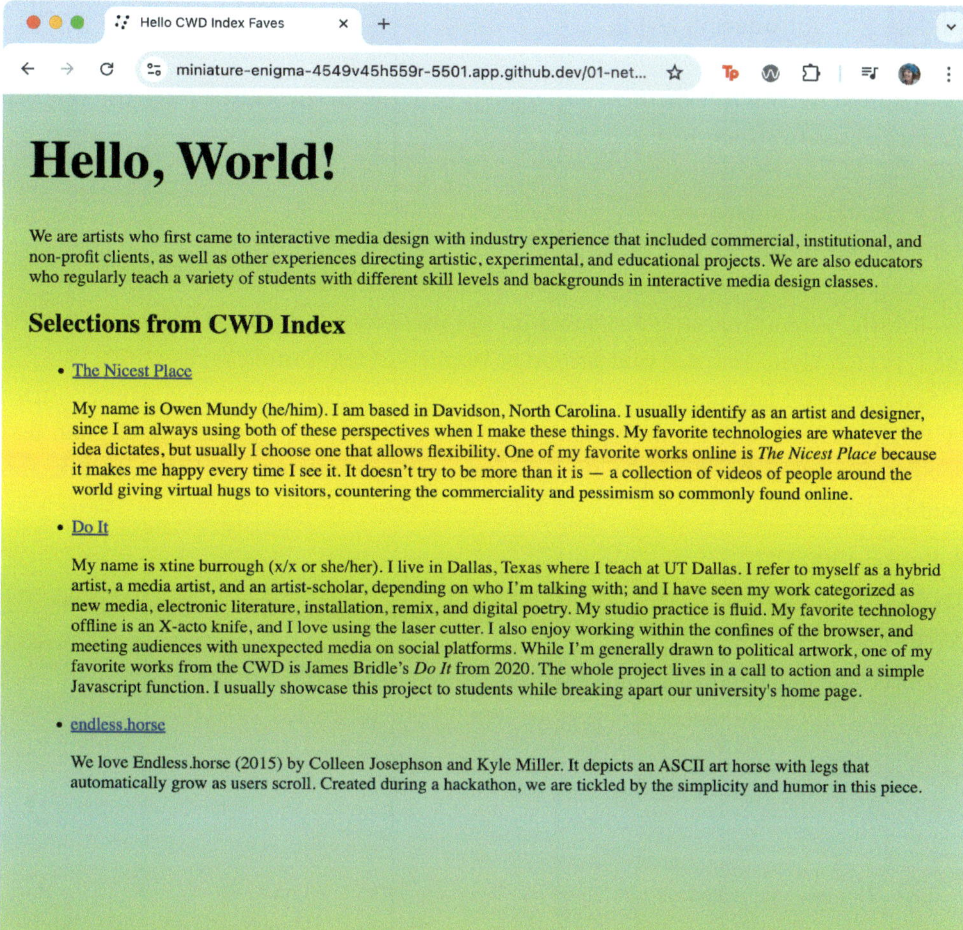

Figure 1.4

After finishing the modules, we made a web page with some of our biographical information and selections we chose from the *Critical Web Design* index. We added a background gradient color, increased the size of the heading, and added margins to the web page. View our code in the repo to see how!

Module 1.1 Introducing HTML

In this module you'll learn how to create a basic webpage with HTML, the markup language used to structure and display content for the web.

1.1.1 Markup Languages

A **markup language** structures, formats, and/or defines text through special characters that can be read by both humans and computers. The term comes from traditional publishing, where "marking up" a manuscript involves adding annotations to indicate the typeface, style, and size that should be applied to text during typesetting.

Some markup languages, like **Markdown** (used on GitHub et al.) and wikitext (used by Wikipedia) are focused on making it easy to add rich text formatting to plain text documents online. For example, the following will be displayed as a heading, link, and bold text, respectively.

```
# Hello, World!
[a link](https://criticalwebdesign.github.io/book)
**This is bold text**
```

Other markup languages, like **XML**, structure and define content so that data contained within can be saved, accessed, or sent across networks.

> **History: The HTML Living Standard**
>
> Like software, markup languages also use **version numbers** to keep track of supported features. The last major release of the HTML language was HTML5, in 2019. Since then, the World Wide Web Consortium (W3C) and the Web Hypertext Application Technology Working Group (WHATWG) have worked together to define a single HTML Living Standard. Code standards are essential to help you know which tags and media are supported in which browsers,[6] let you use code validators to check your work,[7] and give you access to the documentation,[8] even the actual (very detailed) language specification.[9]

1.1.2 HTML

HTML (HyperText Markup Language) is the markup language used to structure and display text and media in web pages. Content in HTML (similar to XML) is structured using **elements**. An HTML element consists of an **opening tag**, followed by text or other tags, followed by a **closing tag** (figure 1.5).

HTML elements define how browsers **render** (the process of interpreting and displaying) the content on the page. For example, a block of text is denoted as a paragraph

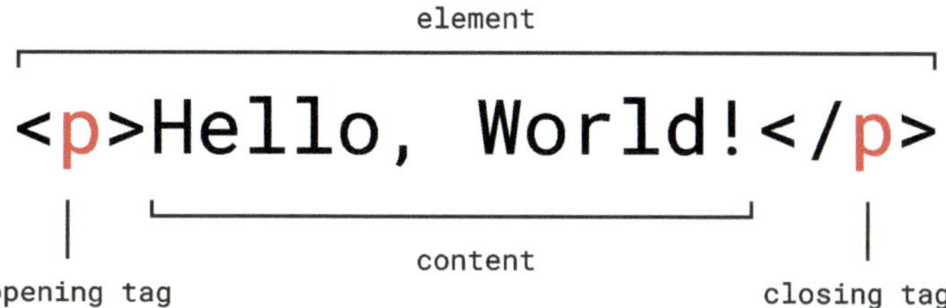

Figure 1.5
This diagram shows the structure of an HTML element, including the opening tag, content contained within, and the closing tag. Tags use predefined names between a less than and greater than sign.

HTML document · head · body

```
<html>
    <head>
        <title>The title</title>
    </head>
    <body>
        <p>Hello, World!</p>
    </body>
</html>
```

Figure 1.6
This diagram shows the required structure of an HTML document.

in HTML code when it is surrounded by the opening paragraph tag, `<p>` and the closing paragraph tag `</p>`. Every opening tag must be closed, with the exception of a small list of **void elements** like `<br>`, `<hr>`, and `<img>`, which do not require a closing tag and cannot have child elements.[10]

1.1.3 HTML Anatomy

The `<html></html>` element is the **root element** that encloses all other tags in an HTML page (figure 1.6). Inside the opening `<html>` and closing `</html>` tags are the `<head>` and `<body>` sections. The `<head>` is the part of the page used to display meta content about the page, like the title which is wrapped inside `<title>` and `</title>`. All visible content on the page is placed between the opening `<body>` and closing `</body>` tags.

1.1.4 Development Environments

While web pages are created using HTML, CSS, and JavaScript, there are many ways you can write and publish them. Below we list some common **development environments** that combine the tools and processes that let you build and publish web pages on the WWW.

- **Code playgrounds** like **codepen.io** (see the first exercise) make it easy to experiment with web publishing and quickly share your results.
- **GitHub Codespaces** (which you will use throughout this book) is a web editor based on Visual Studio (VS) Code. It is easy to manage file versions with Git (an industry standard for version control and document collaboration on the web) and publish documents to the web using GitHub Pages. Used by newcomers and professionals alike, Codespaces is free for students and teachers, requires no software installation, and is accessible for new learners.
- **VS Code + Git + GitHub:** If you are already familiar with coding or version control, or you have long-term goals in web development, we encourage you to adapt the workflow we present by installing the VS Code editor and Git on your local machine. See the wiki to learn to set up a project with Git and GitHub Desktop to allow you to build and test websites on your own computer.
- Combining a development environment capable of implementing Node.js utilities with cloud-based build and publishing tools allows for multiple **advanced full-stack workflows.** Using Node in Codespaces or on your own machine can greatly simplify building full-stack sites and even mobile apps with back ends and databases. Web development is a fast-moving world, where platforms disappear[11] as quickly as they emerge, so we explore the fundamentals in the printed book in chapters 9 and 10 and provide up-to-date introductions for applying those skills on the wiki.

While all of our tutorials can be built and published using any of these workflows, note that we prioritize writing code by hand over a WYSIWYG editor (see callout) because these fundamental tools will always exist and give you the most control over the medium. Additionally, know that you can try installing Git on your own machine and using it with VS Code any time. The more ways you know how to publish web pages the more likely you'll choose the best method for your current project.

> **Author Note: WYSIWYG**
>
> A **WYSIWYG (What You See Is What You Get)** editor describes software tools—for example, Dreamweaver's Design View, Wordpress, or Wix—that let you edit code through a visual interface. These tools often leave users frustrated because clicking and dragging boxes doesn't deliver the detailed control that actually learning HTML and CSS code provides.

Exercise 1.1.1 Hello, World! with Codepen

Code playgrounds like **codepen.io** make it easy to test and share HTML, CSS, and JavaScript in a "web environment."

1. In Chrome, go to **codepen.io**.
2. Click "Start Coding." You will see an area where you can type HTML, CSS, and JavaScript, as well as a preview window containing the outcome of your work. Codepen includes the required document structure so you can focus on adding content to the page.
3. HTML is the language that structures the content of web pages. Type the following code into the HTML section. Codepen will automatically refresh the preview window to show your updates.

```
<h1>Hello, World!</h1>
```

Author Note: Code Block Typography

Blocks of code we write in our exercise instructions will appear in monospace typeface throughout this book. When you see `this typeface`, we are instructing you to write code that matches ours in your editor. Code from previous steps is set in light gray to help you place the new code in the correct order.

4. Type the following code into the CSS section. As you can see, CSS is the language that controls the presentation of web pages.

```
h1 {color: hotpink;}
```

5. Type the following code into the JavaScript section. JavaScript is the language used to control the behavior of web pages. Click the **Console** button to see the output from **console.log();**.

```
console.log("Hello, World!");
```

6. We use **codepen.io** sporadically throughout this book. Feel free to continue experimenting or look through their examples. Create a free account to save your work.

1.1.5 Nested Elements and White Space

Nested elements (elements contained inside other elements) are an essential part of writing HTML. For example, adding a hyperlink to a heading requires you to nest the `<a>` tag inside the `<h2>` element (figure 1.6). The most important rule to nesting is that each tag should be closed before you close their parent tag. Like a set of stacking dolls that must be assembled before they can be fit inside the next larger doll, nested

```
<a href="#"><h2>Incorrect nesting</a></h2>

<h2><a href="#">Correct nesting</a></h2>

<h2>
    <a href="#">Correct nesting (with whitespace!)</a>
</h2>
```

Figure 1.7
The first line shows incorrect nesting (the `<a>` tag is closed before the `<h2>`). The second line shows the proper structure. The third shows how to use whitespace (the enclosed tag is tabbed over) with nesting to make the code readable and easier to see if there are nesting problems.

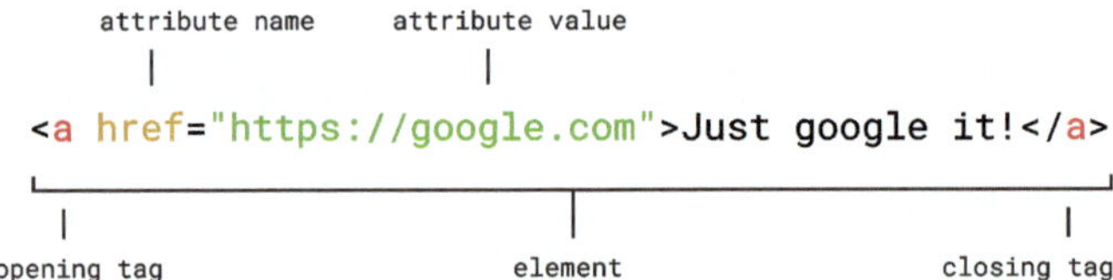

Figure 1.8
An anchor tag with an **href** attribute. The attribute value can be wrapped in single or double quotes.

elements have an order by which they must be opened and closed. If a browser can't interpret your code because of improper nesting, it may not be able to display content to your users. In figure 1.7 you can see how **whitespace** (spaces, tabs, line breaks, and other hidden characters) can be added to your document to make visually clear which elements are children of enclosing parent elements. When a browser renders your page, all whitespace is collapsed and shown as just a single space, making it a helpful way to see if you have formatted your HTML correctly.

1.1.6 HTML Attributes

HTML attributes add information to modify the behavior of tags. Attributes almost always have a name and value (figure 1.8). For example, an `<a>` (anchor) tag adds a hyperlink to the page but requires the `href` attribute to provide a destination for the link, while an `<img>` tag will display an image using the `src` attribute, which provides a path to the image file. Tags can also have multiple attributes. For instance, the `<a>` tag can also include a `target` attribute, which lets you open links in a new window. See MDN, "HTML Elements Reference" for more elements and attributes.[12]

Prompt 1.1 Design Research: CWD Index

Visit the *CWD Index* **criticalwebdesign.github.io/index** for inspirational works of critical web design. Select three coded projects that represent your interests, aspirations, and passions. Add the `<a>` tag with the `href` attribute to the Codepen above to create a link to the projects you selected. Remember that nested elements must be closed in the reverse order in which they are opened.

Module 1.2 File Paths and Version Control

This module introduces concepts for locating pages and assets in and outside your project, then turns to version control, an essential tool for web development.

An **IP address** is a numerical label used to identify and connect devices to the internet.[13] Assigned by your Wi-Fi router or internet service provider (ISP), it is required before your device can send data through the network. For example, if you open Chrome and search "what is my ip" the result will be a number that looks like this: 64.233.177.104.

Each IP address is unique but not easy to remember. For example, type the address above into a web browser and press return. It should take you to Google.com. However, it would be painful to type that every time you wanted to conduct a search. A **domain name**, such as "Google.com," is a human-readable string of characters that points to an IP address or web host. While easier to recall than the numbers in an IP address, domain names must be resolved via the domain name system (DNS) to learn the IP address of the **web host**, the device or server where all the files for the website are stored.[14] If you go to **lookup.icann.org**, you can run a **whois** search for a domain name and see the owner of a domain name, the date they registered it, and the **nameservers**, which translate human-friendly domain names (like "Google.com") into numerical IP addresses.

Throughout chapters in this book, you will publish your web pages on GitHub Pages. This free web hosting makes your content available to the world through a subdomain using your username like: **yourusername.github.io**. You can also purchase a domain name, such as yourname.com, to use with GitHub. Since our aim is to make learning critical web design as accessible as possible, we suggest waiting to purchase a domain name and hosting until after you have developed a foundational understanding of how the web works.

1.2.1 File Paths

Throughout this book you will be editing and testing many different types of files and organizing them into folders. One of the first things you should know is that a **folder** and **directory** are the same thing. When working with web servers you may see one name used more than the other, but these terms are interchangeable.

The files you create while completing exercises in this book will each have a specific **file path**, or address, to describe the location where they are stored on your computer. A path consists of the names of all the containing folders, separated by forward slashes, until the name of the file itself.

⚠ Watch Out!

The Windows operating system shows nested file paths using a backslash character \. This will not work on the WWW, which requires a forward slash / for nested files and folders. Windows users should watch out for this when copying and pasting a file path. You can install an extension to fix this (explained in module 1.3).

Best Practices: WWW Naming Conventions

Whenever you are creating or referencing files or folders for the Web you should always use standard internet **naming conventions** to make the names easier to read and reference in your code:

- Always use lowercase letters. The internet is case sensitive. If you try to reference a file named `cat.png` using title case `Cat.png` you will see an error message instead.
- Don't use spaces or other special characters. Some special characters like forward slashes and colons will be rejected by your computer. Others, like spaces, can make it difficult for web browsers to reference a file. Best practices advise that you should replace any character that is not alphanumeric (letters and numbers) with a hyphen or underscore to make it readable by humans and software.
- Always end the name of the file with its extension such as .jpg, .png, or .html.
- Be descriptive. Use file names that accurately describe the content.

1.2.2 Why Do You Need Version Control?

Imagine you want to update a website with a new feature. You aren't sure if you will like the changes you made, so you duplicate your project folder. This way you can go back to the previous files if you (or maybe your client) change your mind. You make all your new edits in the duplicate files, so if you don't like them, you can just delete that folder to "undo." Your system works so well (since you practice iterative design!) you make a second and third iteration of the new feature to test those, too.

Testing is going great, but while working on one of those iterations you find a bug, which itself takes two iterations to fix. You now have six different project folders, each with many different changed files. But you realize you want to keep some

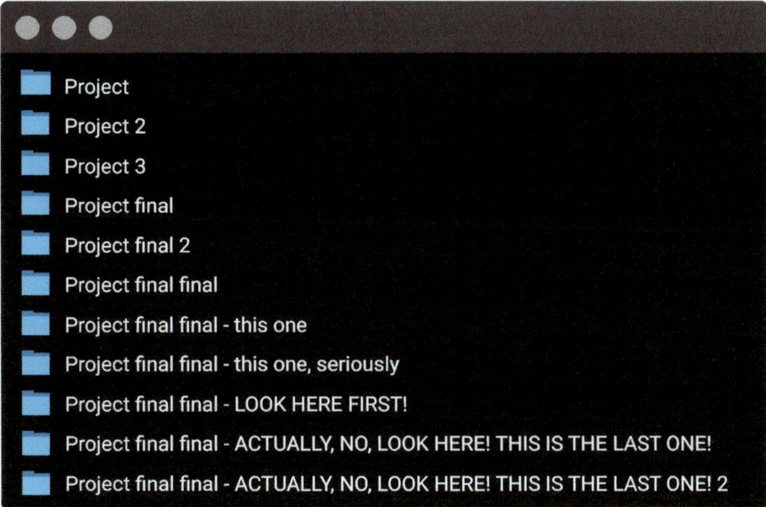

Figure 1.9
Without version control to manage iterations and changes, your project folder may need to employ some creative naming conventions.

changes from several different folders (figure 1.9). Do you see any challenges in this story?

What if you must work on something else for a few weeks and then come back to the project after taking such a break. How will you know which is the most up-to-date version of the files? What if you want to keep just some of the changed files from the third iteration, and some from the bug fix? In other words, what if you want to keep only some changes in some of the files? How would you know which files to integrate back into your project? What if you need to integrate some changes, from some files, from different collaborators?

1.2.3 Version Control to the Rescue

All of these "What if" situations are realities for people who code projects for the web browser. If you are reading this book and working on a project that will be published in a web browser, you will be the protagonist in our hypothetical story. But there is good news, **version control** provides solutions for the problems we've described. With a version control system, you can review changes to documents over time, manage changes you want to keep, and track and name the versions you create. Version control also lets you incorporate work from collaborators, automate the integration of your updates with others', and much, much more.

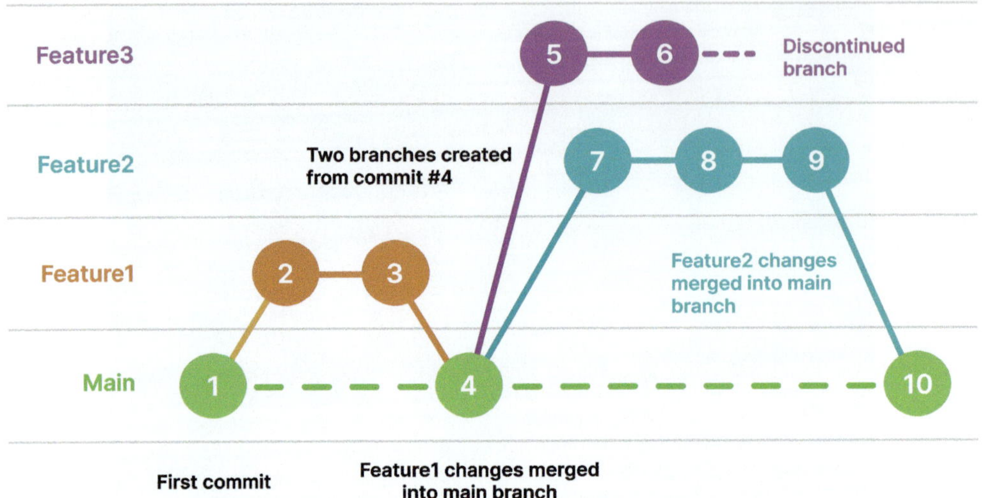

Figure 1.10
Git uses the concept of branches to let multiple creators add features to a project asynchronously, and then it automatically merges the changes (in this case, each numbered commit) into the project for you.

1.2.4 About Git Version Control

Git is a free and open-source distributed version control system, and it is the one we will be using in this book. A Git project is called a **repository** (or "repo"). Git offers a manageable way to collaborate while maintaining control over many versions of a project and its parts. Saving sets of changes to one or more files is called a **commit.**

Git uses **branches** to give you or your collaborators a space to develop features, much like the story about copying the project folder. However, unlike our story, branches or even parts of branches can be merged back to the main project branch. By default, each repo contains a main branch (figure 1.10). When you (or a collaborator) add a new feature, you create a new development branch so that you can preview the whole project as you make changes. When the changes or new features are ready, you perform a **merge**, which automatically integrates all updated files into the main branch and checks for any conflicts in your new edits.

Speaking of collaborators, **GitHub** is a place to share code repositories. Developers **push** their commits to a single code repository and **pull** the changes that others make. Git keeps track of who made the changes and merges the changes together so that everyone can edit the same code. Other code repositories include BitBucket and GitLab.

In our story, we had to remember which folders held parts of the project that were different or places where we had fixed bugs. Git handles this for you, and offers additional commands, such as:

- You can see file-level changes before each commit (or in your history) using **diff** (as in "different")—to see what was updated, deleted, or added in a single file, or the whole project.
- To view the history of work performed in your project, use Git **log**, which lists each commit, the text you added to describe the commit, and the commit date.

Exercise 1.2.1 How to Set Up a New Web Project with Git

This exercise establishes best practices for setting up a new website project, including the **index.html** page, and tracking and publishing with Git. While you are working through this book, you will create a new repository for the prompt in each chapter. This allows you to publish individual projects with unique URLs and keep your files organized. See the wiki for a video demonstration of this exercise.

1. Login or create an account at **GitHub.com**.
2. Click the **plus** button at the top right of your page to create a **New Repository**.
3. Name the repository "hello-world" and enable "Add README."
4. Click "Create repository."
5. Click "Add file" to create a new file in your **hello-world** repo, and name it "index.html" (without the quotes).
6. Add the html, head, and body elements that define the structure of an HTML file. Your code should look like the following:

```
<html>
<head>
    <title>Hello, World!</title>
</head>
<body>
    <h1>Hello, World!</h1>
</body>
</html>
```

7. Return to your **codepen.io** project from module 1.1 and copy the code you wrote in response to prompt 1.1 creating links to inspirational works of critical web design. Paste this code into your **index.html** file below the heading. It might look like the following—notice we used the line break tag `<br>` to create a new line for each link:

```
    <h1>Hello, World!</h1>
    <a href="https://anatomyof.ai">anatomyof.ai</a> <br>
```

```
        <a href="http://endless.horse">endless.horse</a> <br>
        <a href="https://thezen.zone">thezen.zone</a> <br>
    </body>
```

8. Press **Commit changes . . .** and add a commit message about your changes, such as "Create new file." Press Commit and the code you added to your file will be saved. You can verify this under the History tab.

Congratulations! Not only have you created your first web page; you have also completed a basic Git workflow to edit and commit changes to a repository. In the next exercise you will set up GitHub Pages to publish this site to the WWW.

Pro Tip: Work on Your Computer with GitHub Desktop.

You can download website projects to your computer from **GitHub.com** using GitHub Desktop. See the wiki to learn how.

Exercise 1.2.2 Enable GitHub Pages

GitHub Pages is a service that lets you publish web pages for the world to see. In this exercise you will publish the contents of your repo as a live website. See the wiki for a video demonstration of this exercise.

1. Go to your `hello-world` repo page on **github.com**, click **Settings** from the top menu, then select **Pages** from the side menu.
2. Under the "Build and Deployment" heading ensure the Source option is set to "Deploy from branch."
3. Choose the **main** branch and press the **Save** button (figure 1.11). You only need to do this once to publish your site in each repository, as GitHub will republish it automatically each time you push commits to the repo. Note that you may need to wait a few minutes before changes you push are redeployed.
4. To view your published website, click **Code** from the top menu to return to the main page of the repo. Under the **Deployments** section in the callout, you should now have an "Active" deployment. Clicking the link to github-pages takes you to your Deployments page where you can view details and the time of each deployment. There will be a link at the top of the page to open your live website. Note the address for your repo on **github.com** is **https://github.com/<username>/hello-world** and the address for the published site is a slightly different arrangement using the **github.io** domain **https://<username>.github.io/hello-world**.

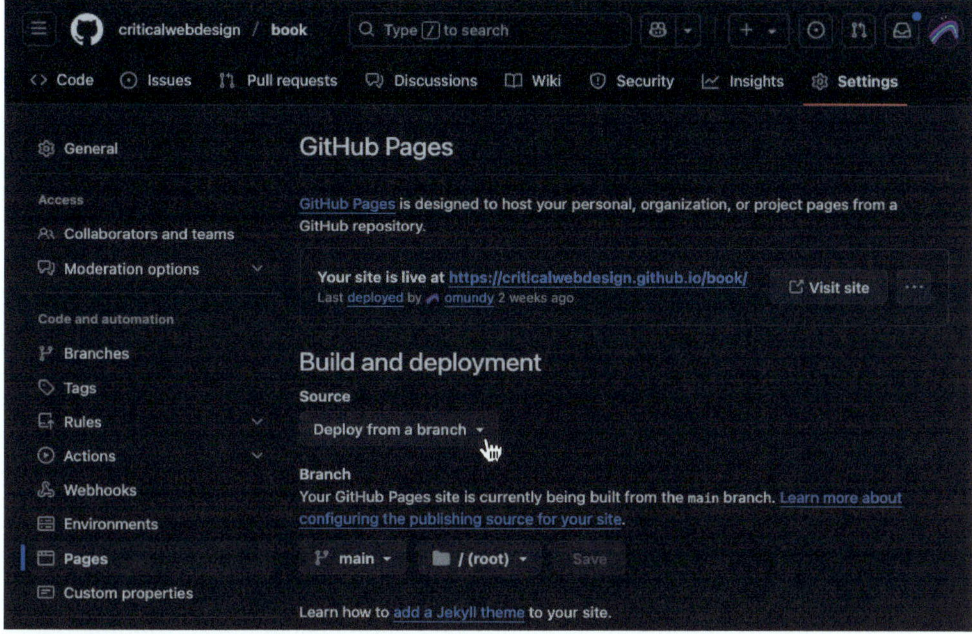

Figure 1.11
Build and deploy your website with GitHub Pages.

You have covered quite a bit of ground in this module to learn Git and publish your first website on github.io. These terms may feel unfamiliar, but you'll become proficient at using Git and GitHub to build web pages throughout this book. The practice and knowledge of Git you develop will benefit you not only within web development but will allow you to use version control, collaborate with others, and even incorporate code from GitHub across any other environment on the network.

Prompt 1.2 Code: Add Information to index.html

For each project you linked to following prompts 1.1 and 1.2, add its title and a few sentences describing why they are remarkable in your **index.html** page. Hint: You may use the **`a`**, **`ul`**, **`li`**, **`headings`**, and **`p`** tags to complete this prompt.

Module 1.3 GitHub Codespaces

You may have noticed a lag between the time you commit changes to your repo and deploy them to your GitHub page. Here we introduce GitHub Codespaces to the rescue.

Exercise 1.3.1 Edit Your Website with Codespaces

Like **github.dev** or **vscode.dev**, Codespaces lets you edit your project in a web browser. But Codespaces offers the additional advantage of showing changes immediately thanks to a virtual host it runs in the background. See the wiki for a video demonstration of this exercise.

1. While you are logged in to your GitHub account, go to **github.com/codespaces**.
2. Click the **New codespace** button.
3. On the page that opens, **Select a Repository** from the drop-down menu and choose the `hello-world` repo you created above.
4. Leave the default settings for branch, region, and machine type and click the **Create codespace** button.
5. A new window will open with an online code editing environment running the VS Code editor. Thanks to a virtual machine running in the background, you can install extensions and preview your work without waiting for deployments (like when you commit changes and wait for your GitHub page to deploy).
6. Click the **Extension** button from the left sidebar and search for Live Server. We installed Live Server by Ritwick Dey (with sixty million installs). Press the **Install** button, then click **Trust Publisher** to finalize installation.
7. Click the **Explorer** button from the left sidebar. Right-click on your **index.html** file and choose "Open with Live Server" to preview the page in a new browser tab. We recommend you position your editor tab in a new window on one side of your screen and the preview page on the other so you can make see the results of changes you make to **index.html** immediately.

Author Note: Codespaces for Education

Verified students get free use of GitHub Codespaces, up to 180 hours per month, see **docs.github.com/en/education.**

Exercise 1.3.2 Stage and Commit Your Work in Codespaces

Your work is saved in Codespaces, but you will need to commit changes to your files before they are saved in your project repo and republished to your live website on GitHub Pages. See the wiki for a video demonstration of this exercise.

1. When you edit files in Codespaces, you will see that a number corresponding to the number of files you edited appears over the **Source Control** button in the left sidebar.
2. Click the **Source Control** button. All the changed files are shown in a list and have a letter `M` next to them to indicate they have been modified. Click the plus sign **(+)** next to the letter `M` to stage your files. In Git terminology, **staging** a file means you have finished work on the files for now and you are ready to commit those changes, and push them to the files in your repo.
3. Enter a commit message, such as "Testing Codespaces" (or accept the default message if one appears), and press **Commit** to save changes to the files.
4. After you commit, the button will change to a prompt to "sync changes". Press the button now and it will push your changes to your repository and cause Github Pages to start a new deployment and show your latest work on your github.io page.

> ⚠ **Watch Out: Codespaces Sync Error**
> When you have a repo open in Codespaces, you must sync your changes before making edits on **Github.com.** If you edit the same file in two places, you are likely to see an error while trying to push your commits.

Exercise 1.3.3 Practice a Basic Web Page Editing Workflow

You will make and test many changes as you are working in your HTML files. This exercise guides you through a basic web development and publishing workflow. You should keep two tabs open while editing in Codespaces: one for the editor and the other to see the live server preview. You'll become very familiar with this process as you complete the exercises in this book. See the wiki for a video demonstration of this exercise.

1. **Edit** your **index.html** file in Codespaces by adding a new paragraph below the heading "Hello, World!" to share selections from the *Critical Web Design Index* that inspire you:

```
<h1>Hello, World!</h1>
<p>Selections from CWD Index</p>
```

2. **Switch** to your Live Server preview tab in the browser to see your edits.
3. **Stage and commit** your work when you are satisfied with your changes by pushing your edits to the file in your repo (see the previous exercise). Remember, editing in Codespaces is not permanent until you stage, commit, and sync changes. Then the files in your repo will reflect your edits.
4. **Publish** your work. When all of your commits are synced, look at your GitHub pages deployments to see a link to the live page you can share with others (see exercise 1.2.2).
5. You are now ready to complete the final prompt in this chapter, in which you'll add more text (and possibly images) to your web page.

Check Your Work

This concludes the chapter exercises. We invite you to compare your work to the final outcome **criticalwebdesign.github.io#1-3** and code **criticalwebdesign.github.io#1-3-code** in the book repo. Don't forget to enable GitHub Pages in your project and then stage and commit your work to make it live!

Author Note: Refresh

Normally you would need to **Refresh** the browser to see changes using Command+r (Ctrl+r on Windows), but Live Server will automatically do this for you.

Prompt 1.3 Publish: Finalize Your Introduction with HTML Tags

Complete a simple web page that introduces you to an online audience by writing about a type of critical web design that appeals to you. Follow these steps to challenge yourself to add content to your page:

1. Edit **index.html** with Codespaces.
2. Add a new heading and text to describe yourself and your motivations for learning critical web design. The content you add can be descriptive, poetic, abstract, visual, statistical, or however else you would like to portray yourself on a web page. Follow this with the list and summaries of the works you have already noted in the prior chapter prompts.
3. Use the following elements (feel free to explore others):

```
<html>, <body>, <h1>, <a>, <ol>, <br>, <hr>
```

4. Add other tags, such as including an image that represents you. See the Mozilla Developer Network documentation link in the introduction.
5. Commit and push **index.html** to GitHub to publish your work, then visit this URL **https://<username>.github.io/hello-world** to see your work.

Pro Tip: Install an Extension to Format Your Code

Every worthwhile code editor has a function (or option to install extensions like "Prettier") that will automatically reformat and organize your code to make it easier to write and read properly nested code. While you can type tab characters by hand, you can save a lot of time by automating formatting.

1. In Codespaces, click the **Extensions** button in the left sidebar.
2. Search extensions in the marketplace for "Prettier," a code formatter by Prettier.io.
3. Press the **Install** button, then click to **Trust Publisher** and **Install**.
4. Right-click anywhere in your code and choose **Format Document**. The first time you run a formatting extension, you will be prompted to choose a formatter. Press **Configure**, then select **Prettier** at the top of the page. You can also use the appropriate key command on Mac (Shift + Option + F) or Windows (Shift + Alt + F).

2 View Source

> Codes typically serve three main purposes. They are used for communication, clarification, or obfuscation.
>
> —Casey Reas, Chandler McWilliams, and LUST

Context

The primary goal of design is to organize and communicate information. When you modify the format or arrangement of text while sending an email, composing an essay, or jotting down a list, you are attempting to remedy **design problems** that prevent others from understanding the full meaning of your text. These actions, or **design decisions**, are improvements we make every day to balance consistency between the content, intended meaning, and current presentation options.

Graphic design is all around us, helping to communicate and understand all the information in the world. But that doesn't mean we see it. In fact, many design problems you will face in creating web pages lie in how you will prioritize the content of the message for various audiences, while considering their different experiences and access to technology. In other words, design supports the transmission of information, and when that task is done successfully, the users see and understand the message, not the design.

This chapter is about noticing two things at once: the design and visual components of content displayed in the web browser and the seemingly invisible code used in its construction. When you view the source of a web page, you examine the parts of the design that many people overlook. Viewing the source of a web page is like looking under the hood of your car to see how it operates. Critical web designers look beyond what sits at the surface and investigate not just what is presented but how that has come to be. In short, viewing the source is a way to think about the world: to be engaged with EVERYTHING going on, from the shiny surface to the systems and technology that make everything work—every part of it affects our culture.

Free Information

To view the source code that underlies interfaces we see, information must be freely available. Historically, the idea that "information wants to be free" spans many cultural connections. Consider this concept as it relates to the new left and counterculture movement of the mid-twentieth century. For instance, Abbie Hoffman's *Steal This Book!* (1970) reads like a manifesto against corporate control and the government. Hoffman offers a "new left" way of living, and chapter titles read as a list of resources for free goods and services. Prior to this, the slang term, "hacker" can be traced back to the 1959 Tech Model Railroad Club at MIT, led by Peter Samson. From 1968, Steward Brand wrote and published the *Whole Earth Catalog*, a counterculture magazine featuring essays about self-sufficiency, ecology, alternative lifestyles, and DIY practices. In 1983 he reimagined the project for pioneers of DIY computing.[1] The catalog, also a relic of the counterculture, offered advice, diagrams, and resources for participants and communards of the back-to-the-land movement. These pioneers relied on concepts of *free* that include no cost, distribution, and the ability to take and modify something for your own needs. These ideas are referred to in the free software movement as "free as in beer" (free to use and distribute without cost) and "free as in speech" (legal rights). The ability to view the source code of web pages underscores these freedoms.

Activity: Look for ASCII (American Standard Code for Information Interchange) art on the NYT website.

Sometimes web designers add messages meant to be seen by people who know how to view the source code. Go to **NYTimes.com** in Chrome and then open the View menu > Developer > Developer Tools and select the Console tab. Like a portal to a secret message, you should see an ASCII art image of the *New York Times* logo with a message that they are hiring.

Open Source

View source is made possible by the idea (concept) and licensing (put into action) referred to as **open source**. Richard Stallman urged anyone working with code to join the free software movement. He started the GNU project and the Free Software Foundation (FSF) in the mid-1980s to encourage others to **license** their work so that anyone can view, use, distribute, and modify software as it is being developed.[2] The internet is predominantly built on open-source technology. When you visit a website, use a mobile app, or play a multiplayer game, you are accessing data on a server powered by open-source software. This philosophy made actionable by these license formats enable remixability. Viewing the source of a web page offers you an opportunity to study it, copy it to your own editor, modify it, and then republish it as a new version

Additional Materials and Resources

Explore links and other content related to this chapter: **criticalwebdesign.github.io#wiki-02**

that you have authored. Thus, your remix of any source code starts with the practice "view source." Legally, you can make your work accessible for others to remix by licensing it with an open-source license. This licensing practice sits at the core of making software truly free and remixable. Open-source licenses include Apache, BSD, Creative Commons (CC), GNU, MIT, and others. These licenses continue to offer attribution rights (in other words, the work is still attributed to the person who holds the license), while also allowing for (or not) remix and distribution. There are many types of licenses that enable the holder to decide how freely the work is available.

Author Note: Blank B-side

Side B of the Dead Kennedys' 1981 album, *In God We Trust, Inc.* features the message "Home taping is killing record industry profits! We left this side blank so you can help." This cassette tape encouraged sharing and free distribution before the rise of Napster and other digital sharing websites (figure 2.1).

Figure 2.1
Dead Kennedys, *In God We Trust, Inc.* cassette tape.

Hacking

Steven Levy defined seven principles of the "hacker ethic" in his 1984 book *Hackers: Heroes of the Computer Revolution*. While these principles are now thirty years old, they continue to resonate:

1. All should have access to computers.
2. Always yield to the Hands-on Imperative!
3. All information should be free.
4. Mistrust authority—promote decentralization.
5. Hackers should be judged by their hacking, not bogus criteria such as degrees, age, race, or position.
6. You can create art and beauty on the computer.
7. Computers can change your life for the better.[3]

This list of principles relates to the free software movement, the counterculture's mistrust of authority and demands for "free," and an excitement for hands-on experimentation while creating art on the computer, all without judging others based on "bogus criteria." In the third module of this chapter, you will perform a temporary and local (on your computer only) hack on a preexisting website.

Closed Source

Closed source describes software that (unless you have privileged access) is created with code the public cannot see or alter. Examples include desktop software like Adobe Photoshop or Microsoft Word; platforms like Facebook and Google's search engine; or **firmware** (code that is embedded on and enables device hardware) like that on Tesla vehicles or an internet-connected smart TV: The source code that makes up these software and their internal logic are proprietary, shielded from examination or scrutiny. When you look at such closed-source systems, the view of their internal workings is opaque, a technological **black box** where the functions, except for their inputs and outputs, are hidden from public view. Like closed source, code inside a black box cannot be seen, altered, or redistributed. But perhaps more importantly, the operations inside a black box can include algorithmic bias, reselling of user data, or other unsavory actions. And since the decisions it makes are hidden, you don't know what the source code is doing "under the hood."

Case Study: MSCHF

MSCHF: Founded in 2019, MSCHF is an American art collective based in Brooklyn, New York. MSCHF's output is aggressively medium agnostic and deliberately difficult to define, spanning shoes to chat platforms to gun buyback programs. Their work accelerates the aberrations of twenty-first-century capitalism by laying bare twentieth-century cultural tropes—Duchampian humor, "Medium is the message," guerilla marketing, interactive performance art, and celebrity culture. MSCHF's work forces viewers to reconsider the contexts in which art can exist and weaponizes its pop appeal—and its own corporate existence—to drive its critical practice into mainstream spaces.

What does it mean to "hack" capitalism?

MSCHF: Hacking capitalism entails exploiting the infrastructural quirks of our surrounding capitalist environment—and perhaps also the crowd psychology produced by that environment.

Back in 2019, before we were permabanned from the platform, MSCHF used Venmo to broadcast our work, sending our audience one-cent payments with a project link in the

Figure 2.2

MSCHF, web interface for crowdsourced drawing, *The FREE Movie*, 2019 (ongoing).

transaction notes. Because Venmo is a payments app, and therefore heavily prioritized, most users would get a Venmo notification, an email confirmation, and sometimes even a text message (depending on their settings) from this one action.

A MSCHF project from 2020 called *The Blue Donkey* was a shell restaurant on the Seamless platform. Items named "burger" and such did not deliver food, but instead donated money to Elizabeth Warren or Bernie—candidates pushing anti-big-corporate policies. Because (tech) companies in NYC provided their employees with generous expense cards for food delivery—the better to keep workers in the office late at night—*The Blue Donkey* was a way to spend these companies' own money against them.

In *ATM Leaderboard*, 2022, we rigged an ATM to save the bank balances of everyone who used it, take their photo, and rank them all on a digital leaderboard on top of the ATM. The higher you were on the leaderboard, the more the piece was making fun of you. *ATM Leaderboard* literalized wealth flaunting and did so by using clout as bait. As the piece gained traction, the leaderboard spots became more and more desirable, until rich Miamians' attention-seeking impulses overwhelmed the taboos around exposing financial information.

How important is free media to MSCHF?

MSCHF: Much of MSCHF's work radically alters the original intent and significance of objects, from defacing famous artworks to wholesale appropriating Nike sneakers. MSCHF views cultural elements—a brand, a logo, an artist—as building blocks to construct our work, in a radical expansion of sampling-, remix-, satire-based artistic creation. There is a dramatic disconnect between art-historical attitudes toward such appropriation ("Hasn't this been normalized since at least Warhol?") and the state of copyright law. Since MSCHF started in 2019, a series of court cases have progressively shut down and restricted such use—especially where artistic use of corporate-held copyright is concerned. Projects like *The FREE Movie*, in which the crowdsourced hand-redrawing on *Bee Movie* becomes an extended metaphor for media passing into broad cultural ownership and taking on new meaning, hold special significance for us in light of the stakes for this larger mode of working (figure 2.2).

Author Note: More About MSCHF

Visit **thefreemovie.buzz** to watch the finalized movie. Readers should also view other works by MSCHF like **pyramid.chat**, **cdgrandprix.com**, **onlybags.biz**, **antirobocall.com**, **screamclub.club**, and more that you can find at their website **mschf.com**.

Prompt 2 What You'll Make
Transform a Design Manifesto into a Concrete Poem

Throughout the modules in this chapter, you will create an experimental typography project for the web browser. You will start by previsualizing your page using pencil and paper, then code your design using HTML, CSS, and JavaScript. Start by choosing an important phrase or sentences from one of the texts in the list of manifestos in the callout. Select writing that speaks to you. Our sample concrete poem riffs on Apple's "Think Different" slogan.

View the results of our manifesto-turned-concrete poem at **criticalwebdesign.github.io#2-3** (figure 2.3). You can see the final code for every chapter on the CWD repo, **criticalwebdesign.github.io#repo**.

Figure 2.3
Our example uses inline and block styles as well as some negative values for margins to emphasize repetition and contrast in scale, value, and form (rotation).

Author Note: Design Manifestos

A list of manifestos by artists, designers, and engineers:

- **molleindustria.org/files/BIG-DATA.html**
- **designmanifestos.org**
- **designmanifestos.org/first-things-first-a-manifesto-2020-edition/**
- **criticalengineering.org**

Module 2.1 Design Fundamentals

A **focal point** is part of a design composition that stands out to the viewer. It is often the first thing a viewer sees, and typically (although not always) it is designed to be easily legible. A design usually contains multiple focal points that intentionally direct viewers' eyes through essential information in the composition. In design, this **eye movement** across each successive focal point is like a thesis statement. It's the main idea of the visual presentation, and it is supported by other design elements that surround it.

We will explore several ways to create focal points throughout the book. One method you might consider is through **contrast**, such as differences in scale, color, and position.

2.1.1 Concrete Poetry (Before the Web)

Concrete poetry is a genre in which text and imagery hold equal value as contributors to concept and form. Unlike prose, concrete poetry challenges the reader to view the text as a design composition. Sometimes referred to as **visual poetry**, concrete poetry dates back to Greek Alexandria, though modern references to it may allude to the image-text formations of the Futurists, Dadaists, and Surrealists, for instance, found in Guillaume Apollinaire's book *Calligramme*. Concrete poetry has its first roots in Brazil, where the movement was founded by Augusto de Campos (figure 2.4), and has a legacy in poetic circles, including the imagists like Amy Lowell and Ezra Pound. In an interview, de Campos explains that concrete poetry gives the materiality of the word a new emphasis that combines the sound the word makes with its visual appearance.[4] Our prompt draws on the legacy of concrete and visual poetry, which can be found online in collections like UbuWeb **ubu.com/vp**, which we encourage viewing for inspiration. Since the layout of a web page is constructed using rectangular elements (much like Legos or

Figure 2.4
Open (Abre), Augusto de Campos and Julio Plaza, Poemobiles 1968–1974, Getty Research Institute, Los Angeles (92-B21581). This work is featured in the Getty Research Institute's 2017 exhibition, *Concrete Poetry: Words and Sounds in Graphic Space.*

bricks in architecture), for now, we suggest you steer away from representative forms that use curves or other imagery that would be difficult to replicate in HTML and CSS.

A more recent history includes Kenneth Goldsmith's vision for how the WWW evolved the practice and distribution of concrete poetry. He writes, "Concrete poetry's move from line to constellation, predicts the parallel move in computing from command line interface to graphical user interfaces."[5] One doesn't need to look far for evidence of computing's impact on this form. There are abundant examples of ASCII art (see callout on Unicode) on the web, and their influence on visual culture can be seen everywhere, including the playful and provocative graphic (figure 2.5) found in the source code of "What is Code?" by Paul Ford.[6]

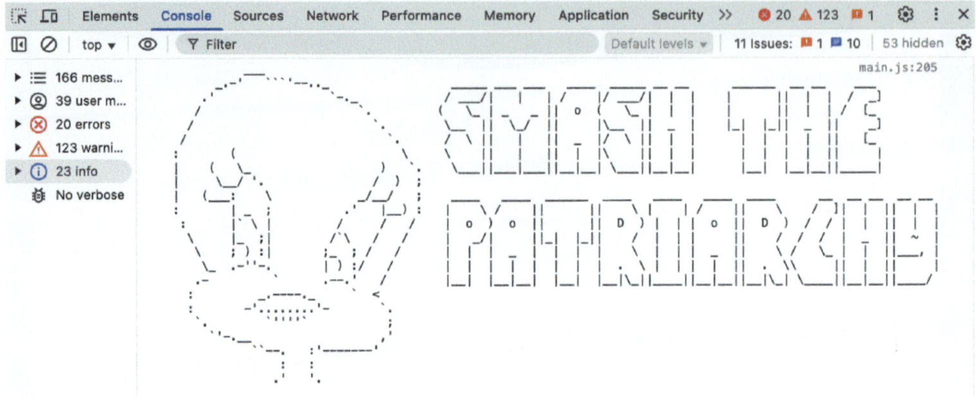

Figure 2.5
"SMASH THE PATRIARCHY" ASCII art found in the DevTools console "What is Code?" by Paul Ford.

This shift to creating and distributing concrete poetry online enables other modern possibilities like rich text, time-based media, interactive components, and new or emergent media forms, all of which can be seen in the works of Young-Hae Chang Heavy Industries. Mark Tribe suggests their work offers "conciseness and captivating clarity" because it "resembles older art forms, such as concrete poetry and experimental cinema, and because its emotionally expressive voices and dynamic visual qualities communicate across disciplinary boundaries."[7]

Exercise 2.1.1 Draw a Wireframe on Paper

A wireframe uses basic shapes and lines in place of content in order to experiment with the placement of elements in a layout. Designers always previsualize layouts before they code because it takes much longer to make changes in a design once it is coded. The tool you use to previsualize a layout should allow you to work fluidly, giving you freedom to be creative, take chances, and experiment. It should be easy to create multiple iterations so that you can save and compare the merits of your previous designs and improve on them. Many professional designers often start with pencil and paper because it is fast, readily available, and easy to manipulate while developing variations. Throughout the next steps, use only a pen or pencil and paper to draw a series of wireframes representing essential components of the design with simple shapes (figure 2.6). We will introduce a professional layout software called Figma in chapter 3.

1. Draw a landscape-oriented rectangle that roughly matches the shape of a browser window. Leave room to draw many of these on the page or draw on multiple pages.

Figure 2.6
Top: Designers create wireframes early in the process using simple geometrical shapes to decide where they will place content in the layouts. Bottom Left: The wireframe drawing for the example xtine designed for this chapter expresses the Apple slogan "Think Different!" It was created in a sketchbook with ink. It's a good idea to leave notes for yourself and a date as you are working. Bottom Right: The wireframe Owen made for the example he designed for this chapter was created with pencil on graph paper. See the result at **criticalwebdesign.github.io/book**.

2. Think about how the meaning of the text you've chosen might influence how it would appear on a page. Look for inspiration in the examples we've supplied above. Imagine the layout in your mind and think about where you want the viewers' eyes to move when they look at the page. For your first visual poetry example, we suggest you avoid creating a figurative work (like a flower or other object) that will be challenging to code and focus on manipulating the flow of text.
3. Draw the characters of the text in the first box to reflect how you imagined it. The drawing doesn't need to be very detailed, or even include every letter from the text,

because you are simply sketching a representation showing the relative size and position of content areas on the page.

4. Every HTML element in a web page is fundamentally a rectangle. Together, these elements create a page similar to how blocks stack to form a brick wall. So, as you draw, position content by including the bounding box of every paragraph, word, or even a single letter to plan how you will control its position.

Prompt 2.1 Design: Draw a Wireframe

Repeat the steps in the previous exercise, trying new ideas and building off the successful iterations in wireframe designs for the manifesto you selected. Use new perspectives to experiment with the layout like looking at inspirational artworks, changing the music you are listening to, drawing with your nondominant hand, or just taking a break. Making substantially different layouts might feel irrational at first, but it is an essential (and fun!) part of the creative process. Remember you can create a focal point by:

- Increasing the size of important design elements (such as a first-level heading) relative to others nearby.
- Using one color that stands out from other hues and values in the layout.
- Placing a design element in a position that isolates it from other elements on the page.

2.1.2 Usability and Eye Tracking

There are several factors that you should consider when comparing design layouts. For example, website **usability** describes the "effectiveness, efficiency, and overall satisfaction" of a user's experience with a digital product.[8] Usability involves many factors, like how intuitive it is to learn to use a new interface, how fast a user can accomplish tasks, and how much they enjoy using the interface.

Author Note: Usability in Chapter 5

You will learn best practices in usability for the web in chapter 5.

Eye tracking is a common method for measuring usability and involves recording the location, order, and duration of focus of participants' eyes as they view a web page. Designers can influence the order in which users will move their eyes across a layout and plan to create web pages that are easy and efficient to scan while finding the most essential information on the page. As a designer, your primary goal is to communicate information in a manner that is legible and easy to use.

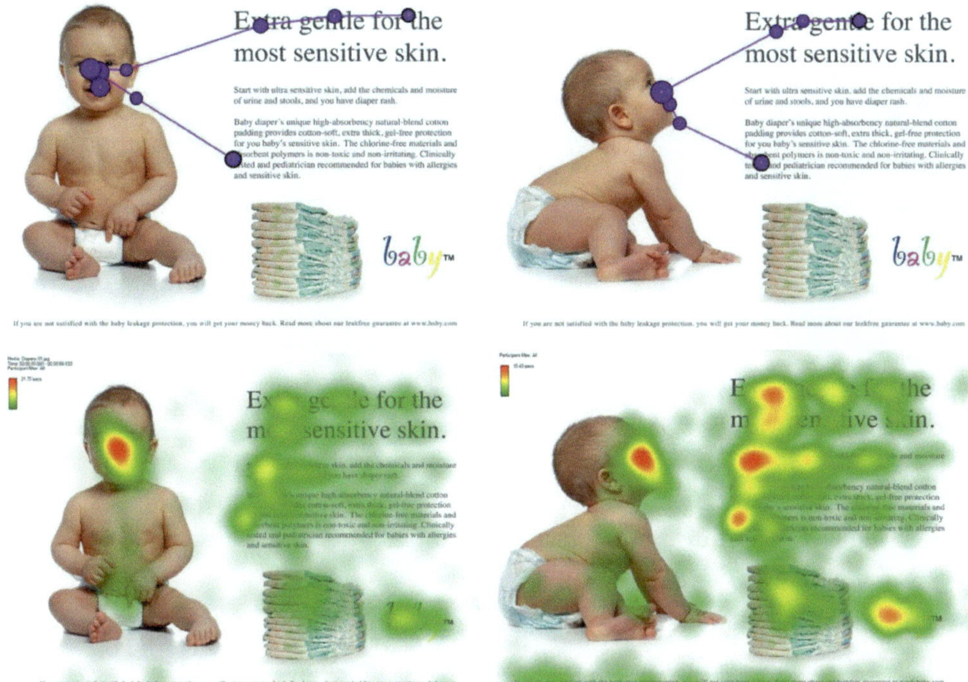

Figure 2.7
In the baby product ad at the top, the results of an eye movement test show the order and location of the test user's focus as they move their eyes around the design. The second row shows a heatmap from the eye tracking test. While the composition on the left shows only one strong heat spot, in the composition on the right, participants' eyes followed the gaze of the baby to increase engagement with important information on the page. This is an example of using leading lines (in this case the baby's gaze) to direct attention. Image appears courtesy of James Breeze, made with Tobii eye tracker.

Eye tracking studies can help a designer learn to design pages that are usable and help users find the most important information. You can learn about eye movements in **heat maps**, which illustrate the duration of participants' eyes when they focus on areas of a composition to navigate or find meaning (figure 2.7).

Activity: Eye Movement Test

Repeat the following activity as often as necessary while assessing your own design compositions or use it to give feedback to others.

1. Choose a composition to assess—for example yours or your peers'—or view a website robust with content.
2. Close your eyes for a few seconds, then open them and look at the layout.
3. Name each element that draws the focus of your eyes, in order of appearance.
4. Review the order. Does it match the relative importance of each item in the context of information in the design?
5. Consider potential issues with how the design leads your gaze. Do your eyes ever get stuck, leave the page, or struggle to find meaning when looking at the design?
6. Update the design to reiterate the hierarchy of information.

Module 2.2 HTML and CSS

In modules 2.2 and 2.3 you will become acquainted with the interplay between all three languages you must know to produce intentionally designed, interactive web pages:

- HTML is the markup language that structures the content.
- CSS is the language that specifies the layout and presentation.
- JavaScript is the programming language that adds interactivity.

2.2.1 Doctype and Meta Tags

The HTML tags we discuss in this section provide meta information about web pages which help define how a page is interpreted. While there are many potential tags to include, we focus here on three essentials.

1. The required **Doctype preamble** `<!DOCTYPE html>` tells browsers which specification to use to interpret your code. Web browsers use this to render your page, so it should be the first line in your HTML file, right before the `<html>` element.
2. The `lang` attribute, which should be added to your opening `<html>` tag, informs the browser about the human language of the text on the page. The value uses an abbreviation like, "en" for English, "de" for German, and so on. A region subtag like "en-US" is optional.[9]
3. In addition to the `<title>` element, **meta tags** in the `<head>` can add other information about a web page. A `<meta>` tag with a `charset` attribute informs the browser about which **character set** (see the UTF-8 and Unicode callout) is needed to represent the chosen language.

Keywords: UTF-8 and Unicode

In the internet's early days, it was not uncommon to encounter web pages using characters that appeared garbled. These strange symbols were more than likely written in a language that used characters excluded by the original 128 (western language) characters of the ASCII character set. This issue has largely been solved thanks to **Unicode**, a universal standard for encoding and representing text.[10] Thanks to this standardization, the **UTF-8** character set is now the most common encoding used across the web to represent, in addition to ASCII, up to 1,112,064 total characters that include all the world's languages as well as emoji 🤩.[11]

Exercise 2.2.1 Create Your Boilerplate Website Template

By following this exercise, you will create the **boilerplate code**[12] for a standard webpage, including important meta information, that you need to begin each prompt in this book. You can also find this HTML page in the website-template repository linked below. See the wiki for a video demonstration of this exercise.

1. Sign in to your **GitHub.com** account and click the plus sign at the top right to **Create a new repository**. Name it `view-source` and enable "Add a README."
2. Click the **Add file** drop-down menu and choose **Create new file.** On the next page, name the file "index.html" (without the quotes) in the field next to the name of the repository. Notice the file path states the name of the repo, then a slash, then the name of your "home page" file, **index.html**.
3. Press the **Commit changes** button and enter a message about the changes you made or accept the default message, "Create index.html."
4. Edit the new file in your preferred code editor, or in GitHub Codespaces. Click the plus sign at the top right and choose **New codespace**. On the page that follows, choose your **view-source** repository. Select **index.html** and edit the file to add the doctype, lang attribute, and meta tags, matching our code below. Note that meta tags are **self-closing**.

```
<!DOCTYPE html>
<html lang="en">
<head>
    <meta charset="utf-8">
    <title>Thththththink</title>
</head>
<body>
    <h1>different</h1>
</body>
</html>
```

5. Click on the Source Control tab and stage and commit your work (as shown in exercise 1.3.2). Now that your changes are committed, you have created a boilerplate **index.html** page you can use each time you start a new project.

> **Author Note: Website Template**
>
> We have also created a simple website template repository containing the above files and directories. Press the **Use this template** button and then from the dropdown create a new repository at: **github.com/criticalwebdesign/website-template**.

2.2.2 URLs and index.html

The hierarchy of folders and files in your project, whether it is on your computer or uploaded and accessed on the internet, can be represented as a path, where directories and files are separated by a slash. Codespaces reflects this path in the Explorer panel (top left in figure 2.8) as a hierarchy of folders, and above the code as "bread crumbs."

If you view the live page from the previous exercise, you will see that the public URL also reflects the hierarchical path down through the folders in your project. A **URL** (uniform resource locator) is the address for a file on a computer or network. Your web browser displays a URL in the address bar so that you know your location at any given moment (except Safari, which unfortunately hides everything but the domain name by default).

You will notice we keep using the filename **index.html** for exercises. This is a special name in web development. Take for example this address:

```
https://criticalwebdesign.github.io/book/02-view-source/2-3/index.html
```

Web servers are usually configured to look for an **index.html** file whenever they receive a request that matches a folder path. If found, the server will display the contents of the file regardless of whether your path includes the file or just the directory name. This makes the address "clean" and easier for humans to read and type. If you go to either of these URLs you will see the same file.

```
https://criticalwebdesign.github.io/book/02-view-source/2-3/
```

If you access a directory without an **index.html** file, although less common these days, a server may show a list of the files, or **index**, of that directory. Without this setting, if a file doesn't exist, the server may just return an error message to prevent access to potentially sensitive files.

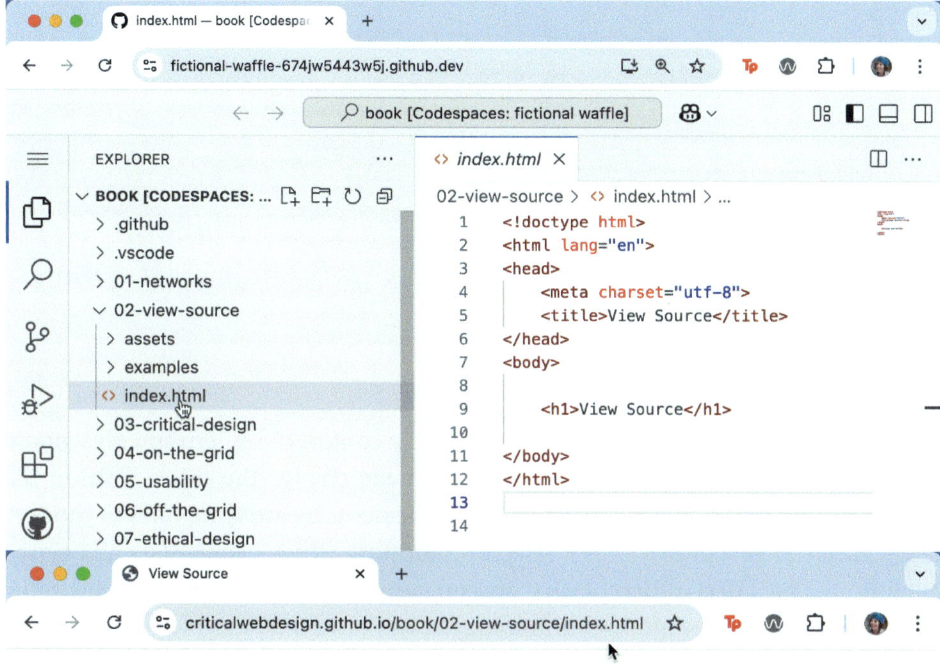

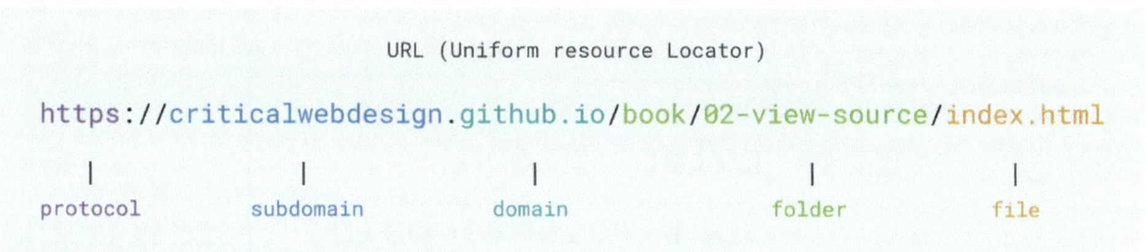

Figure 2.8
Top: The hierarchy of folders and files in your website is the file address or path. Bottom: This diagram shows the primary components of a URL for the **index.html** file in the file directory called "02-view-source" in the *Critical Web Design* GitHub account's repo called "book."

Activity: Explore the Power of CSS

This activity puts your knowledge of paths to work to explore how websites use CSS to change the presentation of HTML files.

1. Visit the CSS Zen Garden website at **csszengarden.com**.
2. Click through the links in the menu on each page. As the design changes, notice the text does not. This site uses a simple but effective trick, loading different CSS files (indicated by the changing number in the URL) to underscore the power to control the presentation of HTML using CSS.
3. Edit the URL of the site so that the number at the end looks like this: **csszengarden.com/000** and press return. You are now viewing the unstyled page, or **vanilla HTML**. Created over twenty years ago, every contributor started with and evolved this basic HTML page, designing and coding layouts to reimagine the original.

2.2.3 Introduction to CSS

CSS (Cascading Style Sheets) is the language used to control the design and presentation of text and media on web pages. With CSS, you can change the color, position, size, and many other visual characteristics of HTML elements by applying **rules** to those elements. Each CSS rule begins with a **selector** indicating which element(s) will be modified, followed by a **declaration block** (between curly braces) that contains one or more declarations. You can see all this terminology at work in the rule depicted in figure 2.9, which selects all `<h1>` tags on a page to change their color to green and font weight to bold. Note how each declaration includes a **property** (color) and **value** (green), separated by a colon and terminated by a semicolon.

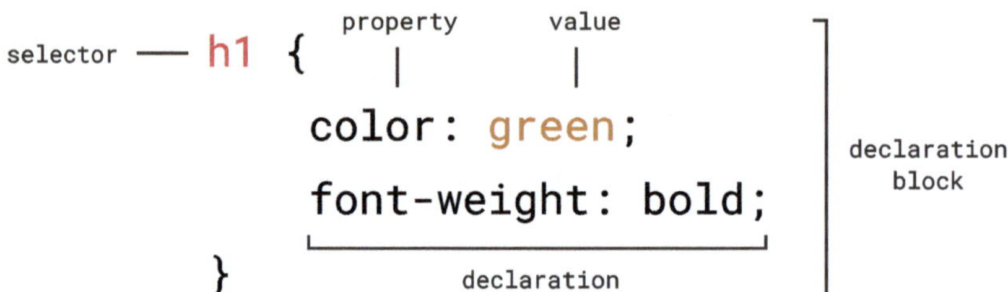

Figure 2.9
This CSS diagram shows the anatomy of a rule, including the selector, and properties and values in the declaration block.

2.2.4 Methods for Adding CSS to HTML

You can apply CSS rules to HTML documents in three different locations:

1. Apply **inline styles** by adding a `style` attribute directly to HTML tags. These styles only affect those specific elements.

2. Apply **internal styles** inside a `<style>` element in the `<head>` of a page. This lets you reuse styles for multiple elements within a single page, making it a simple method for adding CSS.
3. Apply **external styles** using a separate **.css** file linked from the `<head>` of the page. This is by far the most common in production websites. Using separate files allows designers to share the same rules across all the pages of their website, and accordingly, makes it easy to update those rules by editing a single file. We explore this in chapter 3.

Exercise 2.2.2 Add CSS Rules with Internal Styles

Follow these steps to add internal CSS to your file using Codespaces.

1. Open your **view-source** repository in GitHub Codespaces. If you have already opened a project in a Codespace, you should go to **github.com/codespaces** to re-open that previous project. See the callout to learn why this is a good idea.

> ⚠ **Watch Out! Codespaces Limitations**
> Always go to **github.com/codespaces** to **re-open** a previous Codespace project. If you edit the same project files from more than one place (like another Codespace or **GitHub.com**), you could create Git conflicts. If you see a button to sync your changes after you commit, you may have two Codespaces open, or you made changes on **GitHub.com** in your repo. An added benefit to using previously opened Codespaces is that it preserves extensions you have installed like Live Server or Prettier. Also note there is a limit to the number of Codespaces that you can run at once. If you see a message about "Maximum running codespaces reached," you will need to delete a previous Codespace from **github.com/codespaces**. Make sure you commit and push your work from that Codespace to your repo first. You can see this information in the list of messages Codespaces and GitHub will post if you have unpushed changes.

2. Open your **index.html** file. Add opening and closing `<style>` tags to **index.html**, after the `<title>` element and before the closing `</head>` in the document.

```
<style></style>
```

3. Add this CSS rule below inside the `<style>` element. Right-click in your code and choose Open with Live Server to preview your work in a new tab. If you do not see this option, you may need to install Live Server (see exercise 1.3.1). The preview tab will auto refresh if you leave it open, so you can toggle back and forth to view edits on your page. You should see that the background color is pink and all text inside

the **<body>** element is now a sans-serif font and green in color. Like HTML, you can use whitespace as you like when coding CSS styles to make contents readable.

```
<style>
  body {
    font-family: "Helvetica", "Arial", sans-serif;
    background-color: pink;
    color: green;
  }
</style>
```

Pro Tip: Refresh Key Command

As we noted in the introduction, we are writing this book using Mac OS. Thus, when we instruct readers to refresh (or reload) the page using **Command+r**, Windows users will (usually) translate this instruction to **Control+r**. For more information, consult the Introduction.

Author Note: We Asked GitHub Copilot for Help

Codespaces includes an AI agent called GitHub Copilot. We found the "Quick Chat" feature to be less intrusive. We pressed Quick Chat from the Copilot pulldown menu and asked the AI to "make the background of my page pink using CSS." It returned the following code snippet in a separate window, which we could paste, intentionally, into our code:

```
body {
  background-color: pink;
}
```

From here, you can add the other two sets of properties and values that are part of step 3 in our exercise. We know working with AI can be helpful, so we are leaving this note to suggest using it mindfully. We strongly recommend you avoid having Copilot enabled all the while you are coding. We have seen it attempt to autocomplete code in ways that worked against our efforts and/or add code to the page that we did not expect to see.

4. Add the following CSS rule and preview your live webpage. The `h1` tag should now be light green. While the `color` rule for the **<body>** is **inherited** by all child elements on the page, the rule below for `color` applies *only* to the **<h1>** tag and **overrides** other rules. Its selector is more specific, so it has priority over the less specific

rule from the **<body>**. The word "cascading" in the CSS name refers to how the language resolves such conflicting rules using **specificity**.

```
h1 {
  color: aquamarine;
}
```

Author Note: Code Suggestions and Autocomplete

Codespaces and other editors like VS Code are configured to show suggestions based on your input. If you type an "h" inside the **<body>** you will see a list of HTML elements that begin with h, like **h1**, **h2**, **h3**, and so on. Pressing tab or return will automatically add the highlighted opening and closing tags for you and insert your cursor so that you can add content between these opening and closing tags. Sometimes you may need to add your own closing tags if the editor misinterprets your intentions.

5. Add the following **<div>** tags and page content below **<body>**. The **<div>** is a generic container for content. It has no style until you apply CSS.[13] Our manifesto-turned-concrete poem creates an audible pattern highlighting the first two letters in "Think."

```
<div>Th</div>
<div>Th</div>
<div>Th</div>
<div>Th</div>
<div>ThThTh</div>
<div>ThThTh</div>
<div>ThThTh</div>
<div>ThThTh</div>
<div>TTThhhh!!!!</div>
<div>Th!nk</div>
<h1>different</h1>
```

6. Add these styles to the **div** selector in the internal styles. We don't need to use **color: green;** because it is inherited from the **body** rule. We are using the CSS **transform** property to rotate the "Think" phrases by 2 degrees (clockwise). Preview the page to see differences between the div elements and the heading text:

```
div {
  font-weight: bold;
```

```
    font-size: 60px;
    transform: rotate(2deg);
}
```

7. Add typographic styles to the `h1` selector below the color rule and preview the page. We used the CSS `letter-spacing` property to increase the space between letters, adding emphasis to make them stand out from the background color on the page.

```
h1 {
    color: aquamarine;
    font-weight: bold;
    font-size: 220px;
    letter-spacing: 12px;
}
```

2.2.5 Class and ID Selectors

CSS changes the appearance of an HTML element by selecting it, then applying a style to it. Selecting an element by tag name changes all of them, but you can use the **class** and **id** attributes to be more specific about how CSS rules are applied. The `id` is the most specific selector, followed by `class`, and finally, tags by name. A `class` attribute can be reused over and over in your HTML, making them ideal for groups of elements that share a style or behavior. An `id`, on the other hand, can be used only once in a web page. In fact, your HTML will not validate if you use an `id` attribute more than once.

Best Practices: Comments

Comments are lines in your code ignored by the web browser. They let you add notes about the purpose of a code block, which can be helpful if you are collaborating with others or even when you close a file and come back to it after time has passed.

```
<!-- An HTML comment -->
/* A comment in CSS or JavaScript */
// A single line comment in JavaScript
```

Exercise 2.2.3 Use a CSS Class Selector

You have already updated the appearance of your page by adding CSS declaration blocks that target the `<body>` and `<p>` tags. In this exercise you will add styles using a class selector in order to offset the margin on the heading (the word "different") and the row of exclamation marks that appear between a set of div tags.

Author Note: Adding CSS

We are providing the most common methods for adding CSS to your HTML page to explore the power of CSS in the design of your web projects. There are many other clever ways to use selectors (like wildcards!) to add CSS rules. Selectors are also handy because JavaScript can use them to add behaviors to a page, as you'll see in module 2.3.

1. In your Codespace, add the following class selector beneath the last style declaration block in your **index.html** file. CSS rules using class selectors are defined by a period before the name. Any CSS class you define can be applied to multiple elements in your HTML page, however they only affect HTML tags that reference the name of the class with a special attribute, as you will see below.

```
.offset {
  margin-left: 30px;
}
```

2. Best practices include adding comments while you code. Add the following comment explaining what your offset class does on the page.

```
.offset {
  /* Increases left margin to move elements to the right */
  margin-left: 30px;
}
```

3. These rules exist in your file, but they need to be referenced by HTML elements in the body of the page to create a visible effect. Update the `<h1>` and add a last `<div>` tag as follows before the closing `<body>` tag on the page, and preview your work.

```
<h1 class="offset">different</h1>
<div class="offset">
  !!!!!!!!!!!!!!!!!!!!!!!!!!!!!!!!!!!!!!!!!!!!!!!!!!!!!!!
</div>
```

2.2.6 Block Versus Inline Elements

This last CSS concept will prepare you to manipulate text per the chapter prompt. When a page loads, starting from the top left of the page, all HTML elements are rendered in the order they appear in code. Like "building blocks" in an upside-down construction set, these elements fill and expand the page vertically as they appear. This default stacking order of elements is referred to as the page **flow**. You can control how these "blocks" are added in many ways using CSS and even **break the flow** of elements as needed using the **position** property (see callout). You can also use `display: none` to hide elements from the browser interface.

- **Block-level** elements (`div`, `p`, `h1`, etc.) always start a new line and stretch to fill the entire width of their parent, causing later elements to flow downward.
- **Inline** elements (`a`, `span`, `b`, etc.), on the other hand, do not create a new line and only take up as much width as needed for their content.
- **Inline block** elements also fit on one line, but like block elements, they can use width and height properties to change their size.

Figure 2.10
Abstract Browsing by Rafaël Rozendaal and Reinier Feijen (2014).

Inspiration: *Abstract Browsing*

Rafaël Rozendaal and Reinier Feijen's **Abstract Browsing abstractbrowsing.net** is a browser extension that transforms all block-level and inline-block elements on every webpage into colorful abstract patterns.

The CSS **box model** defines the containing box for every HTML element (figure 2.11).[14] It includes (starting from the outside) the margin, border, padding, and the width and height of the content box.

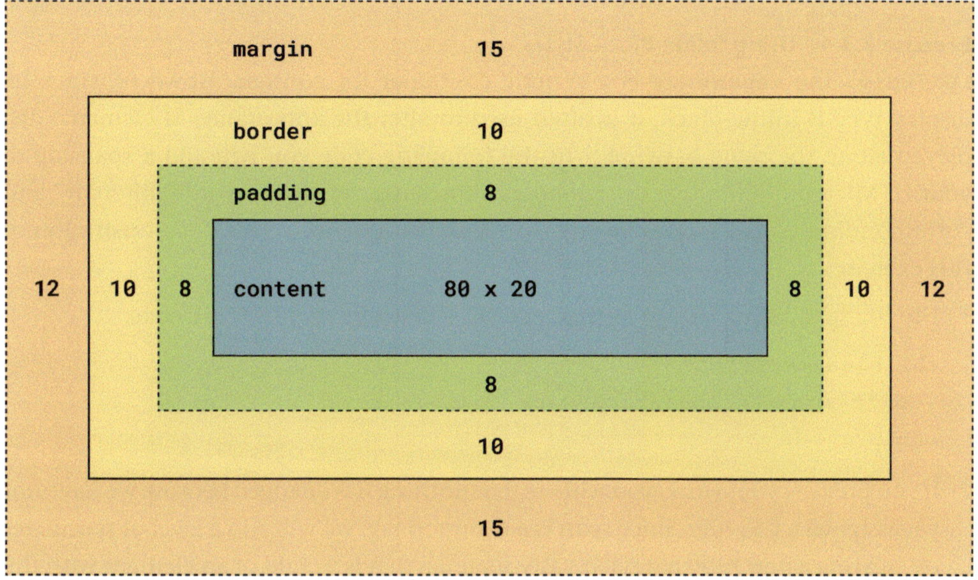

Figure 2.11
A diagram showing the margin, border, padding, and content components of the CSS box model.

These properties can be set using static units like pixels (px), or relative units, like percentage (%), that are defined relative to the size of the browser window.

```
p { margin-left: 10px; }
p { width: 85%; }
```

The values for margin and padding can be set using various **shorthands**. If you use four values separated by spaces (not commas), then the first defines the top margin and moves clockwise, right, bottom, then left. You can also use a single value to set all properties to the same size.

```
p { margin: 10px 20px 30px 40px; }
p { margin: 10px;}
```

The sizes in figure 2.11, for example, would be set using the below rule.

```
p {
  margin: 15px 12px 15px 12px;
  border: 10px solid yellow;
```

```
    padding: 8px;
    width: 80px;
    height: 20px;
}
```

Exercise 2.2.4 Using Inline Block Styles

Like **<div>** the **<span>** tag is a generic container for content. However, since its display type is inline-block, it is often used to alter the appearance of elements displayed along the same baseline.[15] In the following code you will add a span tag to your HTML around the two occurrences of the letter "e" in the word "different" and corresponding CSS to rotate the elements. See the wiki for a video demonstration of this exercise.

1. Use the span tag to "wrap" both of the "e" characters in the HTML code:

```
<h1 class="offset">
  diff<span>e</span>r<span>e</span>nt
</h1>
```

2. If you preview your work, you will see that nothing has changed because we have not yet assigned a CSS rule. Since span is a common tag, we will add a level of specificity by creating a new rule that selects any span tag that is a child of an element with the offset class. Add this block of code right before the closing **</style>** tag to rotate each **<span>** by 12 degrees (clockwise). The rule **display: inline-block** allows us to affect display properties normally reserved for block-level elements.

```
.offset span {
  display: inline-block;
  transform: rotate(12deg);
}
```

3. Preview your code and you will see that both "e"s are rotated in the same direction. Let's make our viewers think even more different(ly) by rotating the second letter e counterclockwise. We will use the style attribute to apply an inline style directly to the HTML element. Inline styles take priority over styles in the internal stylesheet. Add this to your HTML and preview your work:

```
diff<span>e</span>r<span style="transform:rotate(-12deg);">
e</span>nt
```

4. Finally, update the CSS rules for the **h1** tag to fine-tune the heading text using negative margins. Some might say this is a "hack," but ultimately it affects the positioning to reach our intended goal. And it is valid code (see callout)!

```
h1{
  color: #b5edcc;
  font-weight: bold;
  font-size: 220px;
  letter-spacing: 12px;
  /* negative margins decrease space between lines */
  margin-top: -80px;
  margin-bottom: -80px;
}
```

5. Preview your work. If you like what you see so far, this might be a good time to stage and commit your changes.

Best Practices: Code Validation

Validation is a way to check for syntax, nesting, or other issues with your HTML and CSS code. The World Wide Web Consortium (W3C) maintains the HTML **validator.w3.org** and CSS validators **jigsaw.w3.org/css-validator**, which examine the code of a public web page, or code you upload, for errors. Validating your code can save you a lot of trouble by highlighting and suggesting fixes for syntax issues that might prevent your code from working as expected. Validate your code by uploading a document directly, or publishing your latest version on GitHub Pages, and then pasting the public link into the validator.

Author Note: CSS Position

You may find it is possible to code your design without breaking the flow of the page using only padding and margin. However, you may need to use the position property to move elements to match your layout. A common method is to use **position:absolute** with the **top** and **left** properties to move elements to a specific position (figure 2.12).

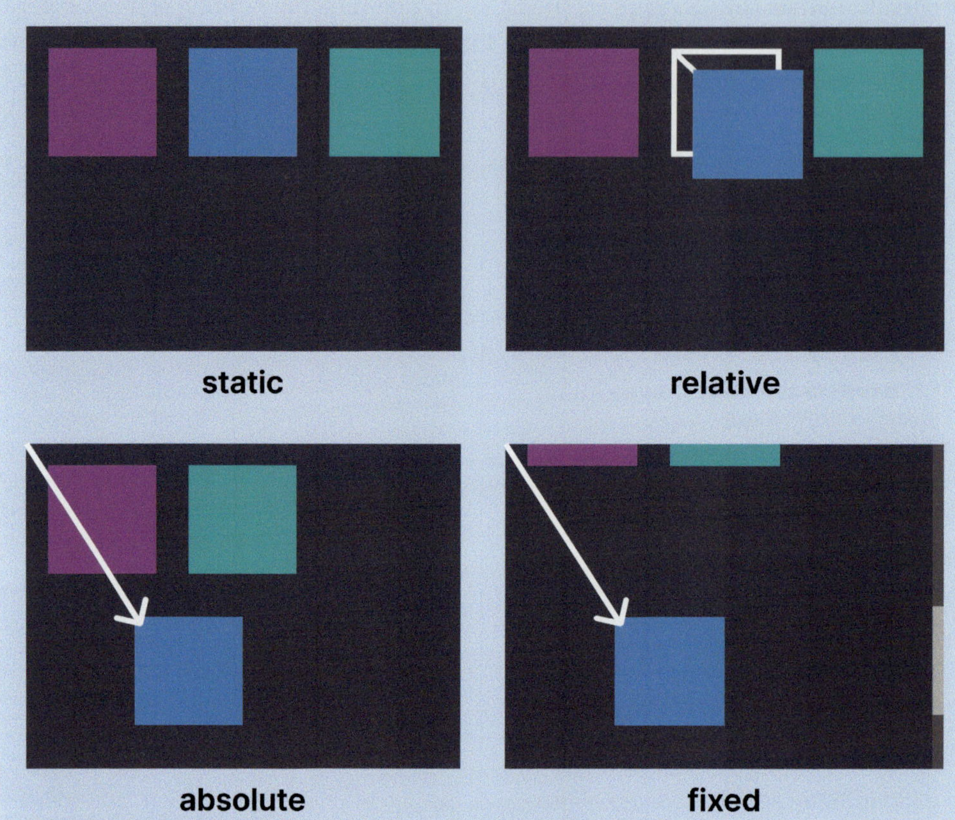

Figure 2.12
HTML elements can be positioned in different ways. **Static** is the default and causes the element to "go with the flow" of the page. **Relative** position allows an element's position to be offset from its original position using the top, right, bottom, or left properties. Absolute position will set the element's origin to the top left of a page before you apply offsets. Fixed position is the same as absolute, except the element will stay fixed even if the page scrolls. Finally, sticky (not pictured) will cause an element to stick to the top of the screen if the user scrolls past its origin. See this example for more **criticalwebdesign.github.io#css-position.**

Exercise 2.2.5 Inspect CSS Rules with DevTools

1. Open your **index.html** page in Chrome.
2. Right-click any location on the page and choose **Inspect** to open DevTools. This will open the **Elements** tab and focus on the line of code corresponding to the area where you clicked.

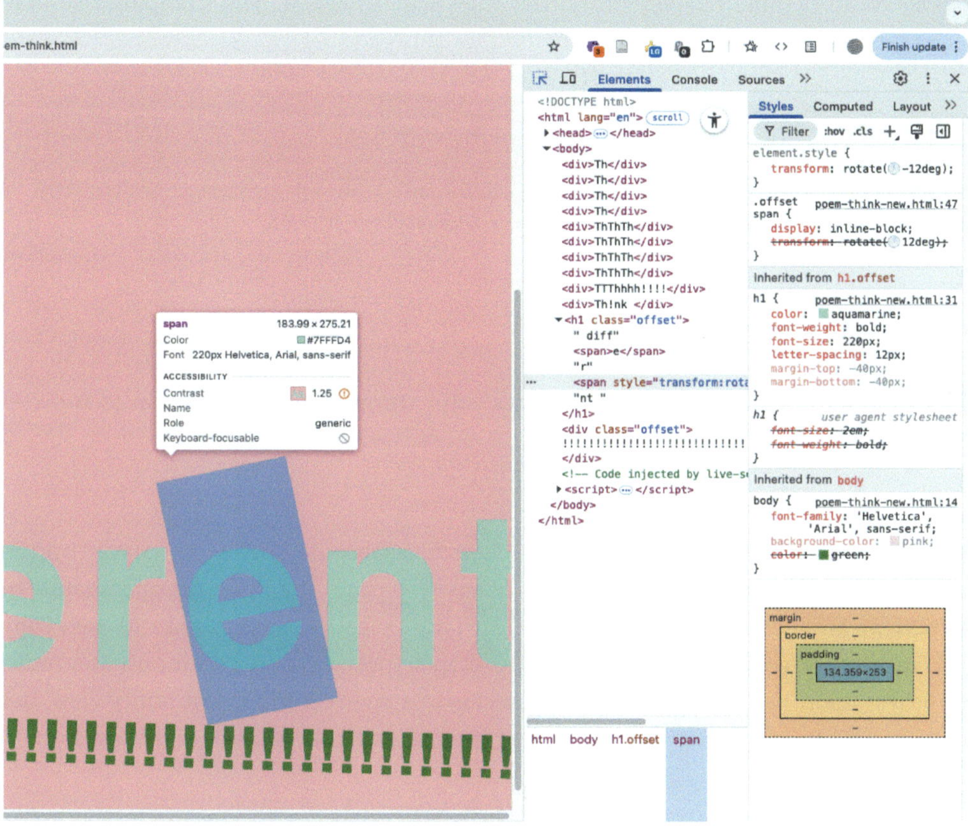

Figure 2.13
Using DevTools, developers can see and manipulate a live version of the page. The element is visualized in the bottom right using the Box Model diagram.

3. Inside DevTools, be sure the Element tool is selected (figure 2.13) then hover over lines of HTML code to highlight them on the page. You will see rectangles appear defining the bounding boxes of components of the CSS Box Model, reflecting the element's margin (orange), border (yellow), padding (green), content (blue), as well as transform and other properties of the box.
4. Select the element in DevTools to see the CSS rules assigned to it under the **Styles** sub-tab. Toggle a checkbox next to any CSS rule to see the element with and without that style applied.
5. If you select the `<h1>` tag in the HTML panel, you will see that some styles have been marked out, like the color rule inherited from body, reflecting the *cascading* nature

of CSS to be able to overwrite other rules when needed. The **Computed** sub-tab shows the styles that were actually used for this page.

Prompt 2.2 Code: Expressive Typography with CSS

Add the text from the manifesto you chose to the **index.html** page. You will need to wrap words or characters with HTML tags to control its display with CSS.

Module 2.3 JavaScript and DevTools

In this module you will learn to use JavaScript through an introduction to browser DevTools.

2.3.1 View Source and DevTools

Accessed under **View** > **Developer** > **View Source** in Chrome, the "View Source" option makes it possible to view the HTML code of any web page. Thanks to the open nature of hypertext, anyone can use this option to learn how a feature was created and even copy and modify the code for their own use. Developer Tools, or more commonly **DevTools**, improves upon this idea to provide *live* access to a page's source to not only view, but edit the HTML and CSS properties in real time to experiment, test, and learn how to improve your page.

Activity: Modify NPR.org using DevTools

Any change you make to a web page using DevTools exists in the local copy in your browser and lasts only until you refresh the page. This means you can experiment and modify the source of any page on the internet!

1. Go to **npr.org** and find a headline on the page that you think could be "improved" with a more optimistic tone. Right-click the headline and choose Inspect to open the element in DevTools.
2. Double-click on the headline text in the Element tab and edit the text. Press the **Return** key to see your changes!
3. Give your headline more emphasis with CSS so that it stands out. Double-click the `size` property of the CSS rule and increase it. Add a rule called `color` and choose something loud to make sure your new, positive headline is more visible than others.

2.3.2 Introduction to JavaScript

JavaScript (often written as "JS") is the programming language for the web. JavaScript can run in any web browser or even on your computer. You can use JS to add or modify content on the page, make forms and media interactive, and even build games and animations for the web. The quickest way to test JavaScript is with your browser's DevTools, which you'll do in the next exercise.

A big part of programming is based around inputs and outputs. When you **input** a command in the Console, the code is executed and returns **output** that you can use. **Expressions** are any unit of code that resolves to a value. For example, if you input a basic expression like `1 + 1` JavaScript will evaluate the text and return (output) a new value (`2`). They are the fundamental building blocks of programming and allow you to use data to perform math, logic, or other interesting things.[16]

Exercise 2.3.1 Test JavaScript Expressions in the Console

While the Elements tab shows live HTML and CSS code, the **Console** tab lets you *run* JavaScript right on the page. You will explore the Console now. See the wiki for a video demonstration of this exercise.

1. Open **npr.org** in Chrome.
2. To open the DevTools Console, either right-click, choose Inspect, and select the Console tab, or use a keyboard shortcut **Command+Option+J** (Mac) or **Ctrl + Shift + J** (Windows).
3. At the bottom you will see a command prompt denoted with a greater than (>) symbol. To run JavaScript, type the following after the prompt and press return.

   ```
   "Hello, World!"
   ```

4. If you pass data to JavaScript, it will simply return the data's value. The data you entered is called a **string**, indicated by the quotes used to wrap it, and is just one of many data types. Try typing a number value in the Console and press return.

   ```
   12
   ```

5. Again, JavaScript returned the same value. If we tell JS to do something with the data using an **operator** it might be more interesting. For example, we can use an arithmetic operator[17] with another value to cause JavaScript to evaluate the code, multiplying the values to return (or output) the new value.

   ```
   12 * 12
   ```

6. JavaScript can do all kinds of things with expressions. For example, it can compare two values and use that output to make decisions in the program. Run this to see what we mean.

   ```
   12 > 12
   ```

7. If an expression is a building block, a **statement** is what uses those blocks. JavaScript statements are like a complete sentence telling the machine what action to take; they even have punctuation (a semicolon;) to note when the instruction is complete. We can use the built-in `alert()` **function** with any data or expression to make JavaScript display an alert message to the user. A function is a type of statement that can be **called** using its name and two parentheses. Try these, one by one, placing data between the parentheses so the alert function will use it. Note that non-numeric characters must be wrapped with quotes to make a string.

```
alert(123);
alert("hi!");
alert(12 * 12);
```

8. Pat yourself on the back. You've just started programming! While it might seem intimidating at first, we believe this introduction is going to give you confidence as you learn more.

Exercise 2.3.2 Explore the Document Object Model

Every time a web page loads it creates a **DOM**, short for document object model (DOM), in order to represent all the HTML elements and content on the page (figure 2.14). The HTML DOM reflects the hierarchy of nested tags and content on the page. Just as you can access and change these elements manually with DevTools, you can use JavaScript to retrieve or set values on the page via the hierarchical tree of the DOM.

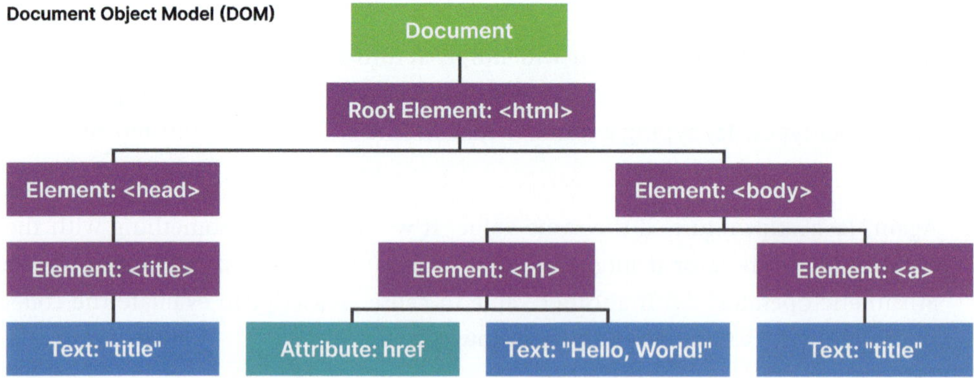

Figure 2.14
The hierarchical document object visualized.

1. Open **npr.org** in Chrome. If you already have it open, you can refresh the page to reset the Console.
2. In the DevTools Console, type **window** and press return. This will log the entire DOM object to the Console. Explore its properties and functions by expanding the drop-down arrows. Note that **alert** is the first function (it has an *f*) in this list.
3. Look for the **document** in the list and expand it to see all the data about the page itself. Scroll down to the **title** property. We can reference properties and functions in this hierarchy using **dot notation**. Refresh the page to reset and run the following.

```
document.title
```

4. Just as we used JavaScript to **get** the value stored in **document.title**. We can **set** the value to something new using an expression (figure 2.15). Run the following and press return. You should see the title of the page (on the tab) change to reflect the new value assigned to the title.

```
document.title = "Hello from the console!"
```

5. JavaScript can also change the presentation of your pages. Run this code to change the CSS code. If you go to the Elements tab you will see this has been added as an inline style to the opening **<body>** tag.

```
document.body.style.backgroundColor = "plum"
```

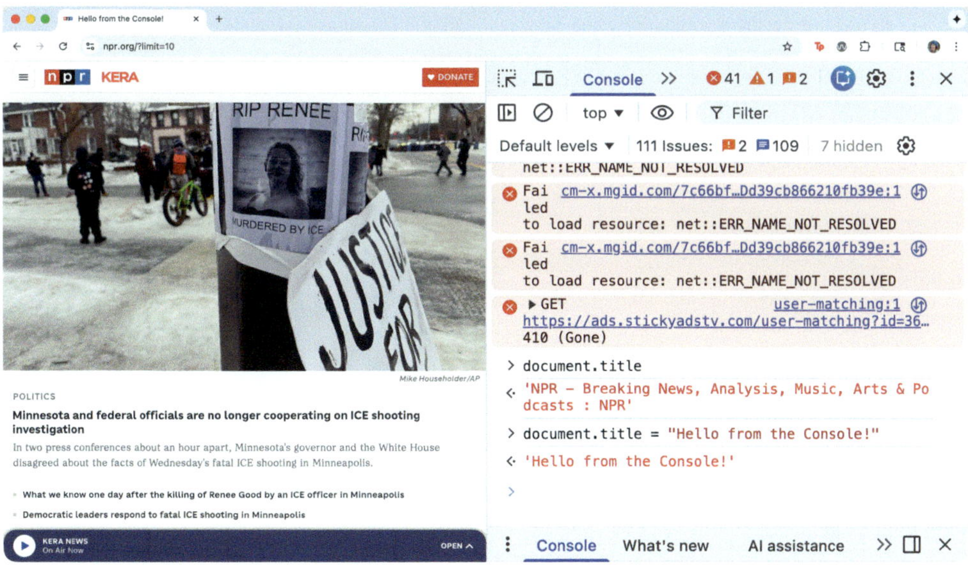

Figure 2.15
Use the Console to test JavaScript before you save it in your script tag.

Exercise 2.3.3 Examine the Console

Testing JavaScript in the Console is a great way to make sure your code is functional before you add it to your pages. As you probably noticed, the Console has an **autocomplete** feature, which can help you learn about what is possible in the language. In this exercise you will learn to use the Console to explore messages, warnings, and errors from the browser.

1. In Chrome, go to this URL: **criticalwebdesign.github.io#errors**
2. Open DevTools using Inspect and click on the Console tab. You should see several messages **logged** in here (figure 2.16), as well as the line number of the file that generated the message. Whether an error or a message you add yourself, these are all helpful for displaying information about the progress and state of variables in your code "under the hood."
3. Add a new message to the Console using the `console.log()` function, placing text inside quotes between the parentheses as you did above with `alert()`. Explore other console functions like `console.warn()` and `console.error()`.[18]
4. Notice that one message, "**Failed to load resource: the server responded with a status of 404 ()**," was logged because the browser could not locate a file. This is referred

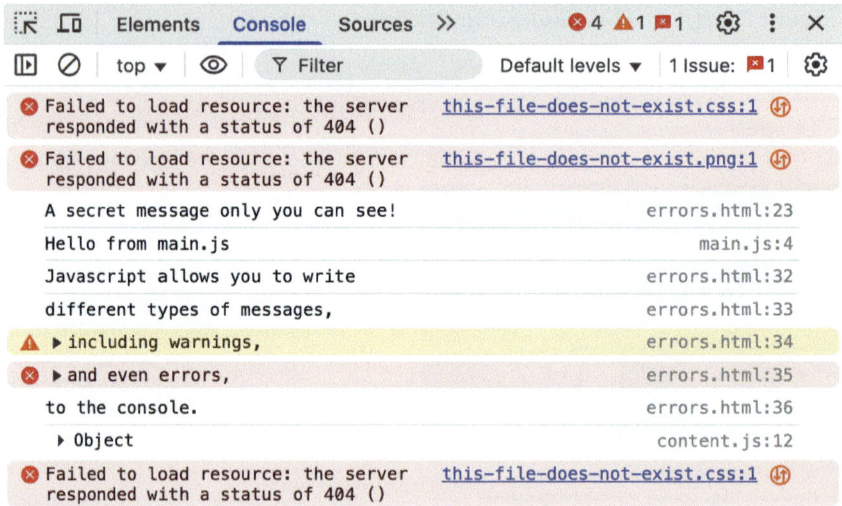

Figure 2.16
The Console can show several types of messages, warnings, and errors to let you know about issues with your page.

to as the **404 File Not Found** error and is one of the most common errors new developers encounter. It might mean that you typed the file name or path incorrectly in your code, or that the file hasn't yet been uploaded to your website. What is important is that we know about this issue *because we have the Console* open while we are coding the page.

5. Click on the **Network** tab inside DevTools and reload the web page. You will see a list of all the files the browser attempted to load while rendering this page, along with each of their HTTP Response Codes (under the Status column), and a **Waterfall** showing when and how long it took to load each resource.

As you can see, there are many other tabs to explore inside DevTools. The Console is one of the most important because it tells you when there might be a problem with a page and where you can fix it in your code.

Best Practices: Leave the Console Open!

Most web developers leave DevTools open while they are coding, and we advise you to do the same. It will save precious time and frustration if you need to see the code or by showing you an error if you mistype a path.

Best Practices: Avoid Smart Quotes

You should always design with smart quotes and code in dumb quotes.

```
<script>
    alert("Hello, World!");
    alert(“Hello, World!“);
</script>
```

Figure 2.17
VS Code and other editors use color to let you know when your code syntax is not correct. The first line in this image uses **dumb quotes** so the formatter changes the color to indicate it is recognized as a string. The second line uses **smart quotes** (aka "curly quotes") so the formatter shows the string does not conform to a single color and adds red underlines to signify the syntax error.

Exercise 2.3.4 Add JavaScript to a Web Page

CSS should be added to the top of a page so that the style rules are available when the browser attempts to render the HTML. JavaScript, on the other hand, should be added to the bottom of a page so that the HTML elements exist when the code tries to access them.

1. Open your **view-source** project in Codespaces.
2. Open **index.html** and add a `<script>` tag to the end, just before the closing `</body>` tag. This ensures the entire document has loaded in the browser, and JS can access the HTML.
3. Add the JS `alert()` function and then between the parentheses () add a string parameter surrounded by two double quotes. When the browser loads the page, it executes this script and sends an alert with the message you added as a parameter for the alert function.
4. Use the `console.log()` function to log the same message to the Console. This is usually the preferred method to test your program, so you don't have to dismiss the alert box every time you refresh the page.

```
<script>
  alert("Hello, World!");
  console.log("Hello, from the console!");
</script>
```

Check Your Work

This concludes the chapter exercises. We invite you to compare your work to the final outcome **criticalwebdesign.github.io#2-3** and code **criticalwebdesign.github.io#2-3-code** in the book repo. Don't forget to enable GitHub Pages in your project and then stage and commit your work to make it live!

Prompt 2.3 Publish: Complete Your Expressive Typography Page

Creating a website that is accessible for all viewers is an important goal. We provide an in-depth look at accessibility in chapter 7, but you can start testing for accessibility now using code validation and by incorporating `alt` attributes.

Continue developing your work using the suggestions below:

- Use DevTools to inspect your page in the browser and experiment with different CSS rules to control its display. Refer back to your wireframe and the CSS box model documentation as needed.
- Incorporate design choices using focal point and contrast to add context or new meaning to the text in your design.
- View the examples in the book repo showing our own responses to this prompt. Use DevTools to explore the source code to learn how we created these.
- Use the W3C's HTML and CSS code validation tools to check your code.
- As you finalize your solution to prompt 2.3, consider using JavaScript's `console.log()` to cite the quote, poem, or manifesto you selected. Include the title, author, date, and a link to the original. You can also log a license for work. We licensed our pages with a Creative Commons and MIT license. If you do not want to attribute your work with a "copyleft" license, you can always use a traditional copyright.

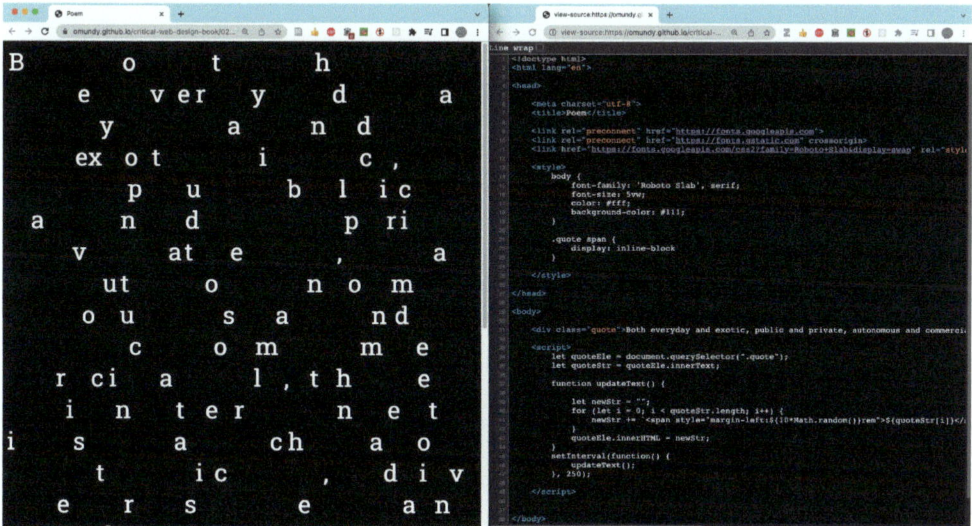

Figure 2.18
This alternative solution to prompt 2, **criticalwebdesign.github.io#poem-chaos**, uses JavaScript to update the CSS of the page to create an animated rendition of Rachel Greene's description of the possibilities and "chaos" of the WWW from her book *Internet Art*. See this example and more at **criticalwebdesign.github.io/book/**.

Author Note: Keep Practicing!

At this point in your web development journey, it's fine to stick with the CSS rules you have seen so far like margin, padding, font size, and color to see how close you can get to your original design. But don't feel like you need to learn all the HTML tags and CSS properties that exist either. Use a search engine or explore examples online using DevTools and keep experimenting. It is also typical for a coded design to vary from your initial sketches. In the following chapters, you will continue adding to your capabilities by using a design layout tool and design grids to control the positioning of elements on the page. As you learn new techniques you will improve your ability to represent the designs you create through code.

3 Critical Design

> Most North Americans now live designer lives—sleep, eat, sit in a car, work, shop, watch TV, sleep again. I doubt there's more than a handful of free, spontaneous minutes anywhere in that cycle.
>
> —Kalle Lasn

Context

Anthony Dunne and Fiona Raby write that critical design "uses speculative design proposals to challenge narrow assumptions, preconceptions, and givens about the role products play in everyday life."[1] Critical design inverts, transcends, or refuses the commercial role that design often plays. Rather than upholding the status quo (which is deeply embedded in capitalist histories and tendencies), critical designs "are testimonials to what could be, but at the same time, they offer alternatives that highlight weaknesses within existing normality" (35). Dunne and Raby coined this term in the mid-nineties, yet the definition intersects with several other concepts and art historical practices like detournément, culture jamming, adversarial design, tactical media, and creative disturbance, to name some. You can locate ideas of refusal in the Dadaists, and transcendence by way of the surrealists, including practices of automatic writing. While this is not an exhaustive list of antecedents to critical design, the spirit of the artists and designers who use creative practice to transform the everyday is alive in each of them. Critical web design also shares in this art and design legacy as it applies to making on, for, and of the WWW.

Culture Jamming

In this chapter you will create a series of "unbranded" designs inspired by the subvertisements (a portmanteau of "subversive" and "advertisement") that fill the pages of

Figure 3.1

Top: The *Adbusters Corporate American Flag* transforms the stars and stripes into a symbol of patriotism for a field of corporations. In money we trust. Search online to see many variations and updates to the corporate logos over the years. Bottom: This spoof cigarette ad from *Adbusters* magazine[2] reinterprets the Marlboro Man as a wistful cowboy who shares nostalgia and regretful longing for his healthy lung. Images appear courtesy of Adbusters Media Foundation.

Additional Materials and Resources

Explore links and other content related to this chapter:
criticalwebdesign.github.io#wiki-03.

Kalle Lasn's *Adbusters* magazine. This form of media art and political communication, a precursor to memes today, twists the content and other properties of designs associated with popular brands to deliver a critical, often contrary or competing message (figure 3.1). It is not the design, per say, that is being critiqued, but the malevolent practices of the company that the logo or ad represents. For example, the critical message might address the way in which a company uses design to obfuscate harmful or false information or intentions. This was the case with some of the most popular subvertisements of the 1980s and '90s, which were made to undo messaging put forward by cigarette companies. Joe Camel becomes Joe Chemo, for instance; or the Marlboro Man is seen standing in front of giant letters spelling the word "impotent" (perform a search for "subvertisement marlboro man" to find it). During this time the public learned that cigarettes were linked to increased risk of lung cancer and emphysema. Soon it became clear that the tobacco industry had been aware of these risks as early as the 1950s but continued to market their addictive substances without sharing this knowledge.[3] Putting a cute camel on the packaging, presumably to make the product attractive to younger audiences/potential future buyers, was an especially heinous strategy played out by corporate marketers and designers to shroud the destructive effects of smoking at the expense of the consumers' lives.

Adversarial Design

Subvertising is a creative practice that is part of the media art and protest genre called "culture jamming"—a term coined by Negativland in 1984 to refer to acts of mass media sabotage. Co-editors Marilyn DeLaure and Moritz Fink write, "At its best, culture jamming is a creative and inventive mode of public engagement: it cultivates critical attitudes toward commercial culture and dominant institutions, and helps foster belief that the world can be different."[4] While culture jamming responds to mass media, as Mark Dery writes, by "boxing with shadows,"[5] Carl DiSalvo's "adversarial design" (from his eponymous book in 2015) involves action along with potential solutions. Rather than responding only in protest, DiSalvo suggests design can do the work of agonism. He writes that artifacts and systems can be adversarial when they "represent and enact the political conditions of contemporary society and function as contestational objects that challenge and offer alternatives to dominant practices and agendas."[6]

In *The New York Times Special Edition*, The Yes Men with Steve Lambert and additional partners produced, printed, and distributed a fake version of *The New York Times* newspaper that celebrates an abrupt, but definitely fictional, end to the Iraq War.[7] Many people involved in this project imagined and wrote "All the News We Hope to Print," a week after Barack Obama was elected into office in 2008, calling forth the work to be done. As a fake, the newspaper employs a verisimilitude (or "truthlikeness") that tricks recipients into believing they have received a free copy of the *Times*. The design of the paper, writing of the fake articles, and distribution by many volunteers contributed to a project (easily categorized as either culture jamming or adversarial design) that surprised recipients in New York City who only had to read a few lines before realizing what they had received was a knock-off.

Speculative Design

Unlike most culture jams, *The New York Times* project refers to the original in order to promote potential improvements to society. It is this emphasis on positive outcomes that is reminiscent of other critical design methods like design fiction (a term that combines design with science fiction[8]) and speculative design. These practices explore possible future scenarios through hypothetical, often provocative, outcomes and objects. As in other works by The Yes Men (for instance, the Barbie Liberation Organization), the objects from *The New York Times Special Edition* were only a way to facilitate meaningful conversations around the unrealized areas for societal improvement. In his book *Conversation Pieces*, the art critic and historian Grant Kester discusses works that involve public engagement, where creating objects, spaces, or scenarios (or potentially, software) "involves the creative orchestration of collaborative encounters and conversations well beyond the institutional boundaries of the gallery or museum . . . these exchanges can catalyze surprisingly powerful transformations in the consciousness of their participants."[9] So, too, can these encounters be had online.

Critical Web Design

Just as tactics can be shared across the domains we mention above, critical web design also has the potential to foster debate through cleverly reimagining how users perceive and know the world. Thanks to hypertext, the public nature of the WWW, and programmable interfaces, critical web design offers new formats and methods for how these messages are shared, and experienced. For example, *Binky*, by Dan Kurz (figure 3.2), is an app that reflects on human-computer codependency in a playful and tangible way. As Kurz describes in the trailer for the project, at first glance, this mobile application looks like Instagram or any other infinitely scrolling social media app.[10] However, the content you see in Binky is completely random. By including all the affordances (things

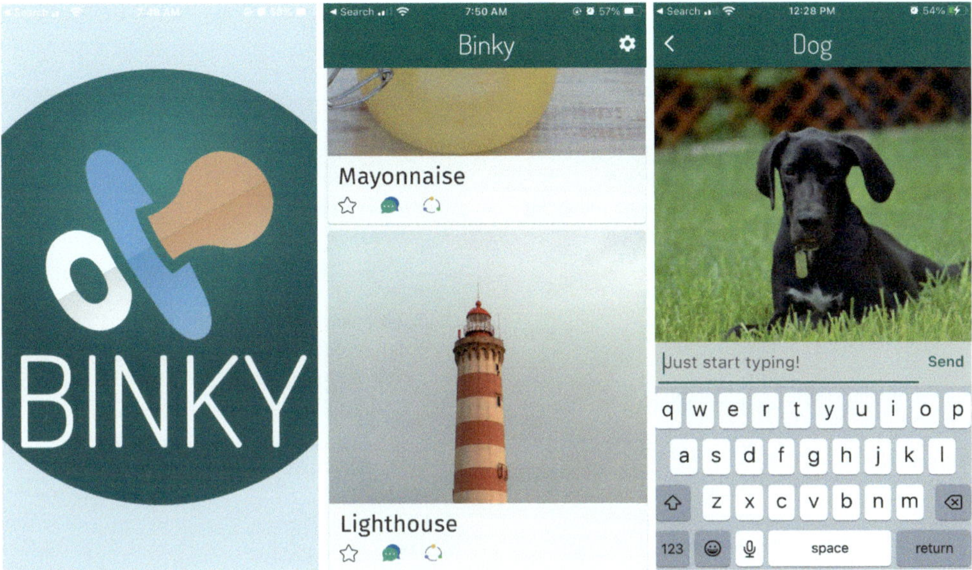

Figure 3.2
Binky by Dan Kurtz is a real, fake mobile app that lets users, like other social media apps, scroll, like, and comment on posts. Like an infant's binky (or pacifier), it satisfies the need to use social media, except it doesn't allow users to upload or save files, and it will not monetize your data. See **binky.rocks**.

you can do) of apps it mimics, letting you "like" photos and type comments (also auto generated and wonderfully cliché regardless of which keys you type), Binky critiques the world of apps and craze around their development ever so common in Silicon Valley. But it also humorously gives us users a way out, offering us "all the pleasure of tapping, scrolling, liking, and commenting without any of the burden of meaning."[11]

As we write above, these works can be appreciated under several contexts. They are clearly designed, yet they are not in the commercial design category "A" that Dunne & Raby identify in their book (figure 3.3).[12] We find them instead in the "B" column, with other speculative works intended to foster debate and ask questions that commercial design is not supposed to address. Very few of the authors might consider themselves to be only "Artists," which is perhaps also under the control of capital, since it is difficult to sell something one freely contributes toward the common good and "Art" is so often hidden away in museums or private collections.

You might think of them less as "Art" and more as media projects that have a purpose (or a purposeful mispurpose). What we appreciate about critical design is that it can encompass art, design, and other media that might seem difficult to categorize if you haven't been exposed to expert language, including some of the genres we have discussed, like culture jamming, adversarial design, tactical media, and others. In fact,

A	B
Affirmative	Critical
Problem solving	Problem finding
Provides answers	Asks questions
Design for production	Design for debate
Design as solution	Design as medium
In the service of industry	In the service of society
Fictional functions	Functional fictions
For how the world is	For how the world could be
Change the world to suit us	Change us to suit the world
Science fiction	Social fiction
Futures	Parallel worlds
The "real" real	The "unreal" real
Narratives of production	Narratives of consumption
Applications	Implications
Fun	Humor
Innovation	Provocation
Concept design	Conceptual design
Consumer	Citizen
Makes us buy	Makes us think
Ergonomics	Rhetoric
User-friendliness	Ethics
Process	Authorship

Figure 3.3
Dunne & Raby's *A/B*, 2009 and ongoing. See **dunneandraby.co.uk/content/projects/476/0**.

as practitioners and teachers of these forms, we often find that specific labels and constraints to categorize or exclude practices get in the way of exploring the messages, forms, and potential positive outcomes contained within them.

Best Practices: Fair Use

If your project is a design experiment that you don't plan to share publicly, you won't have to worry about the legality of modifications you make to a corporate logo. While intellectual property (copyright, patents, and so on) laws vary across territories, in the United States the **fair use**[17] doctrine includes four specific (and commonsense) dimensions that are assessed when copyrighted material is used without first gaining permission:

1. The "purpose and character of use" looks at how you used the original, allowing for creative expressions of critique or parody in noncommercial works.
2. The "nature of the copyrighted work" assesses whether the original is a unique work that deserves protection.
3. The "amount and substantiality" question asks how much you changed or transformed the original in your design iterations.
4. The fourth dimension asks whether the unlicensed use of the original would diminish or affect the value of the original.

Case Study 3.1: xtine burrough, Delocator.net

XB: In 2005 I led a team that designed and launched **Delocator.net**. My goal was to create a tool for locating independent businesses in an era before the "Web 2.0" introduced apps that relied on user-generated content like Yelp and Tripadvisor. Delocator.net initially launched as a space for participants to submit addresses of locally owned coffee shops in their neighborhoods, providing an alternative to the well-advertised Starbucks locations. For their article, "Consumer Exit, Voice, and 'Power' on the Internet," S. Umit Kucuk writes, "Delocator.net is a good example of how consumers can articulate their anti-consumption philosophy by targeting specific corporate brands and connecting with other consumers through the co-creation of messages and inspiring consumers to change their behaviours and create economic pressure on the targeted brand."[13]

Since the website was made to flex, as Kucuk writes, an "exit-based consumer power," the visual reference to the Starbucks brand was an important part of the visual identity. Unbranded iterations on the logo left the green circle around the outside of the recognizable Starbucks identity intact, while drawing the letters with expressive typography signified difference (figure 3.4). In all versions of the logo, the iconic mermaid was replaced.

Figure 3.4
Delocator.net logo variations (2005, 2009) include the distressed type reference to Starbucks, and in later versions stars to emphasize wayfinding.

An important design question was: Has the logo been transformed enough so that the original reference was legible, but the new work of design was not too derivative? Of course, one check we can perform on our work is to consider it within the four factors used to assess fair use (see the Best Practices callout):

1. The work was made for noncommercial purposes and referenced the original design as part of an effort to critique the massive invasion of Starbucks stores in land plots adjacent to local coffee shops.
2. The original is a unique and protected work, and thus our reference to it should be assessed with respect to the other three factors.
3. The amount of transformation is crucial: Leaving the green concentric circles in the design helps the viewer understand the connection to the Starbucks logo, but all other parts of the composition are transformed in the name of parody.
4. This work does not alter the value of the original. In a 2005 *New York Times* article about the project, Kim Severson writes, "Starbucks would not comment on the Delocator directly. But a spokeswoman, Val Hwang, said in an e-mail message, 'We are aware that people use many means to voice their opinions, including fliers, bumper stickers and Websites.'"[14]

In one of the major revisions to the project (2009), I redesigned the site to incorporate all of the data we collected into a Google Map, following a suggestion made by Tom Brickman, a fan and user of the site from the United Kingdom.[15] Pragya Singh programmed the current version of the site (2026).[16] I redesigned the logo, adding stars in place of the beans to reference historical modes of wayfinding that used the night sky.

Prompt 3 What You'll Make
Create a Work of Critical Web Design

In this chapter you will use Figma to unbrand and redesign a corporate brand identity. You will then iterate on your design, considering typographic choices using Google Fonts, and create a web page with interactive images and JavaScript to express your ideas. The web page you will create in the exercises forms a critique of an IKEA advertisement with the tagline, "Everything you need," and corresponding image of the iconic hex wrench used to assemble most IKEA furniture. Our example web page suggests that the one thing the company cannot give you is the abundance of time that it takes to assemble the big-box furniture. You will learn to create a **mouseover** effect to swap the image of the wrench with a clock.

View the results of our unbranded Ikea page at **criticalwebdesign.github.io#3-3** (figure 3.5). You can see the final code for every chapter on the CWD repo, **criticalwebdesign.github.io#repo**.

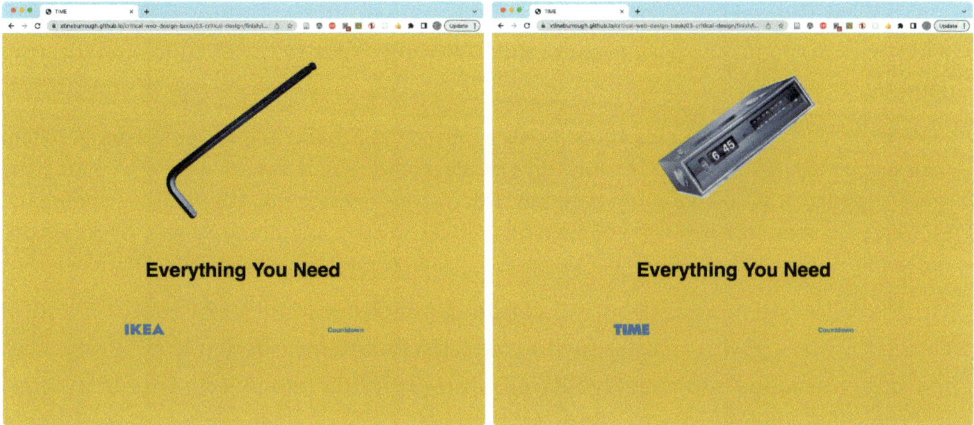

Figure 3.5
Our example uses the CSS `:hover` pseudo-class to swap the image of the Allen wrench with a graphic of an alarm clock. The TIME wordmark is an unbrand of the IKEA logo.

Inspiration: Paula Scher

This chapter's prompt draws inspiration from designer Paula Scher's playful parody of a book cover. Scher's design critiques Swiss design for its predictability by changing the title to a pseudo-German phrase to protest the contemporary design layout standards as, "Boring this is boring." Listen to Scher describe this work and her philosophy of "serious play" in her TED talk, "Great Design Is Serious, Not Solemn."[18]

Module 3.1 Design with Figma

One of the most visible functions of graphic and web design in society is in the service of marketing and public relations for corporations. A corporation is a legal designation that authorizes a group of people to act as a single entity and thereby protects shareholders and board members against repercussions if the entity breaks the law or harms others. Yet thanks to manipulation of the US Supreme Court, corporations still enjoy all the constitutional protections afforded to US citizens, including free speech. With many more resources at their disposal, corporations actually enjoy much "freer speech" than the average citizen, in addition to no indemnity, and of course, potentially hundreds of marketers, designers, and programmers to craft their message.

In the **First Things First Manifesto**, published originally in 1964 and again in 2000, leaders in the field of graphic design wrote the following about the over-commercialization of design:

> Designers who devote their efforts primarily to advertising, marketing and brand development are supporting, and implicitly endorsing, a mental environment so saturated with commercial messages that it is changing the very way citizen-consumers speak, think, feel, respond and interact. To some extent we are all helping draft a reductive and immeasurably harmful code of public discourse.[19]

In the following modules you will continue establishing the foundations of critical web design, starting with an introduction to Figma for interface design, coding with CSS, and using custom fonts in your layouts, all while exploring the subject of "unbranding."

3.1.1 Brands, Identities, and Logos

Where a **brand** refers to the overall perception of a company or organization, the **identity** refers to the visual elements of that brand. While the identity can include typefaces, colors, business cards, websites, uniforms, and so on, the most obvious signifier is the **logo** (figure 3.6), which is a symbol or graphic that represents the organization absent the name. A **wordmark** is the custom design of a brand name and includes the exact typeface, letter spacing, color, and arrangement of a word. A **logo lockup** pairs the logo and wordmark "locked together" in a specific arrangement. Often an organization will prepare other versions of these graphics for special cases, like for social media icons or when localized (location specific) versions are needed.

Figure 3.6
Ben & Jerry's uses several graphics to express their identity including (1) the simple "Arch" logo; (2) the US "Arch" logo with "flavor cloud"; (3) a wordmark, "for when the 'Arch' cannot be used"; (4) a stacked wordmark; and (5) an icon to represent their brand on social media.[20]

Author Note: B Corp

The B Corp Certification[21] is a designation for businesses that demonstrate high social and environmental performance, make a legal commitment in their corporate governance to be accountable to stakeholders (not just shareholders), and maintain transparency on factors like employee benefits, charitable giving, and supply chain practices. Ben & Jerry's attained B Corp status in 2012.

Activity: Why Unbrand a Corporate Logo?

Borrowing, appropriating, and transforming works of art has never been a one-way communicative activity. As much as artists borrow from consumer culture, corporations also help themselves to the work of artists and counterculture groups in their marketing and advertising materials.[22] Additionally, in the "real world" you will have plenty of opportunities to create boring, promotional material, so you should use this chance to create something experimental, fearless, and honest! Start by exploring some reasons why you might want to perform such a critique in your design.

1. Create a list of positive and negative effects of corporations. These can be general or specific. If you are in a classroom, you might work with a partner. For example, a positive effect might be shared wealth in the form of generous donations, and a negative effect might be environmental hazard.
2. Support your ideas by providing one company that exemplifies the effects you listed. For example, TOMS shoes donates a portion of its profit to "grassroots good," while Exxon was notoriously responsible for one of the worst oil spills in US waters. Consult a reputable news article to confirm your ideas with facts.
3. Collect examples of the company's branding, including logo variations, style guides, and in-context uses. How might you alter them to account for the information you explored above? Select a specific representation to use in your unbranding. It may be helpful to identify something about the brand it represents that you feel is inauthentic or could use context.

3.1.2 Design Layout Tools

While we recommend starting with paper, you will eventually need to compose your design using a digital layout tool. Coding a design in HTML/CSS is time consuming, and it is difficult to change and experiment with different layouts. A design tool makes it easy to change and compare typefaces, colors, and compositions across different versions of your design, and pre-visualize the final layout exactly as you intend, before you code it.

There are many design tools, and they vary in complexity and cost. In our classrooms, we use Adobe software and Figma because they are popular with professional designers. Figma is specifically targeted for web design. It contains most of the capabilities found in Photoshop and Illustrator, in addition to several other UX design features to let you preview how your design will look on different devices, simulate user interactions, or collaborate on or share your design with others. Figma also maintains a promise on their website that it "will be forever free for students and educators,"[23] and now that (thankfully) the Adobe acquisition has been abandoned, we are optimistic it will not change. We will demonstrate the basics of digital design in the web-based version of Figma,[24] but you can use a design software with which you are already familiar as well.

Best Practices: The Right Tool

When considering learning a new tool, ask yourself: What problems was it made to solve? Photoshop was made for photo editing. Illustrator was built to create detailed vector graphics. Likewise, you'll find that there are UI/UX design features available in Figma that are not available in other software.

Exercise 3.1.1 Figma Basics

Create a free Figma account before starting this exercise. As software tools like Figma can change often, we encourage you to explore their onboarding tutorials to learn the basics.

1. Login to **Figma.com** either in a web browser or by downloading and installing their client.
2. Create a new Figma file or open the layout we created for exercises in this chapter, **criticalwebdesign.github.io#figma-prompts**.
3. Figma organizes files inside projects, which are further organized under teams. Figma is cloud-based (files are stored on their server), which allows you to collaborate by adding other users to your team. We suggest you create your own new project and try to make it look like our design.
4. You will see a blank **Canvas**. This is the backdrop where you will add frames containing your designs. Select the **Frame** tool and create a new Frame by selecting the Desktop (1440x1024) preset (among others for mobile, tablet, and even paper sizes) from the menu on the right. Like Artboards in Photoshop or Illustrator, Frames in Figma organize and define the dimensions for each composition you create.
5. We are creating a spoof of an IKEA advertisement in this example, so we will sample colors from their website. Create a screenshot from **ikea.com** and paste or drag the image to your Figma canvas (figure 3.7).

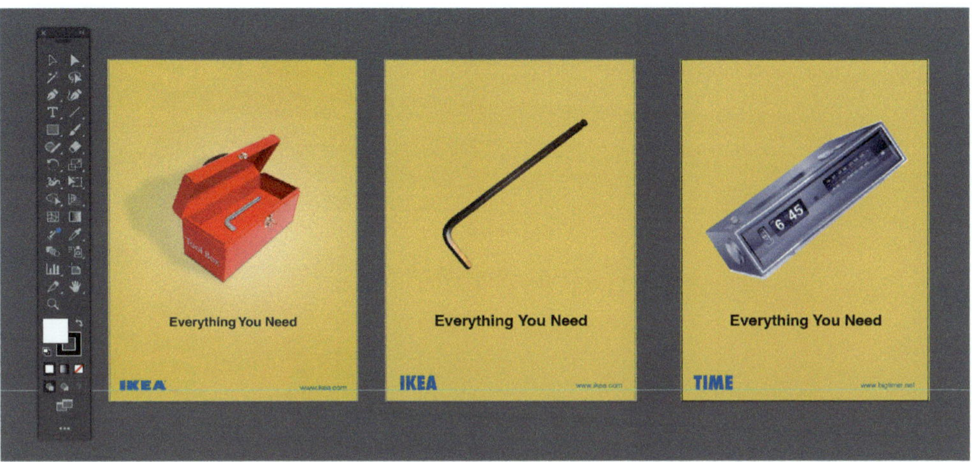

Figure 3.7
This layout shows a screenshot of an original advertisement (left) with mock-up images showing how the company name and graphics might change when the user interacts with the page. Notice that the typeface for the company does not match the original (we'll discuss that in the next section), but the background color and overall layout helps convey the similarities between the original and its transformation.

6. Set the background color of the frame to match the yellow in the company's brand. Select the frame and click on the color chip in the Fill area of the right-side panel. Use the **Sample Color** tool (eyedropper icon) to select the yellow color in the IKEA logo.
7. Use the **Rectangle** tool to make shapes on the page, the **Type** tool to add typography, and the **Move** tool to position objects in your layout. Figma is intuitive, but we created a step-by-step tutorial guiding you through our entire process on the chapter 3 wiki.

Activity: Color in the Browser

As you can see in the case study, color is an essential part of the brand identity. Color enabled xtine's project to reference the original while adding additional information to transform it into a form of commentary.

In the **additive color** model used by computer screens and digital cameras, light is mixed together, rather than pigments or ink, to produce the color humans perceive. Additive color is based on 256 possible values for each channel in the RGB (red, green, and blue) color space. Computers store and use binary data, so these values range from 0–255. Increasing the values in each channel results in colors that appear lighter.

1. In Figma, click the Ikea frame. Notice the color chip next to the fill property of the Design side panel on the right.
2. Click the Color Chip to open the color selector. Change the drop-down under the eye-dropper to RGB (figure 3.8).

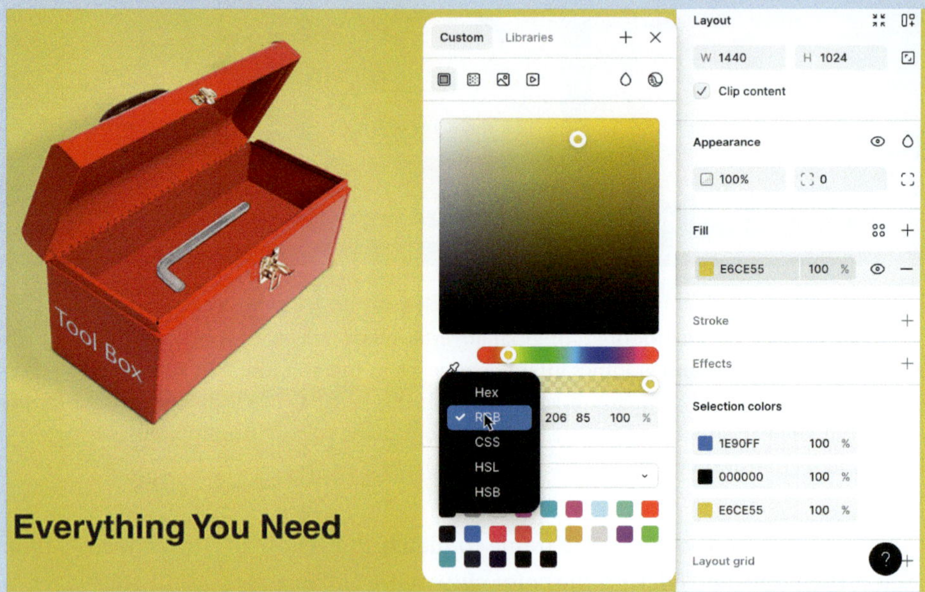

Figure 3.8
Click a Selection color to open the Custom Color panel where you can drag your cursor across a spectrum of hues. Inside the larger (top) box, drag to choose from a gradient of values for each hue from light to dark (as you drag top to bottom) and saturation levels (unsaturated to saturated from left to right).

3. Change the values of red, green, blue channels to 255, 0, 0 and you can see the relationship between the values and the hue it represents. Also notice, when all three are set to the maximum amount of light (255, 255, 255), the result is white, while 0, 0, 0 is black. The values for red can be expressed in CSS like: `rgb(255,0,0)`.
4. Change the drop-down menu to **Hex** to see another popular way to denote colors in CSS. Each character in the hexadecimal system uses sixteen possible values, from `0-9`, followed by alphabetic characters `A-F`, with `F` being the lightest. Hexadecimal colors begin with a hash (#), followed by 2 characters each representing red, green, and blue. So, red is `#FF0000`.

The colors discussed so far are all opaque. To control transparency of your color you can add a fourth **alpha channel** to the RGB colors. To do this in CSS use either the `rgba()` function (the fourth channel is a value from 0–1) or the HEXA notation, which adds a seventh and eighth character to your hexadecimal color values.

```
.red50pct { color: rgba(255, 0, 0, 0.5); }
.red50pct { color: #ff000080; }
```

There are many websites where you can see the relationship between these, including color palette generators like **rgbacolorpicker.com**.

3.1.3 Typography Basics

Typography describes the formal and aesthetic practice of designing and arranging letter forms to produce legible writing. If you are reading this then you have been well trained to see letters as symbols for sounds. But designers must see letters as graphic forms that hold within them shapes, a relationship between the positive and negative space, contrast between line weights, and so much more.

When choosing a **typeface** (a collection of related fonts) and **font** (variations in weight, width, and style of the typeface) for your web pages, you will make choices based on the content of the text, as well as its context on the page. For instance, a **display font** is a typeface variation that sets a mood or inspires specific feelings for your audience and is typically used for the design of headings and titles. However, the characteristics that make them stand out and grab the attention of readers also make their intricate design elements not readable when scaled down, making them a poor choice for large blocks of text. Conversely, the **body font** you choose for large text blocks should be easy to read or scan. It is always a best practice to left-align any text that **wraps** onto multiple lines to create an invisible leading line on the left side. This allows readers to quickly move their eyes with the writing and comprehend the words contained within the text. Ellen Lupton writes that optical sizes for headlines and display fonts are created "to have delicate, lyrical forms," while body text and captions "are built with heavier strokes."[25]

3.1.4 Serif or Sans-serif?

In figure 3.9 you can see that some letters have **serifs**, the small "kickstands" you might find hanging off of certain typefaces like Times New Roman or Roboto Serif; and others, like Helvetica or Open Sans, do not. The serif is a decorative element that can be seen in letter carvings dating back to Roman antiquity, while **sans-serif** fonts are missing these flourishes and present a more "modern"-looking typeface. The serif

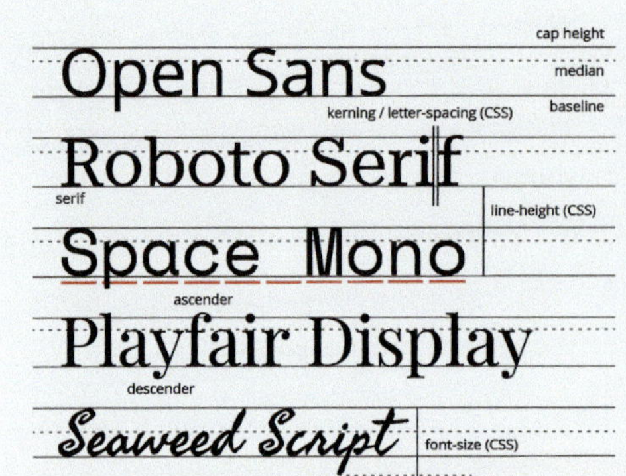

Roboto
Roboto Condensed
Roboto Flex
Roboto Mono
Roboto Slab
Roboto Serif

A **typeface** (or type family) is a collection of related fonts

Roboto Thin
Roboto Light
Roboto Regular
Roboto Medium
Roboto Bold

A **font** is a variation of a typeface; including any particular weight, width, and style

Display Font

A display font is a typeface variation that is good for setting a mood or inspiring specific feelings for your audience. However, because they have features that stand out and grab the attention of your readers, display fonts are hard to read at small sizes, making them a poor choice for large blocks of text.

Body Font

A display font is a typeface variation that is good for setting a mood or inspiring specific feelings for your audience. However, because they have features that stand out and grab the attention of your readers, display fonts are hard to read at small sizes, making them a poor choice for large blocks of text.

Display Font

Conversely, the body font you choose for large sections of text should be easy to read. It is good practice to left-align any text that wraps more than once. The invisible line left-aligned text creates along the left side allows readers to quickly scan the writing and comprehend the meaning of the text.

Body Font

Conversely, the body font you choose for large sections of text should be easy to read. It is good practice to left-align any text that wraps more than once. The invisible line left-aligned text creates along the left side allows readers to quickly scan the writing and comprehend the meaning of the text.

Figure 3.9
Top: These type specimens conveniently use their style in their name, respectively sans-serif, serif, monospace, display, and script fonts. Bottom: Which paragraphs are easier to read? Which headings grab your attention? These examples illustrate proper and improper use of display and body fonts. Explore the typeface categories at **fonts.google.com**.

was designed to finish a letter as it was carved into stone; however for people reading from a screen, sans-serif typefaces are generally simpler to see, especially when produced relatively small as body text.

Activity: Choosing or Matching a Typeface

Much of the time, when selecting a typeface for your web project, you will start by looking at Google Fonts, **fonts.google.com**.

1. Browse by categories, filter for serif or sans-serif fonts, and preview the font in whatever text you type into the box.
2. Once you find a font for your project, click to see its specimen page. Beneath the preview area, select the font by pressing the **Select** button (the plus) on the right side of the

preview. The Selected family menu appears on the right side of the browser. If it doesn't appear, then click on the icon on the top right of the window.

3. You should select several fonts and display them together so you can make a visual comparison.

For our project, we wanted to find a typeface matching the IKEA identity. We started with a search on Google for "IKEA logo font." Often organizations will start with a particular font and modify it to make it hard to copy or better match their identity. Identities also evolve, as you will find with IKEA. We chose the font Jost.

Prompt 3.1 Design: Reimagine a Brand's Message

Draw a wireframe and create mock-ups in Figma that subvert a corporation's messaging using their colors, typography, images, and/or language. Reimagine the messaging of a brand's identity to provide your own alternative commentary. Who is your audience? What do you want them to think about when they see your updated, subversive design? You may want to begin by making a screenshot of the original design and placing it in your composition. Some people like to layer new work on top of the original, thus imagining the original as a template. Your final web page will include a hover effect during which a page element (an image or text) changes when the user interacts with it by hovering their mouse on top of it.

Module 3.2 File Paths, Images, and Pseudo-Classes

In this module you will learn to link assets in your design with absolute and relative file paths. You will understand the difference between vector and raster graphics and learn to add images to your repo through Codespaces. Finally, you will make the image interactive using CSS. We'll begin by setting up a new repo for exercises in this chapter.

Exercise 3.2.1 Creating a New Repo from Our Template

We've created a GitHub repo with a starter template file, similar to the boilerplate file you made in chapter 2 (exercise 2.2.1). Throughout the rest of this book, you will begin your workflow by creating a new repo from our template.

1. Open our website template, **github.com/criticalwebdesign/website-template**. Click the **Use this template** drop-down menu and choose **Create a new repository**.
2. On the following page, name your new repo `critical-design` and press the **Create repository** button.
3. Now that you have your own repo, open it in GitHub Codespaces to build your project. Remember, there is a maximum limit to active Codespaces, see the callout

in exercise 2.2.2. Go to **github.com/codespaces** and click the green **New codespace** button. On the following page, select your repository from the drop-down menu to open it.

> ⚠ **Watch Out! Accessing Codespace**
> In the **Use this template** drop-down menu, you could choose "Open in a codespace" (rather than "Create a new repository"), skipping the steps required to make a new repo first. We found this to be more confusing than the steps we suggest in exercise 3.2.1.

3.2.1 Absolute File Paths

When you add an image to a web page, you need to refer to the location where the file is stored, known as its **path**, so the browser knows where to find the resource. Paths are essential when working with web pages, without which we couldn't create hyperlinks, display media, or link to external files. There are two kinds of paths you will use.

An **absolute path** (aka global path) defines an address from a well-known or "global" location. That might look like this: Go to Earth, find North America, then North Carolina, then go to the center of Davidson, find Ben & Jerry's one block south, and order a cone. This is an absolute path because it starts with a globally known location: Earth. Likewise, the following are also absolute paths, because they, too, start with globally known locations like domains on the internet (https), or the root folder of a filesystem (file:/// or /).

```
https://google.com
file:///Users/username/Sites/index.html
/Users/username/Sites/index.html
```

Exercise 3.2.2 Download Images from an Absolute Path

We will use two images in our project. You could "hard link" to them directly on our *Critical Web Design* repo using the absolute URL. However, you will ultimately want creative control over the images you use in your project, so you should know how to download an image using an absolute path.

1. In Chrome, open **criticalwebdesign.github.io#wrench**. This shortcut link will forward you to an absolute path that displays the wrench image from our book's repo, hosted on GitHub.
2. Right-click on the wrench and save the image to your Desktop or someplace in your hard drive where you can easily find and upload it to Codespaces in the next exercise.

3. Download and save the clock image to the same folder as the wrench: **criticalweb design.github.io#clock.**

3.2.2 Relative File Paths

A **relative path** does not include a global location and instead describes the steps it takes to get from your *current* location to another. If you were in the Edith O'Donnell Arts & Technology building at UTD and we instructed you to go to Ben & Jerry's using a relative path, we would say, "Exit this building, cross the pathway with Magnolia trees, and enter the Student Services Building. Go up the stairs, turn left, and locate Ben & Jerry's in the food court on your left." So for example (figure 3.10), to get from **index .html** to **styles.css**, your path would go "down" (a level in the directory hierarchy) into the **assets/** folder, then into the **css/** folder, to find **styles.css**. The complete path would look like this, where the slashes represent changing a directory:

```
assets/css/styles.css
```

The above path can also be written with a single dot and slash before **assets/**, to refer to the current directory, like this:

```
./assets/css/styles.css
```

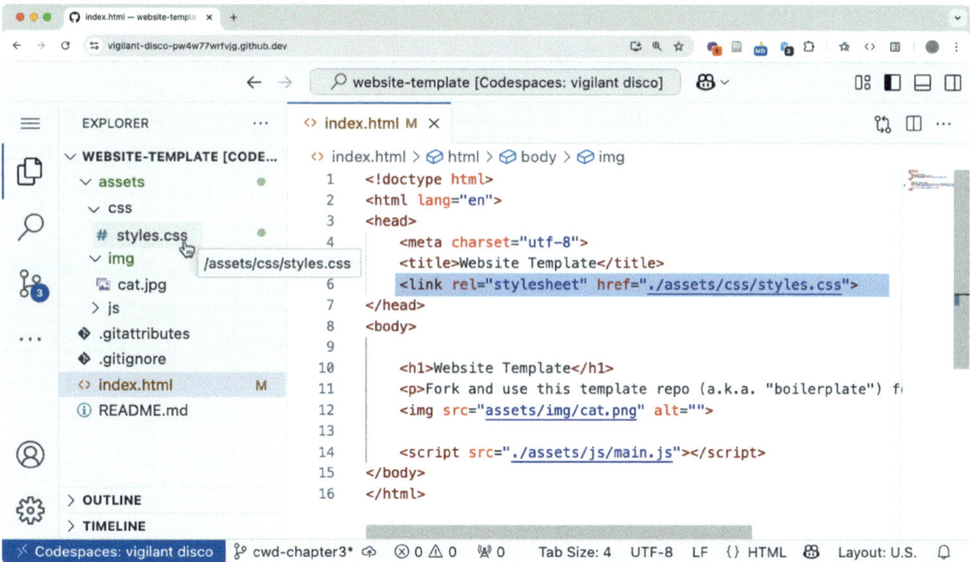

Figure 3.10
The relative link from **index.html** to the stylesheet points to the **assets/** directory, then the **css/** directory, to load **styles.css**.

Changing to a directory that is outside the current location (i.e., "up" a level in the directory hierarchy) is indicated with two dots and a forward slash, or ../. For instance, if you wanted to display the **cat.jpg** image you would use ../ to go up a directory (back to the **assets/** folder), then into the **img/** directory, to find **cat.jpg** like this:

```
../img/cat.jpg
```

Using relative paths to access files inside your website is almost always the best practice since it allows you to move your project anywhere, including to different web servers, without breaking internal links.

Exercise 3.2.3 Point to a Relative Path in HTML

With the wrench and clock images downloaded, you are ready to upload and use them in your project. In this exercise you will add files via Codespaces, then add a path to your image in your HTML document. See the wiki for a video demonstration of this exercise.

1. Open your **critical-design** project in Codespaces and make sure you have installed the Live Server extension.
2. Notice that the template we provided organizes images, stylesheets, and JavaScript files into separate folders inside an **assets/** directory. The following line of code (line 12 of **index.html**) uses a relative path to point to `cat.jpg` inside the **img/** folder, which is inside the **assets/** folder:

   ```
   <img src="assets/img/cat.jpg" alt="" >
   ```

3. In the Explorer section in the left side panel, click on the arrow to expand the **assets/** directory. Click on the arrow to expand **assets/img/** and you will see **cat.jpg** has been saved there. Upload **clock.png** and **wrench.png** by dragging and dropping them from your hard drive to the **img/** directory. When you hover over the **img/** directory you will see a green plus sign (+) indicating these images will be added to your Codespace.
4. Change the image source code on line 12 to point to the clock image (figure 3.11). The relative path from **index.html** points to **assets/img/clock.png**. Also, add an `alt` attribute, which is used to describe images or other media using plain text for assistive technologies such as screen readers.

   ```
   <img src="assets/img/clock.png" alt="digital clock">
   ```

⚠ Watch Out!

The **assets/** directory in our template includes three folders: **img/**, **css/**, and **js/**. If you move files outside of their respective folders, the paths we reference will no longer be accurate (and it will appear that your code is "broken"). Be careful about placing assets in their proper folders!

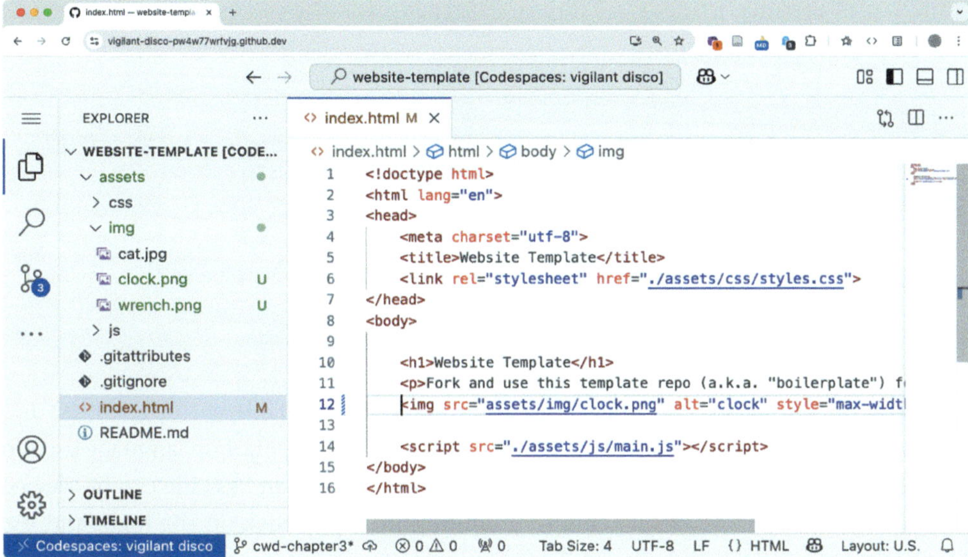

Figure 3.11
Notice the path to **clock.png** in the directories beneath the Explorer area. Also notice that the changes are unstaged, so these new images have not yet been saved in our repo!

5. Stage and Commit your work with a message about uploading the new images. The images will be pushed from the Codespace, which is a temporary working area, to your (more permanent) repository.
6. Go to **GitHub.com** and check your repo to verify the images are now there.

3.2.3 Vector and Raster Graphics

There are two types of images for the web. **Vector** graphics contain information about the position of **points**, **lines** that connect them, and other data (e.g., curves, color, and gradient) describing the appearance of those shapes. Because the representation is defined mathematically, a vector graphic can be scaled up or down without losing quality. This makes them ideal for logos, typefaces, and other line art that may be rendered across different sizes, from small screens to giant printed billboards.

Pro Tip: Digital file Formats, Extensions, and Media Types

When referring to digital files:

- The **file format** describes how data is stored within a file. Data can be stored as binary, plain text, or multipart (a combination). Some use compression to decrease the file size.
- The **file extension** identifies the file format and informs the operating system what software to use to open a file.
- The file's **media type** (aka **MIME type**) identifies the file's media type and subtype. For example: `text/html`, `image/png`, and `video/mp4`.

The most common vector image format online is **SVG** (scalable vector graphics) and is mostly used for logos and icons. SVG is also the name of the markup language used to describe the graphic.[26] As an extension of XML, the source of an SVG file can be viewed in a web browser. Go to **github.com** or **youtube.com**, right-click on the logo, and use inspect to examine the code that defines the image to see what we mean!

A vector is different from a **raster** image, which is constructed of a grid of pixels. The quality and size of a raster image (like a photograph) is defined by its **resolution** or the number of pixels used to represent the image. This means the size of a raster image cannot be increased without losing quality, because new pixels will have to be added using **interpolation** where the computer estimates their color from surrounding pixels. For this reason, when a designer creates a logo, the original file is almost always a vector graphic to ensure that it can be scaled up or down without a loss of detail.

3.2.4 Image Formats

There are several raster formats for the web, each with different characteristics that make them better for some applications over others. These traits usually balance the quality of the image compared to its resulting file size to ensure that the graphic remains readable while allowing it to be downloaded quickly. For example, the **JPG** (Joint Photographic Experts Group) image format (with a .jpg or .jpeg extension) uses a compression algorithm that allows it to display images with gradients (like photographs) at a relatively high quality while keeping the file size low. However, due to how JPEG compression uniquely blends pixels to save color data, a vector art file with sharp edges will appear blurry if saved as a JPEG unless you significantly increase the information in the file.

The **GIF** image format (short for graphics interchange format, with a hard "G") allows you to limit the available colors in a file to save data. This makes it great for line art and logos but terrible for representing the millions of gradating colors within photographic images. GIF is also popular for its ability to store and play multiple frames as an animation. **PNG** (portable network graphics) is a **lossless** format (as opposed to **lossy** formats, which use compression to decrease their size) and is great for both line art and photographs. In addition to the three channels that correspond to the RGB colors of your monitor, it also contains an alpha channel to make the background transparent or even fade to transparency when the image is placed on top of other graphics. Finally, new formats like **WebP** improve on the qualities of PNG to produce readable graphics at lower file sizes.

Again, the raster and vector categories refer to how the image data is displayed, and the format determines the file extension and compression type or schema. There are also some overlaps between types. A vector image can be **rasterized** so that the lines and points are converted to pixels and saved as a raster type. Also, some vector formats **encapsulate** both raster and vector data in the same file, which makes them easier to print and share. For example, a **PDF** (portable document format) can contain both vector and raster data.

Activity: Export Images from Figma

Follow these steps to use your own images in a web page.

1. Make sure the graphic you intend to export is in a frame and the frame is named appropriately, as it will be used with the file extension for the name of the file. For example, "Frame 1" is not descriptive. Remember to avoid using spaces in file and folder names for the Web by using camelCase, or by replacing the spaces with hyphens -or_underscores.
2. Drag the edges of the frame to crop it closely to the edge of the graphic (but not too close!). If the frame is much larger than the actual artwork, the dimensions of the image will be large but the actual graphic will appear small.
3. With the frame selected, click the **Export** button on the bottom right of the Design panel. The **1x** option refers to how large the image will be scaled. Eight hundred pixels on its longest edge will be large enough to look good but small enough to transport efficiently across networks. You can always scale it down with a CSS rule. The **image format** you choose (see discussion above) should allow the highest quality possible with the lowest file size. A PNG is usually a good choice since it is good at representing both line art and gradients.
4. Download each image you intend to use. The image format extension will be added to the end of the frame's name. Upload images to the **assets/img/** folder in your Codespace like we did in exercise 3.2.3 to use them in your designs.
5. If you update the file in Figma, just follow these steps again and "save over" the previously downloaded file using the same file name.

3.2.5 Coding Images in HTML and CSS

It is possible to add images to a web page using HTML, CSS, or even JavaScript. The exercises in this section demonstrate how to export images from Figma and add them to a web page using HTML and CSS.

While using code to point to a file, every character counts. This means that correct spelling is important, as is the inclusion of the proper file extension. Typos in the path ("bat.png" instead of "cat.png," for instance) or erroneously pointing to a .jpg instead of a .png file will result in the image not loading, or worse, the broken file icon in the browser. If you are experiencing trouble loading a file, confirm there are no errors in the DevTools Console.

Exercise 3.2.4 Add an Image with CSS

In this exercise you will add HTML elements to the page to begin building our IKEA spoof web page. Instead of incorporating the clock and wrench using an `<img>` element, you will display these images using the CSS background property in a `<div>` tag, which makes it possible to add a hover effect later.

1. In Codespaces, open **index.html.**
2. Change the `<h1>` tag to the headline "Everything You Need," remove the `<p>` tag and "boilerplate" copy and the HTML `<img>` source code that you altered in the previous exercise.

```
<h1>Everything You Need</h1>
```

3. Notice that, instead of adding CSS inside a `<style>` element in **index.html**, we use the following `<link>` tag to fetch an *external* CSS file. The `rel` attribute tells the browser to use this other document as a stylesheet when it loads the page and the `href` attribute contains a relative path (discussed above) to point to the location of the CSS file:

```
<link rel="stylesheet" href="./assets/css/styles.css">
```

4. With the file linked, click the **css/** directory in the Explorer and then select **styles.css** to view the stylesheet.

Author Note: The 👉 Emoji

Look for this 👉 emoji within code files we provide whenever our exercises instruct you to edit existing code.

5. In the stylesheet, add a class declaration after line 5 named "backgroundImage". When adding a reference to another file inside CSS you must use the **`url()`** function with a relative path to the image *from the CSS file* (not the HTML file) inside the parentheses.

```
.backgroundImage {
  background-image: url(../img/wrench.png);
}
```

6. Before you can see the background image in the web browser you will need to add an element that uses the **`.backgroundImage`** class to the **`<body>`** of the HTML document. Select the **index.html** tab and add the following **`div`** above the **`<h1>`** element.

```
<div class="backgroundImage"></div>
<h1>Everything You Need</h1>
```

7. If you preview your work with Live Server, you will not yet see the image. Where is it? Open DevTools to see if you can find the issue before proceeding to the next step. See the wiki for a video demonstration in DevTools.
8. When working with background images it is important to remember that HTML elements only take up as much space as their contents or style dictates. Since this new **`<div>`** has no text or images adding space within the HTML file, its height and width are zero. A common hack to verify the image is working is to temporarily add some text to the **`<div>`** to expand its size and reveal the background. The better way is to explicitly set the **`width`** and **`height`** of the **`<div>`** in the **`.backgroundImage`** rule to match the image pixel dimensions. You can find the values in your image editor or by loading the file in a browser and using DevTools. Our clock and wrench images are both 400 pixels, square. Add these values to your stylesheet and preview your work with Live Server.

```
.backgroundImage {
  background-image: url(../img/wrench.png);
  width: 400px;
  height: 400px;
}
```

9. To center the image on the page, you can use the margin property. A margin shortcut with two values (below) applies the first value to the top and bottom margins and the second value to the left and right margins. The auto value centers content on the horizontal axis because it takes the total space leftover and divides it by two. Notice that there is no comma between these two values. Your class should now look like this:

```
.backgroundImage {
  background-image: url(../img/wrench.png);
  width: 400px;
  height: 400px;
  margin: 64px auto;
}
```

10. Stage and commit your work. In the next exercise, we will add a hover effect to swap the wrench image with the clock.

3.2.6 CSS Pseudo-Classes

A **pseudo-class** can be added to a selector to change CSS rules during certain interaction conditions. A typical example is the `:hover` pseudo-class, which is often used to update a link color as a result of the mouse hovering over it. The following example shows an anchor tag coupled with a pseudo-class:

```
a:hover {
  text-decoration: underline;
}
```

Pseudo-classes can also be used to change or "swap" images when the mouse moves over the element. Table 3.1 demonstrates examples using pseudo-classes to change the appearance of HTML links in the web browser based on common mouse interactions.

Table 3.1
As you know, the HTML tag and attribute `<a href>` is used to create a link on the page. In CSS you can style this element for each of these states using a CSS pseudo-class.

Code example	Link state description
`a:link {color: blue;}`	The default state of a link on the page.
`a:visited {color: red;}`	A link after it has been clicked (or "visited").
`a:focus {color: black;}`	A link (or form element) when "given focus," usually triggered by either clicking on or tabbing to it.
`a:hover {color: red;}`	A link when a user moves their mouse over it.
`a:active {color: red;}`	A link when a user starts to press it during mouse click.

Exercise 3.2.5 Add a Hover Effect

In this exercise you will apply the `:hover` pseudo-class to create a swap image effect.

1. In **styles.css** add a new declaration block to change the background image when the user hovers their mouse over the element with the original background image.

The cursor property changes the appearance of the cursor to a crosshair, providing feedback that the user's interaction has affected the page.

```
.backgroundImage:hover {
  background-image: url(../img/clock.png);
  cursor: crosshair;
}
```

2. Preview your work with Live Server, then stage and commit your changes.

Activity: Prepare Image Files for a Hover Effect

Notice that the two image files you used in the previous exercise have exactly the same pixel dimensions. This is important, because when the hover effect is enabled, the new image uses the same space as the image it replaces. The following instructions let you create your own images for the swap effect using Figma. If you use Photoshop, you can also explore our PSD file, **rolloverimages.psd** inside the chapter example in the book repo. You will see we used an adjustment layer to tint both images (contained on separate layers) to create visual consistency in hue and tone.

1. In Figma, paste each image onto the canvas.
2. To crop an image, double-click the image and select crop from the drop-down in the options panel.
3. Crop each image so that they are the same dimensions. We chose to make these each 400×400 pixels. You can scale an image if needed to make the sizes match.
4. Export the images using the instructions above and give them descriptive names.

Exercise 3.2.6 From Design to Code in CSS

In this exercise continue coding our design by adding to your stylesheet (figure 3.12).

1. Add the remaining content to the page after the `<h1>`. We created a class called `.text` to hold these two elements. The word "IKEA" is coded with a second-level heading and we are using an `<h3>` for the word "Countdown," which links to an online countdown timer with an absolute path.

```
<h1>Everything You Need</h1>
<div class="text">
  <h2>IKEA</h2>
  <h3>
    <a href="https://www.bigtimer.net/">Countdown</a>
  </h3>
</div>
```

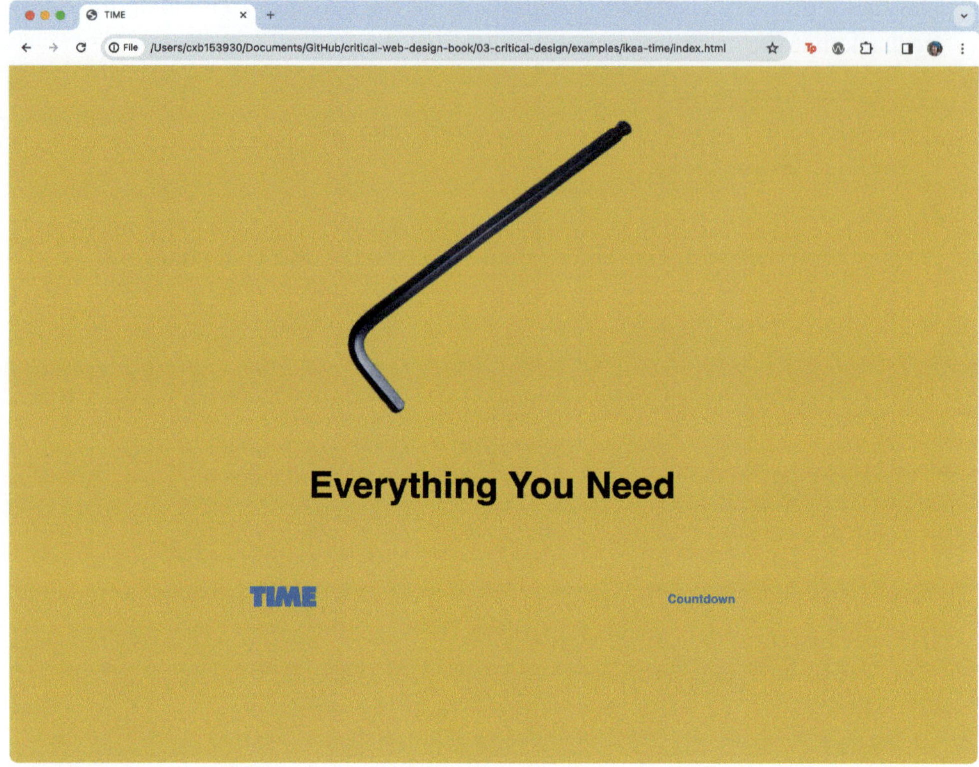

Figure 3.12
This screenshot shows the results of exercise 3.2.6 in the web browser. View it live at **criticalwebdesign.github.io#3-2**.

2. With content finished, edit the stylesheet to reflect the design in our mockup. Add the following rule to the top of the stylesheet to add a yellow background and use Helvetica as the primary font-family for all child elements.

```
body {
  background-color: #e6ce55;
  font-family: Helvetica, Arial, sans-serif;
}
```

3. Update the style of the `<h1>` text with the following.

```
h1 {
  color: black;
  font-size: 48px;
```

```
    text-align: center;
}
```

4. Add a rule for the `.text` class that holds the `<h2>` and `<h3>` elements.

```
.text {
    width: 50%;
    margin: 96px auto;
}
```

5. Add a new rule to affect all the elements *inside* the `.text` class. It makes them inline-block so they will stay on the same line, removes all margins and padding, and centers them vertically inside their parent element. We set the width to 48% to accommodate any whitespace on this line. Since all elements inside `.text` need the same rules, it is efficient to use the wildcard operator (*):

```
.text * {
    display: inline-block;
    width: 48%;
    margin: 0;
    padding: 0;
    vertical-align: middle;
}
```

6. Adjust the color and font size of each heading.

```
h2 {
    color: dodgerblue;
    font-size: 40px;
    text-align: left;
}
h3 {
    font-size: 16px;
    text-align: right;
}
```

7. Add a hover effect to the `<h3>` using a pseudo-class. Notice that we are using a comma to indicate that we want the same declaration block to affect both selectors.

```
h3 a:link,
h3 a:visited {
    color: dodgerblue;
```

```
    text-decoration: none;
}
h3 a:hover {
    color: white;
}
```

Prompt 3.2 Code: Create Your Unbranded Page with Colors and Images

Based on the mock-ups you designed in Figma, begin coding your page in HTML and CSS. Add code for color with CSS and add images to your page.

Module 3.3 Web Fonts and JavaScript Events

In this module you will learn to use Google Fonts, one of multiple ways to add custom fonts to web pages. Then you will understand how to create and use variables in JavaScript to add interactivity to your page.

3.3.1 Using Custom Fonts on the Web

Computers display text by matching each character's unique **codepoint** (see Unicode discussion in module 2.2) to its corresponding **glyph**, or visual representation of a character, in a given font file. To display characters on the screen in a specific font each users' computer needs to access the typeface file containing the glyphs for all the codepoints. If the font is not accessible, the text will be displayed in some other (potentially undesirable) default font.

In the early days of the internet **web-safe fonts** described those typefaces that were already installed across every possible computer and thus safe to use in a web page. The list includes fonts such as Times New Roman, Arial, and Verdana, among a handful of others. To ensure text appears as intended on every user's machine, designers still use **fallback fonts** in the CSS font-family declaration. In the CSS rule below, the browser looks for Helvetica, and then Arial if the first is not found, then finally defaults to any sans-serif font available.

```
body {
    font-family: Helvetica, Arial, sans-serif;
}
```

Nowadays, designers have access to many more typeface options using the CSS `@font-face` rule that makes it possible to link to a custom font just as you would an image or any other page resource.[27] This is the method used by Google Fonts and other typeface services, but you can implement it yourself if you have a font file. See the wiki to learn how.

Best Practices: View Fonts Installed on Your System

To see which fonts are installed on your computer, use the appropriate method below:

- Mac: View fonts in the Font Book application.
- Windows: View fonts in the Font Viewer in the Control Panel.

Best Practices: Clear Cache with Hard Refresh

When your browser displays a page, it saves local copies of the page resources (e.g., CSS, JS, fonts, images) in a **cache** on your computer. This process helps to make other pages on the site load faster because the browser can use the saved files instead of loading the same data over the network. However, this can create confusion when you are coding web pages because you can't see your changes! To make sure you are seeing the newest copy of CSS and other page resources, use a **hard refresh** by holding down shift when you click refresh or use the key command (**Command+Shift+r**) to refresh the page.

Exercise 3.3.1 Add Google Fonts

This exercise shows how to add Google Fonts, a collection of hosted typefaces, you can embed in your projects for free. See the wiki for a video demonstration of this exercise.

1. Go to **fonts.google.com** and search for the font Jost.
2. On the Specimen page, add text to preview variations of the typeface you plan to include in your project. Click the **Get font** button.
3. Press the **Get embed code** button. There are two code snippets to copy. First, copy the code in the "Embed code in the <head> of your html" section and paste it into the `<head>` of your **index.html** before the link to your CSS stylesheet. If you view the URL of the last link in a browser, you will see you are simply linking Google's CSS file with `@font-face` rules (see the wiki for an exercise). The `crossorigin` attribute in the URL tells the Google server to allow anonymous requests like yours. Note that code samples with long URLs will sometimes wrap to the next line. Any amount of whitespace you add to make these readable is fine as long as there is at least one space.

```
<link rel="preconnect" href="https://fonts.googleapis.com">
<link rel="preconnect" href="https://fonts.gstatic.com"
crossorigin>
<link href="https://fonts.googleapis.com/css2?family
=Jost:ital,wght@0,100..900;1,100..900&display=swap"
rel="stylesheet">
```

Author Note: Download vs. Embed

If you download and install Google Web Font files on your computer, the web pages you create using these fonts *will only display correctly when viewed on your own machine.*

4. At this point, you have linked to the font file on the Google server from your page, but you need to add the font to a new or updated selector in your CSS. On the Google Fonts page, copy the declaration block—all of the properties and values—under "CSS class." Paste this block of code into the h2 declaration to add Jost as the font-family and specify its weight:

```
h2 {
  color: dodgerblue;
  font-size: 40px;
  text-align: left;
  font-family: "Jost", sans-serif;
  font-optical-sizing: auto;
  font-weight: 900;
  font-style: normal;
}
```

3.3.2 JavaScript Variables

Now that your type is displaying correctly, it's time to make the `<h2>` element interactive. The following explains how to use JavaScript to add hover and click effects. These are foundational concepts, and allow more precise control over the interactivity of your pages than the `:hover` pseudo-class.

In programming, a **variable** allows you to save data in a computer's memory and access it whenever you need it later. And, like in algebra, the value in a variable can change. In a game for example, you could store the number of coins a player collects to provide feedback about their progress. But you might also use that data in other ways,

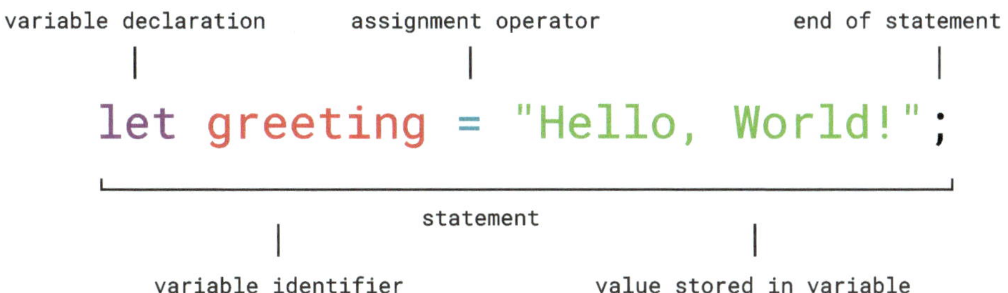

Figure 3.13
This code creates a new variable called `greeting` and assigns a string of text as the value.

like to reward players with a new life when the value reaches a specific amount or progress the narrative or mechanics of the game.

To create a variable in JavaScript, you use a special keyword called `let` with a unique name for the variable. A variable name should not contain special characters or spaces. The variable declaration is usually followed by an equal sign that assigns the data you want to store to the variable (figure 3.13). This process is also referred to as **binding** because the data is stored in the computer's memory, and "bound" to the name you give it.[28]

Exercise 3.3.2 Test a Variable in the Console

Testing is a common part of the coding process. Each time you write a new block of code you should test it. In this exercise you'll learn to test your work in the Console.

1. Open the DevTools Console on any web page. Type the following statement (like in figure 3.13). Make sure you avoid smart quotes as you type.

   ```
   let greeting = "Hello, World!";
   ```

2. You have just saved data in the computer's memory. It will exist until this page is refreshed. You can now use the variable name in place of that data like so:

   ```
   console.log(greeting);
   ```

3. The `let` keyword is required only to create a new variable. Once the variable has been declared, it means (like in our coin example in this section's introduction) you can update the value by simply assigning a new value to the name. Try it out.

   ```
   greeting = "Hey, Universe!";
   console.log(greeting);
   ```

4. Unlike some other programming languages, JavaScript will let you store any data in a variable, including numbers, URLs, or even references to elements on the page.

This means the code below will return the number 123 when **greeting** is referenced. Chapter 5 has a more in-depth description of JavaScript data types and the different variable declaration keywords.

```
greeting = 123;
console.log(greeting);
```

3.3.3 JavaScript Event Listeners

In chapter 2 you learned to apply CSS rules by selecting HTML elements. Below you'll use selectors with JavaScript to make things happen when a user interacts with the page.

In JavaScript, an **event** is anything that happens. An event can be initiated by a user (e.g., click, keypress, mouseover, mouseout, scroll) or something happening on the web page (like when it finishes loading or catches an error). An **event listener** "listens" for the event to happen, then calls an **event handler**, which runs code in response to the event. Much of the time "listener" and "handler" are interchangeable, since they work together to respond to events.

Exercise 3.3.3 Add an Event Li3stener in JavaScript

In this exercise you use **mouseover** and **mouseout** event listeners to change the text of "IKEA" on the page to "TIME" and back again. To create this interactivity, you will add a variable to store a reference to the target element and listen for the mouse events on the page to know when to change the text. You will add code in the document **assets/js/main.js**. Notice that the template HTML document you are using already includes **main.js** using the **src** attribute in the **<script>** tag *just before* **</body>**. It is essential that the **<script>** tag appears below the HTML elements in the **<body>** tag, so that those elements have loaded and are accessible to JavaScript when it attempts to use them.

1. To add an event listener, you first need to select a **target** element. Type the following inside **main.js** to store a reference to the **<h2>** element.[29]

   ```
   let targetElement = document.querySelector("h2");
   ```

2. Log this variable to the Console using the **outerHTML** property and you will see it outputs the HTML code and contents of the element itself (figure 3.14).

   ```
   console.log(targetElement.outerHTML);
   ```

3. Add the listener and handler function code below, paying close attention to the syntax. With the target element properly referenced, you can add an event listener using dot notation (module 2.3). The parentheses of the **addEventListener()**

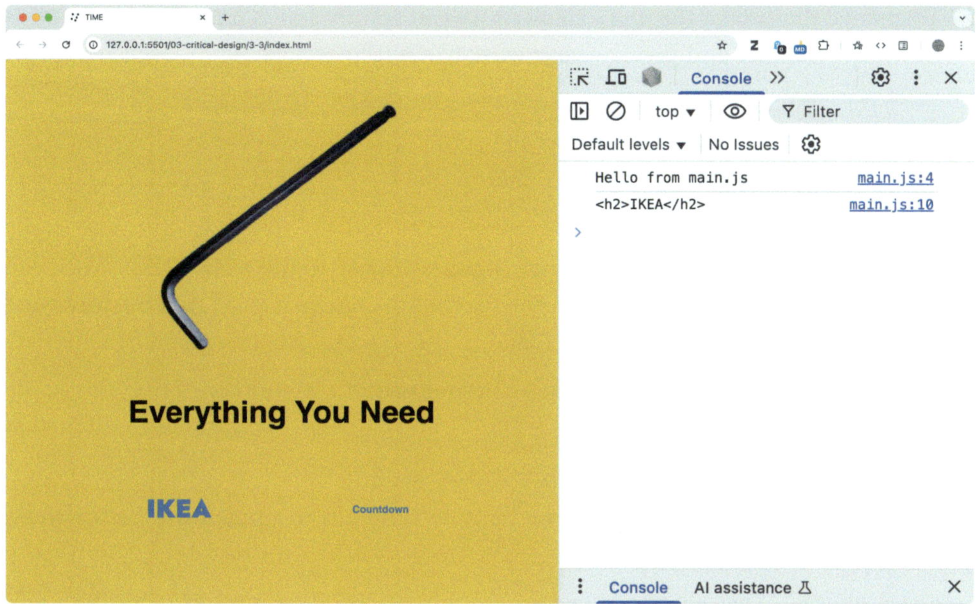

Figure 3.14
DevTools can highlight a target element, which is handy for debugging when you need to confirm that a selector is working.

requires two parameters: the mouseover event in quotes, followed by a comma and the handler, or **callback function**, that only runs *after* the event has happened. The handler function can also be referenced as a separate function (see our examples in the book repo). Preview your page. When you hover over the `<h2>` element, nothing appears to change on your page, but look in the Console. You should see the same reference to the target element thanks to the special `this` keyword, which always provides a reference to the target element.[30]

```
targetElement.addEventListener("mouseover", function() {
  console.log(this);
});
```

4. Since `this` is a reference to the target element, you can use dot notation to access and change its properties. Change the log statement to the following to get the text in the element.

```
console.log(this.innerText);
```

5. To change the text of the `<h2>` element we can simply assign a new value. Add this inside the handler and preview your work to see it in action.

```
targetElement.addEventListener("mouseover", function() {
  console.log(this.innerText);
  this.innerText = "TIME";
});
```

6. At this point your mouseover listener changes "IKEA" to the word "TIME," but you need a **mouseout** listener so the browser knows to change it back. Add the following code to the end of your JavaScript file.

```
targetElement.addEventListener("mouseout", function () {
  this.innerText = "IKEA";
});
```

7. Add this line inside the **mouseover** handler function to update the cursor when users mouse over the target.

```
this.style = "cursor: wait";
```

8. Finally, add this line in the **mouseout** event handler function to change the cursor back to its original icon.

```
this.style = "cursor: pointer";
```

Check Your Work

This concludes the chapter exercises. We invite you to compare your work to the final outcome **criticalwebdesign.github.io#3-3** and code **criticalwebdesign.github.io#3-3-code** in the book repo. Don't forget to enable GitHub Pages in your project and then stage and commit your work to make it live!

Prompt 3.3 Publish: Add Interaction to Finalize Your Project

Continue experimenting with HTML/CSS/JS on your page. You can borrow code from the book repo and edit as needed to create the interaction. We used **mouseover** and **mouseout** events, but there are many more you could listen for in the code. Use the powers of Google and the MDN documentation as needed!

4 On the Grid

> There is a profound and enduring beauty in simplicity; in clarity, in efficiency. True simplicity is derived from so much more than just the absence of clutter and ornamentation. It's about bringing order to complexity.
>
> —Jony Ive

Context

In this chapter we introduce the **design grid,** a tool that designers have used since before the invention of moveable type to structure content on stone surfaces, printed pages, and now the internet. Today the grid is more important than ever, providing the foundation to make it easier to design, place, and align content within responsive layouts that flex and adapt to different device sizes to ensure content remains readable, usable, and consistent across your site. We begin by exploring the idea of "good" design in the next activity and notice how the grid has helped to create consistency throughout the history of design practice.

Activity: Evaluate a Design Using the Thinking Aloud Test

In a Thinking Aloud test, participants use an interface while continuously verbalizing their reactions to that interface. This test was recommended by usability expert Jakob Nielson to assess website usability.[1] For example, while evaluating a website, someone performing this test may say, "My goal is to find the Contact page on this company's website. I'm looking at the header for the link, now the footer, and feeling a bit frustrated because I saw a link previously but now cannot find it." With practice this test can be very effective at understanding and evaluating user experiences, assumptions, and behaviors in response to website navigation, page layouts, or other interfaces.

The following activity asks you to evaluate your response to good design. As an example of "learning through discovery," it works best if you actually do the activity, whether you are reading this section on your own or with a group in a classroom.

1. Think of a company or organization that you associate with "good design."
2. Explore the website of the organization, consider the objects, software, or other things they create. Use this method while you look to evaluate your response to the design.
3. List some reasons why you might have selected this organization. What about their website, products, or other aspects of their brand or identity (see chapter 3) are examples of good design?

On the wiki we share notes from our own response to the above questions, using the Thinking Aloud method to assess **apple.com**. As we state on the wiki, the answer to the question we present above is that there is one solid principle you can take from Apple's brand, products, webpage, everything, it is this: *Consistency is central to good design.*

Design Consistency

Consistency is one of the most important principles in design, and it is achieved by a purposeful attention to unity across design elements such as position, scale, shape, value, and so on. Look again at the site you evaluated above and note everything that appears to use a consistent approach. Consider how the photography, color palettes, typography, even the margins and padding between elements in the layout match each other. When all the aspects are consistent the design feels stable, ordered, and reliable, and nothing stands out as "incorrect."

You may have heard the phrase "You shouldn't see good design." It seems obvious that content should be what your users notice, since navigating and finding information is most often their goal. But what about what users think, experience, and feel? There are seemingly small efforts that transform "a" design into "good" design. It doesn't matter that Apple used brushed aluminum throughout their products and websites just a few years ago or that now they have orange buttons, as long as these elements are the same as each other now. Since all the details pertaining to objects and layouts are rendered with a similar and cohesive treatment, users feel they can trust their expectations in a design.

Style Guides and Design Systems

Professional designers don't make decisions about color, typeface, and margins by flipping a coin. A lot of care and thinking is part of this work, evidence of which can be found throughout the different tools and methods that exist to support it. A **style guide** is a set of rules and examples showing how to implement all the visual elements of a

Additional Materials and Resources

Explore links and other content related to this chapter: **criticalwebdesign.github.io#wiki-04**

brand, including logos, typography, and color. Style guides are often included within comprehensive **design systems**, which can contain standards for usability and accessibility, rules for how information is organized, and principles for all parts of user interfaces (even the animation curves for moving parts!).

The primary goal of these guides and systems is to ensure uniformity in style and formatting wherever a brand is used, regardless of who or when or where they are implemented. As you may guess, Apple (figure 4.1) and other corporations publish these guidelines[2] to help their employees, as well as designers they contract, to ensure cohesion across all the media that represent the company, from billboards, to TV commercials, and even on the products themselves. Their Human Interface Guidelines contain advice, information, and specifications for design to make sure that interfaces

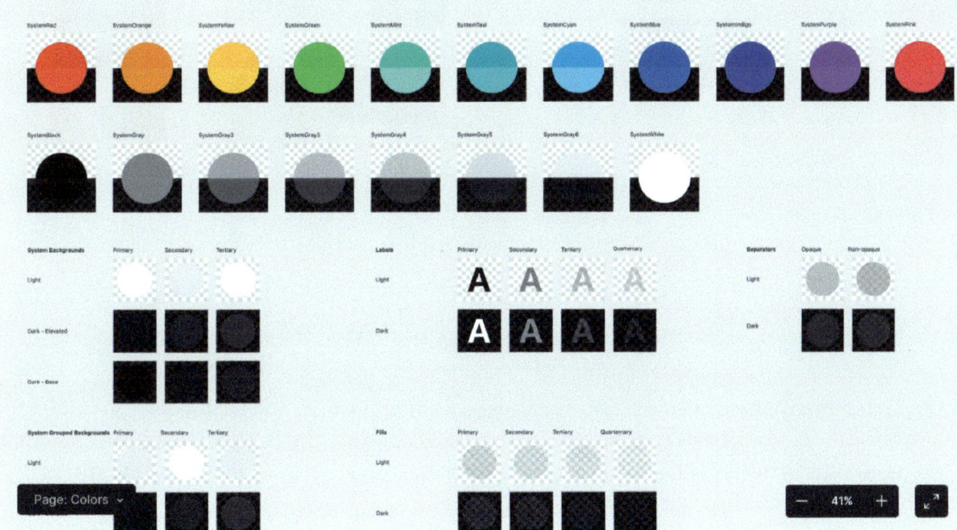

Figure 4.1
A Figma design template published in the Apple Design Resources for iOS 17 and iPadOS 17 **developer.apple.com/design/resources** to help designers and developers ensure consistency with all Apple interfaces.[3]

"remain familiar when [users] rotate their device, resize a window, add another display, or switch to a different device."[4]

Activity: Explore Style Guides

Explore style guides of organizations to see how they plan for design consistency.

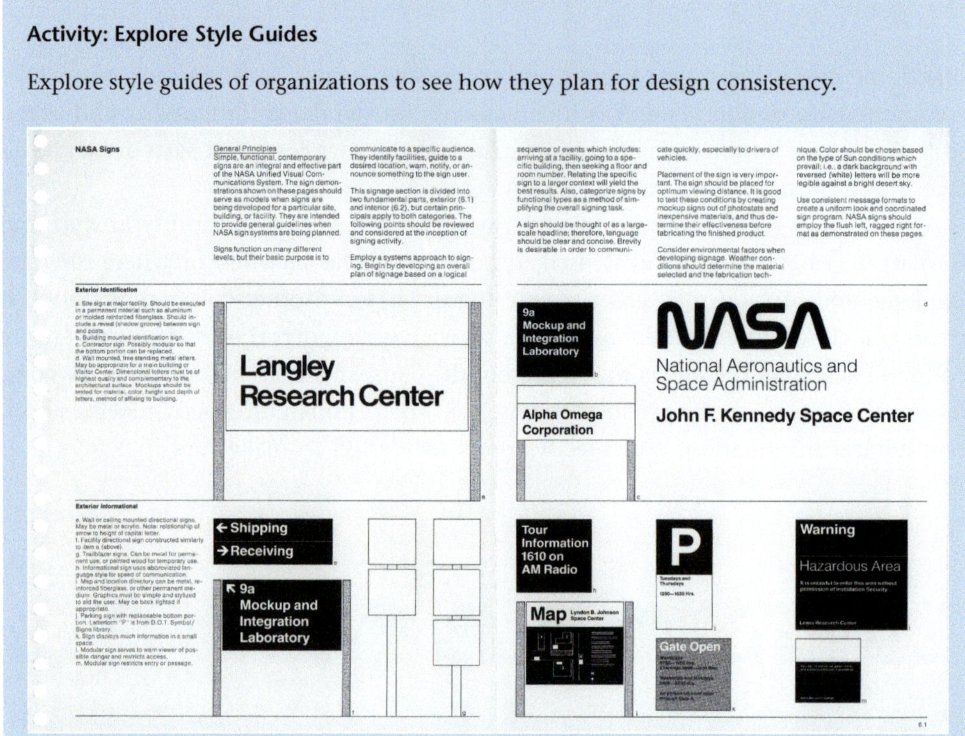

NASA Signs

General Principles
Simple, functional, contemporary signs are an integral and effective part of the NASA Unified Visual Communications System. The sign demonstrations shown on these pages should serve as models when signs are being developed for a particular site, building, or facility. They are intended to provide general guidelines when NASA sign systems are being planned.

Signs function on many different levels, but their basic purpose is to communicate to a specific audience. They identify facilities, guide to a desired location, warn, notify, or announce something to the sign user.

This signage section is divided into two fundamental parts, exterior (6.1) and interior (6.2), but certain principals apply to both categories. The following points should be reviewed and considered at the inception of signing activity.

Employ a systems approach to signing. Begin by developing an overall plan of signage based on a logical sequence of events which includes: arriving at a facility, going to a specific building, then seeking a floor and room number. Relating the specific sign to a larger context will yield the best results. Also, categorize signs by functional types as a method of simplifying the overall signing task.

A sign should be thought of as a large-scale headline; therefore, language should be clear and concise. Brevity is desirable in order to communicate quickly, especially to drivers of vehicles.

Placement of the sign is very important. The sign should be placed for optimum viewing distance. It is good to test these conditions by creating mockup signs out of photostats and inexpensive materials, and thus determine their effectiveness before fabricating the finished product.

Consider environmental factors when developing signage. Weather conditions should determine the material selected and the fabrication technique. Color should be chosen based on the type of Sun conditions which prevail; i.e., a dark background with reversed (white) letters will be more legible against a bright desert sky.

Use consistent message formats to create a uniform look and coordinated sign program. NASA signs should employ the flush left, ragged right format as demonstrated on these pages.

Exterior Identification

a. Site sign at major facility. Should be executed in a permanent material such as aluminum or molded reinforced fiberglass. Should include a reveal (shadow groove) between sign and posts.
b. Building mounted identification sign.
c. Contractor sign. Possibly modular so that the bottom portion can be replaced.
d. Wall mounted, free standing metal letters. May be appropriate for a main building or Visitor Center. Dimensional letters must be of highest quality and complementary to the architectural surface. Mockups should be tested for material, color, height and depth of letters, method of affixing to building.

Exterior Informational

e. Wall or ceiling mounted directional signs. May be metal or acrylic. Note: relationship of arrow to height of capital letter.
f. Facility directional sign constructed similarly to item a (above).
g. Trailblazer signs. Can be metal for permanent use, or painted wood for temporary use.
h. Informational sign uses abbreviated language style for speed of communication.
i. Map and location directory can be metal, reinforced fiberglass, or other permanent medium. Graphics must be simple and stylized to aid the user. May be back lighted if appropriate.
j. Parking sign with replaceable bottom portion. Letterform "P" is from D.O.T. Symbol/Signs library.
k. Sign displays much information in a small space.
l. Modular sign serves to warn viewer of possible danger and restricts access.
m. Modular sign restricts entry or passage.

Figure 4.2
The NASA Graphics Standards Manual (1976). © Danne & Blackburn/NASA, Standards Manual.

1. In the 220-page NASA Graphics Standards Manual (1976), Richard Danne and Bruce Blackburn show how the NASA logo, US flag, and classic Helvetica typeface should be used on vans, confidential documents, and even the space shuttle (figure 4.2).[5]
2. The Apple Human Interface Guidelines explain best practices across all their content. For example, on the Charts page inside Content, they remind readers to "establish a consistent visual hierarchy [to] help communicate the relative importance of various chart elements."[6]
3. Continue exploring the above examples and find one more contemporary or past example online. Make notes about the system, including things that might not be evident at first glance. See the chapter 4 wiki for more examples.

Grid-Based Design

Clearly consistency is not just about making users feel they can trust the information in your design, it also helps them to navigate and use your websites. When designers create consistent layouts across pages, it establishes rules that users can rely on. This is where we turn to grid-based design, which assists users, as well as designers in several ways.

Grids have been used for centuries in the design and layout of text-based compositions. In the 1450s, Johannes Gutenberg used his printing press and metal moveable type to separate text of the bible into four separate columns. In Western languages like English and German, the left-aligned text creates an invisible line that acts as a focal point, leading the reader's eyes down the page to facilitate reading. View the image of Gutenberg's bible on the wiki and you might notice that each text block is the same width. This measurement, the width of a line of text before it wraps to the next line, is referred to as the **measure**. Best practices in typographic design follows an understanding that humans process text in "saccadic" eye movements. That is, our eyes can follow a line for only so long before our brain loses track and jumps backward. Keeping the measure width small enough that the reader's eye can follow the line all the way to the end makes for an easier reading experience. Also note that if a measure is too wide then readers will experience difficulty as they try to find the next line of text when they return to the left side of the page. The general rule for a legible text block is about 45–85 characters (approximately 2–3 "alphabets") per line.

Being able to scan text is even more important today, as users search for information quickly on web pages where the grid is the primary architecture. In addition to creating unity and cohesion, Lidwell et. al. underscore how alignment is "a powerful means of leading a person through a design" thanks to "the rows and columns of a grid or table [which] make explicit the relatedness of elements sharing those rows and columns, and lead the eyes left-right and top-bottom accordingly" in their important book on design principles and usability.[7]

Best Practices: Avoid Center-aligned Text

Left-aligned text has a straight edge, and each line starts at the same horizontal origin. Center-aligned text has a ragged left edge, and each line originates from a different location. To make text readable, you should avoid center-aligning text blocks that wrap more than twice. "The invisible column created by left-aligned and right-aligned text blocks presents a clear, visual cue against which other elements of the design can be aligned. Center-aligned text, conversely, provides more visually ambiguous alignment cues, and can be difficult to connect with other elements."[8]

In addition to increasing usability with leading lines to guide users' eyes through layouts, grids also help users understand the content through the structures and hierarchies they create. In another example from design history, the Swiss design style used grids to organize and structure content on the page. Thanks to the table grid of the Stadttheater example (see the wiki), similar content is arranged into columns, which, along with the invisible line of the left-aligned text, allows readers to scan information along the vertical axis to compare dates, titles, or other categories of the poster.

Responsive Design with Grids

The grid is even more crucial when designing for the web and digital interfaces. Every HTML element in a web page is fundamentally a rectangle (figure 4.3), so creating a design layout using a grid naturally fits the intended medium. This approach also aids the process of translating the design to code when you are ready to make it functional. Grids also help designers by providing the foundation and structure on which to place elements. Using a grid to wireframe and layout pages allows you to work more efficiently, since you don't need to adjust and compare the margins, symmetry, and other basic design principles every time you move something in the layout.

Unlike the static designs created for established paper sizes in their print counterparts, HTML pages are created for the browser, a dynamic electronic page that can

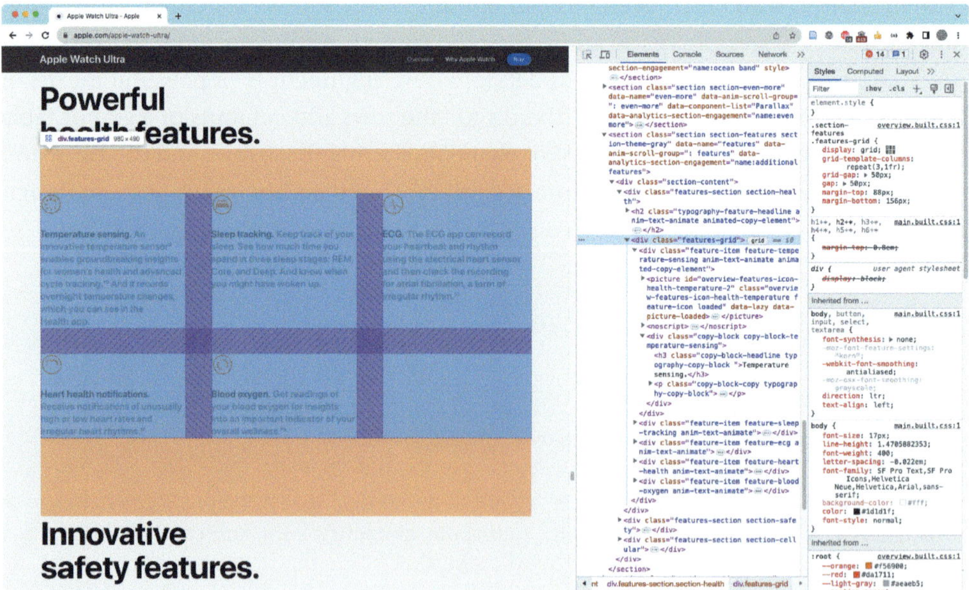

Figure 4.3
DevTools reveal the underlying grid of HTML elements in the Apple Watch Ultra page.

be resized, zoomed, and even modified using script. HTML is **reflowable** so that the content contained within a page automatically fills the space allotted by the size of the browser window. When you resize your browser, you literally edit the page's bounds. Imagine cutting a printed poster by one-fourth of its size. The content does not scale or move; it would simply fall to the floor or be discarded. However, load a web page on your desktop and then view it on a tablet or mobile device. If it was designed to respond to various electronic viewing formats, the content reflows based on the dimensions of the **viewport** or viewable area of the web page in the browser.

Designing and coding web pages that intentionally change (beyond the reflowable feature of HTML) to match viewport sizes is referred to as **responsive design**. The wireframes in figure 4.4 show how a typical responsive layout might transition to three different **breakpoints**, or pre-designed configurations that accommodate specific viewport sizes.

1. First, notice how the horizontal navigation bar (in orange) at the top of the page is condensed to an expandable **hamburger menu** on the smaller sizes.
2. Look at the **billboard** (the large area on home pages that displays the most important information). The desktop shows one row with a left column containing (purple) text and a call to action (CTA) button, and a column on the right with an image. Observe how the desktop and tablet are fairly similar while the phone layout "breaks" the two columns into separate rows that fill the full width and show the content centered.
3. Finally, beneath the billboard, the text with the three (green, cyan, blue) image placeholders in the desktop design has shifted in the tablet layout to a row for each image,

Figure 4.4
These wireframes show how a responsive layout changes across device sizes.

moving text to the right of the graphic. The phone changes layouts again, stacking the text under each image into a scrolling layout.

Keyword: Call to Action

A **call to action (CTA)** is an important and highly visible link from a product or service's web page that moves the user toward learning more, making a purchase, or otherwise meeting the goal put forth by the business or webpage owner. In figure 4.4 the orange rectangle seen prominently on all three responsive layouts represents a CTA button. A CTA can be a link, a button, or any other clickable page element. While CTAs are not exclusive to consumer web pages, they are a standard, measurable tool in the online marketing industry. You will find many examples on sites that include shopping carts.

While there are many types of devices where a user might view your work, designers typically develop for (at least) desktop, tablet, and mobile sizes. The Bootstrap CSS framework that you will use to design and code responsive web pages includes six different sizes (xs, sm, md, lg, xl, xxl) that you can select from.[9] As you will see, using grids allows you to standardize columns, content, and page flow across any number of breakpoints in your responsive designs, as well as when you transition the layout into code.

Activity: Test Responsive Websites

Simulate different device sizes using a desktop browser to see how a design responds to viewport breakpoints.

1. Load a responsive web page built using the Bootstrap framework like **icons.getbootstrap.com**, **owenmundy.com**, or **etsy.com**. Other examples are easy to find with Google (search for "bootstrap" in the source code to confirm if you are unsure).[10]
2. Exit **Full Screen mode** (if you are using it) in Chrome. While it provides you a bit more area on small laptop displays, it will prevent you from changing the browser window size.
3. Drag the side of your browser window to the left and right to change the width of the window. As you do, watch how the page changes and sometimes completely reconfigures itself for each device size you are simulating.
4. As you change the size, notice how Bootstrap "snaps" content into distinct configurations for each breakpoint size.
5. Expand the window to the full width and open DevTools. Look for the small "Toggle device toolbar" icon at the top left. Simulating breakpoints in DevTools adds additional device presets and the ability to change the device from landscape to portrait orientation.

Case Study: Jan Diehm, The Pudding

JD: My name is Jan Diehm (she/her). I live in San Antonio, Texas, with my wife and four cats. My technical title is Senior Journalist-Engineer at The Pudding, but I casually refer to myself as a data/visual journalist. We're a "digital publication that explains ideas debated in culture," but we've also been called "the best internet rabbit hole," "cool shit on the internet," and "data viz about just about everything."[11] Each person on our team can do every step of the process (data analysis, storyboarding, design, and development), but we all have our strengths. Cross collaboration with skilled developers/engineers like Michelle McGhee and strong data analysis/storytelling freelancers like Jennifer Ding is what helps make The Pudding's data visual essays shine. Day-to-day, I symbiotically hop between Svelte/HTML/CSS/JS, Figma, Illustrator, Photoshop, After Effects, and Google Spreadsheets. One thing that I keep coming back to on the internet is Mona Chalabi's Instagram page. It's filled with thoughtfully handcrafted data viz that centers people.

Could you talk us through your design process at The Pudding? What tools or methods did you use to layout articles?

JD: My design approach is heavily influenced by my childhood playing with LEGO, my early career as a newspaper page designer, and my ability to visualize data and patterns. I rarely think about screen sizes or breakpoints, at least not actively. Instead, each web page is a treemap. The hierarchical rectangles can fix together in endless different ways and they're collapsible at their smallest element. I'm bad about committing designs to paper. Once I'm in Figma, I've worked through all the ways things could fit together in my head, so I usually do a single mock that's pretty close to the end product, seen in pieces like "Can Data Die?" (figure 4.5),[12] "Who's in the Crossword?,"[13] and "Votes for Women."[14] From there, I'll start to move to code, adapting the design on the fly as needed. CSS layouts like Flexbox and Grid work seamlessly for this treemap approach.

How do you rely on the grid in the design and code of your pieces in order to connote the themes and information delivered in the article(s)? For instance, in "Can Data Die?" we love the interaction between the cursor location and animated pixel colors. This play on the pixel and the grid feels congruent with the appearance and disappearance of information online.

JD: I use all the standard design tricks like typographical hierarchy, spacing, color, and modular layout, but more than those, I try to think about all the little whimsical details that create an emotional connection with a piece like Lil Nas X sliding down a pole in an article about same-gender lyrics,[15] (figure 4.6) or how the waffle charts are skate decks in an article about skate music,[16] or how the animated squares in the Lenna story

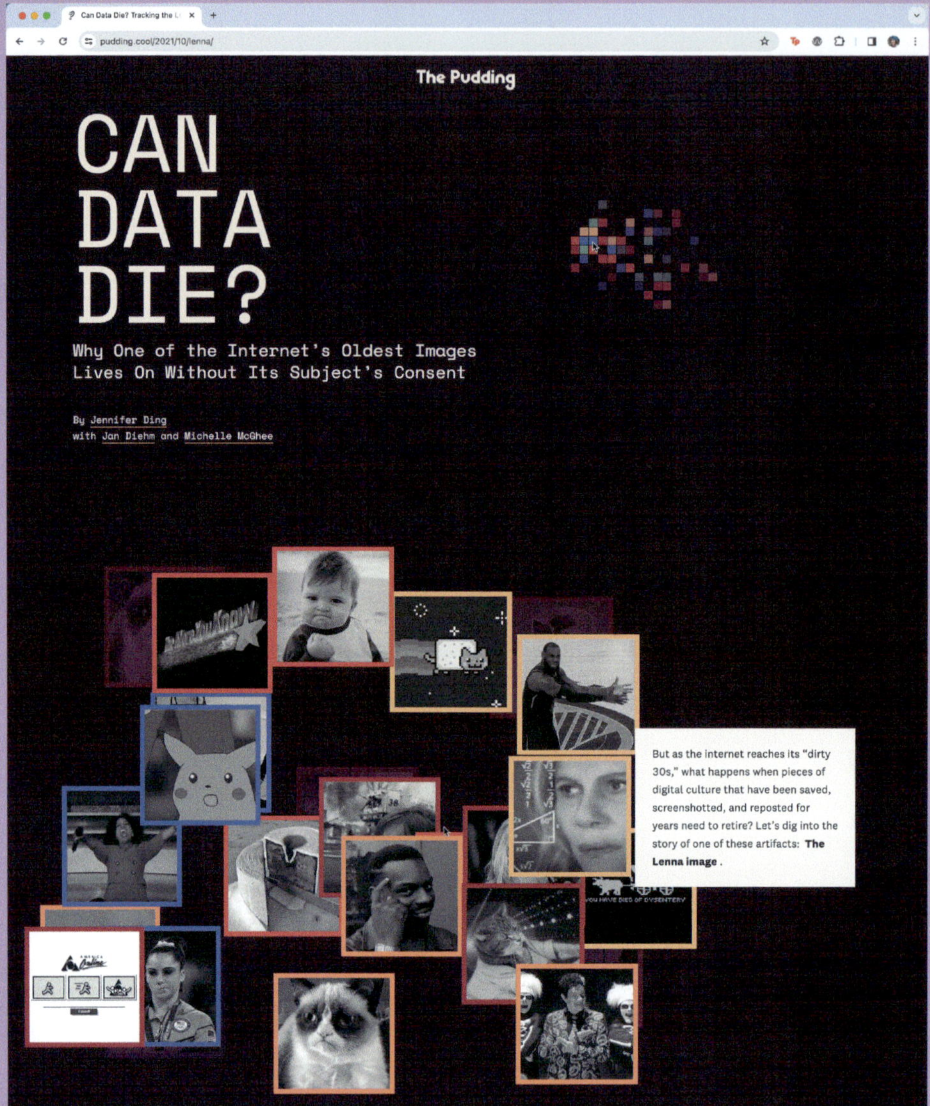

Figure 4.5
Jan Diehm's design for The Pudding's "Does Data Die?" incorporates an interactive grid and explosive image boxes that follow the cursor as the viewer scrolls through the article. The text consistently flows in an easy-to-read, high-contrast single column on the right while graphics animate throughout the page. Just as pixels combine to form an image, the reader combines these elements to understand the history of Lenna's image. Read and interact with this piece at pudding.cool/2021/10/lenna.

are reminiscent of pixels coming together to form an image.[17] It's an approach that's very much in opposition to data-to-ink ratio enthusiasts and pixel-perfect designers. I'm often looking for the smallest tangible unit that the average person would be familiar with—both in my story narrative and the designs. That's what's behind the opening to this piece on country radio, one single song.

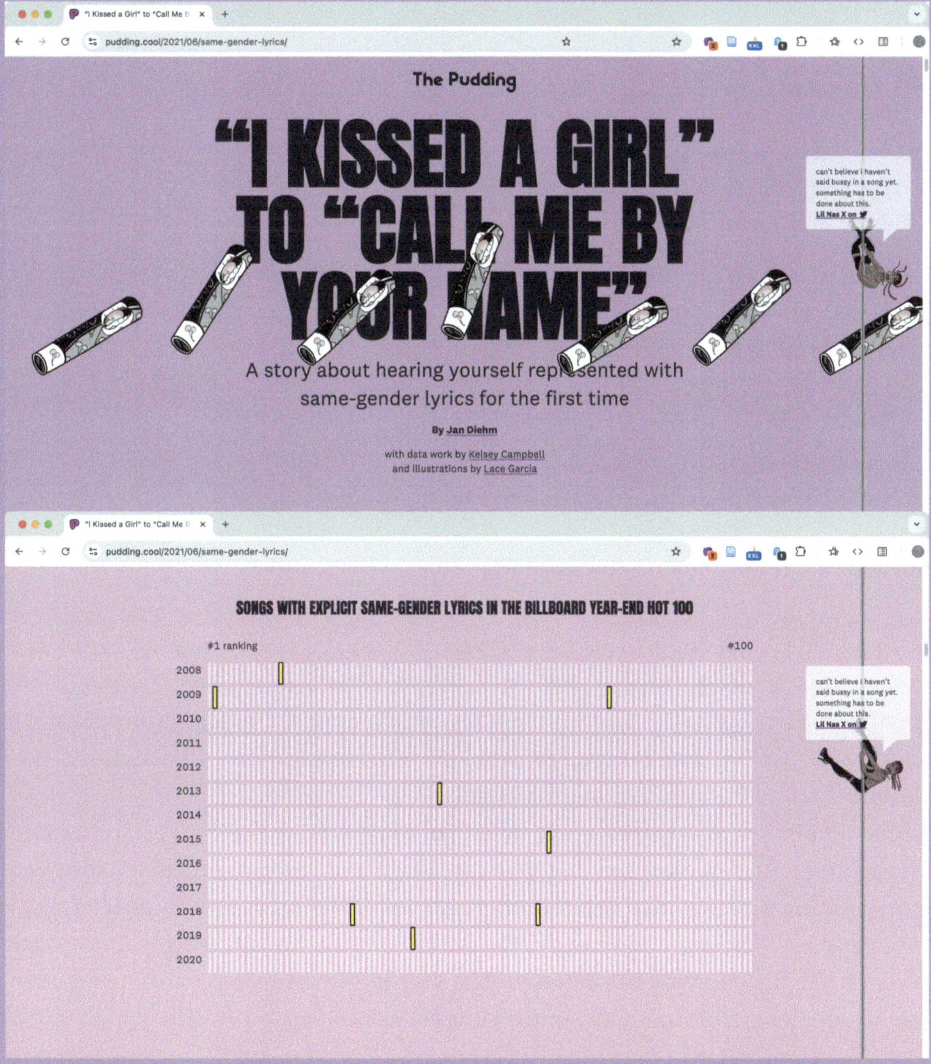

Figure 4.6
Jan Diehm's design for The Pudding's "I Kissed a Girl to Call Me By Your Name" featuring Lil Nas X sliding down a pole as a scrolling interaction.

What do you think is essential for new designers to think about, especially if their first foray into design is with the web browser?

JD: There are a million different ways to get to the same endpoint. You'll learn something one way and then someone on the internet will do it another way. There's no one "right" way! Remember that when you're reading snarky and unhelpful comments on Stack Overflow. As a designer, it's more important to connect with the reader/user than to appease other designers or developers. Stay curious. Stay flexible. Lastly, if there's an error, it is likely in mobile Safari.

Prompt 4 What You'll Make
Design and Code a Responsive Web Page

In this chapter you will design a responsive, multi-column layout for a fictional newspaper. You will use placeholder text throughout your design and code the page using the Bootstrap CSS framework.

View the results of our responsive New York Felines page at **criticalwebdesign.github .io#4-3** (figure 4.7). You can see the final code for every chapter on the CWD repo, **criticalwebdesign.github.io#repo.**

Module 4.1 Responsive Design in Figma

In this module you'll design a responsive web page using a Layout Grid layout in Figma. We show how to design the desktop experience first because it provides more room to experiment than the tablet and phone sizes, which are usually just minimized copies of a full-size version. You will design using a twelve-column grid to match the twelve columns that the Bootstrap framework offers.

You will also use placeholder text called **Lorem Ipsum** in the design. This common passage is used to create layouts that look like English but are presented in Latin. Rather than repeating a phrase like "placeholder text here," using text with differences and contrast better represents **body copy** (the main text in a layout), and will not distract viewers attempting to evaluate a design. Use sites like loremipsum.io or lipsum.com to generate any length of lorem ipsum for your projects.

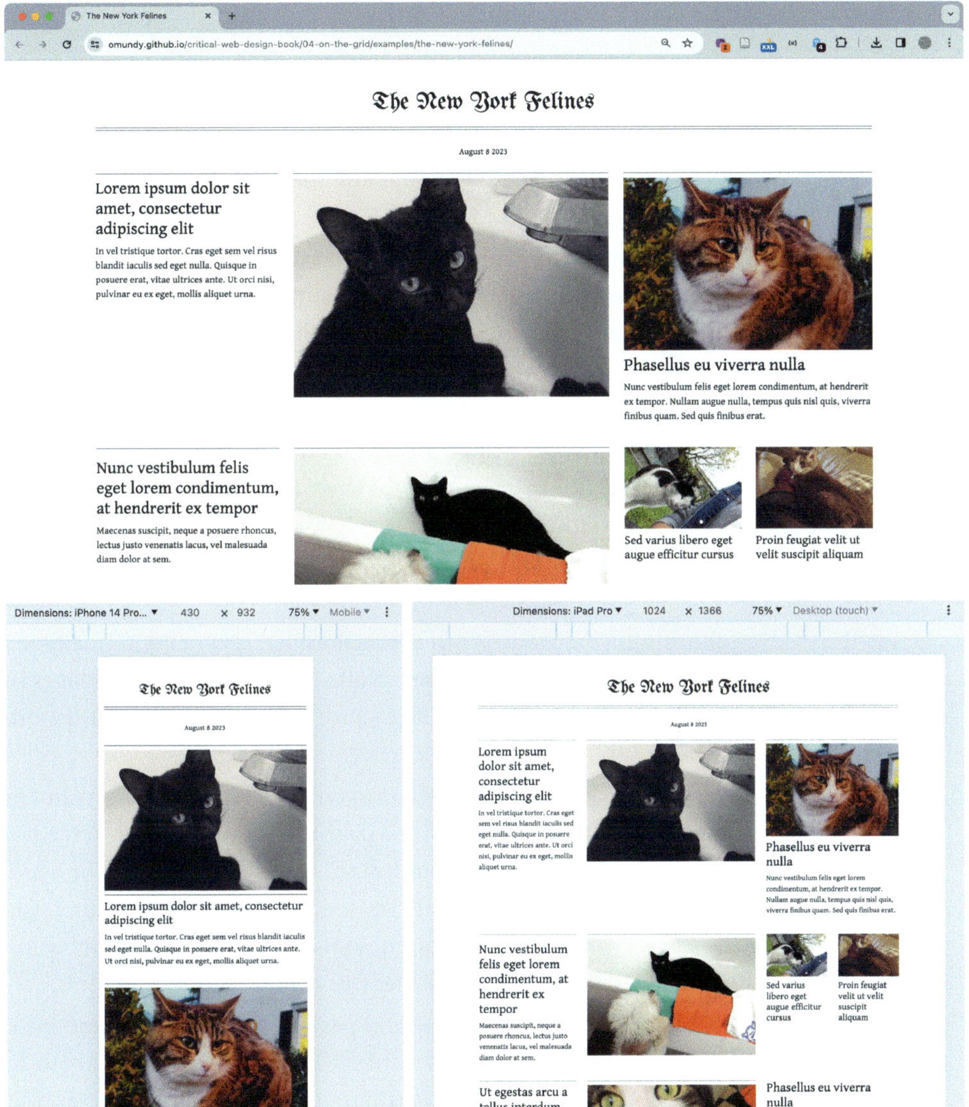

Figure 4.7
Our final composition for multiple breakpoints seen in the browser with DevTools. The Toggle Device Toolbar enables you to view your work across multiple devices in the Chrome Browser.

Exercise 4.1.1 Create a Grid-Based Layout in Figma

Use our grid templates to start designing your own responsive web pages.

1. Create a new Figma file you will use to paste our template into for exercises in this chapter.
2. In a web browser, open our Responsive Templates file **criticalwebdesign.github.io#figma-templates** and click "Open in Figma."
3. Press **Shift + G** to view Layout Grids in Figma. Note that there are twelve columns in each frame, which corresponds to the twelve columns in the Bootstrap CSS framework. Laying out your design with these templates will make it easier for you to translate your design into code.
4. Select the **XL Desktop frame** in our template. Copy and paste it into the Figma file you made in step 1. The Layout Grid will be included. Press **Shift + G** to confirm it is visible. We have added instructions to chapter 4 in the wiki if you want to make the layout grid yourself or understand it in-depth.
5. Make a screenshot (see the Common Key Commands table in the Introduction) of *The New York Times* home page and place it into your Figma file. Center the image across the twelve columns in your frame, with the farthest left text or content aligned along the left edge of the first column (figure 4.8). Note: If you need to scale images in Figma, hold the Shift key to constrain the image's proportions and prevent it from stretching.
6. Similar to the mockup you created for the prompts in chapter 3, use the screenshot as a reference and begin laying out a wireframe of the page using the Rectangle (creating placeholders for images) and Text (using Lorem Ipsum) tools. The goal is to preserve the spirit of the design without trying to replicate their precise grid structure. The home page design of a news website changes often, so it is possible they are not using twelve columns in their own layout grid. Consider this a work of interpretation.
7. When the desktop wireframe is complete, copy and paste the **MD Tablet frame** from our template into your own Figma file. Copy content from your desktop layout to the tablet layout, making adjustments to the position, order, column count, and so on as needed to match not the exact layout of your first design but the way that the layout hierarchy prioritizes content through scale, position, and so on.
8. Repeat the previous step for the mobile breakpoint. You can use the *visual* four- or two-column layout for mobile, since there is less space, though you will always have twelve total when you code it in Bootstrap. You should have three wireframes when you are finished for the desktop, tablet, and mobile experiences.

Figure 4.8
The *New York Times* home page screenshot scaled so the width matches the twelve-column grid in Figma.

4.1.1 Custom Color Palettes

A color palette is essential for ensuring that your design is cohesive and can convey information about your content. Color sparks an emotional response in the viewer. Bright colors can be cheery, while a muted palette is calming, for example. If you are reading this book as part of a design or arts curriculum, you may have taken multiple classes in color theory; however, we often have students from other disciplines who have not heard of **complementary** (opposing) or **analogous** (similar) colors. Color theory is outside the scope of this book, but online generators are not! Not surprisingly, there are many tools for creating a color palette you can use in your news website design as you follow the prompts in this chapter. Create a color palette in the accompanying activity to complete the following exercises.

Activity: Creating a Color Palette with a Hot Color

Open **coolors.co**. View their quick onboarding tutorial if you have never used the site before.

1. Start by selecting a color of your choice or using the random generator to find a color that resonates with your vision.
2. Lock the color, then repeat the process to find the remaining colors in your palette. A mixture of dark and light values in your color palette enables you to create strong contrast among design elements. This palette generator does a decent job of ensuring that the relationship between the colors in the palette provides both contrast and harmony.
3. While experimenting, consider that one of the colors should be a **hot color.** A hot color is a hue that stands out from the other colors in your palette, usually to communicate to users that an item is clickable. You can recognize it in a palette as the "loudest" of the colors and find examples where links appear within website text.
4. If you like a color that you see on the screen but want to include a variation in its value, click the "View Shades" icon to select a lighter or darker tone.
5. Save your color palette when you are finished. Press the **Visualize Colors** button to see your palette in works of art, typography, and layout design.
6. Notice that all of the colors are referenced by a fun name that Coolors assigns to them and their hex value, which you can use in Figma and in your CSS file.

Exercise 4.1.2 Finalize the Layout in Figma

1. Use the Type tool and replace the placeholder text with your own copy to ensure the design accommodates your actual content.
2. For the masthead (where it says "The New York Times"), we used the Google Font—available to you in Figma—UnifrakturMaguntia. This is a Blackletter typeface not too dissimilar from the font used by the NYT.
3. Replace all image placeholders with images in a genre of your choice. In our version, "The New York Felines," we substituted the NYT photographs with internet cats.
4. Once the desktop version is complete, repeat the steps above to create a tablet and mobile design for the same content. Use the instructions in the exercise above to create the designs in new frames, while deciding how the content reflows for the smaller widths.
5. Do not change the width of the frames since they are based on actual device sizes, but feel free to stretch the height of the page as needed in order to fit all the content in the design. Note that you should be conscientious about which content appears on the page **above the fold** when the browser is first opened, and which content is scrolled to, appearing later (or further down) in the page. In figure 4.9 you will see a thin purple line that indicates an important position on the page referred to as the **fold**. This term, coincidentally adapted from newspaper design, refers to how

The New York Felines

August 8, 2023

Lorem ipsum dolor sit amet, consectetur adipiscing elit

In vel tristique tortor. Cras eget sem vel risus blandit iaculis sed eget nulla. Quisque in posuere erat, vitae ultrices ante. Ut orci nisi, pulvinar eu ex eget, mollis aliquet urna.

Ut orci nisi, pulvinar eu ex eget, mollis aliquet urna

Fusce tempus augue nec dignissim sagittis. Aenean pretium dapibus turpis, at vulputate elit pellentesque in. In fringilla massa id ex varius, nec mollis tortor suscipit.

Phasellus eu viverra nulla

Nunc vestibulum felis eget lorem condimentum, at hendrerit ex tempor. Nullam augue nulla, tempus quis nisl quis, viverra finibus quam. Sed quis finibus erat.

Nunc vestibulum felis eget lorem condimentum, at hendrerit ex tempor

Maecenas suscipit, neque a posuere rhoncus, lectus justo venenatis lacus, vel malesuada diam dolor at sem.

Sed varius libero eget augue efficitur cursus

Proin feugiat velit ut velit suscipit aliquam

Ut egestas arcu a tellus interdum, eu sollicitudin justo vehicula

Phasellus eu viverra nulla. Nunc vestibulum felis eget lorem condimentum, at hendrerit ex tempor. Nullam augue nulla, tempus quis nisl quis, viverra finibus quam. Sed quis finibus erat.

Phasellus eu viverra nulla

Nunc vestibulum felis eget lorem condimentum, at hendrerit ex tempor. Nullam augue nulla, tempus quis nisl quis, viverra finibus quam. Sed quis finibus erat.

Phasellus eu viverra nulla

Nunc vestibulum felis eget lorem condimentum, at hendrerit ex tempor. Nullam augue nulla, tempus quis nisl quis, viverra finibus quam. Sed quis finibus erat.

Phasellus eu viverra nulla

Nunc vestibulum felis eget lorem condimentum, at hendrerit ex tempor. Nullam augue nulla, tempus quis nisl quis, viverra finibus quam. Sed quis finibus erat.

Figure 4.9

Use the Text tool and replace images with a genre of your choice. Recreate the masthead with a Blackletter font such as UnifrakturMaguntia. For each grid size, make sure your text boxes and images are aligned with a column on the left and right edges so you can easily set your columns to whole numbers when it is time to code the page.

designers placed the most essential content in the top half of the front page to be visible inside newspaper distribution boxes.

Prompt 4.1 Design: Use a Grid Layout in Figma

Now it's your turn to create the layout for a news website. You can either draw directly on top of the screenshot or you can duplicate the current frame and create the layout next to the original. We performed the latter so you can easily see our work, but if you want to draw on top of your current frame, press the lock icon next to the screenshot image on the left panel to keep from accidentally selecting it while you work.

Pro Tip: Show Your Work

When you make new iterations of a design, don't delete the previous versions. Professional designers always keep the previous iterations by either creating new files or adding new designs to the right and/or below the previous ones as they work. Doing this will help you see your progress and compare improvements against previous iterations, and it will even let you select all or part of a previous successful version as the final composition.

Module 4.2 Bootstrap Introduction

In this module you will understand the Bootstrap framework so you can integrate it into your HTML code.

4.2.1 The Bootstrap Framework

In computing, a library or framework is a collection of code you can use to add additional functionality to a project. You already used a library when you added Google Fonts to your page in chapter 3. In this module, you will add and use the Bootstrap CSS framework in order to tap into its responsive grid system and other features. Bootstrap was originally built by designers at Twitter (R.I.P.) and is one of the most popular frameworks for adding responsive behavior to web pages. It is open source and free ("as in beer" and "as in freedom") to use in any commercial, nonprofit, or artistic project.

Exercise 4.2.1 Add Bootstrap to an HTML Page

Go to the Docs page at **getbootstrap.com** and find the Quick Start with instructions. We provide steps below with links to Bootstrap 5.3.8, but feel free to use the latest version you find on their site. See the wiki for a video demonstration of this exercise.

1. Create a new repo from our template **github.com/criticalwebdesign/website-template** named "on-the-grid" and then go to **github.com/codespaces,** or your preferred code editor, and open your new repository following our steps in exercise 3.2.1.
2. Open **index.html** and add the following `<meta>` tag to the beginning of the `<head>` of your document to add responsive behavior in mobile devices:

```
<meta name="viewport" content="width=device-width,
initial-scale=1">
```

3. Include Bootstrap's CSS by adding this `<link>` tag to the `<head>` of your document. Add it *before* the link to our own CSS stylesheet so that you can override any rules as needed. Adding it to the `<head>` ensures the styles are loaded and ready to be used before the rest of your content loads. If you don't put CSS in the `<head>`, you might briefly see the page unstyled before it displays as you expect.

```
<link href="https://cdn.jsdelivr.net/npm/bootstrap@5.3.8/dist
/css/bootstrap.min.css" rel="stylesheet">
<link rel="stylesheet" href="./assets/css/styles.css">
```

Author Note: Bootstrap Extras

The `integrity` and `crossorigin` parameters you see when copy/pasting the code from **getbootstrap.com** help to ensure remote files are safe to incorporate into your page. You can use our paired-down code or copy the tags directly from their site. Notice also that these files are provided via a **content delivery network (CDN)**, which hosts duplicate content on servers located around the world to decrease load time.

4. Include the Bootstrap JavaScript file by placing the following `<script>` tag at the end of the page just before the closing `</body>` tag.

```
<script src="https://cdn.jsdelivr.net/npm/bootstrap@5.3.8/dist
/js/bootstrap.bundle.min.js"></script>
```

5. Save and reload your page in the browser. After adding Bootstrap, you'll notice that your default font will change. If you don't, then look in the Console in DevTools to look for an error importing their files. If you experience any issues, try copying the CSS and JavaScript import code directly from **getbootstrap.com** using their instructions.
6. Once you've imported the CSS and JS, you can begin using Bootstrap in your HTML document by simply adding any of their predefined CSS classes to an element on

your page. As an experiment, add a regular button to the **<body>**. You will see it appear using the default system style.

```
<button type="button">Primary</button>
```

7. Add the prebuilt Bootstrap **btn** class that manages buttons, followed by any of the specific button classes from their documentation[18] like **.btn-primary**, and you'll see several aesthetic, user experience, and usability improvements when you interact with it.

```
<button type="button" class="btn btn-primary">Primary</button>
```

8. Experiment with the button classes by adding other buttons referenced in the documentation. Then continue reading to learn how Bootstrap improves how you use colors and typography in your site, as well as other vital additions like the responsive grid system.

Best Practices: Check the Version

When you look for Bootstrap tutorials or code examples on the internet, you should always confirm that the version matches the code you are using. There are a few, but important, differences between Bootstrap releases, which are reflected in the corresponding documentation and migration guides for each.[19] The examples in this book use Bootstrap 5.3, which is the current version at the time of this writing. You can see the version you are using by looking at the paths of the scripts you import.

Best Practices: The DRY Principle

One reason responsive CSS frameworks like Bootstrap are so widely used is that they help you adhere to a principle called DRY. **"Don't repeat yourself" (DRY)** is aimed at reducing repetition to make writing and managing code easier. You have already been practicing DRY in this book:

- **More efficient coding**—Writing the same code over and over requires time and energy. Using CSS to define classes that can be reused across your pages ensures you only need to write it once.
- **Easier maintenance**—While it makes perfect sense to reuse code from a previous project (e.g., to make a website responsive), what if you find a bug? Now you have to stop working on the current task to find and fix the issue in every project that uses that code. Bootstrap helps by providing access to a huge amount of thoroughly tested **boilerplate** code with standard features needed for every new site.

- **Avoiding errors**—Think of a program that changes a color on the page depending on user interaction. However, instead of adhering to DRY, the program updates the color from several different locations. This makes it difficult to find where the error originated. Writing a single function will make it easy to debug any unexpected behavior.

In short, when you write DRY code you will be more efficient and encounter fewer errors!

4.2.2 CSS Custom Properties

CSS **custom properties** are another strategy for keeping your code DRY. Custom properties allow you to store values and then reuse them throughout your stylesheet(s). They are also easier to read because they use descriptive names in place of values. A custom property is defined inside a CSS rule using `--` (double hyphens) before a descriptive name. The example below stores the value of a hex color inside a custom property called **`--hotness`** and is then accessed later using **`var(--hotness)`**. We removed whitespace in this example to keep each on one line.

```
html {--hotness: #fb3f7c; --sky: #49c8da;}
h1 {color: var(--hotness);}
h2 {color: var(--sky);}
```

The `<html>` element is considered the **root element** of an HTML document because it is the parent of all the other elements on the page. Adding custom properties to this element makes the declaration **global**. Therefore, it is inherited and used by all child elements in your code. It is also common to see custom properties defined inside the `:root` selector, which is the same but with higher specificity. You can store any CSS value in a custom property, including colors, lengths, and other units, and it is easy to access and change them with JavaScript.[20]

```
:root {--spacing: .35rem;}
h2 {margin: var(--spacing);}
```

Activity: View Bootstrap Under the Hood

Explore the Bootstrap source code to understand how it uses custom properties in its comprehensive color system.

1. Open the **on-the-grid/index.html** page in Chrome. Right-click on the `<h1>` element and choose **Inspect** to open DevTools.
2. In the Styles tab you will see several CSS rules imported from different files. You can observe, based on filenames like **_buttons.scss** and **_root.scss**, that they have a specific

role in Bootstrap. Also note the **.scss** extension, which indicates they use the Sass language, a version of CSS that adds features but requires additional setup (see the callout for more).

3. In the Styles tab, scroll down until you see the reference to the `:root` selector. You can use the search bar under the styles tab to filter elements with "root." You will notice one rule set that contains the custom properties defining the pixel sizes for breakpoints. We will discuss this in depth in the next module. The other rule set for `:root` contains the predefined colors of the Bootstrap theme, also stored as custom properties that can be used everywhere.
4. Inspect the blue button on the page and filter the Styles for the `btn-primary` class (figure 4.10). Each of these button classes have the same set of custom properties that can be overridden as needed. See our tutorial on the chapter 4 wiki that shows how to override Bootstrap styles for your project.

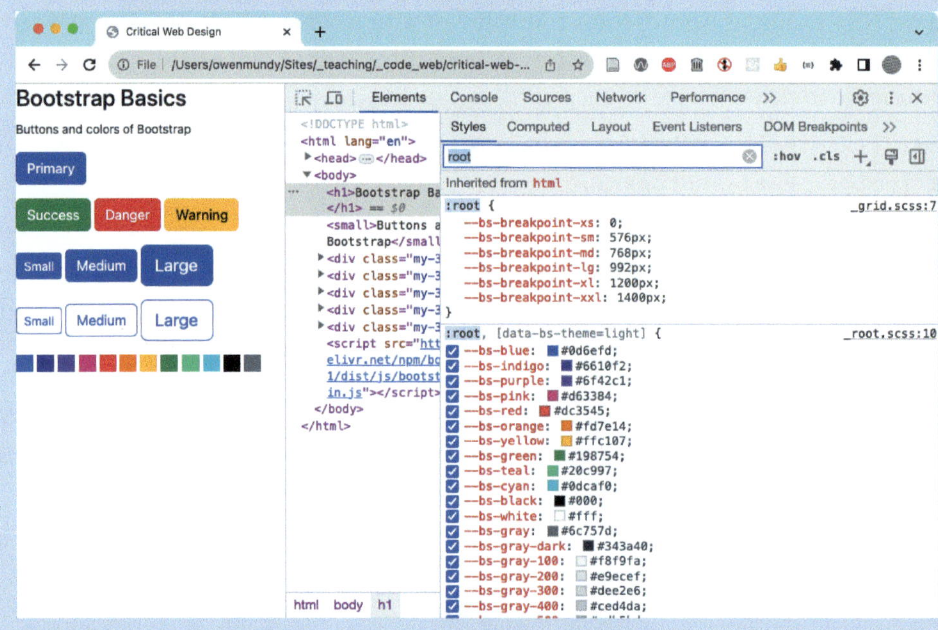

Figure 4.10
Use DevTools to see Bootstrap's `btn-primary` class custom properties.

⚠ Watch Out! Dynamic CSS Is Sassy

The file extension **.scss** is used for **Sass** files, a stylesheet language that adds advanced functionality to CSS like variables, nesting, functions, and more.[21] Sass, **sass-lang.com** (and Less, another type), provides benefits when working on large projects but requires additional setup and adjustments to how you write CSS. In the Bootstrap documentation and online code samples you will see references to Sass code (look for a $ prefix) like the following:[22]

```
@each $color, $value in $theme-colors {
.swatch-#{$color} {
  color: color-contrast($value);
  }
}
```

To use these in your code you will have to set up a Sass compiler. Adding Sass (or Less) to your CSS without installing a compiler will produce errors. We recommend you try that in the future, after you've learned the foundations presented in this book.

⚠ Watch Out! Bootstrap Themes

A **theme** is a collection of coded files that modify the appearance or behaviors of an interface. Themes can be installed in code editors, WordPress websites, and even Bootstrap. For example, we have been using the one-dark theme in the graphics for the book as an homage to the Atom (R.I.P.) editor we used before VS Code. Bootstrap 5.3 has something like a theme in their in-progress color modes[23] feature to let you select between light (default) or dark modes. It goes without saying that *practicing design* yourself is the most important path toward becoming a designer. So, we recommend you avoid using "bootstrap themes" for now, so you learn the foundational concepts we present and avoid getting stuck. While third-party themes appear to be fast solutions, they usually create more work due to little documentation or support. And, perhaps more importantly, they lock you into choices someone else is making. In *The Language of New Media*, Lev Manovich describes this problem, stating that the "interface shapes how the computer user conceives the computer itself."[24] In other words, the tools you use ultimately affect the choices you can make (or even imagine) due to the limits imposed by their creators.

4.2.3 Relative Units in CSS

So far you have used pixels (px) to set CSS values. The pixel, as well as physical units (in, cm, mm, pt), are **absolute length** units because they are fixed to the current display's resolution.[25] For example, setting `font-size:16px;` sets the height of a line of text to 16 pixels regardless of the resolution or display used to view the site. As we noted earlier, this can make using absolute units incompatible with the wide variety of resolutions and devices available.

The `rem` ("root em") unit is the most common **relative length unit** used in CSS. Unlike other relative units like `%`, `em`, `vw`, and `vh` (see table 4.1), the `rem` is based on the font size of the root element, which is equal to the browser's default font size. On desktop computers the value for the rem is usually `16px`, however this can change depending on the device and resolution. Importantly, users can also adjust this preference to accommodate their vision needs. Units that specify lengths (fonts, margins, padding, and other sizes relative to other lengths) can more easily scale to different resolutions and thus be readable across a variety of device sizes and preferences.[26]

The other argument for using relative units over absolute units in responsive design is that relative units are easier to use because they keep your code DRY. Instead of repeating pixel values throughout your code, you can make all sizes either the same, or percentages smaller or larger, of the root em. For example, you can use `1rem` for all text, knowing it will be the correct size for your viewer, and, assuming the default font size is `16px`, you can know that `1.5rem` will be (16 * 1.5) 24px, `2rem` will be (16 * 2) `32px`, and so on.

4.2.4 Bootstrap Typography

If you explore the Typography page in the Bootstrap documentation,[27] you will find that all text is relative to a single font size, declared as a custom property along with all the colors you saw previously in the `:root` rule:

```
--bs-body-font-size: 1rem;
```

You will also notice Bootstrap uses the rem unit to define the precise font sizes for the headings and scale consistently across each level (figure 4.11). The consistent mathematical relationship between these sizes is more than convenient—it creates a visual hierarchy in headings and thus helps you add an implicit structure to the content of your page through their use.

While it is possible to override Bootstrap styles, we will share an important caveat regarding font sizes. The folks that contribute to this open-source project have spent

Table 4.1
A summary of the most popular relative length units in regard to font size

Unit	Name	Description
%	Percentage	These units are based on the size set in their parent elements. Each can create issues when used with nested elements because they compound the unit values.
`em`	Em	
`rem`	Root em	Based on the size of the root em. The most popular unit because it allows measurements to scale across devices and is easy to change by updating the root element.
`vw` / `vh`	Viewport width and height	Based on the width of the viewport. `1vw` = 1% of the viewport's resolution width.

Heading	rem	px	Example
<h1></h1>	2.5rem	40px	h1. Bootstrap heading
<h2></h2>	2rem	32px	h2. Bootstrap heading
<h3></h3>	1.75rem	28px	h3. Bootstrap heading
<h4></h4>	1.5rem	24px	h4. Bootstrap heading
<h5></h5>	1.25rem	20px	h5. Bootstrap heading
<h6></h6>	1rem	16px	h6. Bootstrap heading

Figure 4.11
The headings in the Bootstrap framework scale at consistent values.

a lot of time making the text look great while remaining legible and accessible regardless of the operating system, browser, or device used to access your website. The rules that control Bootstrap text use relative units for font size, font weight, line height, margins, and so on to create "a more inclusive and accessible type scale" to make it possible to let "visitors customize their browser defaults as needed."[28] Since you have a finer understanding of how typography is integrated into design thanks to the content of this chapter, you will appreciate the following recommendation: Do not override Bootstrap's font size(s) or line height and let the text flow as the professional designers intended.

Exercise 4.2.2 Export a Color Palette from Coolors

Export colors and use custom properties in your project.

1. Open any palette at Coolors. We will be using this one in the example: **criticalwebdesign.github.io#coolors**.
2. Click the **Export** button in the upper right menu. This opens a **modal** (a window inside the browser window) with several choices (figure 4.12).

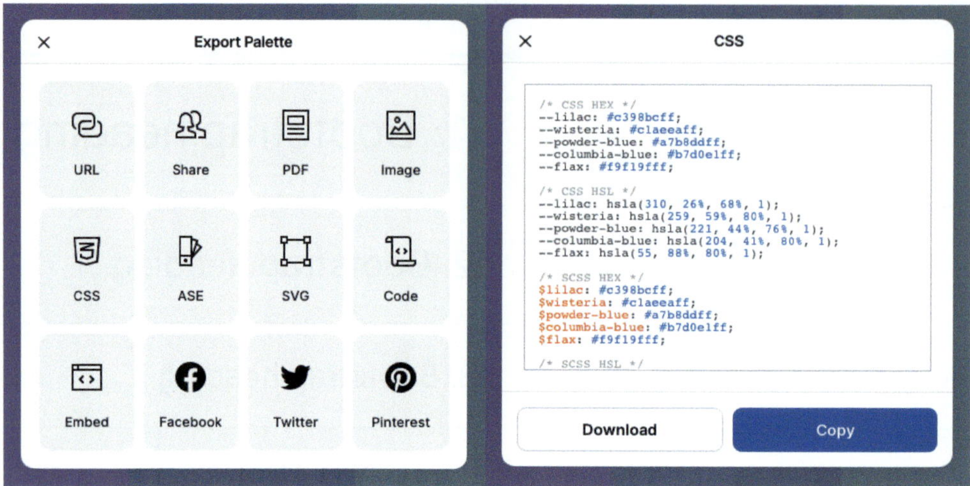

Figure 4.12
Coolors.co export options and CSS formats.

3. Select CSS from the export options. A new window appears with coded color values in several CSS and Sass formats, including Hex and HSL (hue/saturation/lightness) notation.
4. Copy the CSS Hex custom properties and paste them into your root element to use them in your CSS stylesheet.

```
:root {
  /* CSS HEX */
  --lilac: #c398bcff;
  --wisteria: #claeeaff;
  --powder-blue: #a7b8ddff;
  --columbia-blue: #b7d0e1ff;
  --flax: #f9f19fff;
}
```

Prompt 4.2 Code: Bootstrap Buttons, Text, and Colors

Use the Bootstrap documentation to change the color, size, outline of your buttons. Implement colors from Coolors or other palette generators. Continue experimenting with Bootstrap, referencing the documentation as needed. In the next module you'll learn how to use the grid system to make responsive columns.

Module 4.3 The Bootstrap Grid System

In this module you will learn to use Bootstrap's built-in grid system to code three breakpoints into a single responsive web page.

4.3.1 Containers

The first thing you need to use in Bootstrap's responsive grid system is a container that defines how your content will scale with the viewport. To do this, add a **<div>** using either their **.container** or **.container-fluid** classes. The **.container** class always centers content within a maximum width for each responsive breakpoint, while **.container-fluid** fills the entire width of the device or viewport, stretching the twelve columns and their gutters across the width.[29]

Inside the **.container**, add a **.row**, and then a **.col** for each column in your design. Bootstrap's grid system provides twelve columns to use or combine however you like. The basic column class **.col** will fill all horizontal space on each **.row**, automatically adjusting to share space as you add more columns (figure 4.13, section 1). For example, the code below will create a three-column layout with horizontal space equally divided across one row using **container**, **row**, and **col** classes.

```
<div class="container">
  <div class="row">
    <div class="col">1</div>
    <div class="col">2</div>
    <div class="col">3</div>
  </div>
</div>
```

4.3.2 Column Spans

The Bootstrap grid is twelve columns wide, but you choose how you divide these by using the **.col-{span}** classes. To use these, replace **{span}** with the number of bootstrap columns you want to include across the width of the page. For example, the following code will create two columns, with the left spanning four of the twelve default Bootstrap columns, and the right spanning eight columns. This means the left column will be exactly ½ the size of the right column, on any device. This is represented in figure 4.13, section 3.

```
<div class="container">
  <div class="row">
    <div class="col-4">4</div>
```

```
        <div class="col-8">8</div>
    </div>
</div>
```

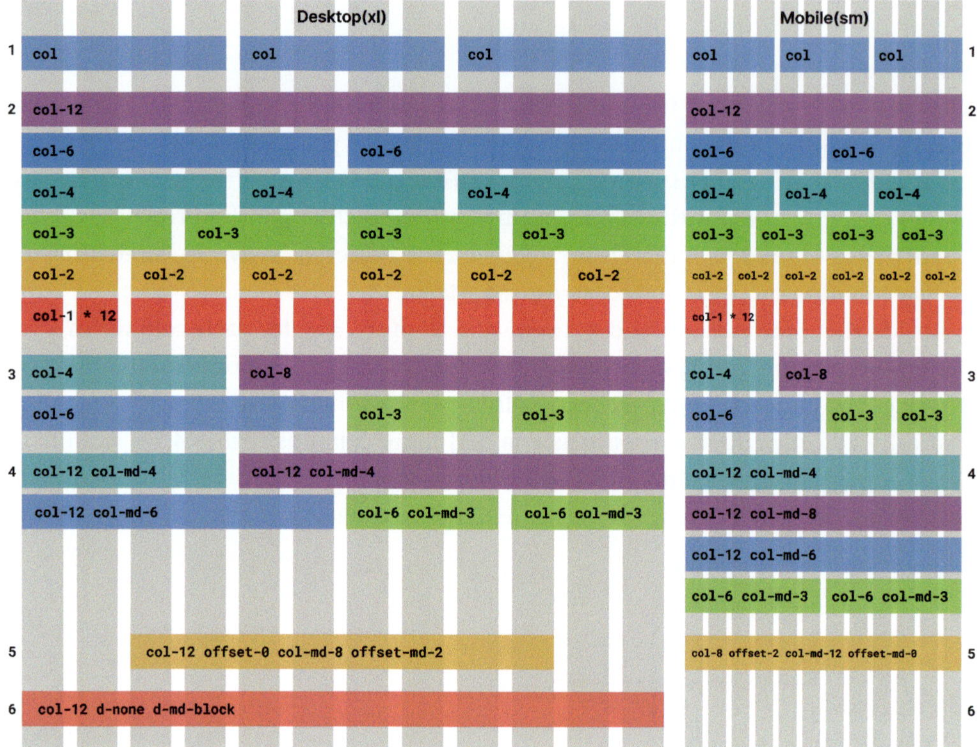

Figure 4.13
A design with Bootstrap grid system showing equally sized columns per row (section 1), specific column widths (section 2), different size columns (section 3), different size columns with their breakpoints (sections 4 and 5), and other breakpoint-specific classes like "display none," for desktop and mobile. Notice that (section 4) you can mix and match Bootstrap column sizes however you like, including the offset set class, which can center the columns in a container. The only rule is that the column and offset spans together add up to twelve. View the coded, responsive, version of this graphic here **criticalwebdesign.github.io#bootstrap-grid** and be sure to change the width of the browser window to see the effect.

> ⚠ **Watch Out!**
> In Bootstrap, the sum of your columns (or column spans) for each row, for that specific breakpoint, should always be twelve or they will "break" and wrap to the next line.

4.3.3 Responsive Column Spans

Finally, we arrive at the responsive versions of these column classes, which look like `.col-{breakpoint}-{span}`. In the example below, there are now two classes for each column. Bootstrap is a "mobile first framework," so these additional classes instruct Bootstrap to span the specific number of columns, for each specified device size *and larger*. Meaning, if this code is viewed on a small device like a phone, these divs default to span twelve columns. But, viewed on a medium device size like tablets, as well as all sizes larger than medium, the first column will switch back to four and the second column is again displayed using eight Bootstrap columns (see figure 4.13, section 4).

```
<div class="container">
  <div class="row">
    <div class="col-12 col-md-4">md-4</div>
    <div class="col-12 col-md-8">md-8</div>
  </div>
</div>
```

Best Practices: Tinkering

While you are learning to code, sometimes it's easier to understand the impact of the instructions in the book by tinkering with examples. For instance, to get a better understanding of the way Bootstrap handles responsive column spans, change the span numbers after `col`, `md`, and `lg` directly using the browser DevTools. Another method is to create a simplified example using codepen that live updates, like this **criticalwebdesign.github.io#bootstrap-grid** to experiment with example Bootstrap grid combinations.

Exercise 4.3.1 Nesting Bootstrap Rows and Columns

In this exercise you will code our example layout as a responsive web page.

1. Confirm that you have added Bootstrap to the **index.html** file in the **on-the-grid/** folder (see exercise 4.2.1).
2. Delete any test code you added to the `<body>`, so that you just have a blank HTML page with the link to Bootstrap's CSS and JS files.
3. Use the code auto completion feature in Codespaces to type `div.container` just after `<body>` then press the **Tab** key. It should add the following Bootstrap container, inside which we'll add all the rows and columns.

```
<div class="container"></div>
```

4. Press **return** to add a new line and then type `div.row` to add a nested element inside the container, repeating the process from above. This is the first row of content.
5. Press **return** again and add three columns nested inside the row. You can count the number of Bootstrap columns each of your columns should span. The first will be `div.col-3` followed by `div.col-5` and finally a `div.col-4` to match the twelve total Bootstrap columns in the design.
6. Add the headers in `<h3>` tags and the lorem ipsum inside a `<p>` to the first and third column. Download the file **cat-34.png** from the **on-the-grid/4-3/assets/img/** folder in the book repo, upload it to the **img/** folder in your Codespace, and add the image to the second column using the `<img>` HTML tag and path of your uploaded file. Your code should look like the following:

```
<div class="container">
  <div class="row">
    <div class="col-3">
      <h3>Lorem Ipsum</h3>
      <p>Lorem ipsum dolor sit amet, consectetur adipiscing
      elit.</p>
    </div>
    <div class="col-5">
      <img src="assets/img/cat-34.png">
    </div>
    <div class="col-4">
      <h3>Lorem Ipsum</h3>
      <p>Donec vel magna sem. Quisque eget quam facilisis,
      eleifend tortor id, faucibus nisl.</p>
    </div>
  </div>
</div>
```

Best Practices: Avoid "Full Screen Mode"

While working on a laptop with a relatively small display it may be tempting to use "full screen mode" to maximize screen space. However, when building and testing responsive websites you need to be able to resize the browser window to preview how your work will look across different display resolutions and devices.

Figure 4.14
The image in the second column is not scaling or reflowing like the text.

7. Preview the HTML file with Live Server in Chrome. Grab the edge of the browser window and scale the horizontal size of the page to the left and right. You will notice an issue because the image is not scaling with the column that contains it (figure 4.14).
8. To fix this issue add Bootstrap's built-in `img-fluid` class, which scales images proportionally to scale to the size of the columns in which they are placed. Your image tag should look like this. Preview your page to confirm it worked.

```
<img src="assets/img/cat-34.png" alt="black cat"
class="img-fluid">
```

9. Update the heading and body copy typeface with a Google Font (see exercise 3.2.2). We used a variety of **Gentium** from Google Fonts in this layout for everything except the masthead. Remember to add the stylesheet links and CSS rule declaration *after* you import Bootstrap's CSS (that is, on a later line of code) so that you override their default font with this new one.
10. Download `cat-81.png` from the repo, upload it to your Codespace, and insert its image tag in the top of column three. Notice that the heading of this column is too close to the image, and it feels "cramped." It needs a margin above the header to match the amount of space below the text to provide balance (figure 4.15). Remember the importance of consistency in design in the Context section of this chapter? Well, Bootstrap has you covered with their prebuilt spacing utility classes,[30] which add padding or margins in ratios that scale at rates consistent to other sizes in the framework. Add an `mt-2` class to the `<h3>` to add a top margin that is equal to `(.5 * $spacer)`. If you are wondering: What is the size of the default `$spacer` variable in Bootstrap Sass? We hope you guessed it is `1rem`!

Figure 4.15
Notice the difference in negative space before and after we added the top margin to the heading.

11. You have now finished adding content to the top row. Preview your work and resize the browser window to approximate the size of a phone. Since you haven't added breakpoints the three columns continue to scale, making the text unreadable at smaller sizes. To fix this, update the classes of the three columns to look like the code below.

```
<div class="col-12 col-md-6 col-lg-3">
. . .
<div class="col-12 col-md-6 col-lg-5">
. . .
<div class="col-12 col-lg-4">
. . .
```

12. Preview your work, then resize the window and watch carefully as the page snaps to each breakpoint. Here is the explanation of what changed:
    a. All three columns now default to take up the full 12 Bootstrap columns. This is for **`xs`** and **`sm`** sizes.
    b. On **`md`** sizes the first two columns split the full width (6 | 6) while the third column continues to take up the full width of the next row.
    c. The previous column layout (3 | 5 | 4) is now only applied to **`lg`** and **`xl`** sizes.
13. Don't forget to stage and commit your changes. Remember that images will not be added to your repo until you commit your changes from Codespace.

Check Your Work

This concludes the chapter exercises. We invite you to compare your work to the final outcome **criticalwebdesign.github.io#4-3** and code **criticalwebdesign.github.io#4-3-code** in the book repo. Don't forget to enable GitHub Pages in your project and then stage and commit your work to make it live!

Prompt 4.3 Publish: Add Columns and Rows to Your Page

Add the next row, including the columns, content, and breakpoints. View your work by using the "Toggle Device Toolbar" in DevTools. Continue experimenting and follow these guiding methods:

1. Organize the page in HTML.
2. Use the Bootstrap documentation.
3. Test the responsiveness of your page in Chrome often.
4. Validate your HTML and CSS—especially when you are having trouble getting code to work as you intend.
5. Explore our example as needed **criticalwebdesign.github.io#4-3**.

⚠ Watch Out! Bootstrap Validation

Bootstrap uses several hacks to ensure your design will look the same across different browsers. When checking CSS validation, look for issues on your own file and ignore the warnings from Bootstrap's CSS.

5 Usability and Forms

Don't make me think.

—Steve Krug

Context

Don't Make Me Think is the title of Steve Krug's classic book and guiding principle for creating usable websites. He writes, "It means that as far as is humanly possible, when I look at a Web page it should be self-evident. Obvious. Self-explanatory."[1] Krug draws a parallel between wayfinding in a mall and navigating a website. His scenario has our protagonist (possible web user) entering a department store to purchase a chainsaw. A user might read the large signs dividing the store into sections, narrowing down the aisles to power tools, and only then looking at singular objects to find the tool. This, Krug suggests, is the same process people use when they are wayfinding online. Starting with obvious cues provided by the menus, users make assumptions about the information architecture (see callout) about where to locate material in the content hierarchy or possibly use a search function if it exists. He writes (and you likely know this experience yourself), "Eventually, if you can't find what you're looking for, you'll leave."[2] This ability to way find through a perceived content hierarchy is crucial for the usability goals of a website.

Best Practices: Information Architecture

A website's **information architecture** describes how pages are organized throughout a website or application to (ideally) help users make sense of content and achieve their goals. Sometimes referred to as a "sitemap," the architecture should reflect the primary categories and hierarchy of information within a site to make browsing as intuitive as possible for users. Creating an information architecture should be done at the beginning of a website planning phase so that the structure of information makes sense and can be used for the main navigation of the site. If you are redesigning a website, it is a good idea to make two sitemaps, one for the existing site and a new version to reflect changes to the content since the previous implementation. Planning a website's architecture can be done visually by drawing a network of interconnected pages (figure 5.1) or by using a simple numbered, hierarchical list in a text document.

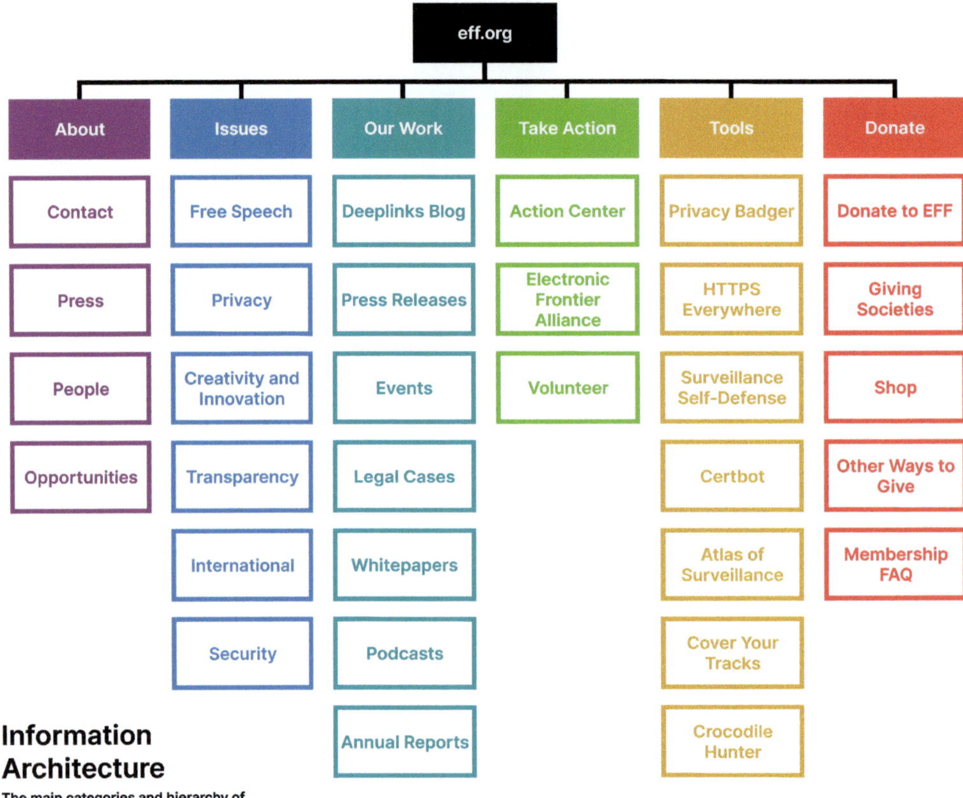

Figure 5.1
Example information architecture from the Electronic Freedom Foundation website **(eff.org)**, a nonprofit organization defending civil liberties in the digital world.

Additional Materials and Resources

Explore links and other content related to this chapter:
criticalwebdesign.github.io#wiki-05

This chapter focuses on usability, helping you to create, deliver, and reflect on results from a usability test that you can apply and reuse across any project. We will also introduce web forms, a common pain point for web users, and learn how to make them usable and functional through input validation and JavaScript variables. Later in this book we will focus on accessibility, which has an impact that overlaps with usability. Taken together, these chapters will encourage you to design websites that are both usable and accessible for a wide range of audiences.

Design Thinking Processes

By now you have developed a sense of how page layout and coding figure into the web development process. In this section, we provide an overview of the entire process, emphasizing how each can affect the usability of the sites you build.

As you've seen, the design process must balance creativity with the requirements for the final outcome. A finished website must be written in valid HTML/CSS/JS code for the browser, tested for usability and accessibility for its intended audience, and published on a live web server. Yet, each project introduces new design problems that require the designer to seek to understand the use cases, invent novel and experimental solutions, and build and test **prototypes** (a "proof of concept" demonstrating just the working, functional parts of a website or application) that can be implemented in the coded site. Interface designers must also generate novel ways of presenting information to make it stand apart in our data-driven world, again working within the constraints of software development, usability, and deadlines. Like the layout grid, design processes exist to help designers consistently create usable interfaces while encouraging creativity and experimentation. The term **design thinking** is commonly used to describe a series of strategic and repeatable steps that can be used to frame problems and develop solutions. However, hundreds of such methods have been conceived and used across architecture, engineering, industrial, software, and other design fields.

The history of processes used across design reveals how creativity and constraints have been accounted for systematically. In the first half of the twentieth century, the increased scale of manufacturing during industrialization spurred design processes and methods in engineering projects, production, and operations research. The acclaimed interaction designer Hugh Dubberly, who held leadership roles at Apple and Netscape,[3] found evidence of repeatable design processes used in the 1920s in research for the design of Royal Navy battleships and other military endeavors. Dubberly writes, "Academic designers imported both methods and philosophy in what became known as the design methods movement (1962–1972)." Concepts that led to the development of design thinking are woven throughout a 1969 book, *The Sciences of the Artificial*, by the cognitive scientist Herbert A. Simon. It was also in the 1960s that Horst Rittel, the design theorist, wrote about the problem-solving aspect of design thinking to address what he called "wicked problems"—problems that are multidimensional and require varying methodologies to understand human needs, motivations, and behaviors.[4]

Evidence of design thinking processes in education can be found as early as 1958, in a seminar titled "Creative Engineering" taught by John Arnold at Stanford University as part of a Joint Program in Design incorporating art and engineering. In this course Arnold attempted to "bring about a union between the physical sciences, social sciences and the arts," where the creative results should be "future-oriented and useful to society, functional rather than recreational."[5] The use (and promotion) of design thinking has exploded in recent years thanks to the rise of start-up culture in and around Silicon Valley. Nearly fifty years after Arnold's course, the Hasso Plattner Institute of Design at Stanford, known as the "d.School," continues the multidisciplinary tradition, promoting design thinking to train students to accommodate the fast-moving software industry.

Applying Design Thinking Methods

While design thinking is a useful approach to understanding problems, there are many such methods. The most useful of these we find are those that emphasize research, creativity, and iteration throughout the process. Hugh Dubberly offers an inspiring selection of diagrams from throughout the twentieth century in his book *How Do You Design? A Compendium of Models*. One example from the book by Bruce Archer, a mechanical engineer who worked in industrial design, shows how creating solutions likely involves repeating a creative activity for which there are no objective or predefined answers (see **criticalwebdesign.github.io#dubberly**). In "Systematic Method for Designers: Part Five: The Creative Leap" (1964) written by Archer for *Design* magazine, he discusses the moment in the process where the engineer/artist/designer must use their imagination rather than rely on step-by-step processes. He writes, "When all has been said and done about defining design problems and analyzing design data, there still remains the real crux of the act of designing—the creative leap from pondering the question to finding a solution."[6]

Design thinking today is actually an amalgamation of different methods developed throughout the twentieth century. The processes almost always emphasize iteration and creativity within logistical constraints. Example diagrams for "design thinking" are prevalent and varied on the internet. The d.School publishes resources for design thinking on their website, including their Design Thinking Bootleg,[7] which narrates five modules in the design process: (1) Empathize, (2) Define, (3) Ideate, (4) Prototype, and (5) Test. The Nielsen Norman Group (NNG), known for establishing the standards for usability testing that we reference in the next section, utilizes the same stages of the design process with the addition of a sixth step: Implement.[8]

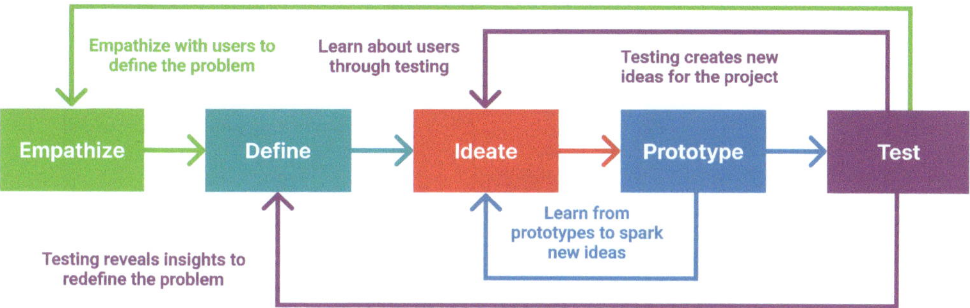

Figure 5.2
The common stages of a design thinking process are represented most often as a series of iterative loops that inform each other to improve your outcomes.

In figure 5.2 we show an example design thinking process diagram drawing on these various design thinking systems with the following sections:

1. **Empathize**—Start by learning about your users, identifying your audience, and developing example scenarios that describe the goals they will attempt when visiting your website.
2. **Define**—This in turn helps to know about the project itself, including how information will be organized throughout the site and potential design problems you will encounter. A **competition scan** (figure 5.3) will show you how other designers have already built similar projects and solved design problems you will encounter. It also helps clients to describe the design, style, content, functionality, features, and so on, as they may not be familiar with the language to describe these elements.
3. **Ideate**—The fun part of the process involves additional research, creating new ideas, and developing wireframes that incorporate the research, scenarios, and goals you have created so far.
4. **Prototype**—The prototype phase usually includes both designing versions of the interface as well as coding simple, bare-bones versions of any programmed interfaces.

5. **Test**—The testing phase follows up the iterative approaches in ideate and prototype, considering increasingly more developed versions of each to learn if they will solve all of the problems from the define phase.

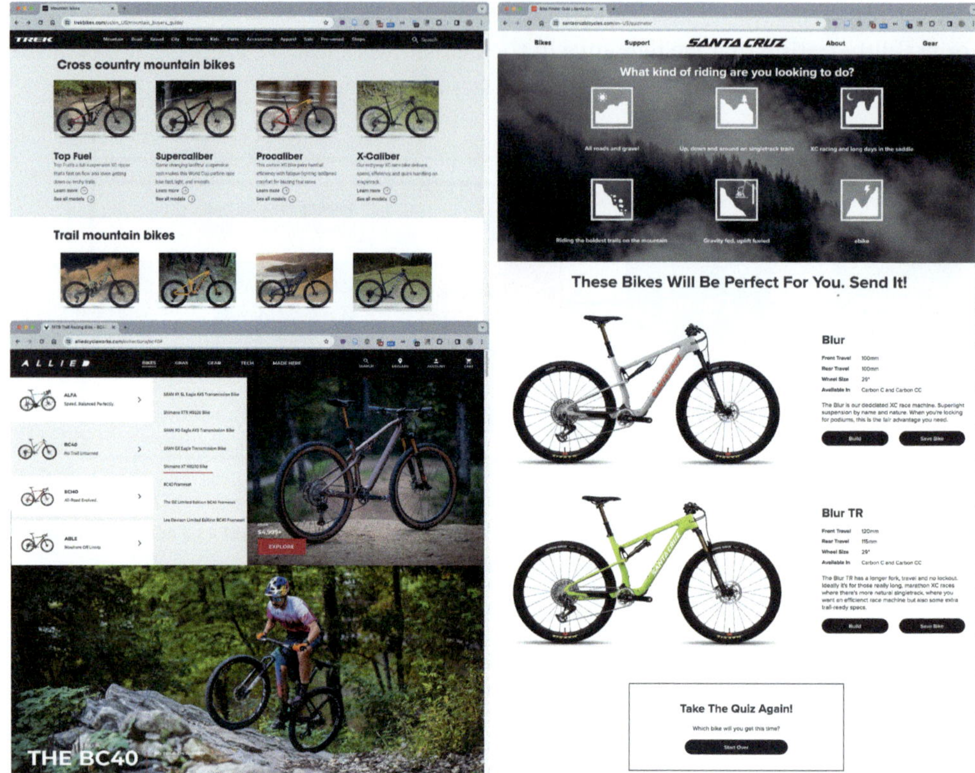

Figure 5.3
A competition scan shows how different mountain bike manufacturers have created varying solutions to the same design problem. Each company has to communicate bikes by intended terrain, wheel size, frame material, suspension, weight, and so on using menus, filters, images, quizzes, information hierarchy, and other methods.

Case Study: Alexei Shulgin, Form Art

AS: Alexei Shulgin (he/him, Алексей Шульгин) lives and works in Moscow, USSR. Artist, curator, educator; Alexei was one of the pioneers of internet art in the 1990s. He is the frontman of 386 DX cyberpunk rock band (starting in 1998). His approach to art making rests in the paradoxical usage of found photographs, html, corporate websites, midi files, text-to-speech software, electronics, and product design. When asked for a favorite work of online art, Alexei says: "**Jodi.org**. And another is (Heath Bunting's) **irational.org**. They both were very inspiring to me (and still are, I guess)."

Could you talk about your inspiration for using web forms as an aesthetic device?

AS: There were two things: (1) work by **Jodi.org** that deconstructed computer and web interfaces, and (2) my thoughts about interfaces that were (and still are) mostly taken for granted, without critical reflection. What did usability look like (or feel like)? Hardware and software were breaking all the time, the internet was very slow, screen resolution was low, my eyes hurt from looking at CRT monitors, but the keyboards were great (figure 5.4)!

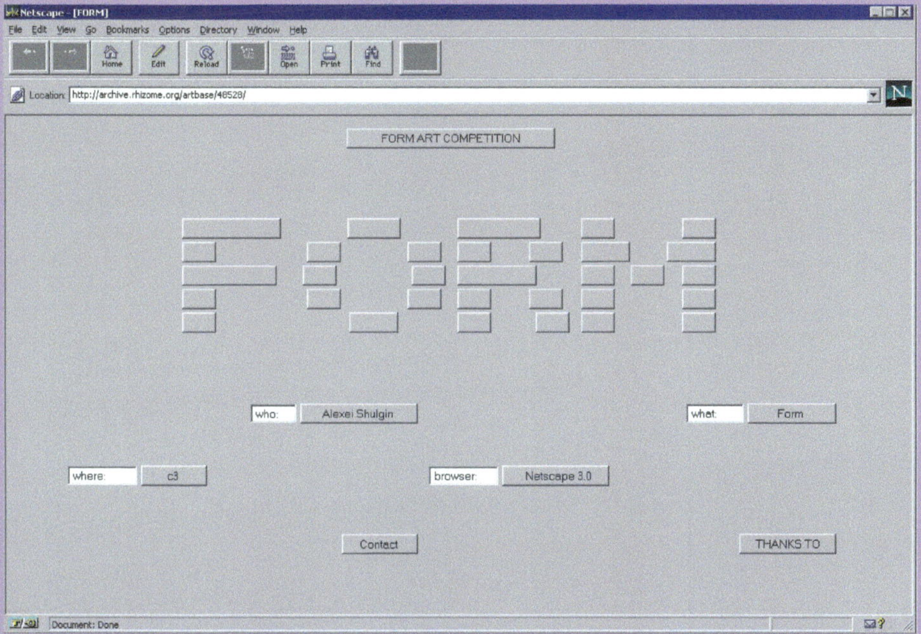

Figure 5.4

Alexei Shulgin, *Form Art*, 1997, c3.hu/collection/form presents various functioning form elements, including inputs, radio buttons, and checkboxes. When clicked, scrolled, or checked, the elements animate, provide context, or link to new pages in a continuous narrative of virtual paperwork. You can interact with the project here sites.rhizome.org/anthology/form-art.html as it was originally published using a browser emulator.

How was Form Art received?

AS: Well, it has become famous within a narrow circle of the net.art crowd. I think it was included in some curricula in art schools and universities.

If you were to remake the project today, would you do anything differently?

AS: I don't think I would remake it today, just because web design changed dramatically and most of the form elements now are either substituted by images or come in various shapes and colors (figure 5.5). Back in the '90s everything was "plain html." Also, I believe the purpose of art has changed a lot since then (in part, because of the internet and net.art), and shifted very much from aesthetics and representation towards new ethics.

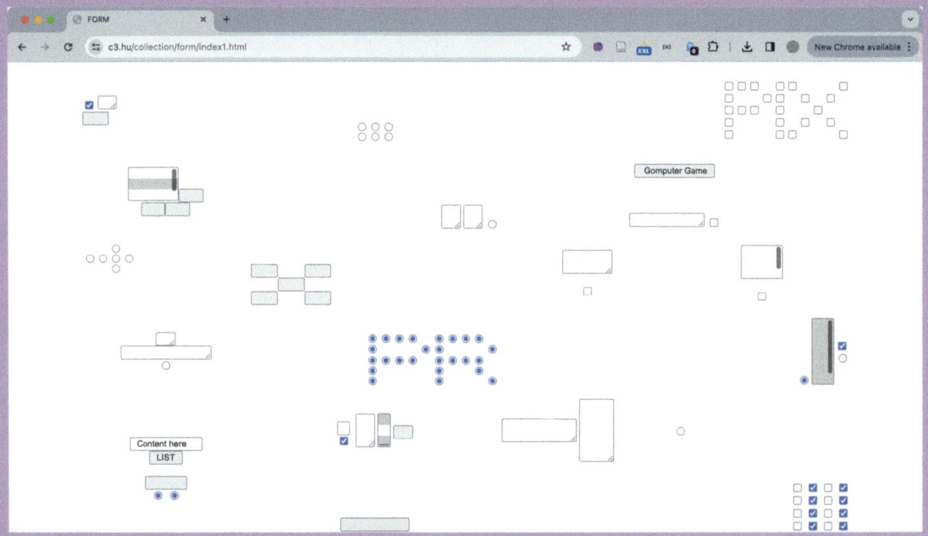

Figure 5.5

Alexei Shulgin, *Form Art*, 1997, c3.hu/collection/form/index1.html as seen today. You can also view a list of the project's content c3.hu/collection/form /list.html to provide order to your experience.

How does your recent work take this new ethics into account?

AS: As for my recent work, together with my wife Ianina Prudenko, we coauthored the Art Footprint manifesto.[9] We are teaching at a technical University (NITU MISIS) and at Rodchenko Art School here in Moscow. Our course is called Sustainable Creative Practices and is based on the Manifesto ideas. Also, we curate one municipal gallery, called Krasnokholmskaya, focused on technology and ecology. I consider these activities as extended art practices.

Activity: Userinyerface.com

Visit **userinyerface.com** and attempt to complete the form on the second page of the website as fast as you can. Made by Bagaar, a software and hardware company based in Belgium, this game presents the opposite experience that you might expect in a chapter on web usability. The tongue-in-cheek 2018 User "in yer face" design is "a challenging exploration of user interactions and design patterns."[10] This game exploits typical reusable **design patterns** common to user interface design that tend to make a website usable, such as high contrast between areas of the page, a top navigation tool labeled with clear hierarchies, and a grid layout structure that creates hierarchy among page sections. Bagaar subverts or even denies these design patterns, to create an unusable and harrowing experience.

The feeling you get from using a website like this aligns with John Brooke's understanding of usability, outlined in his article "SUS: A quick and dirty usability scale." Brooke writes, "Usability does not exist in any absolute sense; it can only be defined with reference to particular contexts. This, in turn, means that there are no absolute measures of usability, since, if the usability of an artefact is defined by the context in which that artefact is used, measures of usability must of necessity be defined by that context too."[11]

Prompt 5 What You'll Make
Create a Web Page with Results from a Usability Test

In the following prompts and exercises you will begin by creating and implementing a usability test. Then, apply design thinking concepts and our "less is more" critique and revise your layout before coding a responsive web page that reflects on your findings. You will make the design responsive using Bootstrap and create a working web form with JavaScript that outputs the score from the System Usability Scale (SUS) survey.

View the results of our usability test of the AIGA website in our own outcome at **criticalweb design.github.io#5-3** (figure 5.6). You can see the final code for every chapter on the CWD repo, **criticalwebdesign.github.io#repo**.

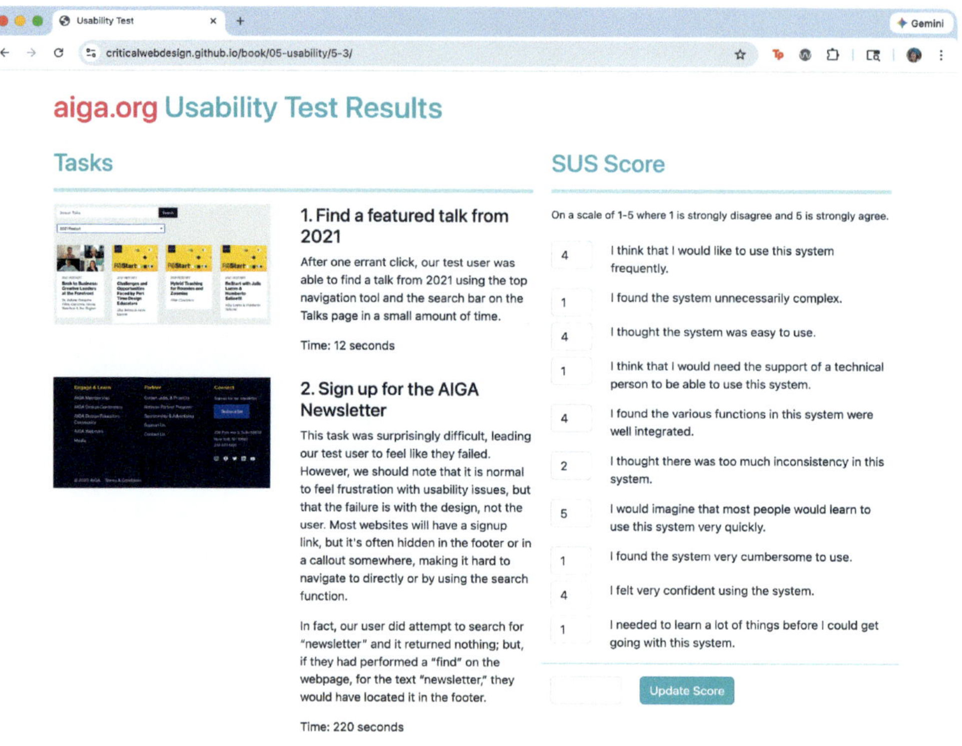

Figure 5.6
Our result shows the usability test coded using the Bootstrap framework with a form that computes our SUS score.

Module 5.1 Usability Testing

These exercises step through the process of creating, performing, and compiling data to understand the results of a usability test.

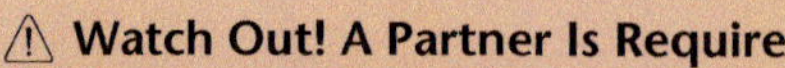
⚠ Watch Out! A Partner Is Required

To complete these exercises you will need at least one other person to fulfill the "user" role. If you are reading this book as part of a class, perform them with a group. If you are working on your own, then find a friend or roommate to be your test user.

Exercise 5.1.1 Create a Usability Test

The empathy phase of a typical design thinking process for website production includes seeking to understand potential users. A typical approach for this is to create a **user story** that helps designers imagine each user, including details about who they are, their technical capabilities, and importantly, understand their specific goals in using the website.

1. Select a website to test that is relatively popular, locally or on the internet. For instance, check out The Moz Top 500 Websites.[12]
2. Imagine a typical user and their motivations for using this website. Create a list of five realistic tasks for them to complete. The tasks should be specific, such as asking a user to find information or perform a specific function. For example, Marieke McCloskey suggests asking a user to "buy a pair of shoes for less than $40." Read her article for detailed guidelines in identifying usability tasks.[13]
3. If you are creating this test in the classroom, designate someone from your group to be the test user. This person will switch with a test user from another group so that completing the five tasks is a new experience. If you are completing this exercise on your own, ask a roommate or friend to be a test user.

Exercise 5.1.2 Perform the Usability Test

Follow these steps to implement your usability test.

1. Ask your new test user to complete each task, one at a time. From this point on, your test user has switched groups, and they are now a member of your (new to them) group.
2. Before you begin the test, note that:
   a. Your goal is to test *the website* (not the user) to discover issues. It is, therefore, helpful if your test user has trouble with any of your tasks.
   b. Watch your test user and make notes, but do not help or interfere with their process. Observe their eye and mouse activity (recall the discussion on eye tracking and focal points from chapter 2). Empathy in design is about accepting users for who they are and how they use your system; allow them to provide honest feedback through their actions.
   c. Ask the user to use the "thinking aloud" method we discussed in chapter 3 to help your group understand why they are making specific choices.
   d. Use other suggestions from the NNG for gathering data, like "Talk less and learn more."[14]
3. For each question, record the following information:
   a. **Time:** How long does it take to complete each task?

b. **Accuracy**: How many mistakes did the test user make, and how fast did they recover from the mistake?

c. **Recall**: How much did your test user remember on multiple uses? Did they improve at using the website over time?

d. **Emotional response**: How did your test user feel after using the website?

4. Finally, ask your user to complete the ten-question System Usability Scale (SUS) survey **measuringu.com/sus** and record the data.

Exercise 5.1.3 Compile Data

Reflect on what you observed and compile information from the usability test with your group into a single report. Write it in a shared document so you can access it later when you create your page designs.

1. List your name(s) and a link to the website you chose to analyze.
2. List the test user's responses (a number 1–5) to each of the ten prompts in the SUS at **measuringu.com/sus**. You will use JavaScript later in this chapter to perform the math required to tally the score.
3. List the five tasks you gave the user, along with the following information:
   a. Add all of the data you collected in the test.
   b. Add a discussion about the result of each task. Was the test user successful? Why or why not? Cite information on the NNG website to inform your report and communicate your findings.
   c. Write what recommendations you would make to the website owner. Refer to the **digital.gov/topics/usability** website for advice on how you might phrase these recommendations.
   d. Create a screenshot for each task focusing on the aspects of the website that led to the success or failure of the task.

In the next section you will define your own design challenge and code a responsive web page to share your findings. Usability should be performed early and often in order to help guide design decisions.

Activity: Create a Post-it Note Wireframe

Create an analog wireframe of the page that will display the results of your usability test, and then update it in a new version in Figma.

1. Write a two- to three-sentence user story to describe a person who will be reading the results of the usability test you created. Who are they, and why will they visit your web page? What goals do they hope to achieve?

2. Using Post-it Notes, index cards, pencil and paper, or drawing boxes on a whiteboard, record each "chunk" of information that should be included on the page (figure 5.7). For example, use cards or boxes as placeholders for the title, descriptions, credits, and web form as well as each of the five tasks, screenshots, and other data points.

Figure 5.7
Students drawing wireframes.

3. Arrange the notes on a large piece of paper or rectangular area to reflect a rough wireframe for the page you will design. Think about the structure of information on the page and how the intended user will move their eyes around the page to achieve their goals.
4. Indicate the fold (chapter 4) beyond which users will have to scroll to see information. Consider this line as you arrange items.
5. After you feel confident you have the items in roughly the right position, take a picture of your notes. Open Figma on your computer and drag that image into the canvas.
6. Add a desktop-sized frame and create a digital wireframe by adding and resizing solid color rectangles matching your photo. Use text to note the content in each area.

Prompt 5.1 Design: Iterate on a Responsive Design in Figma

An iterative approach is essential to the design process. In this prompt you will create multiple versions of your design by duplicating the previous layout to compare how your experiments improved upon the previous iteration. Here are some considerations to make while you work:

1. In Figma, next to the wireframe you created in the above exercise, add a new desktop frame and continue creating the next iteration of your design.
2. Experiment with formal elements of the design like color, line quality, value relationships, contrast, shapes, and text and image relationships.

3. In this version you should copy and paste all the content you created when you compiled the data from your report. Add all the text and images and then move them into the positions and sizes using the content areas you identified in your wireframe.
4. Copy and paste your frame to create a duplicate, and continue to iterate on your design choices. Make several variations of the desktop design before selecting a version to use to develop the designs for smaller devices.
5. Use a twelve-column Bootstrap layout grid to align your items. Update color, typefaces, and positions as needed to continue creating a layout to represent your findings while considering your users' goals.
6. Use screenshots of web forms and other components from the Bootstrap documentation to show the position of such elements on the page.

Module 5.2 JavaScript Data Types

In this module you will learn more about the structure of a JavaScript program, as well as how to recognize and use different data types and functions to code a web form in the final module.

5.2.1 What Is Programming?

Programming is the act of "writing instructions for a computer to execute." At a high level, this involves using a special language to tell the computer how to manage the flow, state, logic, and events that happen when someone uses your program. Look at the diagram in figure 5.8 and consider the descriptions below:

- The **flow** describes the order in which instructions are executed when your program runs.
- The **state** of your program includes information stored in variables that are used by your program to make decisions.
- **Logic** is how you instruct your program to make decisions based on the state.
- **Events** are things that happen, like user input, that may change the state.

You will notice that some of these concepts are already familiar to you. You used variables (state in our diagram) to store and update information on a web page in chapter 3. You also created event listeners and then ran other code to handle the events. We will soon discuss logic, which will give you more control over the program flow. First, you should know more about how JavaScript uses data.

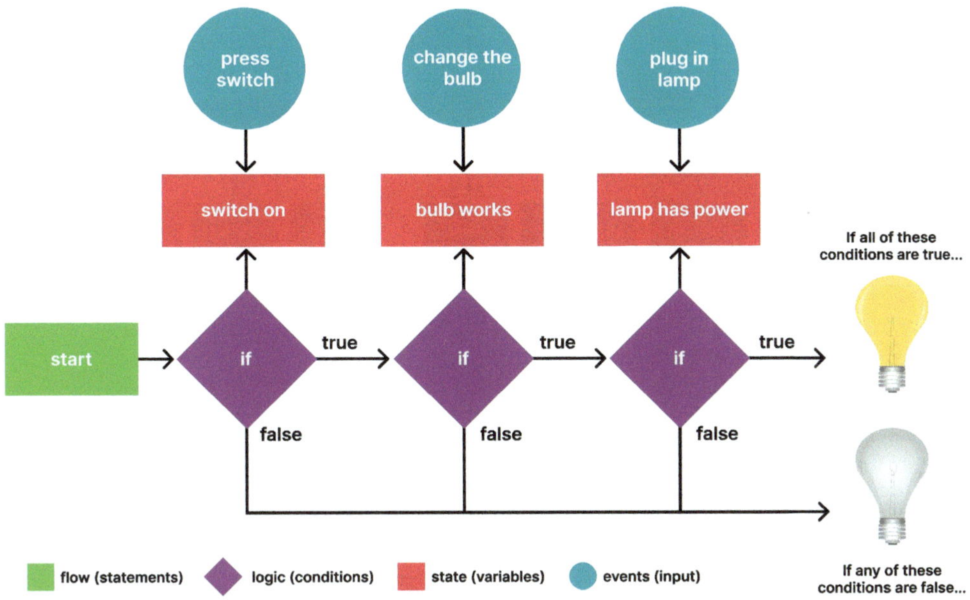

Figure 5.8
This graphic shows the flow, state, logic, and events of a program, **criticalwebdesign.github.io#lamp**, that "turns a lamp on or off." The logic (decisions the computer makes) is based on the state (the status of variables in the program) and events (e.g., user input) directing the computer toward its goal.

Pro Tip: Node.js

Node.js (aka Node, **nodejs.org**) allows you to create JavaScript programs that run on your computer, outside of the web browser. Node is widely used to run web servers, connect to databases, create mobile apps, and much more. Node is not only fast but incredibly versatile, and it is the reason why JavaScript is one of the most popular programming languages in the world.[15] Node also has its own package manager called **NPM** (Node Package Manager). **Package managers** are an essential component of open-source software, letting you install, configure, and use software packages created by others, or create and share your own. For example, you can use Node to build and publish desktop and mobile apps with the Electron framework (which was used to create Slack, Discord, GitHub Desktop, and even VS Code!). You'll learn more about Node as you complete more advanced projects in the final chapters of this book.

5.2.2 JavaScript Data Types

All programming languages store data in your computer's memory to keep track of their state. Like other languages, JavaScript organizes the data into two categories of

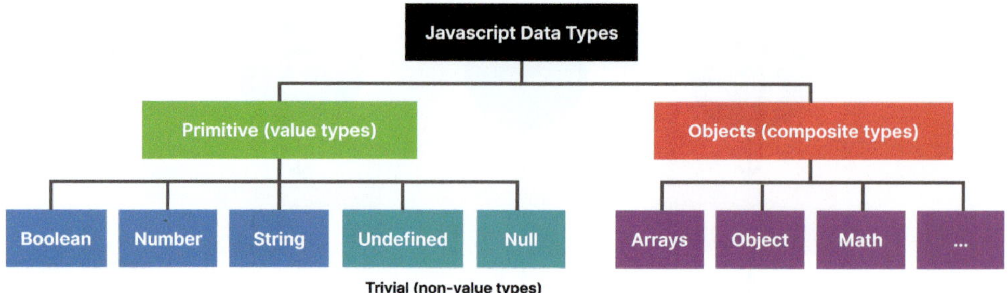

Figure 5.9
JavaScript organizes data by primitive and nonprimitive types.[17]

data types (figure 5.9) that determine both how the data is stored and how it can be used in your program.

When you create a variable in JavaScript, the data type is inferred from the **value** first assigned to it. For example, if you create a variable and assign the value `true`, then JavaScript will create a **boolean** data type. A boolean can only have one of two values: `true` or `false`. The JavaScript **number** type can be any integer or floating point value.[16] All of these are valid JavaScript numbers:

```
1
3.14
-8675309
```

The **string** type can store any alphanumeric character as its value, but it must be wrapped using any of three types of quote symbols: single quotation marks ('), double quotation marks ("), or backticks (``). The number 3.14 in the below list of examples has been converted into a string type because it is wrapped in quotes:

```
'3.14'
"Hello, World! 😍"
`strings wrapped using backticks
can span multiple lines`
```

Later in the book we will discuss those data types categorized as **Objects**, which include data collections like arrays, and complex objects, like Date, Math, and so on.

```
[4,1,2]
{key: "value"}
new Date()
```

Activity: Explore Data Types in the Console

The quickest way to test JavaScript is with the console in your browser's DevTools (module 2.3). In this activity you will use the console to try to guess the return value of each of the expressions below. Check your answer by typing the expression in the console and pressing return.

1. Use the **`typeof`** operator to return a string describing the data's type.[18]

   ```
   typeof 12
   ```

2. Comparison operators such as **`>, >=, <, <=`** (and more) return a Boolean (truth) value, expressed as true or false, after performing the comparison in the expression.[19] Thus, the following will return the value **`false`**.

   ```
   4 > 5
   ```

3. The equality operator `==` checks to see if two values are equal, returning the value **`true`** if this is the case.[20]

   ```
   1 == 1
   ```

4. Likewise, the inequality operator `!=` returns **`true`** when its two operands are *not* equal and **`false`** when they are.[21]

   ```
   1 != 1
   ```

5. The strict equality operator `===` will compare the value *and type* and is unique to JavaScript.[22] Can you guess what value the following will return?

   ```
   1 === "1"
   ```

6. If you guessed the above will return **`false`** because `1` is a number and **`"1"`** is a string, then you are correct! While their values appear the same, their data types are different: `1` is a number, while **`"1"`** is a number wrapped in quotes, and is therefore a string. Finally, if you combine expressions using parentheses, JavaScript will evaluate each in order starting with the innermost expression. What will these examples return?

   ```
   typeof (4 > 5)
   typeof (typeof (4 > 5))
   ```

7. The solution: `4 > 5` uses a comparison operator so it will return **`false`**. But since **`typeof()`** returns a **`string`**, the first line will return **`"boolean"`** (note the double quotes), and the second line will return **`"string"`**.

Pro Tip: Check for Type and Value

JavaScript, unlike other languages, is "weakly typed" so it will infer the type of data you store in a variable. But that doesn't mean you can't make mistakes based on type. Whenever possible it is a good idea to check the value and the type using the `===` triple equal sign operator.

5.2.3 JavaScript `var, let, const`

In chapter 3 you learned how to declare variables using the `let` keyword. There are three different keywords you can use in JavaScript to create new variables. See table 5.1 for a comparison. For example, with **var** (the old method that still works), variables can be redeclared in a script and maintain a global scope, which makes them accessible anywhere in your program.

Table 5.1

A comparison of the three types of variable declarations in JavaScript. The keywords `let` and `const` are practically the same except for the "constant" value of `const`, which means its value cannot be changed once declared.

Keyword	Constraints	Scope
`var`	Variables can be redeclared later in your program.	Variables maintain a global scope, so they are accessible anywhere in your program.
`let` and `const`	You cannot use a variable before it is declared, and you cannot redeclare the variable later in your program.	You can only access a variable within the statement block, between the curly braces where it was declared.

Author Note: The ES Standard

The older method to declare variables (`var`) allowed you to create and reuse a variable anywhere (table 5.1) in your code. However, as JavaScript programs became more complex this flexibility posed issues. For example, imagine if two `loggedIn` variables exist and they hold different values. Suddenly, a user both can and cannot access their account, depending on how they try.

In 2015, the **ECMAScript (ES)** standard, on which JavaScript is based, added the new variable declaration keywords, `let` and `const`, to provide slightly stricter requirements and improve the language. The ES language specification is updated with new features nearly every year, but browsers are not always as quick to update their functionality. You can check whether features are supported by your target browsers using the website **caniuse.com**. For example, view the results for the `let` keyword at **caniuse.com/?search=let**.

Activity: Concatenate Strings and Numbers

To practice understanding how the plus operator works with different data types, on your own or with a partner, try to guess the value of the variable after each line of the following script. Check your answers using the DevTools Console.

```
let num = 1000;
num = num + 10;
num += 10;
++num;
num++;
num += "10";
```

In these lines of code you assign the numeric value 1000 to a variable called num. The first two expressions offer two methods for adding 10 to the number variable. Both of the `num++` and `++num` expressions will increment the variable by one, with a key difference: When `++` comes before the variable (`num`) it increments and returns the *new* value. But, when the `++` comes after the variable (`num`), it will return the *original* value and then increment each time thereafter. So at first, it appears to do "nothing" in the Console. What is different about the last expression in the script? (Hopefully you noticed that the value appears in quotes.) Whenever a string is present in an expression the plus operator changes all other value types to strings and **concatenates** the values, returning a new string with each value merged into a larger string.

Best Practices: Using Quotes

In programming, the order of quote characters is important. For example, paste or type and run this quote from the interaction designer Brenda Laurel in the DevTools console:

```
console.log('"Design isn’t finished until somebody is using it.
"—Brenda Laurel');
```

Her words are wrapped in double quotes, while the entire string is wrapped in single quotes. You can wrap single quotes inside double quotes or vice versa, but, like HTML nested elements, you must close the nested string before closing its parent. The single quote in "isn't" is a smart quote, so it has no effect on this order.

5.2.4 Web Forms

Forms are the primary method through which users can submit information on a website. Coding a form requires writing a combination of HTML, CSS, and JavaScript to work together in the browser. If the website saves information submitted by users, server-side scripts and potentially a database are required to preserve that data. For example, when you sign up for a newsletter, you type your email address into an **input** field and click the submit button. The page sends a request to a web server to save your information in a database. Data in a web form can be transferred using one of two different **HTTP methods**, called GET or POST.

- The **GET** method sends data from a form as a string of characters in a **URL parameter**. Its length is limited, so you cannot, for example, upload an image using `GET`. And, because the data is visible to you, and potentially any node on the network that sends the request, it is also not safe for secure information like passwords.
- The **POST** method sends data in the body of the request and, thus, is encrypted on secure websites ("secure" websites show a lock next to their URL because they are using the **HTTPS** protocol). The `POST` method supports images and long strings of text but is harder to test because you cannot see the data that is being sent "under the hood."

Activity: Explore `GET` Requests with DevTools

Learn how to examine and change `GET` parameters using the browser's URL bar.

1. Go to **google.com.** Type the word "cat" into the input field of the page and press the **Search** button. The browser will load a new URL to display the results of the search.
2. Look at the new URL. It should contain the domain name (google.com) and the word "Search" followed by a "?" and more characters. The text that follows the question mark is a list of URL **parameters** and **values** separated by "&" ampersands. Notice the parameter named "q" (short for query), and its value, "cat." When you submitted the form, the data you added to the input field was included in the new request as a URL parameter and sent to the Google server which performs a new search using your data.
3. Knowing this, you can query Google's search engine directly by editing the value of "q." Simplify the URL bar of Chrome to match the below text and press return. This removes all of Google's tracking parameters, but the actual page content won't change: `https://www.google.com/search?q=cat`
4. Edit the URL bar to change "cat" to "dog" and press return again. You've just sent a new `GET` request to Google to return search results for this new phrase.
5. Open DevTools on this page and click the Network tab. Reload the page and watch as all the page resources are displayed in both the browser GUI and in the list of files in the Network tab (figure 5.10). Click on the first resource in the Name list, which should be the page itself, `search?q=dog`, to see the meta information stored in the **request header.** You can see the status code is `200` to indicate it was successful, and that the request method is `GET`, which we discussed above.

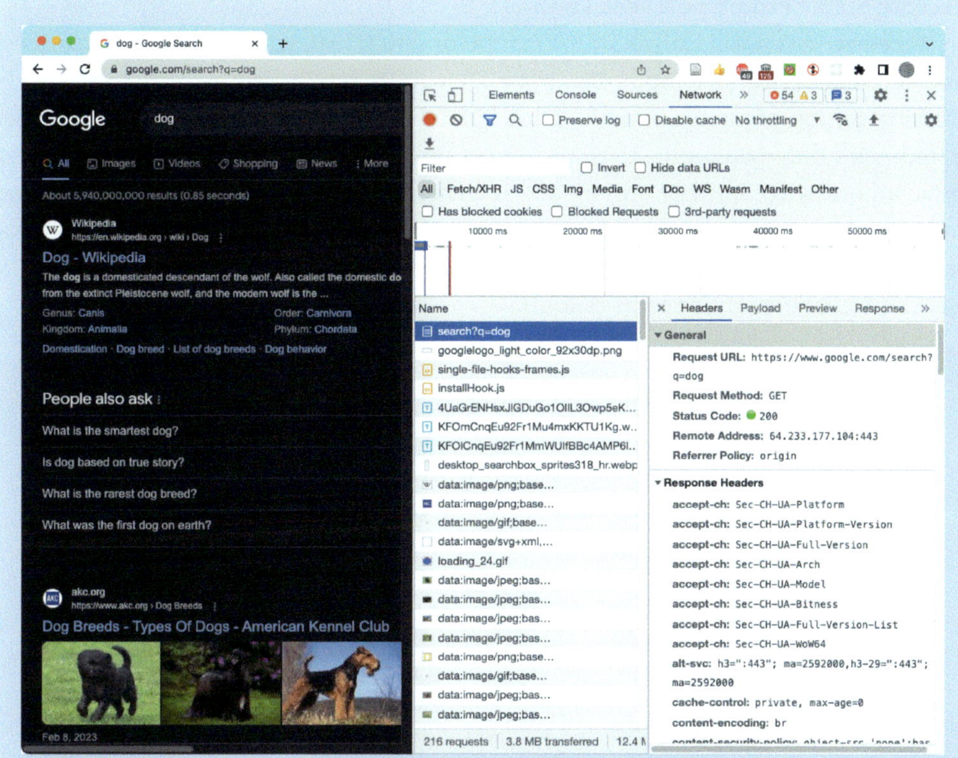

Figure 5.10
Inspecting the headers of the GET request using a Google search for "dog."

Author Note: Search Engines

It's worth noting that although Google boasts about the speed in which it performed the search for the word "cat" ("About 6,100,000,000 results (0.80 seconds)"), it didn't search the entire internet in such a short amount of time. The results that Google displays were collected or **indexed** by their software (aka "Google Bot"), which follows links to pages on the internet to store in their databases. So when Google says their results were returned in 0.8 seconds, they are really describing the time they retrieved information they already copied from other websites into their databases. And Google's results only include web pages they can access (ignoring censored content, as well as the "deep web" and "dark web") and, thus, are not even close to all the potential results from the whole internet.

Exercise 5.2.1 Prototype a Web Form

In this exercise you will learn how to create a form in HTML and use JavaScript to access and summarize the user input. Below we show only how to create a prototype, or a working version of just the functional part of a website. In our prototype we will make a form with only two inputs to test for functionality. Once it is working, you will add more inputs by completing prompt 5.2. In general, especially as your projects become more complex, we suggest keeping the code for the functional part of your project separate from the presentation code to make it easier to develop and test each independently (see the **Separation of Concerns** callout).

Best Practices: Separation of Concerns

Separation of concerns is a common coding strategy that aims to arrange parts of complex projects into smaller, more manageable files. For example, moving your styles and logic into separate CSS and JS files makes it easier to find and edit those aspects of your project.

Likewise, it is a good practice to create design and prototype iterations separately before merging them together, as we show in figure 5.11. This strategy makes it easier to create and edit designs in Figma that echo and imagine the work you do in your prototype. And, since you haven't coded the design yet, it is much easier to make changes to it in Figma to match the ultimate functionality that you build in your prototype. Equally, keeping the prototype free of design code will simplify your testing and iterations. After multiple iterations you can bring the coded design and prototype together into the final coded version of your project.

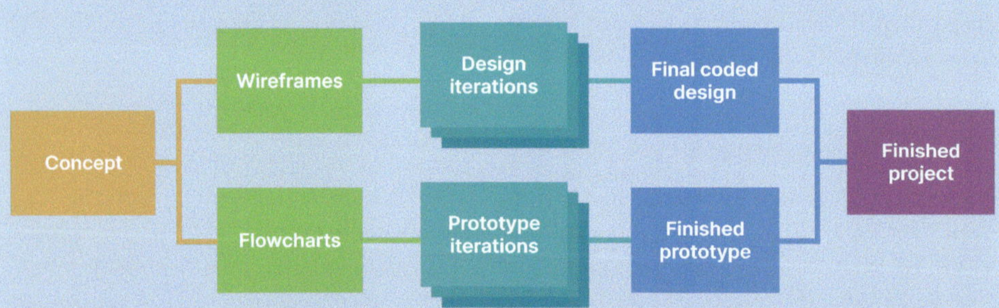

Figure 5.11
Diagram separating design and coding processes during iteration.

We find it helps to use a code playground with instant feedback for quick testing of these functional parts of a project. For example, you could use it to test the form and paste the code into your project later. This is what we did when working on this chapter prompt, see **criticalwebdesign.github.io#sus-prototype**. You will need to click the **Console** button in Codepen if you do this. Create a free account to save your work.

1. Create a new repo from our template **github.com/criticalwebdesign/website-template** named “usability-test” and then go to **github.com/codespaces** or your preferred code editor, and open your new repository following our steps in exercise 3.2.1.
2. Open **index.html** and, in the `<head>`, change the title to “Usability Test.” Remove all the HTML tags inside the `<body>` except for the `<h1> and <script>` tags and change the heading to “SUS Score.” Following the new heading, add a `<form>` tag with autocomplete by typing “form” and pressing the **tab** key. The resulting code is:

```
<body>
  <h1>SUS Score</h1>
  <form action="" ></form>
  <script src="./assets/js/main.js"></script>
```

3. The `action` attribute in the form tells the browser the URL where this form data should be submitted. Since we are using JavaScript to edit the data within the client only, add a hashtag (aka number sign #) placeholder value so the form doesn’t reload the page. Add an `id` attribute set to `myForm` so that JS can listen for the submit event and access the form values. Thus far, your code should look like this:

```
<form action="#" id="myForm"></form>
```

4. Between the opening and closing form tags, add a new `<input>` element by typing “input” and pressing **tab**. Set the input `type="number"` and add an `id` attribute set to `q1`.

```
<form action="#" id="myForm">
    <input type="number" id="q1">
```

5. After the `<input>`, add a `<button>` element using autocomplete. Add a type attribute set to `submit`. Add instructional text to the button like “Submit” between the opening and closing `<button>` tags. So far, our HTML form code is:

```
<h1>SUS Score</h1>
<form action="#" id="myForm">
  <input type="number" id="q1">
  <button type="submit">Submit</button>
</form>
```

Preview your form, and you should see a simple input that lets you click, add data, and press a button. Notice how the `type="number"` attribute adds validation to reject non-numerical entries. If you click the button, the page will try to submit the form—since there is no back-end code, nothing will appear to happen. We will fix this in a moment.

6. In **main.js** replace the `console.log()` with the code below. As with previous chapters, you are using `querySelector()` to store a reference to the element in a variable.

```
let myForm = document.querySelector("#myForm");
```

7. Now add an event listener to the `myForm` reference to check for a `submit` event. As you did in chapter 3, you'll add the event type as the first parameter, followed by a callback function that runs when the event happens. Notice you are doing something slightly different than when you previously listened for a mouseover event. First, you are using the "fat arrow" syntax that replaces the word "function" with the fat arrow operator `=>` after the parameter. The second is that you are adding a variable called `event` as a parameter to the callback function. This variable will receive an object with information about the event from the page when the event listener is triggered. JavaScript, like HTML, does not mind whitespace in your code, so you can format this however you like to make it readable.

```
myForm.addEventListener("submit", (event) => {
});
```

8. As mentioned above, when a user submits a form, the `action` attribute describes where to send the form data. In other words, the default behavior of a form is to load a new page to handle the form submission. Since you are using JavaScript you want to prevent this from happening. Add the code below inside the curly braces of the callback function to use the `preventDefault()` function of the received event object to prevent the default behavior of the web form.[23]

```
myForm.addEventListener("submit", (event) => {
  event.preventDefault();
});
```

9. On the next line, declare a new variable called `q1` and store the value of the `<input>` inside it using the `this` keyword (see exercise 3.3.5), which allows us to refer to elements in the form itself. Use JavaScript's `Number()` method to wrap the form `input` references. This ensures that when we use the plus operator later it will sum the numerical values, instead of concatenating string values (see the above activity). Finally, use `console.log()` to show the value in the console. Preview the page with Live Server and test the form by adding a number and pressing the **Submit** button. Open the DevTools console to see the value (figure 5.12).

```
myForm.addEventListener("submit", (event) => {
     event.preventDefault();
     let q1 = Number(this.q1.value);
     console.log(q1);
});
```

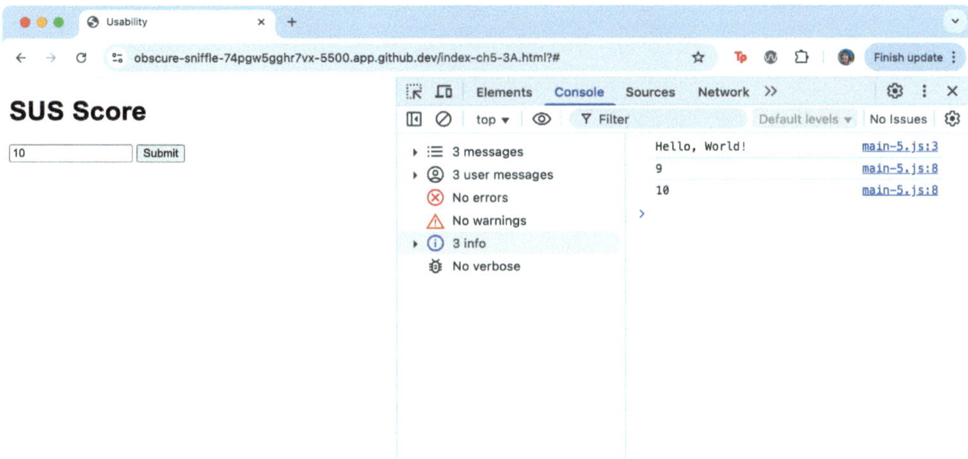

Figure 5.12
Test your form in the browser using the DevTools Console to see the form values have been logged.

10. Open **styles.css** and change the `<input>` elements to display as a block so they appear one per line.

```
input { display: block; }
```

11. In **main.js** duplicate and rename the JS variable declaration once so that you have two inputs. Change the name and id for each line (`q1` and `q2`).

```
let q1 = Number(this.q1.value);
let q2 = Number(this.q2.value);
console.log(q1);
```

12. In **index.html** duplicate or create a second `<input>` element with an `id` set to `q2`.

```
<input type="number" id="q1">
<input type="number" id="q2">
<button type="submit">Submit</button>
```

13. Add an answer field to the HTML.

```
<button type="submit">Submit</button>
<input type="number" id="answer">
```

14. In **main.js**, create an **answer** variable containing the sum of the values, display the value in the <input>, and print it to the console. Thanks to the **Number()** function used above, JS will read those values as integers and calculate their sum, rather than concatenate them.

```
let q2 = Number(this.q2.value);
// add all converted responses
let answer = (q1 + q2);
// store in a new input and log to the console
this.answer.value = answer;
console.log(answer);
```

15. Test your form in the browser by filling in the fields and clicking submit.

⚠ Watch Out! Code Formatting Can Reveal Syntax Issues

Generally, we advise you to type out code from the book because it helps you to become more familiar with the text and thus increases understanding. If you do copy and paste, be careful because the characters used to describe code in a book aren't always the same characters that work in code (see module 2.3 for the discussion of smart vs. dumb quotes for example). If you notice the code editor showing warnings or if some of the color formatting seems off, then try retyping the code or examining it closer to fix the issue.

Prompt 5.2 Code: Expand Your Web Form

Expand your form to ten inputs. You will create eight more **<input>** elements in HTML, as well as the matching JS **let** variable declarations for a total of ten each. You can duplicate existing lines, but be sure to change the name and ID of each so that you have **q1-q10** inputs and variables. Don't forget to add all converted responses in the answer variable!

Module 5.3 JavaScript, Bootstrap, and Web Forms

Now you can use JS to compute the SUS Score by modifying the stored input values from exercise 5.2.1. Then you'll add Bootstrap classes to validate the input and expand upon the design of the form elements.

Exercise 5.3.1 Code the SUS Score with JS

The formula for the SUS Score in "Measuring Usability with the System Usability Scale" by Jeff Sauro includes the following math:

> For odd items: subtract 1 from the user response.
>
> For even-numbered items: subtract the user responses from 5.
>
> This scales all values from 0 to 4 (with four being the most positive response).
>
> Add up the converted responses for each user and multiply that total by 2.5. This converts the range of possible values from 0 to 100 instead of from 0 to 40.[24]

To get started, consider these instructions as **pseudocode**, an often-utilized method for drafting programmatic code. Simply describe exactly what you wish for the computer to do as plain instructions in human language, writing them as comments in your JavaScript file. This provides an overview of the steps, to clarify the process, and also provides an outline for you to follow as you write the JavaScript code. See the wiki for a video demonstration of this exercise.

1. If you did not complete prompt 5.2, you will need to copy our HTML and JS code from module 5.2. See **criticalwebdesign.github.io#5-2-code** to complete the prompt.
2. Add expressions that transform the values of the odd and even numbers based on the pseudocode. For odd number items, subtract **1** from the user response; and for even-numbered items, subtract the user responses from **5**. You'll notice we use the `-=` expression to subtract **1** from the odd variables.

```
let q9 = Number(this.q9.value);
let q10 = Number(this.q10.value);
// For odd items: subtract 1 from the user response
q1 -= 1;
q3 -= 1;
q5 -= 1;
q7 -= 1;
q9 -= 1;
// For even-numbered items: subtract responses from 5
q2 = 5 - q2;
q4 = 5 - q4;
q6 = 5 - q6;
q8 = 5 - q8;
q10 = 5 - q10;
// Add all converted responses
let answer = (q1 + q2 + q3 + q4 + q5 + q6 + q7 + q8 + q9 + q10);
```

3. Modify the answer to multiply it by 2.5 and test your page. For example, if you enter 4 into each field the result would be 50 (a total of 20 * 2.5).

```
// Add all converted responses; multiply the total by 2.5.
let answer = (q1 + q2 + q3 + q4 + q5 + q6 + q7 + q8 + q9 + q10)
* 2.5;
```

Activity: Use the "Less Is More" Critique and Redesign

Remember when we said earlier that "you shouldn't see good design"? A good rule of thumb for achieving this is to question everything you add to a layout. If it's difficult to explain how a text treatment or graphic element makes it easier for your users to understand the content and achieve their goals, then it likely shouldn't be added to the design.

Thus, we introduce the "**Less is More**" design critique. By now you may have noticed that content and graphical elements are often added through each design iteration but rarely removed. This feedback activity can be used with later versions of a design to help to simplify a layout and rely on the content itself to move viewers' eyes to key focal points. It is written as a group activity so that you can gain new perspectives from others who might not be attached to elements in the design. If you are working on your own, then ask a friend to help you. A design critique is a way to generate helpful feedback, but remember the comments are not directed at you, but toward understanding how the *design* might be improved.

1. In Figma, duplicate and rename the frame containing the latest version of your desktop design so that you can let others edit it at will.
2. You (the designer) should watch and take notes (without speaking) while members of your group discuss the design and prioritize items that can be removed to improve, simplify, and make the layout easier to code. Again, the designer should not speak but focus on listening to the group's feedback.
3. Your partners should select items (e.g., graphics, text treatments, colors) to remove and "speak out loud" (see chapter 4) about their motivations as they hide or change the items. While working, they should explain: "How does removing this improve, simplify, or make the design easier to see, use, or code?"
4. After you have taken several notes, you can ask your partners for more information or suggestions on any of the items they brought up.
5. Feel free to repeat with others as often as you like. You can see our outcomes from a similar activity in the wiki. After you have finished, code a new version of your desktop design and, finally, a mobile version of the layout as well.

Exercise 5.3.2 Use Bootstrap to Code Your Usability Test

The following steps provide an overview for coding your usability test. See chapter 4 for setting up Bootstrap (module 4.2) and use the built-in `container`, `row`, and `column` classes. Refer to section 4.3.1 for a discussion on containers.

1. Copy our HTML from the module 5.3 start code at **criticalwebdesign.github.io#5-3-start-code** and paste it into your **index.html** file to complete this exercise. You'll add images in the following step. If you are designing your own page, open **index.html** and add the links to Bootstrap CSS and JS from the Quickstart at **getbootstrap.com**. Then add a Bootstrap container, rows, columns, and the content of your usability test results to match the layout you created in the twelve-column grid.
2. Add the screenshot files you created from your usability test to your repo and point to them using **<img src="">**. Download our images from the book repo if you didn't make screenshots. We are using the Bootstrap **img-fluid** class to make the images scale to the different breakpoints.
3. Test the page in the browser as you work to ensure the page looks correct. Scale the browser window to simulate different device sizes to ensure your content is readable at all breakpoints.

Exercise 5.3.3 Add Form Validation and Labels

The HTML **label** elements help users locate the correct fields to enter data, while validation ensures the data they enter is what is expected by your code. Add the following four steps for each of your form inputs to improve usability, accessibility, and overall functionality.

1. In **index.html**, add the **min** and **max** attributes to each **input** element to constrain the values that can be added to the form, matching the SUS form requirement (a score between 1–5 for each question). While the attribute **type="number"** constrains the field to numeric input values, attributes **min="1"** and **max="5"** make sure submitted data is within the correct range.
2. Add a **name** attribute to each input to make it easier to reference the fields and their data. The name should be the same value as the **id** attribute.
3. Add a **value** attribute to pre-populate each input with the actual score your test user gave. This can be changed later by the user to experiment, but since your page is presenting your test results you will want to display them.
4. Add a **required** attribute to each input. This is a **boolean** attribute, so you just add the word **required** without a value to indicate to users that they must input values before the form can be submitted (see figure 5.13 in the callout).[25] After these additions each input will look something like this:

```
<input type="number" value="4" name="q1" id="q1" min="1" max="5"
required>
```

5. Wrap the text of each prompt from the SUS form with a **<label>** element.[26] Include a **for** attribute with a value that matches the **id** of the corresponding **<input>**. This

adds a caption for each element to identify the content that users should add. It also increases usability because a user can click either in the form field or anywhere on the label text to **focus** (see the Focus and Blur callout) the `<input>` and be able to enter text in the field. Here is an example of one `<label>` element we added to our code.

```
<div class="col-10">
  <label for="q1">I think that I would like to use this system
  frequently.</label>
</div>
```

Keywords: Focus and Blur

Have you ever used the Tab key to change between form inputs on a web page? When you click or tab to an interactive element, it is said to gain **focus** so that you can type in the field. An element can also **blur** when it loses focus when you tab or click to focus a different element. The corresponding **:focus** and **:blur** pseudo-classes apply CSS rules to the elements, like the blue outline in figure 5.13, to give visual feedback to let you know you can type.

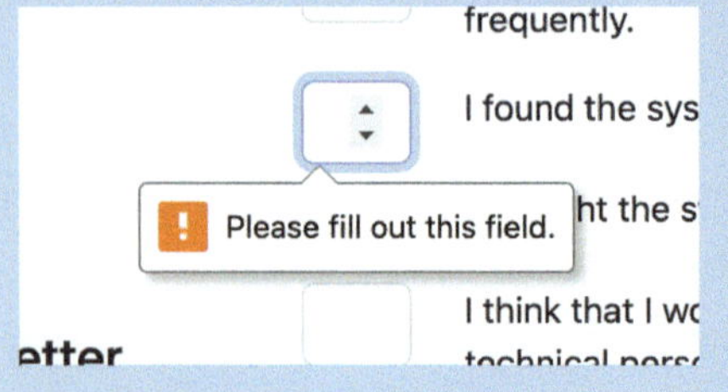

Figure 5.13
An example of form validation thanks to the required attribute.

6. Add a Bootstrap **form-label** class to each **label** to improve accessibility.

```
<label for="q1" class="form-label">I think that I would like to
use this system frequently.</label>
```

7. Bootstrap form classes[27] improve the style and provide a consistent appearance for inputs in the form. Add a `form-control` class to each `<input>`.

```
<input type="number" class="form-control" value="4" name="q1"
id="q1" min="1" max="5" required>
```

8. Add a `form-control` class and `step` attribute with the value `any` to the `#answer` input so that it can accept floating point values.

```
<input type="number" step="any" class="form-control"
id="answer">
```

9. Add a Bootstrap **`btn`** class and our custom button class (see **styles.css**) to the submit button. We discuss how to customize Bootstrap classes in the wiki.

```
<button type="submit" class="btn btn-custom">Update
Score</button>
```

10. Stage and commit your work, enable GitHub Pages on your repo, then **validate** the HTML and CSS of your usability results page at **validator.w3.org**. You should always validate your finished work to be certain there are no issues. You can also do this any time you encounter an issue that could be the result of a hidden syntax mistake.

Check Your Work

This concludes the chapter exercises. We invite you to compare your work to the final outcome **criticalwebdesign.github.io#5-3** and code **criticalwebdesign.github.io#5-3-code** in the book repo. Don't forget to enable GitHub Pages in your project and then stage and commit your work to make it live!

Prompt 5.3 Publish: Create a New Design, Then Code and Test It

Now that you understand how to code all the parts of this page, create a new version of your design following a Less is More critique. Code the page to display the results of the usability test and form you created above.

Author Note: Use the Eye Movement Test

Remember to use the eye movement test we described in chapter 2 (exercise 2.1.2) as you design to create strong and intentional focal points in your layout.

6 Off the Grid

> Collage...[is] a kind of catch-all metaphor for our overly technologized lives.
> —Jessica Helfand

Context

Now that you know how to use a grid to previsualize and code layouts for responsive web pages, this chapter will take a detour "off the grid" to explore experimental design practices that question, or critique, established formats for presenting information in web browsers. This is not to say that prioritizing the form of design before its function by eschewing common rules necessarily removes the grid from the process (nor does it suggest that one cannot experiment with the function as well). Rather, the expressive possibilities for design to excite and surprise viewers, push up against the boundaries of the everyday, or generally encourage users to enjoy the pleasure of looking, can extend from a variety of creative processes that don't always involve organizing content along columns and rows. The designer Jeffrey Keedy posits that knowing the rules is, in fact, the best way to break them.

> The first thing one learns about typography and type design is that there are many rules and maxims. The second is that these rules are made to be broken. And the third is that "breaking the rules" has always been just another one of the rules. Although rules are meant to be broken, scrupulously followed, misunderstood, reassessed, retro-fitted and subverted, the best rule of thumb is that rules should never be ignored.[1]

In his writing and work, Keedy, like the critical designers Dunne and Raby, advocate for designers to push against the grain and test the status quo with their work. Also a signatory on the 2000 edition of the *First Things First Manifesto,* he and others recognize the benefits of deconstructing implicit assumptions within design's position in society and exploring its potential, embracing "a mindshift away from product marketing and toward the exploration and production of a new kind of meaning."[2] Throughout this chapter we discuss the dialectical relationship between design that upholds the steady rules of an underlying grid and compositions that betray a uniform structure, speak out against the hierarchies implicit in layouts, and test users to consider new perspectives in the interpretation of such visual works.

Deconstruction in Design

The theory of **deconstruction** is attributed to Jacques Derrida, who described it in his seminal book *Of Grammatology* as a strategy of critical questioning that removes assumptions when deriving meaning from text. Derrida's proposition has influenced artists and designers who incorporated his method of philosophical analysis in their work. In *Design Writing Research: Writing on Graphic Design*, Ellen Lupton and Abbott Miller devote a chapter to explaining the nuances of Derrida's philosophical breakaway. They write, "Deconstruction is a crucial mode of research, a manner of questioning that frames the nature of its object."[3] As a concept, deconstruction has a lineage connected to post-structuralist philosophies put forth by Roland Barthes, Michel Foucault, and Jean Buadrillard. In the essay "The Death of the Author," Barthes suggests that text and meaning are open and fluid experiences.[4] That is, once constituted or put forth by an author, the meaning of a work of art (or writing, or any expressive medium) is reconstituted by the reader/viewer/participant/listener.

This fluidity, Lupton and Abbot write, gives way to "a romantic theory of self-expression: as the argument goes, because signification is not fixed in material forms, designers and readers share in the spontaneous creation of meaning."[5] However, an understanding of post-structuralist theory narrates the personal experience as one that cannot evade the hierarchical structures that both govern and are external to lived experiences. Thus, Lupton and Abbot write, "Invention and revolution result from tactical aggressions against the grid."[6] For designers, especially web designers, these "aggressions" against the grid can result in experimental and poetic designs that speak back to the content embedded in the author's (or designer's) work.

Note that we are careful not to talk about deconstruction as a style, though many young designers who learned from these artists sometimes use the word as shorthand for the aesthetic it sometimes yields. To briefly detour from what may appear as "**art speak**"[7] (also known as "International Art English"[8]) and provide concrete examples, know first that deconstruction as a methodology does not indicate that the output will be visually messy and illegible. Rather, a work using deconstruction might reconfigure

Additional Materials and Resources

Explore links and other content related to this chapter: **criticalwebdesign.github.io#wiki-06**

graphic and typographic imagery to emphasize the semantic relationships within the information to be communicated. This is the case with the example in figure 6.1 by Jacqueline Casey while working for Murial Cooper, who also designed the logo of the publisher for the book you are reading.[9] In the catalog cover, the text is readable, but the design conveys additional meaning, feelings even, that support the ability for the graphic to communicate and resonate with viewers. Cooper, who was the first tenured female professor at the MIT Media Lab, produced a number of experimental early computer works within her Visible Language Workshop. Her information landscapes project includes examples that reconfigured and arranged text in 3D landscapes, filtered and sorted data based on algorithmic processes, and generally expanded the possibilities for creativity using software so common today.[10]

During the late 1980s and early 1990s, artists and designers new to producing graphic layouts with digital tools utilized the freedom that comes with graphic manipulation to carry out the line of formal questioning put forth by the post-structuralists and the concept of deconstruction. Art and design students in the United States were introduced to these ideas at the Cranbrook Academy of Art under Katherine McCoy's leadership in the 1980s, when Jefferey Keedy was a student at the school. In "OK Identity" (figure 6.2), Mr. Keedy redistributes the authority that corporations wield through their slick visual identities. While created for a real client in Los Angeles, it appears like he may have inadvertently imagined a fake company called "OK" with no established rules or standards to guide its visual imagery. The potential identities in his logos for this seemingly non-brand brand are compelling and alluring, yet without the continuity of the visual indicators upon which a corporate brand relies, they intentionally unbind the viewer from the urge to consume. His use of deconstruction is similar, though more subtle, to the reconfigurations seen in the subvertisements that appear in chapter 3. Transformation and appropriation are common methods for reinscribing meaning.

April Greiman (figure 6.3) was an early adopter of computer-aided design processes when its use was still considered experimental and provocative. Her work incorporated not only the new processes but the often-unexpected results of digitization and computer errors to embrace and reflect on the changes in the medium itself. Instead of using the grid to direct viewers to the most essential content, her outcomes suggest that

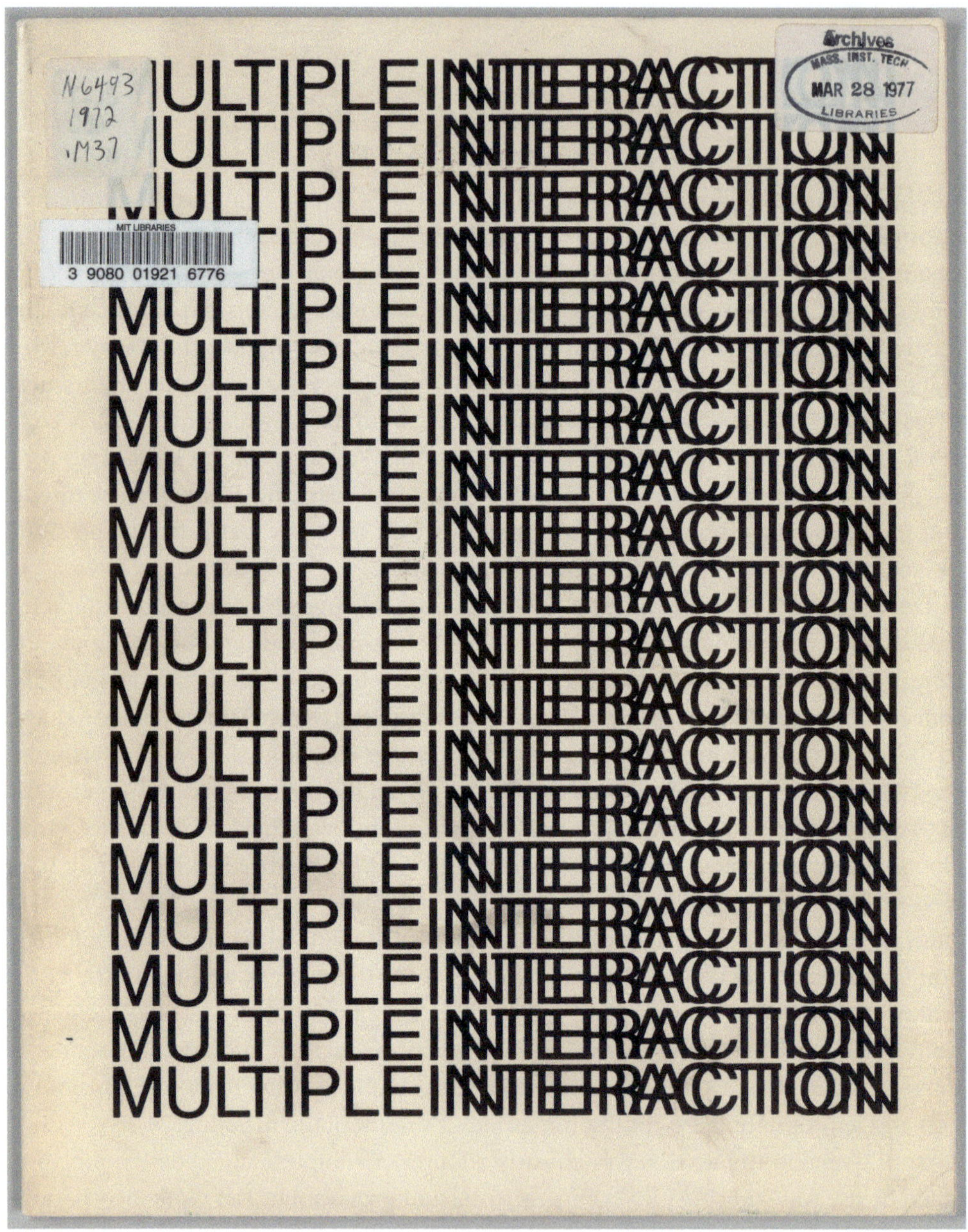

Figure 6.1

"Multiple Interaction Team: an exhibition-event to travel (cover image)," MIT Libraries, Cambridge, Massachusetts, 1972. Call no. N6493 1972.M37. This 1973 exhibition was organized by Gyorgy Kepes and prepared by the Center for Advanced Visual Studies at MIT. The catalog is credited to designer Jacqueline Casey, who worked with Murial Cooper in the Design Services office.

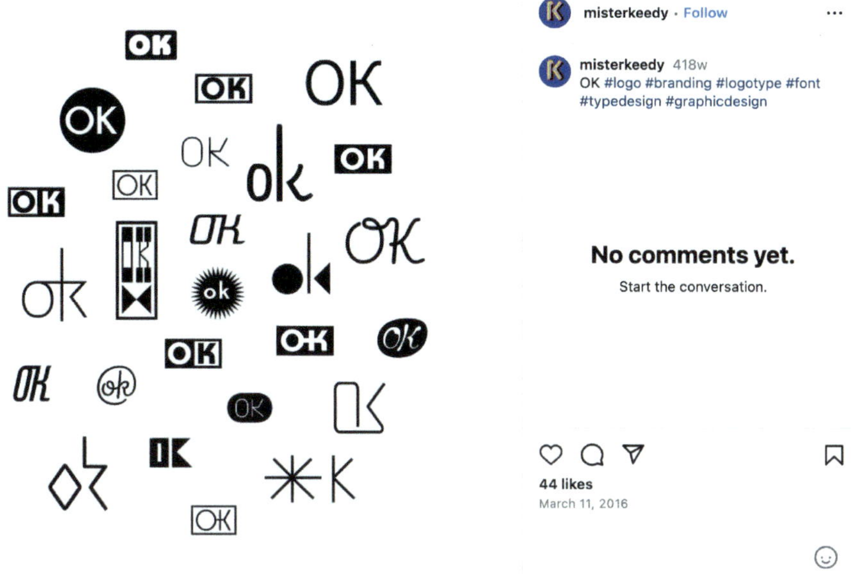

Figure 6.2

Mr. Keedy, "OK Identity" (1999) is an exciting yet pluralistic take on brand identity that neither accepts nor denies the constraints of corporate logo designing.[11]

Figure 6.3

April Greiman, *Think About What You Think About* (2004), Cal State Sacramento Lecture Poster.

we should look everywhere at once, explore the changing nature of communication, and take in the richness of what it means to see as a human.

David Carson is another designer from this period known for breaking the accepted rules for conventional design. The covers and spreads that Carson created for *Ray Gun* magazine grasp the viewer's attention with the surprising discredit to content, all the while asking for meaning to be made by interpreting formal disarray (see wiki).[12] Carson and others' work extend an abundant history of manipulation and collage in the twentieth century, including the visual artists Kurt Schwitters and Hannah Höch, the architect Frank Gehry, and the musicians and composers Laurie Anderson, Steve Reich, and Brian Eno.

A continuation of experimental works that question or amplify the formal boundaries apparent in hierarchical layouts can be found in those made for the internet. In chapter 1 we discuss Olia Lialina's *My Boyfriend Came Back from the War* (1996), which pushed against the expected formats of the web page with a creative use of HTML frames (a deprecated technology we will not discuss here!). Alexei Shulgin's *Form Art* is the case study in chapter 5, which similarly understands the creative potential of utilitarian digital objects. Émilie Brout and Maxime Marion's **goldandglitter.net** (2015) transformed the commonplace meme into a visual treasure trove of several hundred meticulously assembled golden animated GIFs that expands beyond the screen, spilling into the physical world on gallery pedestals (figure 6.4).

Like in magazine pages, building planning, and even musical composition, collage on the internet is an intentional act. The creators know the rules before they break them, and they do so to engage and distract the user from not only the rectangular basis for building layouts but the slick and corporate spaces that subsumed the WWW. Lorna Mills presents animated GIFs with rough-looking pixelated edges that expose the production process. This "cut and paste" approach to image-making has a punk, do-it-yourself (DIY) aesthetic that displays imperfections over "perfect form," in one-of-a-kind (not mass produced) pieces. Herdimas Anggara refers to himself as a "ritual engineer" in performances that center artifacts of digital and online culture. His performances often result in drawings created from files and folder icons that march across the screen to accompanying music (see wiki).[13]

Finally, we address a few contemporary commercial websites that tap into these experimental methods to render their content. While these examples might be seen as "cutting-edge web designs" today, remember that contemporary trends are often built upon a legacy adopted from avant-garde circles of artists, designers, musicians,

Figure 6.4
Émilie Brout and Maxime Marion, *Gold and Glitter*, Installation, website, found GIF and objects, 30×30×130 cm, 2015, see **criticalwebdesign.github.io#goldandglitter**. This work was presented on and offline, where the unique frame counts of each found GIF file made the composition feel alive and more present than most things seen on the flat screens used to access the web.

philosophers, and other thinkers and makers at the fringes of the commercial domain. As we wrote in chapter 3 (prompt 3.1), there is a fluid, give-and-take relationship between the production of mass media and the arts. Experimental practices include a critique of the media, borrowing its tools and paradigms to expand methods of expression, while professional practices in turn borrow again from these expanded forms. For example, the adaptation of features of brutalism, an architectural style that promotes minimalism and a focus on bare materials over decoration, into web design can be seen as a critique of decorative websites. The domain **brutalistwebsites.com** characterizes works in its collection as "rugged" and a "reaction by a younger generation to the lightness, optimism, and frivolity of today's web design." Looking through this collection and other works of so-called rebellious web design, it is clear they have embraced an experimental ethos, ignoring slick campaigns with predefined rules and conventions for keeping aspects of their designs consistent. These methods later show up in professional web design, including sites that use it to project their membership in the avant garde.[14] Business-focused websites with familiar content have jumped on the "rebellious design" bandwagon, too.[15] The Brutalist approach, including its rhetorical claim, has become another trend as more and more such sites copy and dilute the previously original approach, often with results that present usability and accessibility issues. Regardless of your own stylistic leanings, it's impossible not to appreciate all the ways a website can be designed and coded for the chaotic and commercial world.

While we are limited by chapter word count to include every example we love, there are many more fabulous works to explore and incorporate into your understanding of what is possible in this medium. We encourage you to seek out images of the other members of First Things First and read about their motivations and influences to be inspired as you experiment and grow your practice. Then read through the following modules which provide technical underpinnings for such experiments on the web, explaining CSS grid, transformations, animation, and more.

Case Study: Kate Compton

KC: Kate Compton (she/her) is Director of Play at Lego. She lives and works in Vejle, Denmark, and defines her research interest as playful creativity toys. Kate is interested in all web technologies because they go together so easily, such as P5 graphics, hand-and-face tracking with MediaPipe, datasets of words, Tracery, and SVGs because she can take them apart and rebuild them. One of her favorite works of online art and design is *The Barnacle Goose Experiment*. She says, "It's a clear and heartbreaking story told in a very unusual medium."

Can you tell us about your quest to create spaces and tools for all people, especially those who may or may not identify as artists, scientists, or programmers?

KC: All people are creative. But when we reach the age of about eight to ten, we discover "disgust" as an emotion, and become aware that our creativity can be *disgusting* socially, so we start suppressing ourselves creatively. You could dance as a six-year-old, but at twelve, you "can't." This is convenient for me as a tool-builder because I don't have to "make people creative," just lift their self-doubt for a moment, and their natural creativity will reemerge. I take a lot of wisdom from improv—they know that you need to give people "invitations" to participate or create. Invitations let folks know that they can contribute, that their contribution will be "right" and welcome. We want to be "right" socially, especially when we feel like we're trespassing already. So inviting people to make something small, and telling them (through the system) that they have done well, is really effective; and people open right up.

Will you talk about your work (e.g., Tracery and other tools) as a manifestation of getting "off the grid"? For example, relating to previous designers and computer artists like April Greiman and Muriel Cooper.

KC: Web dev is a hot, complicated mess right now. Because I work with students, and "off grid" (i.e., no internet), I keep everything aggressively simple and low dependency. I like the style of web dev where you drag your HTML file directly into the browser, because then you aren't gating it behind tech knowledge. Making simple old-style web tools is a small act of rebellion and liberation. It's a statement that there's still power in small, low-tech things.

Tracery is a small, easy-to-import JS file, and it takes JSON as its data format.[16] So it's a very *polite* little library—it won't fight other software or make demands, and it does its one small job quickly and without fuss. Tracery was based on an old technique, context-free grammars, that was declared insufficient and useless for a generation in the 1980s. But a magical thing happens when you provide an easy tool with "unsatisfying" power. People feel like they are in control, so they make stranger and more playful explorations. And by trying and sharing as a community of artists, we discovered a lot of big powerful things that could be made even with a small, simple tool (figure 6.5).

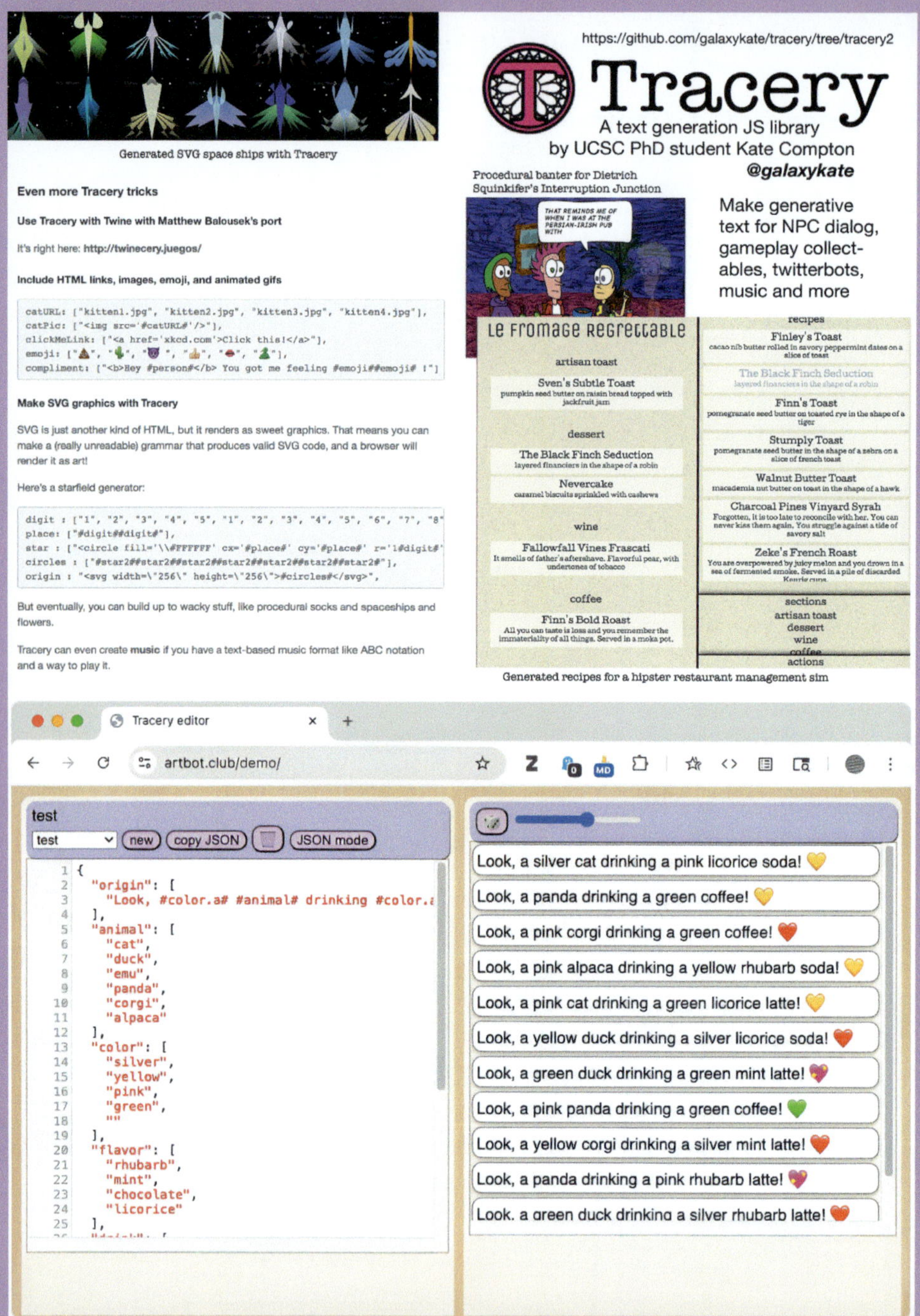

Figure 6.5

Top: Kate Compton, *Tracery* zine used as a teaching tool. Bottom: *Tracery* user interface (editor) used to build most of the bots on Twitter. See: artbot.club/demo.

> **Prompt 6: What You'll Make**
> **Organize a Layout, Then Explode It!**
>
> As you complete the modules in this chapter, you will use design iteration to create two layouts. One will use a grid to align text along rows and columns. The second will use the same content in an experimental composition. For the text in your layout, you could sample a different line from a manifesto that you liked in chapter 2 or create your own using the haiku exercise below while taking a break from the internet.
>
> View the results of our exploded page at **criticalwebdesign.github.io#6-3** (figure 6.6). You can see the final code for every chapter on the CWD repo, **criticalwebdesign.github.io#repo**.

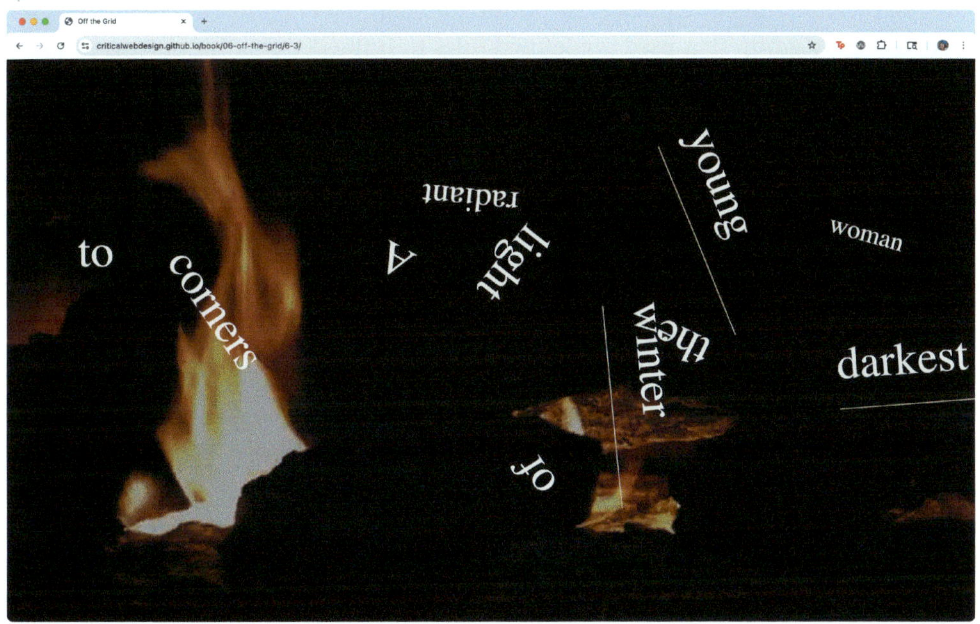

Figure 6.6
Our example uses JavaScript with CSS transformation properties to explode a grid into a surprising, dynamic composition.

Module 6.1 Brainstorming and Experimentation

This module introduces creative tools developed in academia and commercial industries that you can use to generate potential solutions for all types of design problems.

We present activities to develop your own poetic content to code in the following modules. Alternatively, you can use the poem that we provide.

6.1.1 Adjust Your Thinking

The critical web design projects we highlight in this book are most often situated around ideas first, which in turn dictate the appropriate materials or methods needed to realize the concepts. Thus, we start by discussing techniques for brainstorming and creative thinking. We then turn to visual creativity to show how one might move from a concept to envision what an initial spark might grow to become.

Rules and Limitations

Sometimes limitations inspire creative responses. **OuLiPo**, a portmanteau derived from Ouvroir de Littérature Potentielle (Workshop for Potential Literature), is the name for a French literary group that used predefined rules to influence creative outcomes. Starting in the 1960s, inspired by the Dadaist and surrealist art movements, this group of artists, poets, and mathematicians developed several techniques using mathematical constraints to generate poetic writing:

- **N+7** is a writing formula in which every noun is replaced with the seventh noun listed after it in the dictionary.
- The **snowball poem** is a formula in which each line in the poem starts with one word and each successive word is one character longer than the one before it.
- The **lipogram** is a text that purposely excludes one or more letters. For example, George Perec's 1969 novel *A Void* (translated to English in 1994) is a three-hundred-page lipogram novel that excludes the letter "e."

Resting Your Brain

When all else fails, it may just be time to reset. We have found some of our best ideas come to us just after sleeping (or maybe in a dream state), while we are walking our dogs, riding our bikes, at the end of a yoga or meditation class, while cooking, driving, or otherwise not intentionally thinking about our projects. Sometimes ideas seem to flow "in the background" while you are occupied with other activities. When an idea comes to you, pause briefly to make a note and consider it once you go back to work. Do your best to stay present in the moment.

Exercise 6.1.1 Write a Haiku

In this exercise you will disconnect from the internet and write a short poem. We chose the haiku style to minimize the **project scope** (the extent and span of effort) of the work to realize the idea. We suggest you read these instructions and then leave your digital devices and go outside. The weather might be nice, or not, but hopefully you can go somewhere where you can sit and experience the moment. Unplugging from the internet and the work of computers is good for your physical and mental health, and we hope you will find time to reflect and find something beautiful in your environment.

The **haiku** is a Japanese poetry form dating back to the seventeenth century. Traditional haikus include three elements: a word that references the natural world or seasons (kigo), a word that implies you should stop and be reflective (kareji), and sensory imagery.[17] Your haiku will help you to generate imagery and feeling (or mood) for your project. The haiku format adheres to three non-rhyming lines, with five syllables in the first line, seven syllables on the next line, followed by five syllables on the last line, as seen in the haiku xtine wrote for Avi Carmoega, which we use throughout the exercises in this chapter:

A radiant young
Woman to light the darkest
Corners of winter

Here are additional examples that follow the syllabic format in Japanese (though the 5-7-5 syllable count often does not hold in English translations):

I write, erase, rewrite
Erase again, and then
A poppy blooms.
—Katsushika Hokusai

Spring is passing.
The birds cry, and the fishes' eyes are
With tears.
—Matsuo Basho[18]

Notice how these poems speak to their environment while also making an emotional connection with the reader. In just seventeen syllables, your words can elicit rich imagery and feeling.

1. Go outside and bring only a pen or pencil and paper. Read the next two steps, then start with either the haiku or drawing, as described in the next two steps.
2. Write a haiku about your experience using language that inspires imagery in the 5-7-5 syllable count on three sequential lines. You can employ one of the OuLiPo strategies mentioned in section 6.1.1 if you feel stuck.
3. Create a drawing or series of drawings inspired by your haiku (or, if you are drawing first, write a haiku inspired by your drawings). It doesn't need to be a work of "Art" but rather forms that express the imagery, observations, or mood you felt. You will eventually use the text and sketches to create a design that expresses the sentiment in the poem.

Exercise 6.1.2 Create a Text Layout on a Grid in Figma

The first step in resisting any structure is to familiarize yourself with it. Once you understand and know how such a system functions, then your resistance can be focused, specific, and effective. In this exercise you'll complete four layout variations using only the text you've chosen and a layout grid in Figma.

1. Create a new desktop-sized frame in Figma using the templates you used in chapter 4, **criticalwebdesign.github.io#figma-templates.**
2. Add the text that you have created in the haiku or sourced elsewhere. If you like, you can place an image of your poem to experiment and mock up possibilities over the top of it.
3. Experiment with font, position, color, and so on.
4. Duplicate and rename the frame for each new iteration. Even though you are aligning the content on the grid, you should try to make them significantly different (figure 6.7).

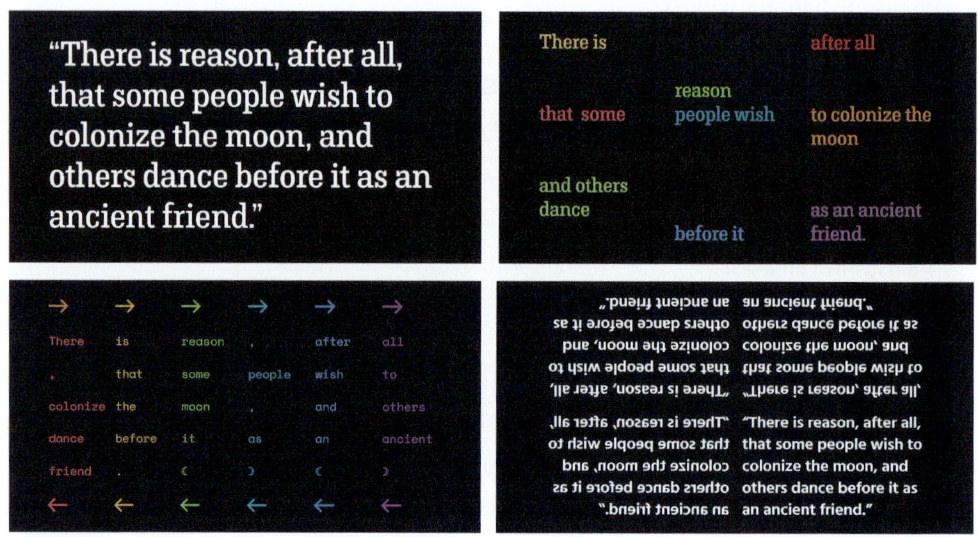

Figure 6.7

Owen used a quote from the poet and author James Baldwin to create four distinct grid layouts. The Figma layout grid is hidden in this figure, but it is clear that the columns and rows provide structure to the text.

6.1.2 Find Inspiration in Existing Works

With your grid-based layout in hand, your task now is to represent the text or experience using a more expressive method that escapes the grid. But understanding the world by organizing its parts into identifiable categories is part of being human. Where does one begin to create a design like the experimental examples discussed in the Context section of this chapter? A common method used across creative fields is to start with research, finding inspiration in existing works, and then using iteration to envision possible outcomes.

In the chapter "Improvisations and Limitations" of his book *The Shape of Design*, Frank Chimero writes about finding inspiration in the work of others. Using examples from both (interestingly) Japanese poetry as well as jazz music, Chimero suggests adopting improvisation to facilitate the creative process. He describes the instructions that Miles Davis gave the other musicians when recording *Kind of Blue*, the groundbreaking album that redefined improvisation across jazz music, by providing them only a "loose framework of limitations to focus them [and] plenty of space of exploration."[19] However, the music they produced at that moment could only have happened thanks to those who established so much of the language and patterns in this musical form. Davis and his group were informed by a history of jazz greats, like Dizzy Gillespie, Billie Holliday, and Louis Armstrong. While you should always seek to define your unique perspective in what you make, creativity is made possible thanks to others' *Giant Steps*.[20] We can "accept the light contained in the work of others"[21] to find our own way.

6.1.3 Design Research: Organize and Analyze Visual Information

The following methods for comparing works of art or scholarship can help to organize your thinking and perform analysis and synthesis with greater clarity. Organization is a research strategy that supports clarity of thinking. In design programs and commercial work, you might be asked to create a mood board or a competition scan, while in other academic settings, a literature review is the standard for assessing a field of work. These methods for gathering and presenting information are similar in scope but may differ in approach, as follows:

- A **competition scan** involves researching competitors to gain insights into standards and practices within a given industry or field. It usually is performed by businesses to understand products, markets, trends, and so on.[22]
- A **competitive website analysis** can yield insights into UI/UX features of a website, including how competitors organize information, maintain usability, and deal with potentially similar design problems.[23] Ask yourself, "Has someone already solved this design problem?" and learn from their work.
- A **critical review** demonstrates extensive research, including analysis and critical evaluation of literature or other published works within a given topic or field, while a literature review usually only describes published works and may or may not include a degree of assessment.[24] This type of analysis often includes developing an annotated bibliography of works, meaning that a full citation of the work is collected along with a brief summary you write to describe its significance to your research.

- A **mood board** is "a collection of visual materials that evoke a certain style or concept" that can be used to collect and explore examples, record specific typefaces or color palettes, and experiment and set the visual direction of your project.[25]

Activity: Create a Mood Board

While we have used all these methods, we focus here on developing a mood board (figure 6.8) as it fits the experimental nature of this chapter:

Figure 6.8

This mood board includes a selection of text and image works made by women artists and designers. While some present easily found grid structures, all of these works use intentional expressive typographic design or juxtapose text and image to animate their ideas.

- It supplies a competition scan to understand what design problems you will encounter as you work in a particular subject or outcome.
- It reveals some of the common solutions others have used to solve the design problems you can anticipate.
- And, it provides you with inspiration to put your ideas into recognizable forms.

Create a mood board by starting in Figma or an application of your choice. A design layout tool will allow you to work directly on top of the examples you collect, but you could use any online space like WordPress or Are.na, or even an offline method, for recording your research.

1. Copy and paste screenshots of inspirational works into a new design file in Figma. Start your visual research by exploring art and design by the signatures on the 2000 edition of *First Things First*. While you are viewing these works, think about how you will express your text visually. Make notes about your inspiration.
2. Resize your frame or add more as needed to accommodate or organize new examples.
3. Return to your mood board often whenever you get stuck in the design process. Ask questions as you view the works you have collected:
   a. How do the works in my mood board compare with the design I am making?
   b. What can I borrow to create connections between my work and those that inspired me?
   c. What is my original contribution to the design I am presenting? How does my work differ from what I collected in my mood board?
   d. What are the relationships between text and imagery working to help communicate in these works?

6.1.4 Generate Possibilities for Text and Image

One common strategy for designers and artists is to create as many possible sketches or iterations that demonstrate how an idea could be executed. In *The Art of Seeing*, the novelist, poet, and philosopher Aldous Huxley wrote, "We see best the things about which, or the likes of which, we have a good stock of memories."[26] Huxley's argument is summarized by the well-known catchphrase "The more you know, the more you see." This eight-word statement summarizes how *seeing* is an activity that incorporates your mind and body. While sight is a physical sensation, perceiving activates the mind. Thus, as your mind expands and your understanding grows, you are more able to "see," perceive, or synthesize connections as you are sensing with vision.

Seeing is, ultimately, one of your primary goals as a visual artist or critical designer. To develop your ability to know and see more involves iterating on concepts and conducting visual research. Relatedly, Mike Bostock, a graphics editor for *The New York Times* and creator of the D3.js data visualization library, characterized design as "a search problem."[27] He reflects that there are too many unknowns for design principles to be sufficient to tell us exactly what we need to do to create successful outcomes. You need "to explore as many possibilities as efficiently as possible," including "things that aren't going to work in order to find the things that do."[28]

Best Practices: Owen's Design Process

Use these steps to iterate on and improve any design.

1. Seek out, collect images, and make notes about works that inspire you or solve a design problem you are contemplating.
2. Duplicate a previous version of your design. After looking at finished works, you might already see areas for improvement.
3. Draw from your inspiration to create a completely new attempt at your design.
4. Take a break so that you can approach the next iteration with a clear mind.
5. Repeat the process!

Prompt 6.1 Design: Iterate on Your Layout

It's time to put the tools you've learned so far into action using your own materials.

1. Add an image to the background of your design. You can use a photograph, animation (see callout), or drawing. There are many resources for open licensed images online like **openverse.org** and **commons.wikimedia.org**.
2. Revisit your mood board. Reflect on design methods, styles, and content you find in these works that inspire you. Be specific about such items as typography, color, lines, negative space, and so on.
3. Use the repeatable iterative design process (above) and draw inspiration from—or even work on top of—examples you've found in your mood board.
4. Continue to experiment with new compositions that break the rules of the grid.

Pro Tip: Create an Animated GIF from a Video

An **animated GIF** used as a background image can make your page dynamic. Here are two methods for converting video to animated GIF that we like to use:

- Giphy Capture **giphy.com/apps/giphycapture**.
- Turn videos uploaded to Vimeo into GIFs.[29]

Module 6.2 CSS Grid and Animation with CSS Transform

Now that you have created assets and design iterations, you'll explore CSS layout tools that let you break the normal flow of a web page and position items however you like. Although you (probably) adhered to the conventional 5-7-5 structure of haiku poetry, you will abandon those formatting rules to experiment with new aesthetic and unconventional treatments of the form.

6.2.1 CSS Grid

In previous chapters, you used the Bootstrap framework to arrange content into responsive columns on your web page. The prebuilt classes in Bootstrap's grid system are based on **flexbox**[30] (as in "flexible box"), which is just one of several CSS layout modules you can use to make rows and columns in a web page.[31] While Bootstrap makes it simple to code responsive layouts "out of the box," flexbox on its own requires in-depth knowledge to implement grids properly. An easier and more capable method for constructing basic two-dimensional grids from scratch is the **CSS grid**.

Exercise 6.2.1 Add Columns with CSS Grid

Use the CSS grid module to add text from your haiku to the first version of your HTML page.

1. Create a new repo from our template **github.com/criticalwebdesign/website-template** named "off-the-grid" and then go to **github.com/codespaces,** or your preferred code editor, and open your new repository following our steps in exercise 3.2.1.
2. Open **index.html** and change the `<title>` content to "haiku."
3. In **styles.css** add the following rule for the `<body>` element. These properties are all familiar to you by now, except `overflow`, which determines what happens to content that does not fit in its parent container. The default value for an element's `overflow` property is `visible`, except on the `<body>` element, which uses scrollbars for content that overflows. Since we know we will radically break the grid in a later exercise, we do not want scrollbars to appear when our poem flows off the page.[32]

```
body {
  margin: 1rem;
  background-color: black;
  color: whitesmoke;
  font-size: 5rem;
  overflow: hidden;
}
```

4. In **index.html**, replace everything inside the `<body>` tag except for the `<script>` tag with your poem or the poem below. Add a new `<div>` element with a class named `grid-container`. This will be the container for your poem. Inside the container, surround each word from your text (or ours) with new `<div>` tags. When you preview your page, you will see the text appears line by line following the normal flow of the page.

```
<body>
  <div class="grid-container">
    <div>A</div>
    <div>radiant</div>
    <div>young</div>
    <div>woman</div>
    <div>to</div>
    <div>light</div>
    <div>the</div>
    <div>darkest</div>
    <div>corners</div>
    <div>of</div>
    <div>winter</div>
  </div>
<script src="assets/js/main.js"></script>
```

5. In **styles.css** add a `.grid-container` class with a single rule, `display:grid;`. Preview your page in the browser. Once an element's display property is set to `grid`, all of its direct children become **grid items** that you can align, justify, or stretch as the parent container size changes. By default, it creates a one-column grid, so your items will continue to display one below the other as they do in normal flow.

```
.grid-container {
  display:grid;
}
```

6. Add to the `grid-container` class a `grid-template-columns` property. This defines the number of columns as well as how available space in the container should be used. In this case, there are three values with the `fr` (or **flex unit**), so each column will use an equal fraction of space regardless of its container's overall dimensions.[33] The `gap` property sets the space between the columns using the `rem` unit so that the space between columns changes with the text size. Preview your work (figure 6.9).

```
.grid-container {
  display:grid;
  grid-template-columns: 1fr 1fr 1fr;
  gap: 2rem;
}
```

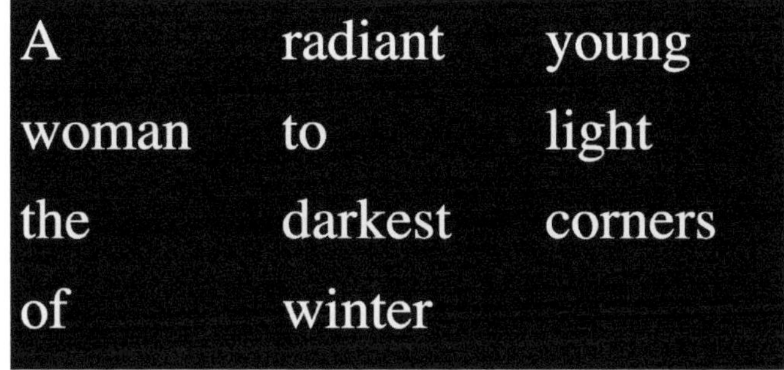

Figure 6.9
The lines of the poem presented in rows and columns thanks to the CSS grid.

7. While the above step adds three columns, your grid is not yet responsive. Change the **grid-template-columns** property with the code snippet below. This new value uses the CSS **repeat()** and **minmax()** functions to set a minimum size for each column and automatically adjusts the number of columns based on the viewport size. Preview your work and change the size of the browser window to see how the columns, like Bootstrap's grid system, adapt to different viewport sizes.

```
grid-template-columns: repeat(auto-fit, minmax(320px, 1fr));
```

8. Since this grid is now responsive, it is difficult to see the haiku structure. Add a class called **last** to the **div** tag containing the last words of each of the haiku lines.

```
<div class="grid-container">
  <div>A</div>
  <div>radiant</div>
  <div class="last">young</div>
  <div>woman</div>
  <div>to</div>
  <div>light</div>
  <div>the</div>
```

```
    <div class="last">darkest</div>
    <div>corners</div>
    <div>of</div>
    <div class="last">winter</div>
</div>
```

9. Add a CSS rule for the class, **`.last`**, with the following code in **styles.css**. The **`border`** property translates the line into a thin, solid rule with a light orange color that will blend when it is juxtaposed with the flames we will use in the background.

```
.last {
  padding-bottom: 2rem;
  border-bottom: 2px solid rgb(220, 200, 180);
}
```

10. Finally, add this **`margin`** property to the **`.grid-container`** rule to increase whitespace around the container. It uses the "top, right, bottom, left" shorthand you saw in module 2.2 to keep the container's top margin relative to 10% of the overall window height.

```
margin: 10% 4rem 0 4rem;
```

Exercise 6.2.2 Use a Background Image

You initially learned to use the CSS **`background-image`** property in module 3.2. This exercise will introduce you to new possibilities for inserting images into the background of block-level HTML elements. See the wiki for a video demonstration of this exercise.

1. Download **flames.gif** from the CWD repo at **criticalwebdesign.github.io#flames** and add it to your project in **assets/img/flames.gif**.

> **Author Note: Uploading Images in Codespaces**
>
> See exercise 3.2.3 regarding uploading images to your repo using Codespaces. You can drag and drop or right-click on the **images/** folder to upload a file.

2. Update the CSS rule for **`body`** to include the following code, placing the image in the background of the page.

```
background: url("../img/flames.gif");
```

3. When you preview your work, you will notice the background image repeats across the page. You can control this default behavior on horizontal, vertical, or both axes. Or you can disable it as we have done below using **`no-repeat`**. Likewise, you can align the background image with the **`background-position`** property. It is most commonly used with two values (x and y) like: **`center center`** or **`top left`**. Finally, **`background-size`** can be used with **`contain`** to stretch to fill the parent element, or **`cover`** to scale the image, fitting the parent while preserving the image's aspect ratio. Add these sets of properties and values to the **`body`** declaration block:

```
background-repeat: no-repeat;
background-position: center;
background-size: cover;
```

4. Finally, if you test this page on a large monitor, you will see the background image only extends to fit the content it contains, which may or may not be the full height of the viewport. This is because the **`<body>`** is actually bound by the height of its parent, the **`<html>`** element. By default **`<html>`** is 0 px high unless you explicitly set the value or fill it with content. Add this rule to set the **`<html>`** element values to 100% before the **`body`** rule in **styles.css**, then preview your work (figure 6.10).

```
html {
  width: 100%;
  height: 100%;
}
```

6.2.2 Animation on the Web

Throughout the rest of this chapter, you will learn how to use the CSS **`transform`** and **`transition`** properties with JavaScript to explode your grid-based design to explore, and potentially adapt, new layout configurations.

Exploding the page by immediately moving each element to a new position will be exciting, but abrupt. In video game coding, this effect is known as **teleporting**, because like the transporter in *Star Trek*, objects unexpectedly reappear at new locations. To make the transitions smoother you can use animation, changing property values over time to simulate motion. In traditional animation, an illustrator draws keyframes to define the movement and then passes the work to an animator to finish the "in between" frames of a sequence. In computer animation, the term **tween** still describes this process, except that the in-between frames (the phrase from which "tween" is drawn) are created with code.

Figure 6.10
The background image is centered in the browser. It appears only once, and the text is juxtaposed on top of it as a well-organized series of divs controlled by CSS grid.

While you can animate any CSS property, the transform is the easiest way to move, scale, or rotate elements on the page. See the callout for more about CSS transform.

Activity: Experiment with CSS Transform

Similar to geometric transformations used in math and computer graphics, the CSS `transform` property lets you translate, rotate, scale, or skew elements by modifying their coordinate space. The following rules will achieve the results seen in figure 6.11.

```
.ex1 {transform: translate(30px, 30px)}
.ex2 {transform: rotate(45deg)}
.ex3 {transform: scale(.5, .5)}
```

Notice that some transform functions require specific units, such as the number of pixels an element should move (translate) or how many degrees an element should rotate. Also, just like in geometry, know that the order of transformations matters.[35]

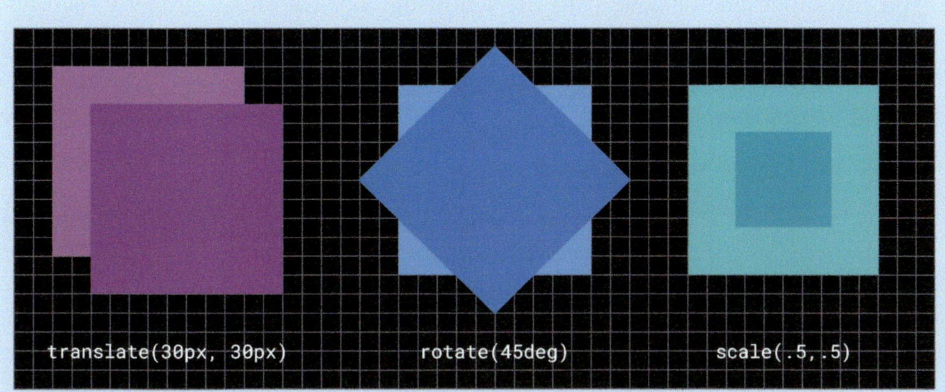

Figure 6.11
The CSS transform property allows for several fundamental geometric transformations.

See this Codepen to experiment with this example, **criticalwebdesign.github.io#css-transform**.

Exercise 6.2.3 Create a Simple Animation with CSS and JavaScript

There are many excellent libraries for animation, like **anime.js** or **p5.js**, which we will explore later in the book. This simple exercise shows how to use JavaScript to create animation by changing CSS properties over time (see the CSS Animations callout).

Author Note: CSS Animations

CSS transitions are great for simple movements, but there is another type that lets you add multiple animation states. A **CSS animation** uses the `@keyframes` rule to define the start and end values of a tween and the browser renders the frames between. We share additional methods on the wiki.

1. You can use the `style` property in JavaScript to access and change the presentation of elements on the page. Add this code to **main.js** and preview the results. This single line of code will change the opacity of everything on the page using a decimal value between `0` and `1`. You could select any element, but we are using the `<body>` to keep the example simple.

   ```
   document.body.style.opacity = .5;
   ```

2. Edit the above line of code with the following. The transform property requires a string containing one or more transform functions. The `rotate()` function requires a numeric value and a `deg` (degrees) unit between parentheses. We are using **backticks** so that we can later use a feature in JavaScript that makes concatenating strings easier.

```
document.body.style.transform = `rotate(90deg)`;
```

3. While JavaScript can change values repeatedly using `setInterval()` (see the wiki), CSS has two methods that create motion automatically. A **CSS transition** lets you animate properties as they change to their new values. Add this transition to your CSS body rule. If you missed the transformation, refresh the browser!

```
body {
  margin: 1rem;
  background-color: black;
  color: whitesmoke;
  font-size: 5rem;
  overflow: hidden;
  background: black url("../img/flames.gif");
  background-repeat: no-repeat;
  background-position: center;
  background-size: cover;
  transition-property: transform;
  transition-duration: 3s;
}
```

4. Replace all of the code in **main.js** with this code. It creates a new variable for rotation and sets it to zero. The `click` listener triggers a callback function that changes the transform style on the `body`. The existing value of the rotation `transform` is incremented using a random number between 10 and 40 (see the callout) degrees, which the CSS transition will animate to the new value. You can see we use a dollar sign with two curly braces (`${}`) to insert the variable's value directly within the string wrapped by backticks. See the callout for more about template literals.

```
let rotation = 0;
document.addEventListener("click", function () {
  let min = 10;
  let max = 40;
  rotation += Math.floor(Math.random() * (max - min + 1)) + min;
  document.body.style.transform = `rotate(${rotation}deg)`;
});
```

Best Practices: Template Literal

You already learned to concatenate string values using the + operator. But this method can become messy when working with nested quotes and many variables. In the snippet below, the first string contains a single quote so it must be wrapped in double quotes, while the second string needs single quotes to wrap the double quotes in the HTML attribute.

```
let str = "Sally's" + count + '<a href="#pic">' + shells + '</a>'
```

The **template literal** makes working with multiple quotes easier.[36] Simply wrap the entire string using backticks and you can use any single or double quote without additional + operators. To add a variable, just use a dollar sign and curly braces **${}**.

```
let str = `Sally's ${count} <a href="#pic">${shells}</a>`
```

The simpler syntax is easier to type and debug and can even span multiple lines to make it more readable.

Author Note: Inclusive, +1

By default, the output of `Math.random()` includes the **min** value, but not the **max** value. So, to make our range "inclusive," we added 1 in our random number generator, ensuring we can output all possible integers, but then round down using `Math.floor()` to be sure we don't return a value outside the correct range.

Prompt 6.2 Code: Develop a New Page and Explode It

Code a web page in a grid using your own text and image. Then create animation using the method discussed above or explore one we demonstrate on the wiki. You will notice there are several additional features we did not discuss, like the CSS `animation-timing-function`, which controls easing. See **easings.net** for a range of possibilities and MDN for details.

Module 6.3 JavaScript Functions, Arrays, and Loops

In this last module, we use functions, arrays, and loops to explode each element on the page to random positions off the grid! The pseudocode for this process is as follows:

1. Get a reference to all the elements on the page.
2. Loop through each element.
3. Create a random value within a specific range.
4. Assign each value to the transform style of each element.

6.3.1 JavaScript Functions

In the CSS transition exercise above, you animated the document's rotation using a random value between a minimum and maximum number. How then, might one move *each* element on the page to different, random positions? You might imagine that to animate other properties you would have to retype the same code for every element. Repeatedly writing identical code is not only inefficient but also complicates code maintenance. Whenever you find yourself doing this, consider creating a function to organize and reuse your code.

Exercise 6.3.1 Write a Custom Function to Generate a Random Number

You've already used many built-in functions throughout this book to perform common tasks like displaying alerts or rounding values, such as the following:

```
alert("hello world!");
Math.ceil(1.3); // -> 2
```

Following the DRY ("Don't Repeat Yourself") principle we described in module 4.2, functions allow you to reuse blocks of code, making them easier to write and maintain. A custom function (one that you create yourself) uses the `function` keyword, one or more **parameters** to customize its task, and optionally, the `return` keyword to send data back to the location where it was called. To use a function, **call** it with the function's name and two parentheses **()** as shown in figure 6.12.

1. Write this function at the end of **main.js** and compare it to the script you used to start the CSS transition in exercise 6.2.3. In the new function, the `min` and `max` variables are now parameters, which the function uses to return a new random number greater than or equal to `min` and less than or equal to `max`.

   ```
   function randomNumber(min, max){
     return Math.floor(Math.random() * (max - min) + 1) + min;
   }
   ```

2. Now edit the event listener to look like the code snippet below. Delete or comment out (as we do) the min and max variables. Packaging the random number

code in a new function makes it easy to use and customize the value with different parameters.

```
let rotation = 0;
document.addEventListener("click", function () {
  // let min = 10;
  // let max = 40;
  rotation += randomNumber(1, 200);
  document.body.style.transform = `rotate(${rotation}deg)`;
});
```

3. Preview your work. Check the syntax or the console if you encounter errors.

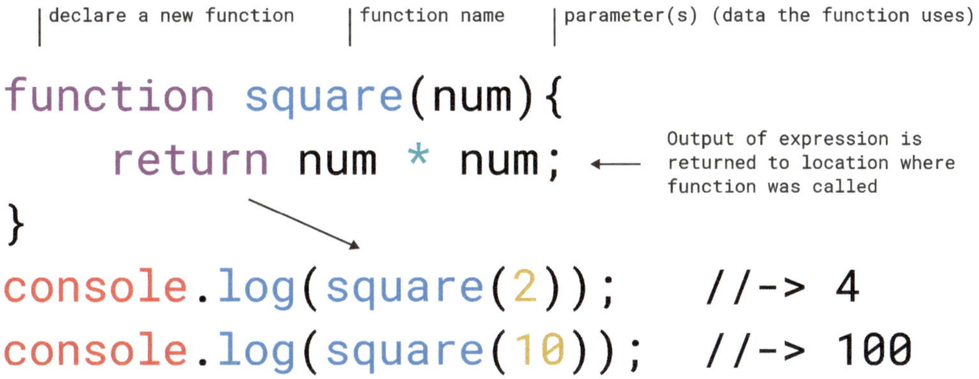

declare a new function | function name | parameter(s) (data the function uses)

```
function square(num){
    return num * num;
}
console.log(square(2));    //-> 4
console.log(square(10));   //-> 100
```

Output of expression is returned to location where function was called

Figure 6.12
A diagram of a custom function.

6.3.2 Arrays and Loops

Before we turn to the "Explode the Web" animation, revisit the data type diagram in module 5.2. In addition to primitive data types, JavaScript can store collections of data. An **array** is an example of a collection type, letting you store multiple values inside a single variable. For instance, this array contains a list of colors.

```
let colors = ["purple", "green", "blue"];
```

You can access the value of any item in an array using its **index**—the position or order of the data in the array—between two square brackets. Note that arrays are **zero-indexed** so the first data value is stored at **0**, and then **1**, and so on. Even though array indexes start at zero, their **`length`** property reflects the total number of items in the array. So, while the length of the **`colors`** array is 3, the indexes are 0, 1, 2:

```
colors[1] // -> "green"
```

Arrays make it possible to step through the indexes or even randomly select values, using our function from above with the JS **`length`** property.

```
colors[randomNumber(0,colors.length-1)]
// -> random number between 0 and 2
```

You can store any type of data inside an array. For example, we will create an array to store references to HTML elements in order to explode the page later in exercise 6.3.4.

One of the biggest benefits to working with arrays is that you can write code that automatically repeats some task using the data stored in each index location. There are a few types of **loop** statements in most programming languages, but all of them do essentially the same thing: repeat a block of code until a condition is met (figure 6.13).

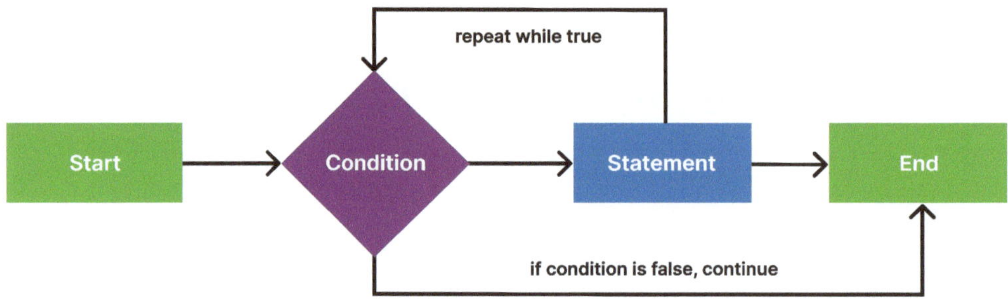

Figure 6.13
A loop is a kind of control structure that will repeat until a condition is met.

In the final code we create for this chapter, we use a **for** loop to transform each element in the page. The **for** loop represents the three essential components of all loops (figure 6.14):

- A **control** variable counts the number of loops.
- A **condition** checks to see if the loop will continue (usually using the length of an array).
- Finally, we **increment** the iterator on each loop.

```
             | control variable    | loop condition        | increment iterator
for (let i = 0; i < colors.length; i++){
    console.log(i, colors[i]);
}          Log the iterator and value at each array index...
//-> 0, "red"
//-> 1, "green"
//-> 2, "blue"
```

Figure 6.14
A JavaScript `for` loop includes a control variable, loop condition, and iterator. If the condition is true, then the code in the statement block will continue to run.

See the activity to experiment with arrays and loops in the DevTools console.

Activity: Array and Loops

Explore a simple array in the DevTools console.

1. Open the DevTools console and create the following array with a variable declaration, a name, and multiple comma-separated values between square brackets. This introduces a new array with three values. The variable name is written in plural form, a best practice for naming an entity that holds multiple values.

```
let colors = ["purple", "green", "blue"];
```

2. Run this code, line by line, in the DevTools console to retrieve each array index, and then its length.

```
colors[0] // -> "purple"
colors[1] // -> "green"
colors.length // -> 3
```

3. Arrays are also like variables in that you can not only retrieve, or `get` stored values, you can `set` values by assigning them to an array index. Run these on the console to see this in action.

```
colors[0] = "red";
colors[0] // -> "red"
colors // -> ["red", "green", "blue"];
```

4. This simple **for** loop logs the value of the iterator to the console. Try it now in the DevTools Console.

```
for (let i = 0; i < 10; i++){
  console.log(i);
}
```

5. Now try this loop from figure 6.14, which logs the all values in the **color** array using the **length** property in the loop condition.

```
let colors = ["purple", "green", "blue"];
for(let i = 0; i < colors.length; i++){
  console.log(i, colors[i]);
}
```

Exercise 6.3.2 Use CSS Transform to Explode Any Page

This exercise was originally written to accompany a chapter for *Signal Culture Cookbook vol.2.*[37] Here we are summarizing it to explode the grid and let you test your knowledge of functions, arrays, and loops. Once you test this in the browser, we will return to **main.js** and implement it in our project. See the wiki for a video demonstration of this exercise.

1. Go to any web page and open DevTools > Console.
2. While **querySelector()** retrieves just the first instance of an element, **querySelectorAll()** returns an array containing references to *every* matching element. Add this code, using JavaScript's **querySelectorAll()** function to create a new array containing references to all the elements on the page inside the **body** using the * (asterisk) as a wildcard selector. Press the Enter key.

```
let elements = document.querySelectorAll("body *");
```

3. Type the following code to see how many elements you selected. Depending on your page, you could have hundreds, or maybe even thousands.

```
console.log(elements.length);
```

4. Use JavaScript's **forEach()** method to loop through the array of elements and apply one or more CSS transforms to each. Press Shift + return in the console to add a single line break if you need to. We are applying the **rotate()** function using a random variable multiplied by 360 within backticks to each element. Press the **return** (Enter on Windows) key to run the code. You may need to scroll to show the transformed result in the viewport.

```
elements.forEach(function(ele){
  ele.style.transform = `rotate(${Math.random() * 360}deg)`;
});
```

5. Most command line interfaces, including the browser's JavaScript console, let you press the up arrow on your keyboard to cycle through previously entered commands. Click in the console and press up to see the **forEach()** command again and press **return** to run it, again, and again, and continue until you achieve some results you like (figure 6.15).

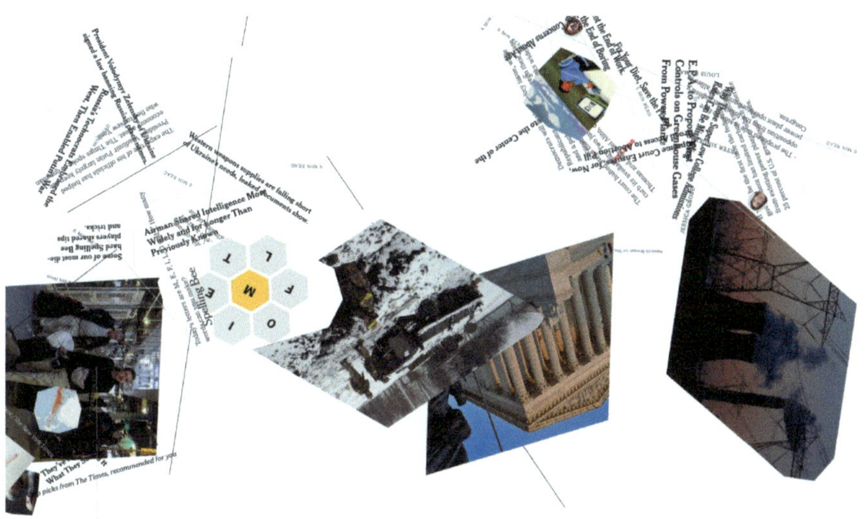

Figure 6.15
The *New York Times* website gets a redesign with two lines of code in the Console.

> **Best Practices: Bookmarklets**
>
> A **bookmarklet** is like a regular browser bookmark except it contains JavaScript in the URL field that runs when you click the link. See this Codepen for more information about bookmarklets, including instructions to save the above "Explode!" script or an HTML/CSS validation tool as bookmarklets: **criticalwebdesign.github.io#bookmarklets.**

Exercise 6.3.3 Explode Your Page!

Now that you have seen how to use functions, arrays, and loops in JavaScript, it's time to put this information to use and explode your page!

1. Return to **main.js** and remove everything except the `randomNumber()` function you wrote above. Add the following line to select all the elements inside your grid.

```
let divs = document.querySelectorAll(".grid-container div");
```

2. Use the `function` keyword to declare a new function called `randomize()`. Make sure to add the two parentheses and curly braces like below. Use `console.log()` inside the function body to test the number of `<div>` tags found. Your script should look like this:

```
function randomNumber(min, max){
  return Math.floor(Math.random() * (max - min + 1)) + min;
}
let divs = document.querySelectorAll(".grid-container div");
function randomize(){
  console.log(divs.length, "randomize!")
}
```

3. To call the function, use the name followed by two parentheses and a semicolon to end the statement. Preview your work and check the console to confirm you see the number of `<div>` tags selected and the word "randomize!".

```
randomize();
```

4. After ensuring that all of your `<div>` elements are selected, you can now loop through them to change their transforms. Update the `randomize()` function with the below variables.

```
function randomize(){
  divs.forEach(function(div){
    let scale = randomNumber(.5, 1.2);
    let translateX = randomNumber(0, 50);
    let translateY = randomNumber(0, 20);
    let rotate = randomNumber(0, 360);
    div.style.transform =
      `scale(${scale})
      translate(${translateX}%, ${translateY}%)
      rotate(${rotate}deg)`;
  })
  console.log(divs.length, "randomize! ");
}
randomize();
```

5. Replace or comment-out the line where you call the **`randomize()`** function and add a **listener** to the page to call it every time a **`click`** event happens. Note that you don't add parentheses when you reference the function as a callback, because you only want it to be executed *when the click happens*, not immediately.

```
//randomize();
document.addEventListener("click", randomize);
```

6. Finally, in **styles.css** cut the two lines that create your CSS transition from the **`body`** selector and paste them to a new rule so the transitions affect **`div`** tags:

```
div {
  transition-property: transform;
  transition-duration: 3s;
}
```

7. Preview your work in Chrome, clicking in the browser several times to watch the poem explode. Stage and commit your work. When you see a composition you like, you can make a screenshot to document the process and inform your adjustments to the parameters.

Check Your Work

This concludes the chapter exercises. We invite you to compare your work to the final outcome **criticalwebdesign.github.io#6-3** and code **criticalwebdesign.github.io#6-3-code** in the book repo. Don't forget to enable GitHub Pages in your project and then stage and commit your work to make it live!

Prompt 6.3 Publish: Get Off the Grid by Adding Functions

Incorporate what you learned throughout module 6.3 to update your poem. While you are exploding your grid, you might create a function to select a random color for elements when the page loads or on-click. After you are finished, consider creating a bookmarklet that explodes any web page. See the other examples, like **criticalwebdesign.github.io#birds**, in the book repo. We started this chapter with an offline module and ended with JavaScript to disassemble the grid. While these are small steps, we encourage you to consider how they take a critical approach to design for the web.

7 Ethical by Design

For most of us, design is invisible. Until it fails.
—Bruce Mao

Context

In this chapter you will learn strategies for producing ethical design and avoiding deceptive practices. While an in-depth discussion of ethics is outside the scope of this book, we believe an "ethical" design practice is one that involves creating interfaces that are intuitive and easy to use, making content accessible and inclusive regardless of ability or person, and employing technology that respects the rights, agency, and civil liberties of all users. These ideas are summarized in the "Ethical Hierarchy of Needs"[1] (figure 7.1) created by Aral Balkan and Laura Kalbag, which intentionally places human rights[2] at the foundation of the diagram to underscore the importance of respect for others' humanity over monetary gains. Below, we highlight several strategies that align with a core philosophy that maintaining respect and compassion for your users' rights, abilities, and goals is a fundamental part of any design process. Later in the Context, we show how design patterns help to achieve these objectives, and how anti-patterns and deceptive design are incompatible with ethical design.

User-Centered Design

There are several concepts and methodologies that run adjacent (or even counter to) ethical design practices. In chapter 5 we introduced design thinking, which encourages creators to empathize with and accommodate users' goals throughout the design process. You created and implemented a usability test to understand and improve the ease with which others can use your layouts. **User-centered design (UCD)**, which includes usability testing, places the user at the center of the process, going beyond creating intuitive

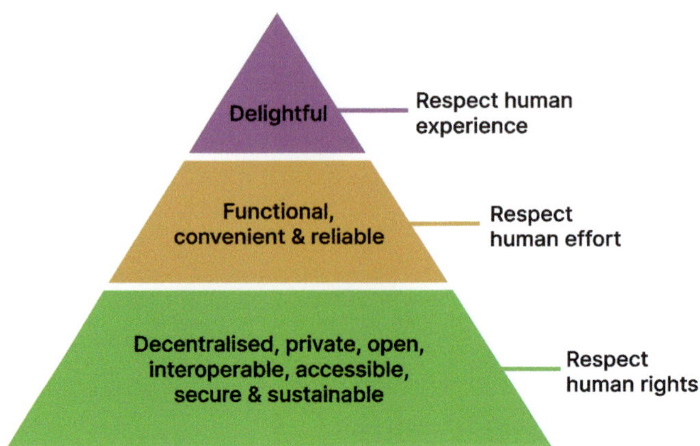

Figure 7.1
Our interpretation of the "Ethical Hierarchy of Needs" (CC BY 4.0) from the "Ethical Design Manifesto," created by Aral Balkan and Laura Kalbag **ind.ie/ethical-design**.

interfaces to make transparent to the user the structure, information, and **affordances** (see callout) of a system.[3] More than the design problem–focused approach of design thinking, UCD addresses the user experience by involving users throughout the whole affair. A related concept, **Design for All**, incorporates a wide range of design approaches (like Accessibility and Universal Design, which we discuss below) "to help address [a] diversity of needs and requirements in the design of interactive technologies."[4]

Keywords: Affordances

In interaction design and **Human-Computer Interaction (HCI)**, the concept of **affordances** refers to what a user perceives they can do with an object. For example, a coffee cup provides an affordance through its handle. But its use also relies on how it **signifies** its function to users. The stacked bars of a hamburger button invite users to click because it informs them of an expandable hidden menu. "Affordances determine what actions are possible. Signifiers communicate where the action should take place. We need both."[5] An affordance is equally defined by the relation between the user and the object. Thus, it is based on a user's capabilities: what they can and cannot do.

Universal Design

Universal design is a framework for creating experiences, architecture, objects, and interactions that can be "accessed, used, and understood by all people regardless of

Additional Materials and Resources

Explore links and other content related to this chapter:
criticalwebdesign.github.io#wiki-07

their age, size, ability, or disability."[6] Established in 1997 by a working group of design researchers, their seven principles of universal design[7] can be used to guide or evaluate design processes within a wide range of disciplines and environments. Like Balkan and Kalbag's "Ethical Design Manifesto," these principles emphasize design that accommodates a wide range of abilities and is simple and intuitive to use. They additionally contain guidelines for minimizing hazards, accommodating low physical effort, allowing for diverse body types, as well as other conditions based on potential physical distinctions.

You have likely benefited from design choices made with these considerations in mind, even if your **positionality**—that is, your subjective relationship to the communities with which you are engaging—is an able-bodied person. For instance, have you ever pushed a stroller up a curb cut or read closed captions on a screen? **Curb cuts** were designed for disabled veterans after WWII to make sidewalks accessible for wheelchairs.[8] But they are also used by cyclists, skateboarders, strollers, and others on wheels. Similarly, **closed captioning** was first invented for the deaf and people with hearing loss, although today people read them on screens at the gym, the airport, on their own devices, or in other situations where noise or quietness presents a situation in which reading is preferred to listening. Originally targeted to assist people with disabilities, these innovations have improved experiences for all users. Likewise, everyone benefits when you apply universal design principles throughout your design process to create an environment that "is accessible, usable, convenient and a pleasure to use."[9]

History: The American Disabilities Act (ADA)

The ADA prevents discrimination against people with disabilities. Over time, updates to the ADA have been made to account for advances in technologies. **Section 508** of the Rehabilitation Act of 1973 required Federal agencies to make their electronic and information technology accessible to people with disabilities. It states, "Agencies must give disabled employees and members of the public access to information comparable to the access available to others."[10] While it is important to consider federal regulations, our motivations for accessibility are guided by a universal and ethical approach to making content accessible for all audiences.

Accessibility

Accessibility describes the degree to which a design is usable by the broadest range of individuals, regardless of ability. An accessible design provides equal access and opportunity regardless of whether a user's ability is permanent, temporary, or situational.

Removing barriers that make it difficult or impossible to access information is good for everyone, not only for people with vision, hearing, mobility or other impairments. A user with a temporary disability like a broken wrist can benefit from a site's accessibility features by tabbing through its menu with their opposite hand. Situations may also present obstacles that can be overcome when interfaces are built to accommodate everyone. A simple, clear, and usable design is always easy to use, but it is also readable under different lighting conditions, and helps people in various life stages, including those who may not identify as disabled.[11] Accessible interfaces can provide other benefits as well. Websites that focus on presenting text over images and video can be used by those who are vision impaired via a **screen reader**, a technology that provides access to meta content of web elements. This in turn increases download speeds, access for people in rural areas or developing countries, and even **Search Engine Optimization (SEO)** (see callout).[12]

Keywords: Search Engine Optimization (SEO)

Perform an internet search for the word "cat" on Google and you'll likely see information at the top of the page regarding the number and speed of results like "About 5,680,000,000 results (0.62 seconds)." While this is impressive, know that when you use a search engine you are not actually searching the internet in real time, nor are you searching the whole internet. Rather, the results come from databases of content that Google's "bot" has previously **indexed.** Most search engine bots index the web by following links between pages. They create searchable records by storing real text (you can select with your mouse), as well as meta information found inside `<title>` and `<meta>` tags, `alt` attributes that describe images, and **semantic** HTML tags, like `<header>`, `<article>`, and `<footer>`, that help to define the meaning of the content they contain. Obviously, raising your **search rank** by getting your service or product to show up on the first page of Google can be profitable, so there are hundreds of (often spurious) companies that provide SEO services. There is also the possibility to increase a page's rank using a **google bomb** if enough people tactically search and click on a specific link to raise its rank.[13] While some of the more suspicious methods employed may actually cause Google to *decrease* your search rank, many tactics that increase your site rank also conveniently align with making your web page accessible to screen readers.[14]

Inclusive Design

Like accessibility, **inclusive design** is an approach that seeks to provide equal access. However, where accessibility may address problems by removing specific barriers based on ability, inclusive design recognizes that exclusion happens in other ways. A design that is inclusive is not only *able* to be used by all, but it will *want* to be used by all because it incorporates diverse perspectives throughout the process. This can include representing the experiences of excluded people in your text and media, incorporating their feedback in the design process, and likewise influencing the culture of the organization where the work is created.[15] We recognize that designers should aim for accessibility and inclusion not just in the way a website is coded but also in how your design inspires actions for your users. One of the ways this materializes is through design patterns you utilize.

Figure 7.2
A selection of common design patterns for website navigation presented across these four sketches (in color) includes (clockwise from top left) the "main menu," "breadcrumb," "pagination," and "fat footer."

Design Patterns

A **design pattern** is a reusable solution to a design problem. For example, the **main menu** (figure 7.2) is a design pattern that offers a common approach to the problem of communicating to users how the content of a website is structured while allowing easy navigation to that content. The main menu works by presenting the most important pages or sections of a website in a unified horizontal or vertical list. But it also works because it is an accepted standard that is applied across the internet. Web users look for and even expect to find a main menu (or in a mobile browser, the hamburger menu) on each website because it is the accepted standard for communicating and linking the overall content to users. Knowing and applying design patterns is essential to interface design because they offer standard methods for organizing information that users have come to expect, not to mention that implementing free and reusable methods make your task easier. In module 7.2 you will learn more about design patterns and choose a standard solution to make your user experiences more intuitive. However, just as there are patterns that improve usability and accessibility, there are those that manipulate and coerce user behavior.

Keywords: Design Smells and Anti-Patterns

Among all the helpful patterns that exist in design and programming are those that are not solutions at all. An **Anti-Pattern** is "a commonly occurring solution to a problem that generates decidedly negative consequences."[16] Despite appearing to be appropriate, these actually cause more problems than they solve because they are either not repeatable or not actually good solutions. In UX design you have likely experienced "hover and cover," or variations where content or controls of the interface are hidden by other interface elements, or "erasing information on error," when completing a web form and your hard work disappears because you missed a single item.[17] Anti-Patterns are also sometimes referred to as design smells or code smells, but there is a subtle difference. While anti-patterns are common "bad" solutions, a **design smell** is an indication of a lack of quality, issues, or potential for improvement in a design or code.

Deceptive Design

While antipatterns (see callout) are ineffective attempts at design, **deceptive design** refers to intentional manipulation tactics used in websites and apps to encourage users to do things against their own best interests, like making a purchase, enrolling in a subscription, or signing up for endless promotional emails. Harry Brignull coined the term (originally "dark patterns" in 2010) to describe "a user interface that has been carefully crafted to trick users into doing things they didn't mean to."[18] The website **deceptive.design** identifies several such patterns intended to exploit users through design, many of which you have, unfortunately, probably encountered.

Some of these deceptions are obvious by their name, such as **Hard to Cancel**, **Hidden Costs**, and **Hidden Subscription**. Other deceptive patterns identified by Brignull include those that deceive by interfering with someone's ability to use interfaces, such as the **Obstruction** pattern. **Disguised Ads** trick users into clicking on advertisements by impersonating native (mobile or desktop operating system) interface elements. While encountering deceptive design most certainly inspires an emotional response, some examples are specifically designed to trigger a reaction to abuse users' psychological state like **Confirmshaming**, which "works by triggering uncomfortable emotions, such as guilt or shame, to influence users' decision-making."[19] **Fake Social Proof** uses fake reviews, testimonials, or notifications about activity on a website to increase clicks and sales. **Fake Scarcity** (also called **Fear of Missing Out** or **FOMO**) is when a site pressures users into completing an action by presenting false information about limited supply or popularity.[20]

It is important to note that the implementation of dark patterns, in addition to being nasty moments of hypercapitalism where "business interests penetrate every aspect of human experience,"[21] also present inequitable experiences due to the accessibility issues they create. "Dark patterns don't affect all users equally—users with different abilities, or who are using software in a new language, or are new to technology, are disproportionately affected by dark patterns."[22] Why would someone use deceptive patterns? Put simply: It's profitable. In Harry Brignull's "A List Apart" essay on deception in UI design, the author shows how deception "tests" better than ethical design in A/B testing (see callout). He writes, "This kind of trick question is like a trammel net used in fishing, which uses different layers to entangle prey in different ways."[23]

Keywords: A/B Testing

A/B testing is a practice most often used to learn which version of a design or experience best increases sales or engagement metrics. A/B testing is performed all the time without users' knowledge by presenting one group with a "control" web page (like the original design) and another group with some variation on it. Users' actions are recorded, including data about whether or not the updated interface increased specific **conversion goals**, like transforming visitors into subscribers or paying customers. After the test, the preferred design may be updated to retest or be permanently implemented as the control. While A/B testing can provide important data for website use, it also presents ethical issues as the tests are almost always employed without participants' knowledge and often are targeted at manipulating users to benefit the site conducting the test. For example, in 2012 Facebook curated information presented to nearly 700,000 users in order to discover whether or not they could create an "emotional contagion" and influence users' behavior. Not only was Facebook able to cause specific emotions and actions but they performed the test without users' knowledge or consent.[24] The Dunne & Raby chart in chapter 3 (figure 3.3) riffs on A/B testing to discern between commercial and critical design.

⚠ Watch Out! Design and Psychology

The fact that user thoughts and actions can be manipulated through dark patterns shows that there is significant overlap between psychology and web design. The user experience specialist Chris Nodder's concept of *Evil by Design* demonstrates how website design can generate profit by leveraging human weaknesses. Nodder's book uses the seven deadly sins to show how human psychology accounts for the success of dark patterns in web design. For example, he highlights that our very human temptations, desires, and pride are all at the root of the influence of these design tricks. Depending on your perspective and motivations, you could join Brignell and Nodder to show how these are problematic. Or you could promote the use of these to exploit users. In fact, the website **ui-patterns.com**, which provides several examples of design patterns to help designers create usable websites, unfortunately also includes a section on "Persuasive Design Patterns" intended to manipulate user behavior. They describe patterns such as **Decoy Effect**, **Loss Aversion** (which aligns with the term FOMO in common language), and **Sunk Cost Effect** among others. The inclusion of these patterns on the same page as seemingly innocuous among other helpful UI design patterns such as Captcha, navigation tabs, and dashboards, communicates the degree to which deceptive design is sadly integrated into the practice of user interface design and online marketing.[25]

Ethical Principles

Design based on deception and evil ambitions that prey on human weaknesses may leave you feeling cynical and asking, "What can be done?" Awareness of these issues is a first step toward understanding the intention behind many sites and interactions, especially in the commercial web. While we have highlighted many counter methods and best practices, to end this section in a positive direction, we offer the following actionable ethical principles from the UXPA Code of Professional Conduct[26]:

1. Act in the best interest of everyone.
2. Be honest with everyone.
3. Do no harm and, if possible, provide benefits.[27]
4. Act with integrity.
5. Avoid conflicts of interest.
6. Respect privacy, confidentiality, and anonymity.
7. Provide all resultant data.

In their "Ethical by Design" manifesto, Mulvenna, Boger, and Bond write, "Design thinking should and can be 'ethical by design'; and design should inherently support the ethical development, selection, deployment and use of products and services."[28] We urge readers to likewise practice accessibility, inclusion, and ethical design patterns and deliberately avoid using deceptive design patterns in their various practices.

Case Study: Reginé Gilbert

RG: Reginé Gilbert is an industry assistant professor and James Weldon Johnson Professor at NYU in the Integrated Design & Media program of the Tandon School of Engineering. She lives and works in New York City. Reginé is the author of *Inclusive Design for a Digital World: Designing with Accessibility in Mind*. Her favorite examples of digital accessibility can be experienced on the websites Equal Entry (**equalentry.com**) and National Federation of the Blind (**nfb.org**). Reginé teaches classes in User Experience Design and Assistive Technologies in which her students have worked on real world projects with clients or companies such as Twitter, Microsoft, NASA, and the New York Public Library.

What is the difference between being "compliant" and best practices in designing with accessibility in mind?

RG: There are guidelines that exist, such as the WCAG (Web Content Accessibility Guidelines) that laws are built around. When making a website that is accessible, you take those guidelines into account. However, the WCAG doesn't take into account, completely, usability. So even though you can make something compliant, it may not actually be usable. The challenge for businesses, designers, and developers is not only to uphold the compliance guidelines but also to make sure things are usable—and not steer too far into the compliance piece without thinking about usability. More importantly, one of the things helpful to think about is: "Who are we excluding from the start?" So, even before you write a line of code, you'll want to think about who is excluded from the start and make a list. As you create, revisit that list to be more inclusive with who you left out from the very beginning. As you test for usability, you should look to see if you cause friction (friction = frustration). In my book, I write, "If it's annoying, it's probably not accessible." When things are annoying, they're difficult for people who are non-disabled. These same tasks can be impossible for people who are disabled.

For example, a few weeks ago I had my students learn to use a screen reader. The person who taught them is blind and was teaching through Zoom. While they were trying to teach the lesson, even before they started, they ran into complications and the students were baffled as to why this person couldn't get to the next step. It was because of the design of the site they were trying to use. For instance, when there are multiple headings in place, it is impossible to use a screen reader to navigate the page in a way that makes sense. After class, students reported how insightful it was to witness how the avid screen reader, our class leader, had a hard time using the very software that was designed, in theory, for them.

If you think about creating anything on the web from an accessibility perspective, you will more than likely make it accessible as you go along. For instance, if something is purely visual, what is it like when you take away those visuals and how might somebody experience that thing? How would somebody navigate your project with a keyboard only, or with voice only?

What tools do you use in your class?

RG: I co-teach a class called Looking Forward, teaching students about assistive technologies that blind and low-vision folks use. In the class, students are shown JAWS (Job Access With Speech is a popular screen reader) and they learn VoiceOver (included in Apple products and mobile devices). One of the things we emphasize is the importance of headings. A good example of things done right is the American Federation of the Blind website (AFB.org), an organization for the blind that a lot of blind or low-vision people use. What you will notice if you view this page is that **accessible design does not need to be boring or ugly**.

For the last three years my students have been working on a NASA-funded UX/UI project to make soundscapes of the eclipse accessible for blind and low-vision folks. ARISA Labs received the grant to collect sounds from the eclipse for their Citizen Science project, **eclipsesoundscapes.org**. This project uses technology to study how solar eclipses affect life on earth. For instance, we know that before and after a solar eclipse you won't hear crickets, but during the eclipse you will, because we have heard recordings of the crickets made by citizen scientists (participants with recorders). These recorded sounds are uploaded to the Zooniverse platform and shared through the Eclipse Soundscapes web page. In spring 2024 (the semester including the April 8, 2024, solar eclipse) my students conducted an accessibility audit on the soundscape website and on Zooniverse. I do stress that my students are not experts, and that a complete audit should be conducted manually, which includes viewing the code and back end of the site. For instance, if I see a page with a bunch of divs, it is not accessible! In the class, the students' job was to review headings, asking: Do they exist? How are they organized? And, are they accessible? Then students developed an accessible onboarding experience teaching people how to use the Zooniverse platform and listen to the uploaded sounds (figure 7.3).

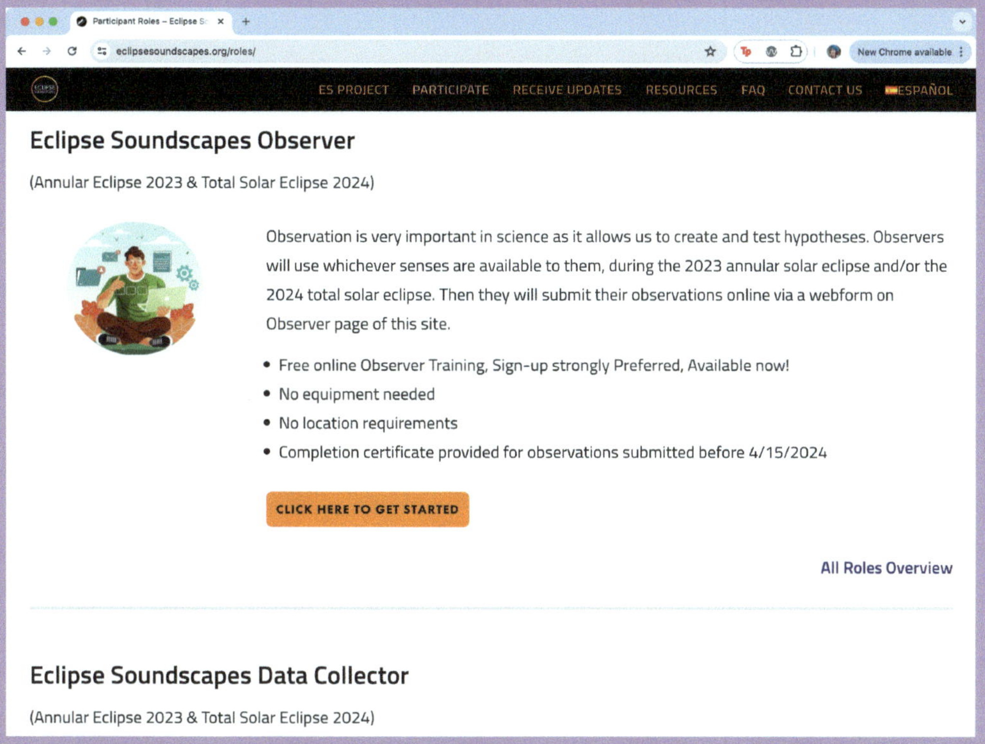

Figure 7.3
Eclipse Soundscapes Observer web page, 2024.

Prompt 7: What You'll Make
Develop Accessible Design Habits

In this chapter you will evaluate a prior project using validation and accessibility tools and examine a design brief for which you will explore common design patterns. Finally, you will implement code and design choices in answer to our brief that create greater accessibility for all users, meeting accessibility criteria on an accessibility checklist.

View the results of our exploded page at **criticalwebdesign.github.io#7-3** (figure 7.4). You can see the final code for every chapter on the CWD repo, **criticalwebdesign.github.io#repo.**

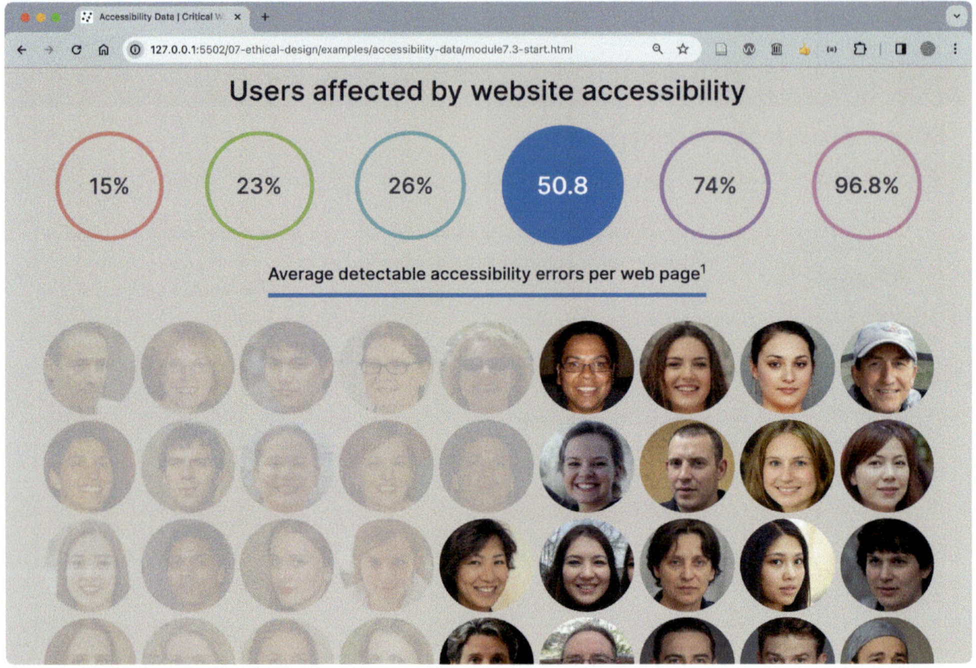

Figure 7.4
You will update the code for the design project featured in this chapter to ensure it follows accessibility guidelines.

Best Practices: Ongoing Accessibility

Accessibility is an area of study and expertise, and while this chapter touches on major themes, standards, and protocols, neither of us are accessibility experts. We honed our own skills through this deep dive. Consider this an ongoing prompt to take with you to design with accessibility in mind, to write code that passes accessibility evaluations, and to implement the A11Y checklist as part of your critical web design practice.

Module 7.1 Accessibility

Achieving accessibility is not just about increasing the amount of meta information embedded within a page. An accessible website helps all users perceive, understand, navigate, and interact with the content and functionality to support the whole experience.

Additionally, know that some methods for implementing meta-content, like the `alt` attribute, are commonly known to increase the understanding of image content via screen readers. Other attributes like `title` are almost completely ignored by assistive technology and can actually *create* issues when mistakenly employed.[29]

Just as companies have style guides to maintain consistency across visual and written aspects of their identity, some also have guidelines for accessibility. Apple indicates best practices for accessibility in their Human Interface Guidelines.[30] Similar to the WCAG (Web Content Accessibility Guidelines) definition of best practices provided by the W3 (table 7.1), Apple's priorities also include components on perception, interaction, and contribution.

Table 7.1

WCAG accessibility guidelines. According to the WCAG, a website (or app or other digital interface) is accessible when the visitor is able to perform the items in this table.[31]

Perceive	A website should make it easier for users to see and hear content. Provide text alternatives for non-text content, including captions for multimedia.
Understand	Make text readable, and content appear and operate predictably. The web experience should anticipate and help users avoid and correct mistakes.
Navigate	Interfaces should support navigation via multiple inputs, including keyboards. The design should allow content to be customized to make it easier to read.
Interact / Contribute	In time-based media, users should have enough time to read and contribute to content. The interaction should allow compatibility with assistive tools.

7.1.1 Lessons from the Web Accessibility Initiative

Web accessibility addresses disabilities that affect access to the web, such as auditory, cognitive, neurological, physical, speech, visual, and learning impairments.[32] Great design often goes unnoticed, and implementing your design with accessibility in mind may not change how your project looks, but it will create a user experience that is useful for everyone, regardless of whether their situation is permanent or temporary. Table 7.2 offers a summary of considerations from the W3C's Web Accessibility Initiative (WAI).[33]

7.1.2 WAVE Findings Walk-Through

In this section we present our own process conducting an accessibility evaluation and then analyzing it for changes we can make to our code.

There are many online tools, including web applications, bookmarklets, and browser extensions, that you can use to check your website content and code for accessibility.

Table 7.2
Web accessibility considerations from the WAI

Consideration	User scenarios
High contrast	Low contrast between the foreground and background decreases legibility for everyone, especially for people with vision disabilities. Create high contrast between the page background and colors for links, icons, buttons, images, and text.
Keyboard compatibility	Make all website functionality usable with a keyboard to allow people to navigate your site with their keys.
Voice recognition	A website coded to allow navigation via voice commands is helpful for people who cannot use their hands to type or operate a mouse.
Text-to-speech	Help those with poor vision or dyslexia by ensuring content can be accessed by text-to-speech technologies.
Clear website layout	Use consistent implementation of design patterns to help users understand how to navigate to the information they are seeking.
Notifications and feedback	Provide feedback during interactions, especially items with latency like web forms or when loading content. This creates clarity and predictability that increases usability, especially for people with lower computer skills, cognitive, and learning disabilities.
Large controls	Large links, buttons, and controls make it easier to see and use navigation.
Customizable text	Every user will have their own preferences for reading. Using relative text sizes gives your visitors greater control over their experience.
Understandable content	Accessibility does not start and stop with visual design. Written content for your website should also be clear and understandable for all audiences.

The W3C publishes a list of 166 utilities to inspect a website's compliance for specific guidelines, abilities, or several categories at once.[34] However, of the fifteen or so "broad compliance" tools we explored, we found that many were unintuitive to use, didn't work at all, or required a fee to try. In the following section we share our experience using the **WAVE (Web Accessibility Evaluation) tool** developed by the Center for Persons with Disabilities at Utah State University. In our opinion, this was the best, free suite of tools for easily checking website accessibility. While you should explore WAVE or other accessibility tools to find one that works for you, keep in mind that these automated tools cannot replace actual knowledge of common issues and accessibility best practices.

Author Note: Accessibility Testing Tools

See the chapter 7 wiki for a list of web accessibility testing tools we found to be helpful and intuitive.

The WAVE tools can be accessed either as a web application on their site, **wave.webaim.org**, or by installing their extension. A **browser extension** is a package of JavaScript, HTML, and CSS files that adds additional functionality to your browser. We found that some websites prevent access to the WAVE web app, so we recommend using the extension when possible. Here we describe our process:

Author Note: Use webaim.org

If you cannot install a browser extension, for example, if you are using a public computer in a lab or library where this is not permitted, you can read through our WAVE findings and then try a URL on the **webaim.org** site such as the address for your favorite shopping, news, entertainment, or school website.

1. We installed the WAVE extension for Chrome **wave.webaim.org/extension**. Then we opened the home page of the AIGA website **aiga.org** and ran WAVE by clicking on the browser extension icon.
2. The WAVE tool evaluates the content of the page, then shows results in a panel on the left, along with corresponding icons within the page about specific errors, warnings, features and other items in the report. At the time of writing, the WAVE tool found the following possible accessibility issues and features: errors (9), contrast errors (0), alerts (11), features (37), structural elements (64), and Accessible Rich Internet Applications (ARIA) (93) (figure 7.5, top).

7.1.3 Analyzing WAVE Results

Now that we've conducted an accessibility evaluation of the AIGA page, we will narrate our method for analyzing those results:

1. Clicking the **View Details** button at the bottom of the WAVE panel opens a tab with the same name to reveal the specifics of the report.
2. The AIGA page included images missing alternative text, so the first items shown in the Details tab are errors (with red icons). Clicking each of the icons in the Details tab causes the web page to scroll to the related item and flash the corresponding red icon in the context of the page.
3. Clicking the red icon within the page shows a pop-up window with a link to more information about the error in the Reference tab and another link to open a drawer showing the code where the error occurred in the page (figure 7.5, bottom). There we can see how the image is referenced in the code and verify that there is in fact no

Figure 7.5

Top: This screenshot of WAVE's summary shows errors and alerts drawing attention to elements one could adjust to achieve greater accessibility. Bottom: There are nine errors found, including missing alternative text, which we can confirm in the code drawer at the bottom.

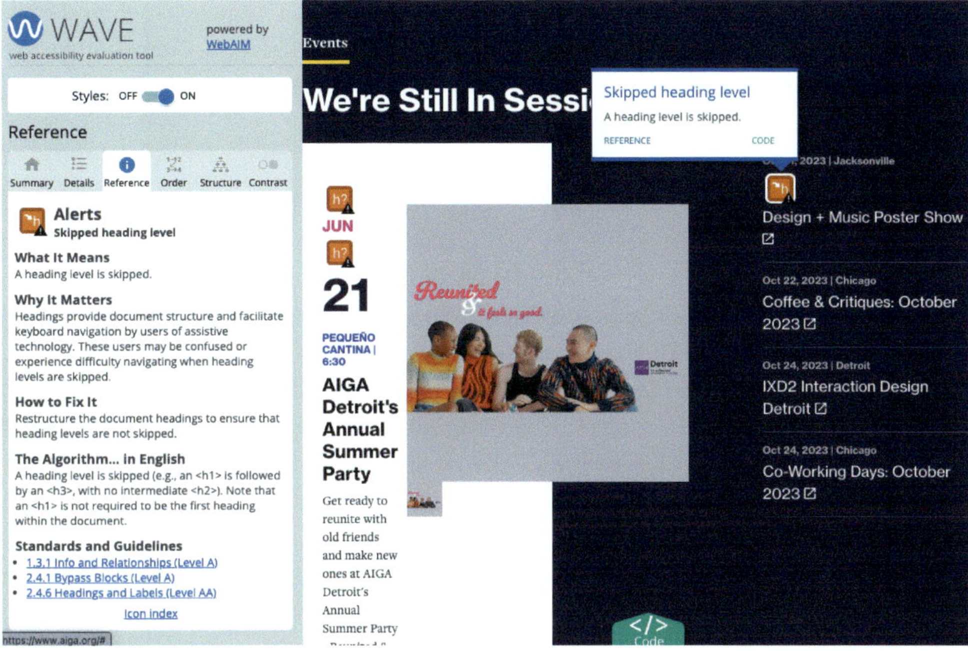

Figure 7.6

The "Skipped heading level" alert shows where the code presents heading levels seemingly out of order.

`alt` text attribute. The adjusted code might be changed to include alternative text, such as `alt="link to AIGA World Scholarships page"` to provide meaningful content for text-to-speech assistive technologies.

4. The Details tab of the WAVE panel also allows you to hide categories of elements by unchecking them. We unchecked everything except "Alerts" to disable other notifications, which made it easier to focus on a single feature of the WAVE tool. We clicked the alert icon for "Skipped Heading Level" (figure 7.6) and clicked the WAVE icon to open the pop-up above the icon in the web page, then clicked REFERENCE in the pop-up. The WAVE panel Reference tab explained the issue was due to the AIGA web developers using an `<h3>` heading when the next logical heading to use within the page (after an `<h1>`) would have been an `<h2>`. You can verify this by clicking CODE in the pop-up. As the WAVE interface explains, "Headings provide document structure and facilitate keyboard navigation by users of assistive technology. These users may be confused or experience difficulty navigating when heading levels are skipped." The recommendation therefore would be to use an `<h2>` in this position.

5. The Features and Structural Elements sections in the WAVE Details panel tend to be indications of "positive outcomes" in the accessibility evaluation. However, we still reviewed these elements to ensure that they appear in their best form. For instance, WAVE found that the AIGA logo image is linked and that it does, indeed, include the `alt` attribute with text attributed to it.
6. Finally, we unchecked all categories except **ARIA**. ARIA includes a set of roles and attributes defined by the WAI to increase accessibility for web content and applications built using JavaScript. ARIA `role` attributes are commonly used to add additional meaning to HTML elements that help define a web page's structure. While ARIA attributes can improve accessibility, developers should be careful not to use them unnecessarily.[35] In fact, developers "should prefer using the correct semantic HTML element over using ARIA, if such an element exists."[36] For example, one of the ARIA icons in WAVE shows that the code includes an **ARIA role attribute** for "article" to label this section of the web page `<article role="article">` for screen readers. This is an example of overuse, since the `article` element itself carries the article role. Therefore the `<article>` tag would be enough, while the `role` attribute creates redundant information and creates more work for users.[37]

This was the last major finding presented by the WAVE tool. If we were adjusting our site, at this point, we would be ready to commit changes, publish the site anew, and run one more WAVE test to make sure we didn't miss anything!

Best Practices: Contrast

Increasing the contrast between text and its background can increase legibility for all readers. Although WAVE found no contrast errors on the AIGA page we reviewed, it does contain a feature you can use to evaluate foreground and background contrast ratios. For large text, the WCAG requires a ratio of 3:1 or greater; and for "smaller" text (like body copy) the ratio is 4.5:1.

7.1.4 Considering Differences in Vision

The CDC reports that "approximately 12 million people 40 years and over in the United States have vision impairment, including 1 million who are blind, 3 million who have vision impairment after correction, and 8 million [with] uncorrected refractive error."[38] With such a large population affected by vision impairments, you should consider how your web page appears for people with common deficiencies.

For example, **color blindness** affects the ability to see differences in color. Among the types of color vision deficiencies, the most common is red-green color blindness, which affects up to 8% of males and 0.5% of females.[39]

Activity: Emulate Vision Deficiencies in Chrome DevTools

Use the DevTools **Emulate vision deficiencies** feature to understand how people with different types of vision deficiencies experience your site.[40]

1. Navigate to the Wikipedia page describing the Ishihara color vision test using Chrome: **en.wikipedia.org/wiki/Ishihara_test.**
2. Open DevTools and ensure the console drawer is visible. This is the smaller version of the console that opens at the bottom of the DevTools window. You can press ESC to show/hide it or find it in the options for DevTools (indicated by three dots).
3. The Console also has a drop-down list indicated by three dots that includes even more tools. Choose **Rendering** to open this tool in the console drawer.
4. Scroll down to **Emulate vision deficiencies** and view the page using each option from the drop-down. Visit different websites and step through the options to compare results (figure 7.7).

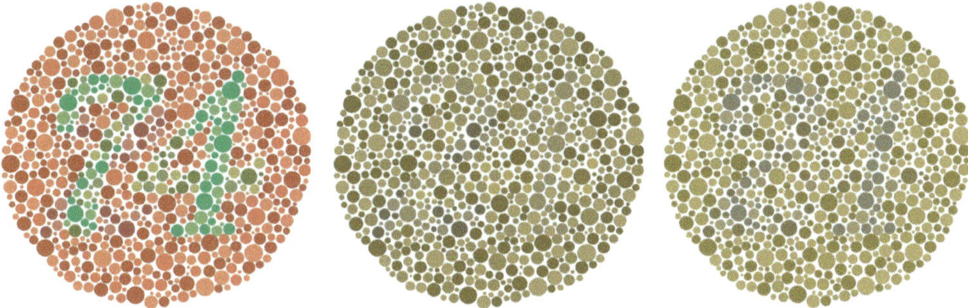

Figure 7.7
Results from using the Emulate vision deficiencies option in DevTools. The original Ishihara test image is on the left, followed by the Protanopia and then Deuteranopia (red-green) emulation.

Prompt 7.1 Use WAVE to Evaluate Your Work

Choose one of your final projects from the previous chapters and evaluate it with the WAVE tool, **webaim.org.** Through using WAVE we found accessibility errors in our final code for chapter 5 and potential improvements for our final code in chapter 6.

Module 7.2 Design Patterns and Prototypes

In this module you will learn to identify and implement common user interface (UI) design patterns to make your websites easier to build and more intuitive to use.

7.2.1 Pattern Languages

In the Context of this chapter, you learned that design patterns are flexible, reusable solutions to common design problems. **Pattern languages** that organize collections of design patterns can be found everywhere that design problems exist. Architecture and city planning are some of the oldest instances of pattern languages, having accumulated repeatable solutions since the beginning of civilization to shelter and cohabitate humans. For example, the "door" pattern and its variations are plentiful across cultures to solve the problem of allowing, limiting, or preventing access to enclosed spaces for people and things. Some languages contain patterns that are intended to work together, such as partnering the "cafe" with the "promenade" planning patterns to provide a "center for public life, where you can go to see people, and to be seen."[41]

Software design patterns are solutions applied to common problems encountered in programming and software design. Sometimes these are formalized and embedded within a programming language, such as the **JavaScript prototype pattern** (see module 9.2), which allows you to copy and reuse the structure and functionality of existing code to save work and increase the performance of your program. For example, `"hello".length` returns "5" in the console because the `length` property is inherited from the string object prototype. Different categories of software development implement distinct patterns that match the specific languages, resources, and applications in each. For example, the **Singleton pattern** is a common method to access global state in game development, while the **Model View Controller (MVC)** pattern helps to simplify and separate web requests, database work, and information display in full-stack web programming.[42]

7.2.2 The Design Brief

Imagine you work at an online publication specializing in visual essays and data journalism, like *The Pudding* (see the chapter 4 case study). Your current assignment, handed to you in the form of a **design brief**, outlines the details and expectations of a project about accessibility:

> *Create an interactive feature that tells a story with data to accompany an article about the human impact of web accessibility. The idea should communicate key statistics (percentages) about accessibility while underscoring how non-accessible websites can exclude users with permanent or temporary*

disabilities. The visual need not be complex, and should avoid common methods for visualization like charts. Every component should be designed with accessibility in mind; the page layout should include recognizable design patterns, large interactable areas, and be visible for a range of users. It should be coded in valid HTML, CSS, JS, be functional through keyboard input and work across every potential viewport size. It will go live in one week.

Also known as a "creative brief," this document usually includes the goals, scope, and strategy of the work to be done. While this hypothetical example includes relatively few parameters, you might already be thinking about different design patterns that could satisfy the requirements. Good! Patterns exist to help designers solve problems, including time constraints.

Activity: Explore Potential Patterns (Jigsaw)

Take a moment to collect some potential solutions to the above brief on your own or with a partner before we explore candidates in the next section. We have collected a list of websites to reference when looking for examples or inspiration at this page **criticalwebdesign.github.io#inspiration**

7.2.3 Common UI Design Patterns

Using the example brief you can now consider potential design patterns. The interface will provide a choice between views showing different statistics, so we need two patterns: one that presents content or data and another to provide options to change, filter, or otherwise select the information to present (see table 7.3).

Table 7.3
Sample data we have been asked to represent in the design brief

15%	World population with a disability
23%	Website images with missing alternative text
26%	Adults in the United States who have a disability
50.8%	Average detectable accessibility errors per web page
74%	Disabled Americans with no high-speed internet, smartphone, or computer
96.8%	Web pages with detectable WCAG 2 failures

A common method for exploring how one might display data is to first imagine it in its simplest or most common form. In this case, the data consists of a percentage and short blurb describing a statistic about users impacted by a specific accessibility issue. A pie chart is a good choice for depicting proportionality and, in this case, would help to emphasize the quantity of affected users.

Figure 7.8
Potential methods for representing proportionality of a value, including (from top) horizontal stacked bar charts, proportional area charts, and icon array charts.

However, since our design brief explicitly asks to represent the data without a chart, we can use a mood board to explore other potential methods that show proportionality. Of such examples (figure 7.8), the **icon array chart**,[43] which is essentially a **gallery design pattern** with a proportion of the items receiving different treatment than the others, might be the easiest to recreate using HTML/CSS. To focus on the human element, we will adapt a method developed by a former student (Kate Hynes, Davidson College '24) and use a collection of portraits to highlight how website accessibility creates a problem for real people. We can represent the percentage by changing the opacity of our hypothetical users' portraits to correspond to the number of actual users affected by each fact or issue. Lowering the opacity of their portraits reflects on the fact

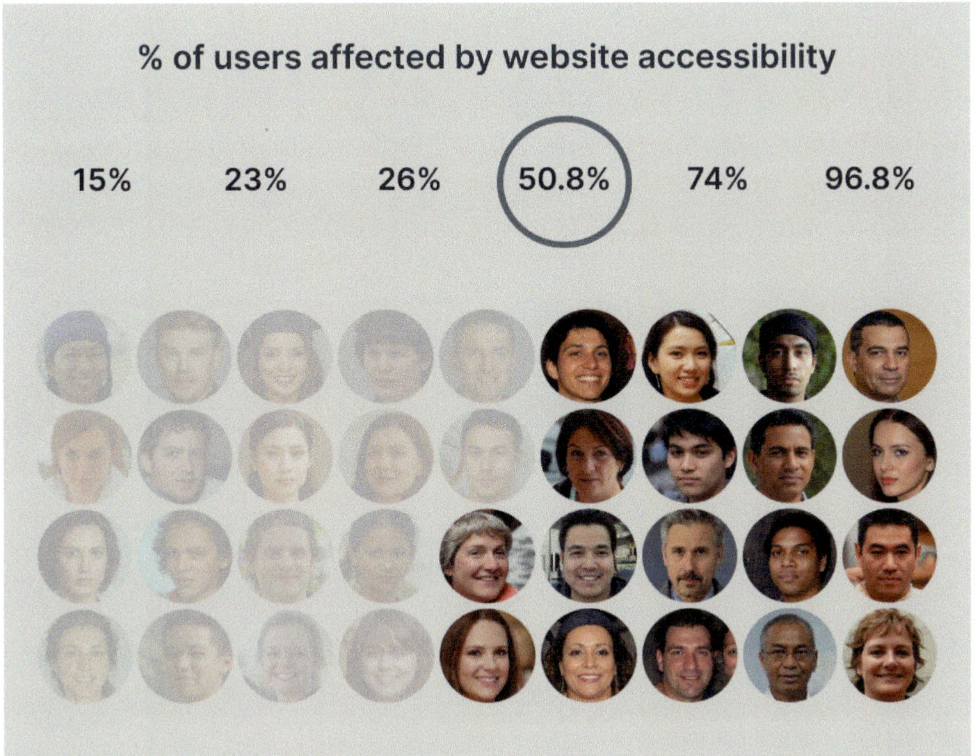

Figure 7.9
A design showing 50.8% of users affected by accessibility issues. The user portraits come from a website called **thispersondoesnotexist.com**, which is a comment on generative AI's ability to reproduce realistic images (see more on AI in chapter 8). We used these specifically because they are not real people but yet appear to be so to inspire viewers to understand the statistics in the design.

that some users are not accounted for due to website accessibility issues. In addition to their lack of representation, the lower opacity also makes more tangible one experience they may face, since it creates an actual vision problem for viewers of this website. Figure 7.9 shows a wireframe of the design, with options across the top and portraits representing each stat from the data.

The second design pattern requires combining the percentage value and corresponding text blurb into a usable menu that allows users to view the representation among the group of portraits. Of the "Content Display" examples found at **ui-patterns.com/patterns** (please do not choose from their deceptive "persuasive pattern" list!), a good

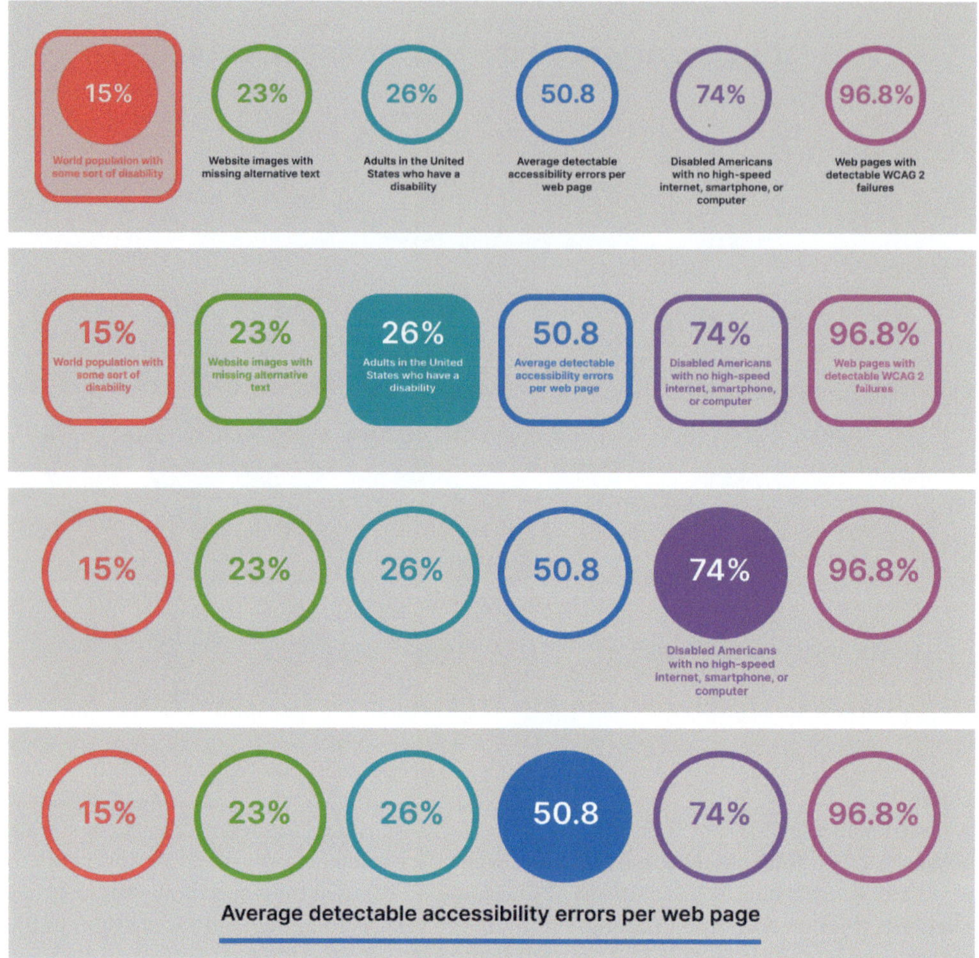

Figure 7.10

Variations of layouts showing the card pattern used to combine the percentage and text blurb into an interactive menu.

choice is the **card design pattern**, which can visually group information of varying types and lengths in order to call for action.[44] While easy to code (common design patterns like the card[45] are available in Bootstrap), we initially found that the text blurbs were too long to be able to be shown at a readable scale using the card (figure 7.10), especially on mobile.

Instead, we decided to use a pattern that invites user interaction to organize and display the text blurbs. The **progressive disclosure design pattern** solves the problem of

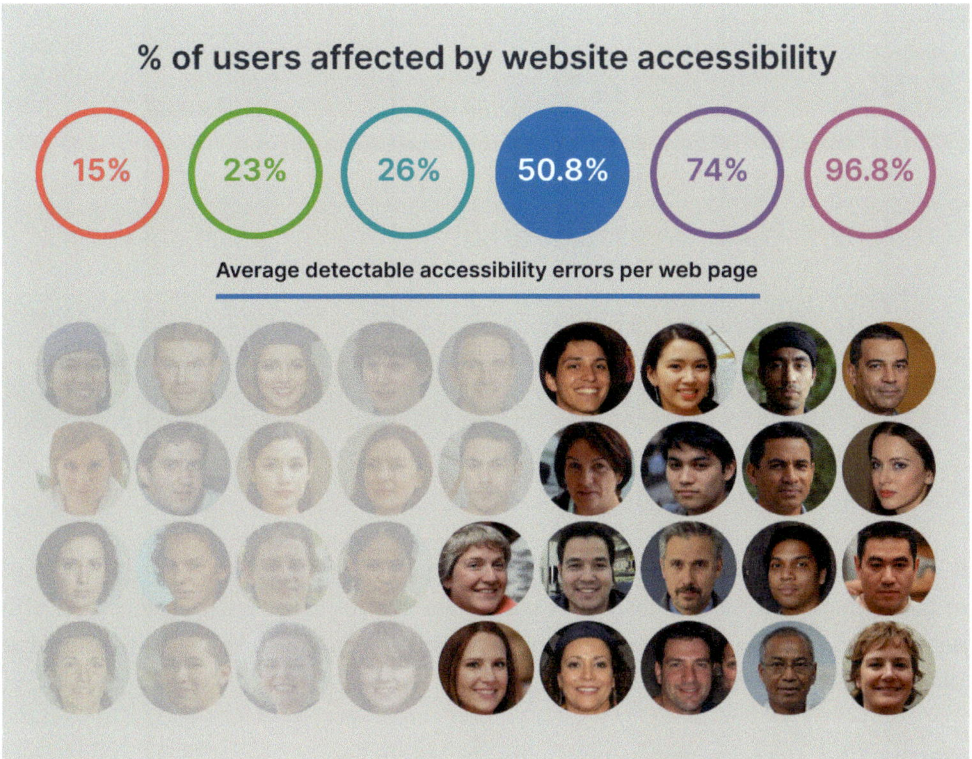

Figure 7.11
This final design departs from the card to use a progressive disclosure pattern. As users hover over the number values, text is revealed underneath to describe the statistic.

clutter in a design, by revealing menu items (like a drop down menu) or content (like our text blurbs) only when necessary.[46] In figure 7.11, you can see how the progressive disclosure pattern allows us to show the text for each percentage as large as possible, to make sure all content would be able to be seen by a variety of users. With the design basics done, we can now turn to creating a prototype to test that our idea will work!

Best Practices: Stay Calm and Iterate!

The example we describe in the text shows how important it is to use a layout tool like Figma to previsualize your design in combination with an iterative approach. While writing this chapter we actually coded the original design with the cards only to discover that it didn't work very well across small layouts. So, we went back to Figma and reworked the design using screenshots of our in-progress coded version and switched to the progressive disclosure pattern. While it took a couple of days to code the original, the updated version is cleaner, simpler to code, and easier to read. You can find both versions in the book repo.

Prompt 7.2 Explore Design Patterns

In the (above) activity, you explored design patterns as methods that could be used to solve design problems. Now turn your attention to the field (that is, published websites and their target audiences). Observe and analyze design patterns to create a mood board using patterns you found on live websites.

Module 7.3 Implementing Accessible Design

Regardless of how much you plan to make your pages accessible, it's always a good idea to incorporate accessibility testing as part of the editing and revision process. In this module you will test a coded design for accessibility issues using the HTML Validator, WAVE tool, and A11y checklist.

Exercise 7.3.1 Improve Accessibility with the WAVE Tool

1. Create a new repo from our template **github.com/criticalwebdesign/website-template** named "ethical-by-design" and then go to **github.com/codespaces,** or your preferred code editor, and open your new repository following our steps in exercise 3.2.1. Copy and paste the code from **index.html** in our **criticalwebdesign.github.io#7-3-start-code** file to the **index.html** file in your repo and enable GitHub Pages.
2. The first item in the **A11y** (short for "Accessibility") WCAG Compliance checklist[47] is to validate your HTML code. This reveals basic syntax errors and confirms that screen readers and other automated accessibility tools can parse your page correctly. Validate your live github.io page at **validator.w3.org**. You will see one error and one warning. The **error** is easy to fix: We mistakenly used the wrong closing tag with the `<h1>`. By now you should know how to fix this. The **warning** tells us that a heading is empty, meaning there is no content between the opening and closing `<h4>`. However, in this page the heading is dynamically populated by the option selected by users. Add an ellipsis to the `<h4>` element to hold space for content that will load and result in a valid page. Stage and commit your changes and validate your URL again to check your work.

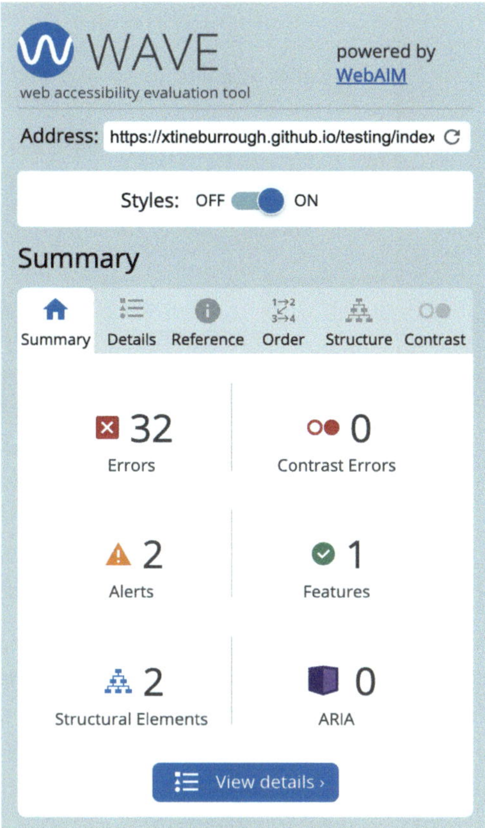

Figure 7.12
The WAVE tool summary shows errors, alerts, structural elements, and more.

3. Use the WAVE web application **wave.webaim.org** to evaluate your live github.io page. Our WAVE Details show multiple errors, alerts, features, and structural elements (figure 7.12). Note, when you are completing this exercise, browsers and/or standards may have changed. You may see more or fewer errors and alerts than what we found at the time of writing.
4. Press the **View Details** button and open the code drawer at the bottom of the page. You can see that the error messages for alternate information occur on the portraits (figure 7.13). If you were inserting one image on a web page, you would surely remember to include the `alt` attribute with a description. Since we are dynamically writing these images to the page using JavaScript, it will be simple to provide the alternate text in one location. You will adjust the JS code to fix this WAVE error in the next step.

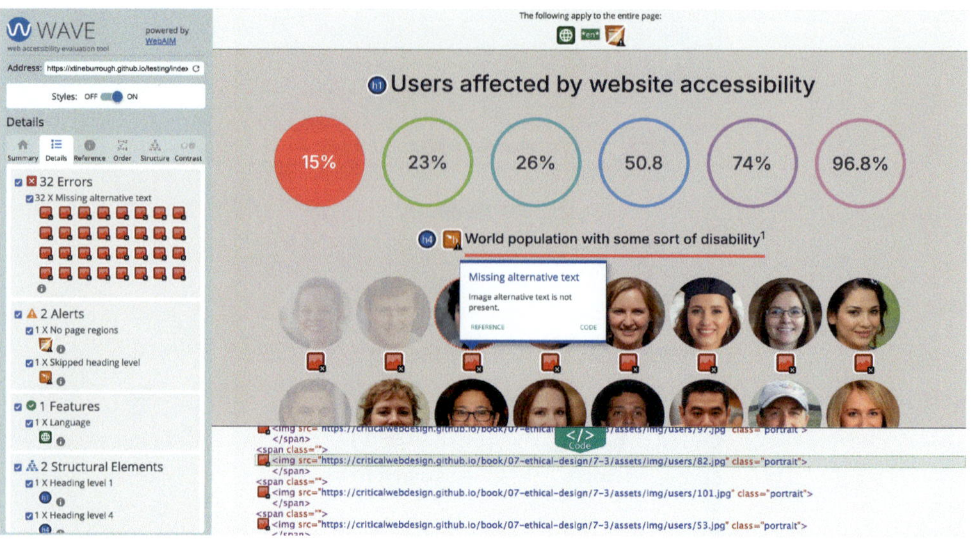

Figure 7.13
The errors are all cases of missing alternative text for the portrait images.

5. In the `<script>` element of **index.html** find the `getUserPortraitString()` function and look for the line that concatenates each `<img>` tag to the `str` variable. Note that we used image files named **0.jpg**, **1.jpg**, **2.jpg**, and so on, to make it easy to randomly select them. Add the below `alt` attribute. This makes the alternate text distinct for each image by appending the counter variable at the end of the text. Preview, stage, commit, and sync changes to republish your page, then refresh the WAVE tool to confirm that there are no more errors on the page.

```
str += `<img src="https://criticalwebdesign.github
.io/book/07-ethical-by-design/7-3/assets/img/users
/${userArr[currentUser]}.jpg" class="portrait" alt="portrait
of a person who does not exist ${currentUser}">`;
```

⚠ Watch Out! Refresh After Delay

Don't forget there is a short time lapse between staging and committing your work and seeing the published results on your live web page. Press the browser **Refresh** button until you actually see the changes in your code appear on your live page, and then you can revalidate your page.

6. Moving on to the Alerts, we were prompted to keep the heading levels ordered. Like the **aiga.org** site, this page skips headings, jumping from `<h1>` for the page title to `<h4>` for the blurb. Since we are not using the `<h2>` tag elsewhere on the page, you can simply change the `<h4>` to `<h2>` so the headings maintain hierarchical continuity. Republish and check WAVE again to confirm this removes the alert.

```
<div class="container-xl text-center">
  <h2 class="blurb"></h2>
  <div class="users grid-container container-xl"></div>
```

7. You may see another alert in WAVE. The improvements are evident if you click on the WAVE Structure tab, which shows the `<h1>` and `<h2>` elements but is missing information to make other common areas of the page structure accessible. We could add an **ARIA label** attribute such as `role="Navigation"` to label the page navigation, but, as we discuss in the callout, using semantic HTML elements is preferable and creates a better experience for users. Instead of using `<div>` tags, we should have used tags intended for the structural role they play on the page and content they contain. Replace the opening and closing generic `<div>` tags just below `<body>` using (in order) `<header>`, `<nav>`, `<section>`, and `<footer>` semantic HTML tags. Don't forget the closing tag for each element. Your code should look approximately like the following:

```
<header class="container-xl text-center">
  <h1>Users affected by website accessibility</h1>
</header>
<nav class="container-xl text-center">
  . . .
</nav>
<section class="container-xl text-center">
  <h2 class="blurb"></h2>
  <div class="users grid-container container-xl"></div>
</section>
  <footer class="container-xl text-center">
  . . .
</footer>
```

8. After replacing the generic divs with correct tags, run WAVE again to ensure that all the issues it found are resolved. WAVE should display a positive report with many features and a notice about structural elements that help users navigate the page

structure with assistive technology. In the next exercise we will dive a bit deeper to make the page easily used with a keyboard. You can confirm the changes by checking WAVE using the finished coded version for this chapter at **criticalwebdesign.github.io#7-3**.

Exercise 7.3.2 Use the Accessibility Checklist

The A11Y Project encourages the development of "beautiful, accessible, and inclusive digital experiences."[48] We have already greatly improved the accessibility of our page, but there is still more to consider using their WCAG Compliance checklist, **a11yproject.com/checklist**, to ensure it can be appreciated by as many users as possible. We'll start with the checklist's Keyboard section, then revise the code to meet accessibility standards in the Controls section of the document.

While the components used to create desktop software interfaces offer keyboard functionality universally via the tab key, keyboard navigation in web pages only works by default on interactive elements like links and form elements—any additional custom interactive items (like our data circles) must be intentionally enabled. By using the `tabindex` attribute, developers can make it possible for users to tab through custom interactive elements using a keyboard, switching the focus to select each item that offers controls. The `tabindex` attribute should be set to either `0`, to make an element focusable by the keyboard, or `-1` to be only focusable by JavaScript.[49] See the wiki for a video demonstration of this exercise

1. First, to make a web page with custom navigation elements navigable by a keyboard, implement the `tabindex` attribute on those elements. This simply enables use of the tab key to focus on each menu option in the navigation. In your code editor, use **Edit** > **Find** (Command +F) to search the page for "option" to find the six nested `<div>` elements in the navigation that contain the `option` class and add the attribute `tabindex="0"` to each like the example below. Preview your page and use the Tab key to jump to each element. You should see a thin blue line surrounding each one.

```
<div class="option rose" data-percentage="15" tabindex="0">15%
</div>
```

Best Practices: Custom Data Attributes

In the code you will see each option contains an attribute named `data-percentage`. This is a **custom data attribute** that allows us to store a value in an HTML element that can be accessed with JavaScript using the **dataset property**.[50]

2. Now that you can tab through the elements (which you can confirm by the blue circle around each option), we need to use JavaScript to update the portraits when the element is selected. Add a `forEach()` loop to the bottom of the `<script>` tag with a `focus` listener to provide visual feedback as follows. This sets the correct option active and updates the number of users to display.

```
options.forEach(function (element, index) {
  element.addEventListener("focus", () => {
    setActive(index);
    displayUsers(userCount, index);
  });
});
```

3. Now that the focus events are recognized, it's time to provide better visual feedback. Add the following to the `<style>` tag in **index.html**. This will make the user's cursor change to a "finger" when they hover these custom interactive elements.

```
.option:hover {
  cursor: pointer;
}
```

4. There is one more thing that we share here as optional, but it is an improvement nonetheless. The blue outline of the focus ring conflicts with the colors in our design (causing confusion) and, in our opinion, is not needed because we make it obvious when an element has focus using CSS. The following additions to the end of the `<style>` tag hides the blue outline and slightly increases the scale of the active navigation item to provide feedback about which item is focused.

```
.active {
  transform: scale(1.1);
}
.option:hover,
.option:focus {
  box-shadow: none;
  -webkit-box-shadow: none;
  outline: none;
}
```

5. Review the A11Y checklist and note how the changes you've made thus far to allow, synchronize, and make visual the keyboard controls, in addition to the earlier adjustments to headings, images, and page structure, account for nearly all the items.

Check Your Work

This concludes the chapter exercises. We invite you to compare your work to the final outcome **criticalwebdesign.github.io#7-3** and code **criticalwebdesign.github.io#7-3-code** in the book repo. Don't forget to turn on GitHub Pages in your project and then stage and commit your work to make it live!

Prompt 7.3 Publish: Fix Accessibility Issues to Finalize Your Web Page

Use the WAVE tool and the A11Y Checklist to edit the page you evaluated in prompt 7.1.

8 Generative Design

> …remixed media may quote sounds over images, or video over text, or text over sounds. The quotes thus get mixed together. The mix produces the new creative work—the 'remix.'
>
> —Lawrence Lessig

Context

In this chapter we explore concepts and processes used across different areas of generative design and consider how these practices are essential to and hold possibilities for web development and creativity online. The term "generative design" is applied in architecture, product design, computer art, and other disciplines, yet the practice of generating outcomes algorithmically (design solutions, art, music, structures, anything!) through an iterative computational process is widespread. The outcomes and applications may be distinct, but the core components—randomness, rules, and repetition—can be observed throughout nearly all creative fields employing generative practices. That is, these systems utilize chance or randomness to vary potential output, rules or constraints introduced by the creators to guide the production, and iteration whereupon the creator repeatedly supervises and refines the procedure to improve on and select from potential experimental outcomes. Throughout this chapter, we'll return often to these concepts and their uses across architecture, video games, art, and design. We'll also touch on the use of generative techniques in AI and machine learning, and recommendation engines. In the exercises, you will use HTML, CSS, JavaScript, and SVGs to create a browser experience inspired by the history of generative art and design.

Chaos and Control

Some of the first examples of randomness in art and design can be found within the Dadaist movement, which in response to the massive death and destruction of WWI, sought to rethink the creation and purpose of art. Jean Arp was a Dadaist who was early to using chance in his creative practice, tearing paper into pieces and letting gravity and physics dictate their landing position. For example, see *Untitled (Collage with Squares Arranged according to the Law of Chance)* on the Museum of Modern Art's website.[1] We can articulate Arp's process to illustrate how randomness can be used in a creative practice:

1. The creator defines constraints or rules as parameters, using a specific number of colors of paper, cut into nearly square polygons at varying but similar sizes, dropped from a specific height, onto a larger paper of a different color.
2. Chance or randomness is employed thanks to the air temperature, potential wind speed, varying drop height, and weight, shape, and initial position of each piece, and combined to create intricate fluid dynamics (the physics of air movement). This, in turn, produces **entropy**, or the degree to which there is disorder or randomness in a system, to affect and vary outcomes.
3. Repeat this action updating the rules and entropy you may add into your system, selecting from several results to publish the one representing your intention.

While randomness was part of Arp's practice, it's likely he made some final adjustments before committing his work with glue. At least that's what we discovered was needed when we built our interactive example inspired by the rules Arp used in his system. Click anywhere on our final project page, **criticalwebdesign.github.io#8-3**, to output a new collage and you'll notice that while it's difficult to find an example without overlapping squares, each iteration of this page is a unique visualization that shows the components of the generative design process we describe above.

While it may seem that Arp's outcomes are not purely random because he probably modified them, consider that artists and designers use chance and often make adjustments later in the production of their work. For example, photography is a practice based on "the decisive moment," when the shutter is released and all the actors in the scene are captured where they happened to be located at that time. Yet, the photographer may crop or improve the image later in the lab, perhaps incorporating potential flaws or other "happy accidents" into the image, or even evolving the concept based on what was captured.

Likewise, other designers incorporate randomness to produce outcomes they might not have considered to inspire decisions in their work. In architecture, various related methods echo our breakdown of Arp's process (figure 8.1). In **computational design**, one creates instructions for a machine to follow, in order to automate much of the manual labor to create output. **Parametric design** involves defining parameters or rules

Additional Materials and Resources

Explore links and other content related to this chapter:
criticalwebdesign.github.io#wiki-08

for a machine to use to inform its own decisions when it creates outcomes. Finally in **generative design**, the machine automates the process of selecting options within constraints but then *generates* many possible outcomes showing the range of possibilities and combinations that the operator may not have imagined.[2]

Inspiration: *Web*

Jan Robert Leegte and Superposition, *Web*, 2023, **opensea.io/collection/web-2023**, is a generative cross-linked network of one thousand web pages.[3] The entire network of pages can be explored using the links on any page as a starting point. In addition to each unique generated composition, including its color palette, interface, and even favicon, each document is "on the chain," making the code for the generated network accessible from any single blockchain record.

Figure 8.1
Heydar Aliyev Centre by Zaha Hadid Architects. The studio for the late architect Zaha Hadid incorporates systems to produce outputs that are then filtered and improved by humans. The computer is not the producer of the design but is used to automate and save time in the iterative process.[4]

Pseudo-Random Numbers

There are generally two ways that precise number-crunching machines like computers create random numbers. **Pseudo-random number generators (PRNGs)** are efficient and fine for creating experiences in video games, screen saver visuals, and even website passwords. But, because they use a predefined algorithm, the numbers they produce can be predicted, and thus are not truly random. While great for creating experimental outcomes in a program, PNRGs only *appear* random. **True random number generators (TRNGs)**, on the other hand, use data from an unpredictable source, like radioactive decay or atmospheric noise, to generate random numbers. The entropy makes TRNGs much more secure for cryptographic and high-security applications because attackers cannot reverse-engineer the method used to produce the password or security token.[5]

Artificial Intelligence and Generative Design

Artificial Intelligence (AI) presumes that machines, rather than humans or other animals, are responsible for perceiving and synthesizing information. However, tasking nonhuman actors with creating and acting on new knowledge presents significant ethical dilemmas regarding potential biases, safety, and accountability.[6] These ideas were articulated in literature, such as Mary Shelley's classic science fiction novel *Frankenstein* (1818), long before the popular rise of technologies such as ChatGPT, Dall-E, or even earlier natural language processing works such as Joseph Weizenbaum's Eliza (1964–1966).

More recently, in Amy Alexander's 2023 *Deep Hysteria*,[7] a text-to-image AI creates artificial portraits of distressed women (figure 8.2). Alexander's portraits create a dialog between two myths: the gendered myth around the medical diagnoses of "hysteria" repeatedly used to control and contain women; and the myth of urgency, accuracy, and neutrality in artificial intelligence, most notably the forms of AI we are experiencing in the twenty-first century. Artificial intelligence learns or is "trained," either through machine learning or deep learning (employing neural networks), to model and improve upon the human mind's ability to comprehend and make predictions from large sets of data. In conversation with historical renderings of female patients diagnosed with hysteria, Alexander created this AI rendering of "distressed women" using Stable Diffusion to illustrate reflective texts that accompany her project.

The motivations to advance AI show how humans consistently develop technologies to extend and automate the capacities of their bodies. Reducing labor through automation has the potential to increase productivity while making life easier for humankind. The wheel allows a person to move more objects and weight than they can carry. The assembly line is the continuation of the wheel, accelerating the production of individual workers through repeated tasks, without requiring the owner to hire an entire factory of skilled workers.

Figure 8.2
Amy Alexander's *Deep Hysteria* (2023) reveals gender bias in artificial intelligence by laying bare how AI describes, and therefore understands or "sees," a series of neutral facial expressions.

Likewise, the history of AI reflects similar progress and compounded integrations to automate processes by computers. Regardless of the fervor surrounding AI at the moment, the promises are unlikely to come to pass. First, it's not as useful as declared. We've seen our students use ChaptGPT to solve isolated programming issues quickly, while others waste hours trying to output something useful. This is due to how such AI is trained by using other data on the internet, which the algorithm then attempts to synthesize into the best potential answer.[8] The linguistics expert Noam Chomsky and colleagues said that

ChatGPT "summarizes [content] by a kind of super-autocomplete," exhibiting something like "plagiarism," not intelligence.[9] If there's anything that could be said about information on the internet, there's a lot of it, but AI's ability to copy/paste new iterations of what it has absorbed into a solid thesis for your midterm paper is still questionable.

Author Note: We Asked Chat GPT to Code an Interactive Albers

At the first time of writing this book, Chat GPT-4 was widely used for generating text, including snippets of web code. Other AI tools like Claude Code can read, write, and debug code in your project repository We asked each to follow this prompt: "Write code in HTML and JavaScript that transforms a Josef Albers painting into an interactive experience." You can find the results and a discussion of these experiments at this link: **criticalwebdesign.github.io#ai-albers**. While Chat GPT understood that Albers' primary contribution to art history revolved around the interaction of color, the browser experience it coded fails to deliver on the prompt. The work is interactive, and colors do change at random when a viewer clicks on a color chip, but it contains none of the aesthetic features of Albers' work like concentric geometrical shapes. The most obligatory failure in the outcome is the lack of intentional adjustment to the hue and value of the color to create a color shift effect based on surrounding colors. Like a lot of AI-produced content, it feels derivative, not intentional, thoughtful, or new. Ultimately, the interactive piece is too uninspired as to be read by a viewer as a work of art in conversation with Albers' studio practice.

Heydon Pickering, the author of *Inclusive Design Patterns*, in his Making Future Interfaces series summarized generative AI like this: "By tokenizing and building a map of all our semi-literate memes and shit posts, LLMs can—when prompted—produce language that sounds like one of us. [. . .] But no part of this process makes the computer intelligent, sentient, or inclined to 'kill all humans.' . . . And that's what generative AI is: not really living, seemingly not dead, a shimmering contortion of what we thought we think and believed we believe."[10]

It's true there is enormous potential for machine learning and AI. But will it enable humans to relax, work less, and care more? Or does it persist in enabling powerful individuals to secure extreme wealth through yet another form of automation? Even if AI can be used as a "super-autocomplete," critical web designers should remain aware of Manuel Castells' networking power inherent to the system and the network-making power used in the creation of the AI and its method for learning. As we mentioned at the start of this section, we have to account for ethical issues, including biases that are part of the structure of the systems we use.

Case Study: Lauren Lee McCarthy

LM: My name is Lauren Lee McCarthy (she/they). I am a Los Angeles-based artist examining social relationships in the midst of surveillance, automation, and algorithmic living using media that spans performance, software, internet, installation, film, and sculpture. I am also the creator of p5.js, an open-source tool that makes learning to code more accessible. One of my favorite online works is Carolyn Lazard's *A Recipe For Disaster.*[11]

Can you discuss advantages and pitfalls you've experienced while working with artificial intelligence in your generative works?

LM: I am captivated by the ways we are taught to interact with algorithms, and how this shapes the way we interact with each other. Central to my work is a critique of the simultaneous technological and social systems we're building around ourselves. What are the rules? What happens when we introduce glitches? I create performances inviting viewers to engage with technology, with AI, and with each other. In *LAUREN*, I become a human Alexa, watching over and controlling your home.[12] In *Voice In My Head* (a collaboration with Kyle McDonald), your inner monologue is replaced by AI.[13] In *Autonomous*, a self-driving algorithm directs the turns of your car as well as your interactions with the other passengers (figure 8.3). The resulting performances call into question how natural vs. synthetic each of our lives and identities actually are. Do any of us have our own point of view? In the interactions there is a reciprocal risk-taking and vulnerability, as performer and audience are both challenged to relinquish control, both implicated. Situated in everyday life, the interventions point to an urgent need to find a sense of agency—to be able to form our own opinions about the systems that govern our lives. As the performer, I am embodying machines, trying to understand that distance between the algorithm and myself, the distance between others and me. There's humor in the breakdown, and also moments of clarity. Who builds these artificial systems? What values do they embody? Who is prioritized and who is targeted as race, gender, disability, and class are programmatically encoded? Where are the boundaries around our intimate spaces? In the midst of always on networked interfaces, what does it mean to be truly present?

For readers who may not be familiar with p5.js, will you describe your role and experience in developing it.

LM: Making our own tools that embody our values can be one mode of response. p5.js is a tool that aims to make creative expression and coding accessible for artists, designers, educators, and anyone else who wishes to learn. Positioned as a free, open-source

Figure 8.3
Lauren Lee McCarthy, *Autonomous*, 2024. Photography by David Leonard.

tool since its inception, we believe that software, and the tools to learn it, should be accessible to everyone. Building upon its predecessor Processing, p5.js allows the creator to sketch with code. Just like making a mark on paper, a single line of code puts a circle on the screen, another changes its color, and a third makes it animate. It's important to understand that p5.js is more than just a code library; it is a project that emphasizes inclusivity and access within its community of users and contributors, holding these as its core values upon which the project is built.

From the beginning, we wanted p5.js to feel welcoming and inclusive. Making p5.js meant starting with deep uncertainty and many questions. It required becoming comfortable with not knowing, with making mistakes, with always being in a process of learning. Following each question until it led us to many more: How do you get started with something new when you're scared? How do we ask for help? How do we think about making a tool? Which users do we prioritize? What assumptions are we making about them? How do we organize our code? Can we value every type and size of contribution? When do we trade the performance of our tool for the legibility of the source code? How do we elevate the role of documentation? How can we teach people to use the tool? Which language are they speaking? Which words are we choosing to use? How do we make decisions with a large group of people? Can we make space for many different people to lead? How do we acknowledge the endless amount of emotional labor required? How do we support each other? p5 is ultimately about community. It is remembering you have other people you can ask to work through questions with you, helping to nurture and grow your skills. We set our own terms. p5 is everything we learn from each other when we make ourselves open.

They wanted us to think technology is a black box. Accept the terms of service. You can't know what's inside. You can't modify it. You certainly can't make your own. We didn't believe it, so we made p5.js.

Prompt 8: What You'll Make
Create a Generative Web Page

In this chapter you'll build *Generative Arp*, a generative web project inspired by the Dada artist Jean Arp.

View the results of *Generative Arp* at **criticalwebdesign.github.io#8-3** (figure 8.4). You can see the final code for every chapter on the CWD repo, **criticalwebdesign.github.io#repo**.

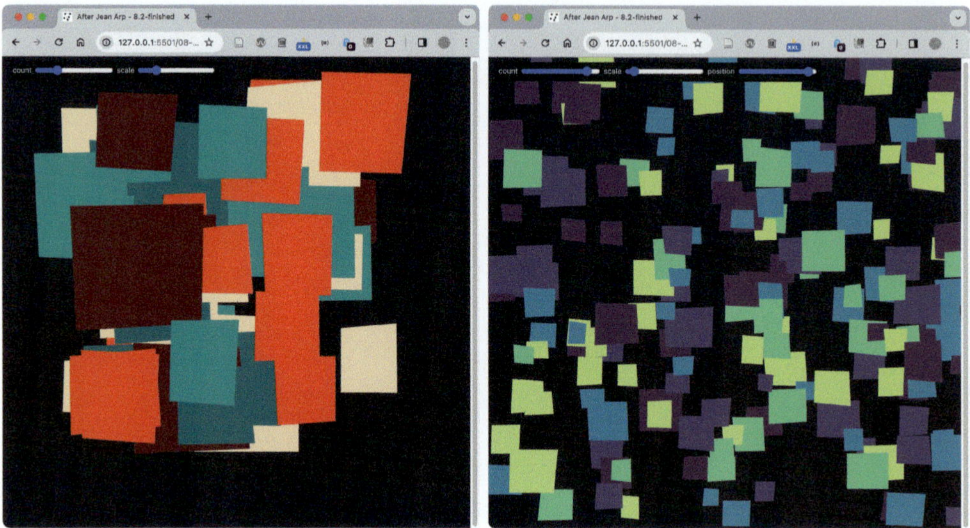

Figure 8.4
Upon completing exercises in module 8.3, your version of *Generative Arp* will include controls for the count and scale of random polygons.

Module 8.1 A Survey of Generative Practices

This module explores historical and current generative practices online, including art, gaming, and generative literature. We also provide a list of creative coding tools and platforms you should experiment with as you develop your critical web design practice.

8.1.1 Early Generative Art

While the term "generative design" may conjure twenty-first-century practices with machine learning or artificial intelligence, its art-historical legacy includes algorithmic thinking without the aid of neural networks. Conceptual themes in art-making during the middle part of the twentieth century leaned into participatory, social, interactive, and other methods incorporating chance. In chapter 2 we referred to the art movements Fluxus and Oulipo to demonstrate how artists were interested in participation, rules, and chance or randomization guiding viewers and participants with instructions for how they might interact with or help to create a performative "happening" as a work of art. During the late 1960s and early 1970s, Sol LeWitt and Stanley Brouwn's instruction-driven art generated visual forms by passing the labor of art-making to their participants, including museum preparators, who drew on the walls, and strangers, approached on the street, who drew maps to nearby landmarks. In the same time period, Georg Nees, Frieder Nake, Vera Molnár, Sonia Landy Sheridan, and Lillian Schwartz were considered pioneers of computer art. Early computational works by these artists rendered geometric forms that morphed through iterative, algorithmic processes.

Inspiration

For Lillian Schwartz and Kenneth Knowlton's film *Pixillation HD* (1970), Schwartz developed an editing technique that synthesized computer code, black-and-white pixels, and hand-drawn colored animation to create abstracted pixel-like movement with a seemingly saturated color palette.[14] We link to a video on the wiki.

Art made with new technologies is often contested, with the commonly raised question "Is it art?" When the computer aids in the generation of visual forms, the boundaries between artistry and authorship may seem blurred. However, in a 2022 interview Mark Amerika conducted with Frieder Nake, Nake is adamant that there is "no creativity on the part of the computer. All of that is always only in the interpreting mind of the human."[15] Throughout exercises in this chapter, you will apply rules using conditionals and iterate with loops and arrays, in preparation for your own dynamically generated concept. We will make one edit to what Nake says: The creativity will take place in the interpreting mind*s* of the human*s*. That is, the creativity will take place both in your mind, as you interpret the prompts throughout this chapter, and in the minds of viewers who respond to your critical web design projects.

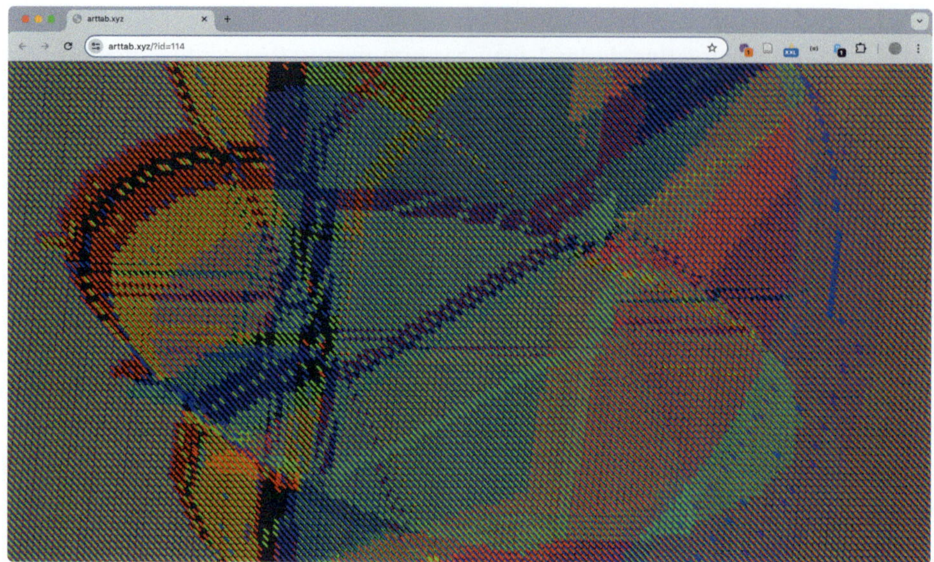

Figure 8.5
Casey Reas created 923 EMPTY ROOMS #874 using p5.js, see **arttab.xyz/?id=114**.

8.1.2 Generative Design

The processes you will use are evident across the fields of art and design. For example, **generative design** is a related cultural trend that, similar to data-driven websites, uses coded rules and algorithms to create (and recreate) concepts and forms for architecture, objects, behaviors, animations, games, and much more. These processes can create new iterations, using varying degrees of input from the creator, to ideate or solve specific design or aesthetic problems. For instance, 923 EMPTY ROOMS #874 by Casey Reas[16] reconfigures itself into new compositions, never stopping in its explorative patternmaking. Using the p5.js framework, the page repeats and continues at a steady rate, transitioning pixels into new colors and patterns using rotating primitive shapes hidden below (figure 8.5). This work and hundreds of others can be viewed using the ArtTab browser extension (**arttab.xyz**). Once installed, ArtTab replaces your "new tab" page with a digital artwork from its curated catalog to provide users a superb distraction that highlights the exquisite visual surplus of the specious NFT bubble.

8.1.3 Electronic Literature

In 1997, Janet H. Murray's *Hamlet on the Holodeck: The Future of Narrative in Cyberspace* paved the way for artists, writers, poets, and digital-literature enthusiasts to reimagine storytelling as a procedural process. She inspired those who create works at the borders of writing and digital art (writ large) to tell computationally informed stories. This work is sometimes referred to as generative literature, computational poetry, or more broadly as electronic literature. Generative literature combines storytelling with algorithmic processes and has affiliations with other art movements that take up chance, instruction, and the role of the artist as the one who sets parameters such as Fluxus, Oulipo, and automatic writing processes common to the surrealists (see chapter 6). A pioneering work demonstrating these connections is Nanette Wylde's *Storyland*. Wylde describes the project as "a randomly created narrative which plays with social stereotypes and elements of popular culture."[17] This work was developed in 2002, revised for a second version in 2004 with the now outdated application and web format Flash, and recently preserved for viewers with Ruffle (a Flash Player emulator written in Rust)[18] by the Electronic Literature Lab in 2023. It is archived in Volume 1 of the Electronic Literature Archive.[19]

Author Note: Flash

Macromedia's Flash was a software tool that combined an animation timeline, a highly intuitive vector drawing and tweening tool, and a code editor that allowed creators to attach scripts to keyframes, objects, or events. Flash files could be exported in SWF (small web format) and then embedded in HTML. Flash was widespread, inspiring international conferences and artists, designers, and game developers across the web. Adobe, who purchased Macromedia, due to performance, accessibility, and security issues on mobile devices, rebranded and reimagined Flash as Adobe Animate. However, you can appreciate the impact of Flash on generative design. See the chapter 8 wiki for examples.

As the description of the versioning and preservation of *Storyland* highlights, generative artworks, literature or otherwise, may not withstand the test of computational updates over time! Artists and designers should take into account if and how their work should be preserved. Organizations like the Electronic Literature Organization and the collections and volumes they publish, as well as Dene Grigar's Electronic Literature Lab at Washington State University, sustain the living history of these projects. A contemporary project in this genre can be seen in the computational poet Allison Parrish's 2021 *The Nonsense Laboratory* (figure 8.6). Parrish writes, "What does spelling sound like? The Nonsense Laboratory uses machine learning to let you poke at, mangle, curate, compress and elaborate the sounds of words spelled in text."[20] To create this experimental, playful, and poetic interface, Parrish developed Pincelate, a machine learning model that integrates with a Python module.[21]

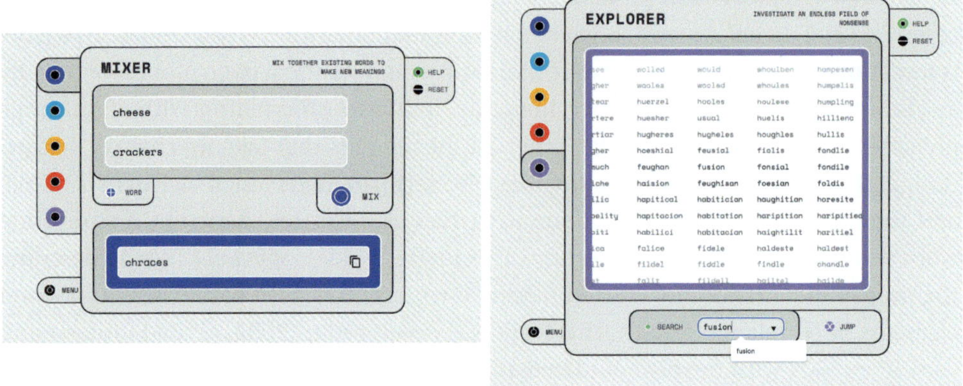

Figure 8.6
Allison Parrish, *The Nonsense Laboratory*, 2021, **experiments.withgoogle.com/nonsense-laboratory.**

8.1.4 Games

Video games and related media rely on random numbers to make the experiences they create feel new, wondrous, and unique for each player every time they launch or replay their favorite games. The unexpected behaviors of an NPC (non-player character), the next puzzle piece that emerges in a Tetris game, or the (mostly) random items you receive during a Mario Kart race are all chosen using random number generators, "under the hood."

Most games use some form of **procedural generation** to create the underlying data that can be used to visualize maps, landscapes, trees, and even characters in games. Playable experiences that use this method execute a human-generated algorithm in combination with PRNGs, to create content that would require massive amounts of work for artists and level designers. Game developers usually output the graphics, three-dimensional forms, and other content while the game is in production, for the level designers to use and build on top of, but some games generate new content when the game code is running, resulting in completely new content each time the game is run. The Game *No Man's Sky* (figure 8.7) used procedural generation to create each planet, creature, ship, ecosystem, everything in its open world universe using algorithms from the game itself. Overall, the game contains eighteen quintillion planets, and most of the worlds have never been seen by humans.[22]

While games use PRNGs throughout to customize the experiences for players, there are a few methods that can make them remarkably varied and unpredictable. For example, some games include **generative systems** whereby the economies, exchanges, and

Figure 8.7
Four screenshots from *No Man's Sky* (2016), which used procedural generation to create over eighteen quintillion planets, each with their own ecosystem and unique flora, fauna, and alien species.

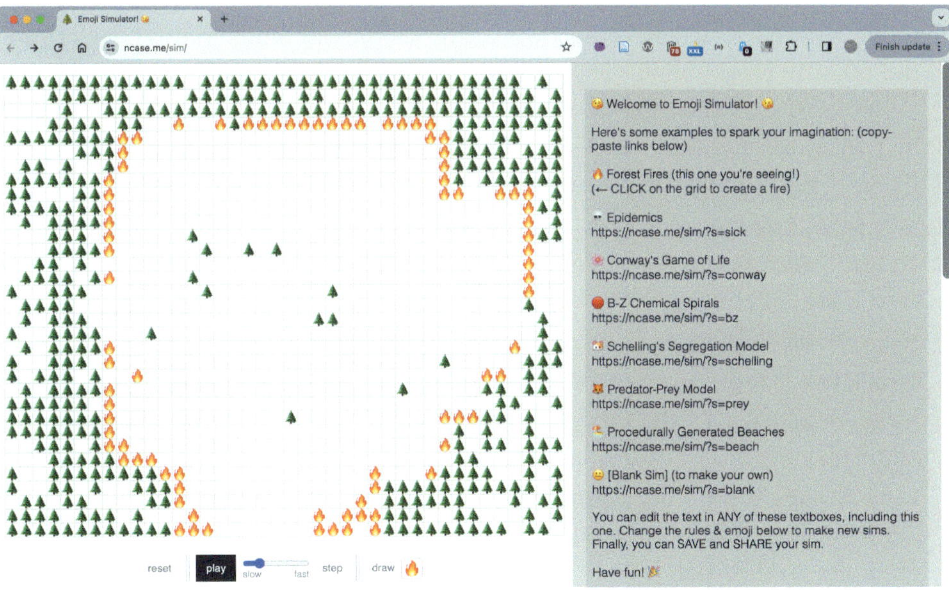

Figure 8.8
Nicky Case, *Emoji Simulator* (n.d.) **ncase.me/sim**, creates generative emoji "worlds" using Conway's *Game of Life* and other systems.

even lives of automated actors in the games use rules and randomness to function independent of player input. One such example is *Conway's Game of Life* (1970)[23], a **cellular automaton** that simulates the birth, life, and death of cells, using only simple rules around the proximity of live cells (dark) to dead cells (light), a two-dimensional grid, and an initial pattern or seed for the system (figure 8.8). Generative systems like this, or *Boids* (1986), a program that simulates the flocking behavior of birds to study the emergence of new behaviors, are used in games to mimic and simulate life, since they effectively work and generate new forms without requiring input from users.

8.1.5 Creative Coding Tools

In this book we prioritize foundational concepts in HTML, CSS, and JS that you can later apply to any project, regardless of what additional tool is trending. Still, we want to share a sample of the many powerful JavaScript libraries and frameworks[24] for creating generative design and art online. Many of these libraries were created by artists or designers, some of whom are featured in the book. We hope you experiment with these tools and continue to seek out others that will advance your critical and creative coding experiences.

1. p5.js **p5js.org** (created by Lauren McCarthy, see the case study in this chapter), and the popular programming environment Processing, **processing.org** (Ben Fry and Casey Reas) on which the JavaScript version is based, have been instrumental in helping artists and designers learn programming concepts to create games, interactive experiences, and data visualizations.
2. SVG.js **svgjs.dev** (Wout Fierens) lets you dig deeper into SVG gradients, bezier curves, and animations. Its powerful functions make manipulating SVG files accessible and enjoyable. Search for "SVG" on Codepen to see what other designers are doing with this versatile format.
3. Two.js **two.js.org** (Jonathan "Jono" Brandel) is a two-dimensional drawing library for the web that also lets you output graphics to the page using SVG, HTML Canvas, and WebGL.
4. Paper.js **paperjs.org** (Jürg Lehni and Jonathan Puckey) is a vector graphics scripting framework that uses the HTML Canvas. As with others, check out the inspiring examples on their site.
5. Three.js **threejs.org** (Ricardo Cabello) is a 3D graphics library for the web using JS and WebGL. This framework, and Cabello's ("mrdoob") personal work, is rooted in the early generative visualizations of the DemoScene (see wiki) and Flash.

6. D3.js **d3js.org** (Mike Bostock) is a multifaceted visualization library popular among interactive journalists for telling stories with data.
7. Twine **twinery.org** (Chris Klimas) is a tool for telling interactive, nonlinear stories using HTML, CSS, and JavaScript. Twine has a huge user base, especially for creating game-like narrative experiences. See **itch.io/games/made-with-twine**
8. The honorable mention goes to some of the popular UI frameworks we discussed in the introduction. "Reactive" tools like React, Angular, Vue, and Svelte can greatly simplify keeping your page content updated (*in reaction to*) changes to data in your code. While we considered incorporating them in the exercises (see our experiment with the Svelte UI Framework here **criticalwebdesign.github.io#string-art-generator**), their setup, complexity, and special syntax can add a lot of overhead, making them only helpful for creating large websites (see discussion in 0.2.3).

Prompt 8.1 Learn a New Tool

The components of the Generative Arp project you will make in modules 8.2 and 8.3 can be used in any of the frameworks we mention above. And while we think they are great, and encourage you to experiment with them, keep in mind that you should not be dependent upon any specific tool. Instead, we encourage you to let the idea dictate the methods you choose.

Module 8.2 Generative Arp Visualization

This module reviews several foundational ideas in JavaScript programming while showing how to build a basic generative page. Our Generative Arp translates Jean Arp's *Squares Arranged According to the Laws of Chance* into an interactive project. Since the design is dictated by Arp's paper collage, we will start with pseudocode. This section is organized by the primary components of the lamp program we illustrated in chapter 5 (5.2.1).

8.2.1 Start by Writing Pseudocode

The first idea we will revisit is the concept of pseudocode in which you break down what your program will do in steps expressed in human language. Writing (and updating as necessary) your intentions like we do below, helps you plan ahead, keeps your code modular and organized, and lets you think of writing code as simply a list of (repeatable) instructions. The steps to make our Generative Arp program are organized into specific tasks that clarify functionality and scope in the program. While we use English, most of the concepts and their JavaScript language equivalents should be familiar.

```
Create global variables
Store a reference to the main HTML element
Create generate() function
  Reset variables, remove previous elements from the page
  Repeat the following for a random number of boxes
    Generate a random size, position, and color
  Insert the boxes into the page as HTML
Add listener to call generate() on page load or when user clicks
Create helper functions
  Return a random number between min and max
  Return a random color
```

As you can see, our code is often nonlinear. While there are global variables that can be accessed from anywhere, all other code is stored in reusable functions to call from user events. The `generate()` function contains a looping structure that repeats instructions as many times as needed.

Exercise 8.2.1 Organize and Retain Modularity in Your Code

In this exercise you will set up your project, adding your pseudocode inside comments to outline and organize the main functions of your program.

1. Create a new repo from our template **github.com/criticalwebdesign/website-template** named "generative-arp" and then go to **github.com/codespaces,** or your preferred code editor, and open your new repository following our steps in exercise 3.2.1.
2. Open **index.html** change the title to "Generative Arp," and replace all of the code inside the body of the page, except the script tag, with a `<main>` element. You can add placeholder text, since you'll be populating the element with JavaScript.

   ```
   <main> this text will change with JS </main>
   ```

3. In **assets/js/main.js** add comments to reflect the main elements of the program we describe in the above pseudocode.

   ```
   // global
   // generate
   // listeners
   // helpers
   ```

4. Add the following code beneath their respective comments. This process, outlining your project with pseudocode then matching it with functions, helps to plan, organize, and retain modularity. The code creates a `generate()` function and adds

two listeners to call the function when the page loads or a user clicks the page. Since you only want the statements in the function to run when the events happen, you don't add the parentheses to the end of the function name in the listeners. If you did, it would execute the function only once, immediately when the page loads.

```
// global
// generate
function generate() {}
// listeners
window.addEventListener("load", generate);
document.addEventListener("click", generate);
// helpers
```

5. Update the `generate()` function now to log a new random number. Preview your page and click anywhere in the browser while watching the JavaScript Console. Notice how the page updates on each refresh with a random number between 0 and 1. This is a common input for a generative work such as this, which we'll use in different ways to modify the output.

```
function generate() {
  console.log(Math.random());
}
```

8.2.2 Variables and Functions

In the diagram for a program that changes the on/off status of a lamp in 5.2.1, we discussed keeping track of state. That is, storing information in memory that you can use to make or influence decisions. We've explained and used variables, which let you store single values, as well as arrays, which can store multiple values, accessible by their index. In the next exercise, you will create a variable that stores a random integer.

Exercise 8.2.2 Store and Modify Random Numbers

Below, modify the random numbers using a function and display it on the page. See the wiki for a video demonstration of this exercise.

1. Add this code to the global section of **main.js**. It will run first, storing a reference to the `<main>` HTML element on the page, which will display the visualization.

```
// global
let viz = document.querySelector("main");
```

2. Now write a helper function to modify the random numbers used throughout the project. JavaScript's `Math.random()` generates a number between 0 (inclusive) and 1 (exclusive).[25] Start by writing the function definition and return the value from `Math.random()`.

```
// helpers
function randomInt() {
  return Math.random();
}
```

3. Use the data returned from `randomInt()` inside `generate()`. Replace or comment out the `console.log()` added previously and add the following to insert the data on the page. Preview your work to see the random number in the top left corner of the page.

```
function generate() {
  viz.innerHTML = randomInt();
}
```

4. The `randomInt()` function needs to create numbers you can use for different items, like each box's position (0–1000), size (100–120), and color (0–255). You can make the function return a number within a specific range using parameters to accept minimum and maximum values. Update the `randomInt()` function to match the code below. The `min` and `max` parameters have default values to prevent errors in the case of missing or undefined values. The math inside the function can be understood by inserting potential values into the formula using the JavaScript Console in DevTools. For example, if `min=1` and `max=100` and the value returned from `Math.random()` is `0.2`, then `Math.floor()` will receive the expression `(0.2 * (100-1 + 1))` or `20.2`. Then, by definition, `Math.floor()` rounds that value down to the nearest whole number, which is `20`. Finally, the value returned adds the min, or `1`. So the result, in our test case, would be `21`. See MDN[26] for a complete description of this JS function.

```
function randomInt(min=1, max=100) {
  return Math.floor(Math.random() * (max - min + 1)) + min;
}
```

Pro Tip: Functional Programming

The `randomInt()` function in exercise 8.2.2 is an example of a **pure function.**[27] That is, it always returns the same output given the same input and produces no **side effects.** Since pure functions are written to perform a single task, all information is encapsulated in the data you give them, and they are easier to test and reuse. With time, you'll see that functions work best as small, single-purpose expressions. You can see we have started to do this by linking to a single JS file called (appropriately) "functions.js" in the main **assets/** folder of the repository in our examples.[28] Pure functions are one feature of a programming paradigm called **functional programming** used by professional JavaScript coders to write code that is easier to understand and more bug resistant.[29]

8.2.3 Loops and Conditions

A loop is any event that is repeated. For example, the design thinking process (chapter 5) improves projects through iteration, repeating attempts at new layouts by changing, experimenting, and incorporating perspectives. Each day, the earth's rotation reveals and then turns away from the sun. This event will be repeated, for as long as it can, with variations in the length of the day or tilt of the earth's axis.

References to loops are abundant across film and literature. Loops, while implying sameness, often include variation. Popular books and movies use loops as a narrative structure to organize possibilities in stories, such as the many versions of a day in *Groundhog Day* (1993) or *Palm Springs* (2020), absurdist parallel universes in *Everything Everywhere All At Once* (2022), and the game-like structure of *Run Lola Run* (1998), to name just a few examples. Matt Haig's *The Midnight Library* (2020), Margarita Montimore's *Oona Out of Order* (2020), and the classic novel *The Time Traveler's Wife* (2015) are examples from literature in which stories span time as the protagonists iterate on possible experiences and outcomes.

A functionality known as *infinite scroll*, when web pages add new content as users scroll to the end of the page, is one of the most visual ways that looping structures can be found online. While infinite scroll has its disadvantages, like contributing to social media addiction, artists and designers use such looping structures for critical and humorous ends. For example, the website **endless.horse** by Colleen Josephson and Kyle Miller (figure 8.9) shows an ASCII art horse whose legs never stop growing regardless of how much users attempt to scroll to the bottom of the page.

Generative design would not be possible without the computational process of iterating over some instruction—generating new parts of an object (text, color, shape, size, and so on)—until a condition is met. While we are sure you can relate to the concept of the loop in your everyday life, from a computational perspective, a loop is a set of instructions repeated until a condition is met.

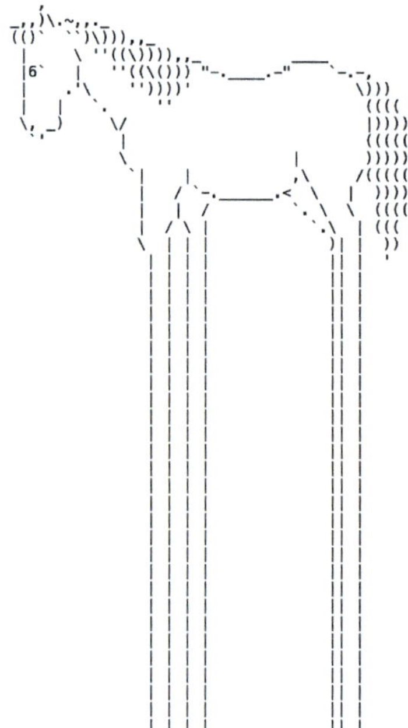

Figure 8.9

Colleen Josephson and Kyle Miller, **endless.horse** (2015), created during the Stupid Shit No One Needs & Terrible Ideas Hackathon (**stupidhackathon.com**), depicts an ASCII art horse with legs that automatically extend as users scroll.

Exercise 8.2.3 Generate Boxes Using Loops and Helper Functions

Author Note: Boxes

We are using the word "boxes" in this exercise as a casual reference to a box-like, four-sided shape produced on the web page. In module 3 you will define these "boxes" as polygon elements in SVG.

1. Update the **generate()** function to match the following code. It creates a random number, then loops that number of times to create a new **<div>** for each box, updating the **<main>** element using a variable called **output**. Preview your work to see the word "box" with a random number between 6 and 12, actually producing that number of **<div>** elements on the page every time you refresh or click (figure 8.10).

⚠ Watch Out! Template Literal

Throughout this chapter you will see blocks of code surrounded by the backtick, `, used in JavaScript to add multi-line strings in the code. Keep an eye out for them as they are small but produce a large impact.

```
function generate() {
  let output = "" ;
  let count = randomInt(6, 12);
  for (let i = 0; i < count; i++) {
    output += `<div>box ${i}</div>`;
  }
  viz.innerHTML = output;
}
```

2. Add the code below before the **for** loop in **generate()** to create a new variable describing the base size of each box. We multiplied the width of the browser window by 0.12 to make it 12% of the viewport (see callout), but you can increase or decrease this value if you like.

```
let size = window.innerWidth * .12;
for (let i = 0; i < count; i++) {
```

Pro Tip: Using Percentages

A common trick for making objects fit and adapt to different screen pixel dimensions is to use **normalization** so that all values are relative to 100%. For example, to place an object in the middle of a screen, you can multiply the width of the window by 0.5 (50% is 50/100 or 0.5):

```
50% of 1200 = 1200 * .5 = 600
25% of 20 = 20 * .25 = 5
120% of 200 = 200 * 1.2 = 240
```

3. Inside the same **for** loop, create variables for the box width (**w**) and height (**h**). We use percentages again to create a random number between 80 and 120% of the **size** variable.

```
let size = window.innerWidth * .12;
for (let i = 0; i < count; i++) {
  // parameters
  let w = randomInt(size * .8, size * 1.2);
  let h = randomInt(size * .8, size * 1.2);
```

4. For the box positions, we will first create two variables defining the center of the browser window by multiplying the width and height by 0.5. Then we define two more variables in order to control the offset from the center on each axis. This allows us to control how boxes float within the window. We'll define **x** and **y** variables by a random number between the center minus and plus the offset on both axes.

```
let w = randomInt(size * .8, size * 1.2);
let h = randomInt(size * .8, size * 1.2);
// viewport center and offset
let centerX = (window.innerWidth * .5);
let centerY = (window.innerHeight * .5);
let offsetX = (window.innerWidth * .25);
let offsetY = (window.innerHeight * .25);
let x = randomInt(centerX - offsetX, centerX + offsetX);
let y = randomInt(centerY - offsetY, centerY + offsetY);
```

5. Now you can use these values. Add a new variable called **`style`** to store the inline styles for the boxes. You can see each line contains a CSS rule to set the position, size, and other properties using a string literal. Finally, CSS transformations to HTML elements are center aligned, so we subtract 50% of the width and height of the box to ensure they won't disappear along the right or bottom edges. Your project should start to take form in various red rectangles on the page (see figure 8.10).

```
let y = randomInt(centerY - offsetY, centerY + offsetY);
let style = `
  position: absolute;
  transform: translate(${x}px, ${y}px);
  width: ${w - (w * 5)}px;
  height: ${h - (h * 5)}px;
  background-color: red;
`;
output += `<div style="${style}"></div>`;
```

6. To randomize the colors, create a new helper function called "randomHex."

```
// helpers
function randomHex() {}
```

7. Add the code below inside this function to create two new variables: the generated hex value and a string that contains all sixteen potential characters of a hexadecimal color. Then use a **`for`** loop to add six new random characters from the list to the hex variable using our **`randomInt()`** function. Finally, **`randomHex()`** returns the value of the color so it can be used with CSS.

```
function randomHex() {
  let hex = "";
  let chars = "0123456789abcdef";
  for (let i = 0; i < 6; i++) {
    hex += chars[randomInt(0, chars.length - 1)];
  }
  return hex;
}
```

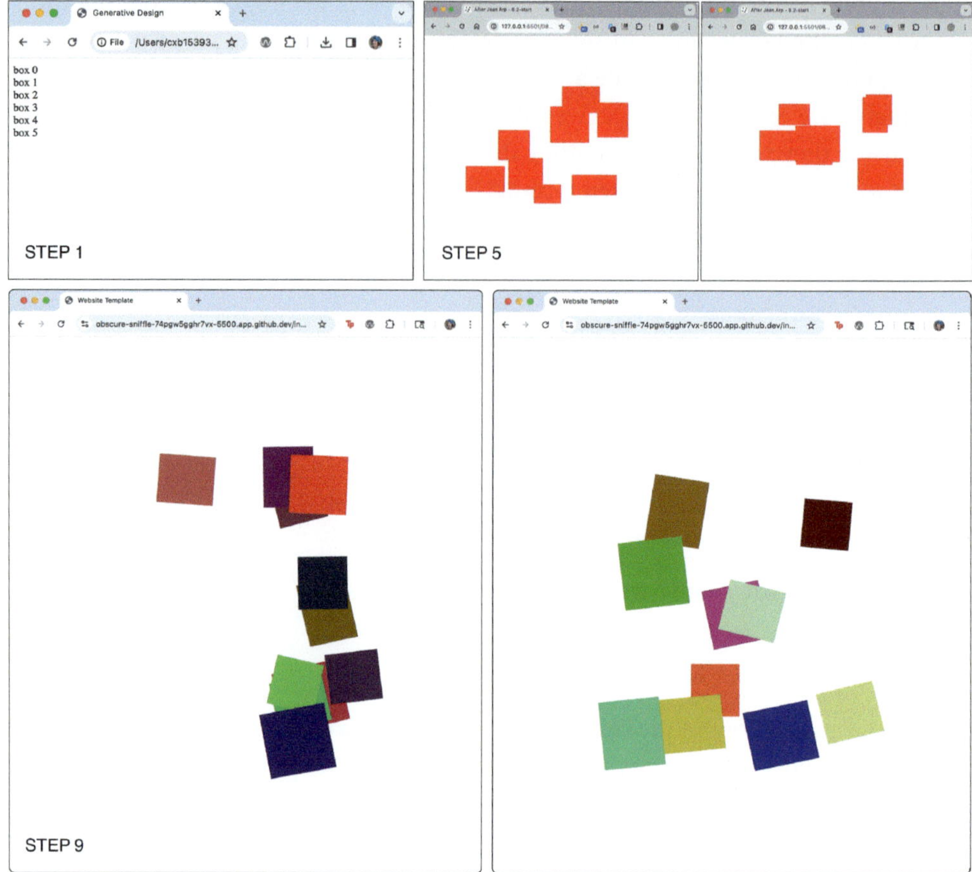

Figure 8.10

The results you should see in your browser as you work through the steps in this exercise. Top left: In Step 1 you will generate random `<div>` elements on the page. Top right: Two instances in the browser showing random red boxes generated in Step 5. Click reload to see a new random number of red boxes. Bottom: Two instances in the browser showing the final results of this exercise (Step 9). Click reload to see a random number of boxes, slightly rotated by a random degree, filled with a randomly assigned color.

Author Note: We Asked Copilot to Create randomHex()

We asked GitHub Copilot to create the `randomHex()` code for us to see if it would produce something like our version of the code. We added `function randomHex() {}` to the helpers area then prompted Copilot with the following request:

In the randomHex function write the code that would produce a random color, or hex value, I can use in my project.

Copilot returned the following line of code, which would technically work in our project by converting the number 16,777,215 to its hexadecimal (16-base) equivalent. But the function is obtuse because it does everything on one line. Our function above would be much easier, for example, if you wanted to skew the colors to be lighter, or more red, by simply changing the values that can be randomly inserted per channel. Our code is also easier to understand, because we wrote and tested it. One of the common problems with AI is that it adds someone else's code to your project without you knowing how to adapt it.

```
return Math.floor(Math.random() * 16777215).toString(16).padStart(6, "0");
```

8. Update the box `background-color` style with the `randomHex` function and include the hash symbol before it. Insert the CSS `rotate()` function in the `transform` property right after the `translate()` function and before the semicolon at the end. This adds a slight rotation to the left or right of each rectangle by one degree to make them appear as if they fell and just (randomly) plopped into that position (see figure 8.10). Check the finished module example file in the book repo if you encounter an error.

```
let style = `
  position: absolute;
  transform:
    translate(${x}px, ${y}px)
    rotate(${randomInt(-1, 1)}deg);
  width: ${w - (w * .5)}px;
  height: ${h - (h * .5)}px;
  background-color: #${randomHex()};
`;
```

This completes the basic generative project for this section. You can visit **criticalwebdesign.github.io#8-2** to see the live web page. In module 8.3, you'll adjust the parameters in code and add a web form to tweak them in real time.

Prompt 8.2 Design: Continue Experimenting

Experiment with the code that you wrote so far. You might change the values in the range for rotation, or the offset or center values, to see how this affects your project. Note that while we were able to create a basic version of Jean Arp's collage, his works often used polygonal or nonuniform shapes, an effect that is hard to replicate with the boxes of pure HTML. Sketch a design for this project using polygonal shapes. The next module will start by showing how to do this with SVG.

Module 8.3 SVGs and Color Arrays

In this module you will add more depth and interest to your version of Generative Arp using SVGs to generate polygons.

8.3.1 SVG Basics

The SVG (scalable vector graphics) image type can display lines, shapes, gradients, and even animations. As a vector graphic they can be scaled to any size without losing quality because their data is described by lines and points, making them a good solution for logos and other line art. SVGs are also unique because they are created with an XML-based markup language of the same name. You can load SVGs into a web page using the `<img>` tag or paste their code directly into the HTML code. Using the `<svg>` tag offers more options because it adds the elements of the graphic to the DOM, making it possible to update their content dynamically with JavaScript.

Activity: Export SVG with Figma

In this activity you will create an SVG file in Figma and view its source code.

1. In Figma, create a new Frame and set the dimensions to 200×200 pixels.
2. Draw some primitive geometric shapes like a rectangle or circle in the frame.
3. Select the frame and click on Export in the side panel. Choose the SVG format and export the file.
4. Open the SVG file you created in Chrome.
5. Open DevTools to see the XML code block defining the SVG file (figure 8.11). It starts with the svg tag: `<svg>`.

Exercise 8.3.1 Generate Random SVG Polygons

Update your generative project to use SVG `<polygon>` elements to match the style of the paper cutouts Jean Arp used in his collage.

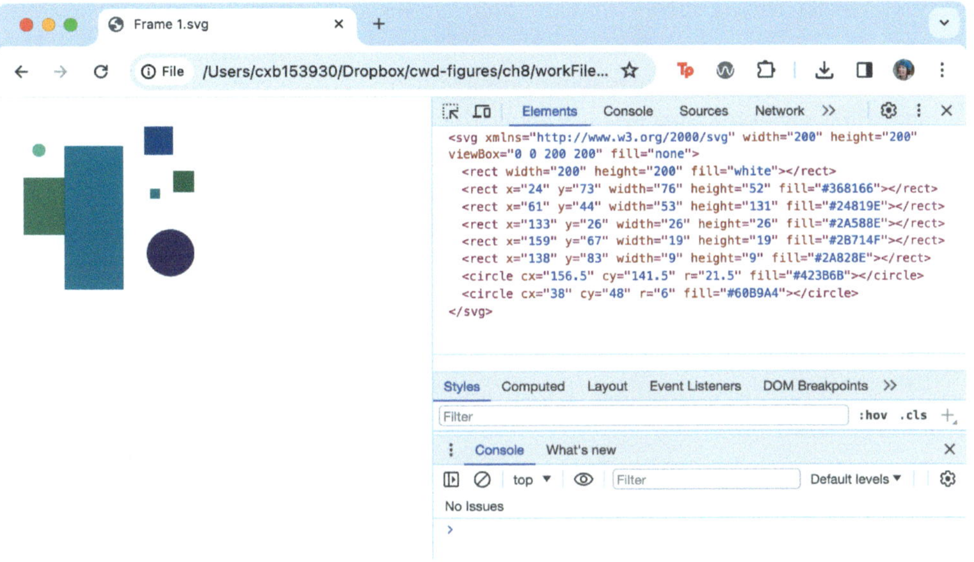

Figure 8.11
The SVG appears as an image in the Chrome browser, but a closer look at its source code shows how this image is composed of coordinates between the open and close `<svg>` tags.

1. Open your Generative Arp project in Codespaces. You can view or download our resulting code from module 8.2 from the repo and use it as a start file.[30]
2. Add a link to our stylesheet in **index.html** to remove the default margin and set the `<body>` to fill the viewport. We also changed the background color to distinguish our work in this module from module 8.2.

```
<link rel="stylesheet" href="https://criticalwebdesign.github.io
/book/08-generative-design/8-3/assets/css/arp.css">
```

3. Replace the `<main></main>` element with an SVG using this code. The `xmlns` (XML namespace) attribute tells the browser what XML dialect it uses, while the size attributes will scale the SVG to always fill the browser window.

```
<svg width="100%" height="100%" xmlns="http://www.w3.org/2000
/svg"></svg>
```

4. Now change the selector used to reference the viz element in the global variables section in **main.js**.

```
let viz = document.querySelector("svg");
```

5. SVG uses its own attributes for many of the styles you previously defined to use with the `<div>`. For example, SVG shapes use **`fill`** instead of **`background-color`**. Now we'll update the **`output`** variable to insert filled SVG polygons on each loop. First, add a new variable called **`points`** above the line where **`output`** is assigned to define a four-sided polygon in the following format: **`"x1,y1 x2,y2 x3,y3 x4,y4"`**. The placeholder numbers we define in points is a square that is 100 pixels on each side. Comment out the **`style`** variable used for the `<div>` since we will be adding attributes directly to the `<polygon>`. To do this, select the code block you want to edit and press **Command** +/ (or **Ctrl** +/ on Windows) to comment out the whole block. The resulting preview should display polygons filled with random colors on a dark background.

```
// let style = ` `
let points = `0,0 100,0 100,100 0,100`;
output += `<polygon stroke="none" points="${points}"
fill="#${randomHex()}" />`;
```

Pro Tip: Use Formatting to Debug

If you experience an error, try formatting your document. Often this will help you to see a missing character in your code. We see syntax errors made obvious by the change in color formatting in the classroom all the time! Keep the DevTools console open too, which will tell you if an issue exists and the line number causing the problem.

6. With that working, we can randomize the `<polygon>` corners to match the style of Jean Arp's cutouts. Add two new variables before **`let points`**. This will be the minimum and maximum variation for each corner position.

```
let min = .75;
let max = .9;
```

7. We'll now use the variables to generate random values that define the distance on each axis (x or y) from the center of the shape. You can translate the first point as a width and height coordinate pair that is: "a random width selected from a range defined by the min and max values as a percentage (here 75% to 90% of the width) coupled with a random height also defined by a range using these same percentages." Figure 8.12 diagrams how **`min`** and **`max`** subtly change each polygon's corner. Update the **`points`** variable to match the code below.

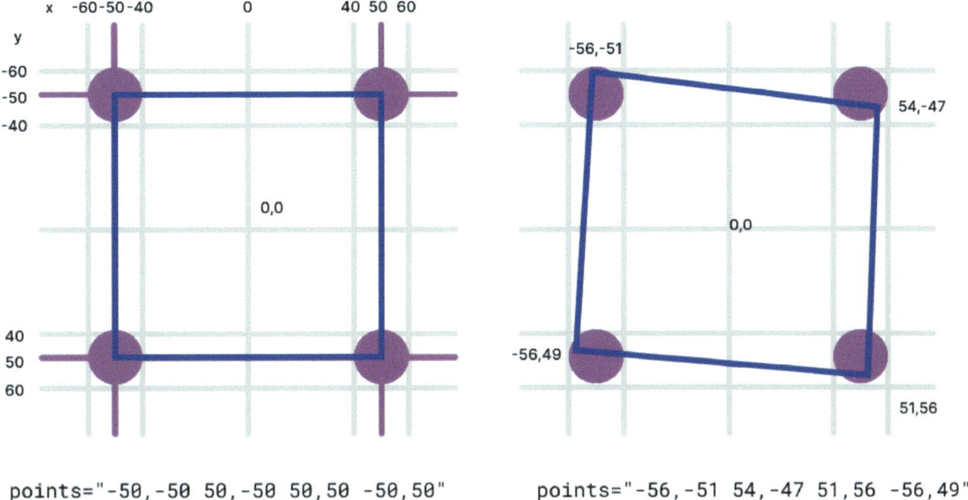

Figure 8.12
This diagram illustrates how the **<polygon>** points are selected. Each magenta circle defines the area within which the **x** or **y** values could be created.

```
let points = `
${-randomInt(w * min, w * max)}, ${-randomInt(h * min, h * max)}
${randomInt(w * min, w * max)}, ${-randomInt(h * min, h * max)}
${randomInt(w * min, w * max)}, ${randomInt(h * min, h * max)}
${-randomInt(w * min, w * max)}, ${randomInt(h * min, h * max)}
`;
```

8. Update the code that stores the **<polygon>** in the **output** variable. Note that the CSS transform rule should include both the **translate()** and **rotate()** functions with only a space between them, and no **deg** after the rotate. Your project should now display polygons filled with a random assortment of colors. Continue adjusting with the parameters and notice how your edits affect the design.

```
output += `<polygon stroke="none" points="${points}"
transform ="translate(${x},${y}) rotate(${randomInt(-1, 1)}) "
fill="#${randomHex()}" />`;
```

8.3.2 Random Values and Arrays

One difference you might notice between our generative version of Arp's work for the browser and the original is seen in the choices we are making regarding the color

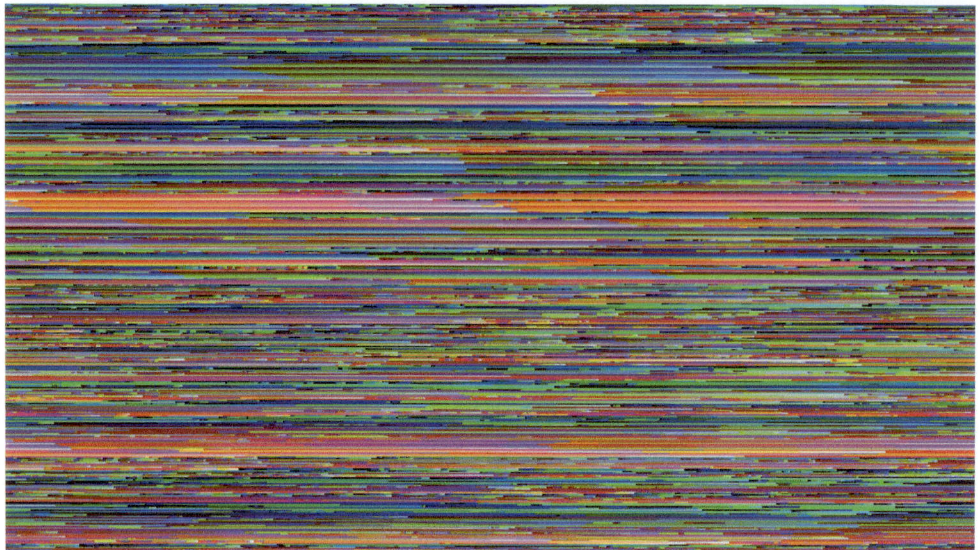

Figure 8.13
The colors in 1:1 (1999) by Lisa Jevbratt are based on rules she created using data collected via web crawlers. She assigned colors to groups of IP addresses that were accessible on the internet at the time, yet a degree of randomness exists in the outcome thanks to the many uncontrollable factors that contribute to the state of each address, such as dynamic software and databases, glitches and system errors, access to technology, and inclination to contribute to the growth by millions of people, to name a few.

palette. Color choices are motivated by many factors across artistic disciplines. For instance, Lisa Jevbratt's *1:1* (figure 8.13) transforms a color palette into a tool for data visualization. So far, the colors we have programmed for this project have been randomized. There are ways we might narrow the colors by light or dark values, or even use random values between 0 and 255 with **`rgb()`**, but we still would not have much control over the palette itself using these methods. In this section we'll demonstrate how to randomly select from a single list of colors using arrays. Recall that arrays store multiple values that can be accessed by their index (see module 5.3). In this exercise you'll populate an array of colors and use it to create boxes on the page.

Exercise 8.3.2 Select Random Values from Arrays

In this exercise you'll create an array of colors and then write a helper function to select random values from the array.

1. Open the Coolors trending palettes page **coolors.co/palettes/trending** and select a palette.

2. Find the "Export palette" menu item (at the time of writing, it's in a drop-down menu coupled with the likes count) and choose Code. Scroll until you see the code marked "array," and copy it. It should look something like this:

```
["bce784", "5dd39e", "348aa7", "525174", "513b56"]
```

   Paste the array into your **main.js** file above the `generate()` function, and add a variable declaration to the start of the brackets:

```
let colors = ["bce784", "5dd39e", "348aa7", "525174", "513b56"];
```

3. Now you can write a function to return a random value from the array of colors. Add this new helper function called `randomFromArray()`:

```
function randomFromArray(arr) {}
```

4. The "work" of this function is so common that it is usually written with many nested expressions on a single line. Add the following to your `randomFromArray()` function:

```
function randomFromArray(arr) {
  return arr[Math.floor(Math.random() * arr.length)];
}
```

   The steps of the function, starting from the innermost expression and working outward are as follows:

   a. `Math.random()` creates a random number between 0 and 1.
   b. `arr.length` is used to scale the random number relative to the length of the array.
   c. `Math.floor` rounds down to a whole number.
   d. `arr` followed by `[]` brackets gets the value from the array using the index.
   e. `return` is the keyword that inserts the result of the function to the place where it was called in the code.

5. To call the function, just pass the array you want to use in the `generate()` function's output. You can easily test different color palettes as well.

```
output += `<polygon stroke="none" points="${points}"
  transform ="translate(${x}, ${y}) rotate(${randomInt(-1, 1)}) "
  fill="#${randomFromArray(colors)} " />`;
```

8.3.3 Parametric Controls

As we described in the Context section, an important component of generative works is the ability to update parameters that control the algorithmic output. For example,

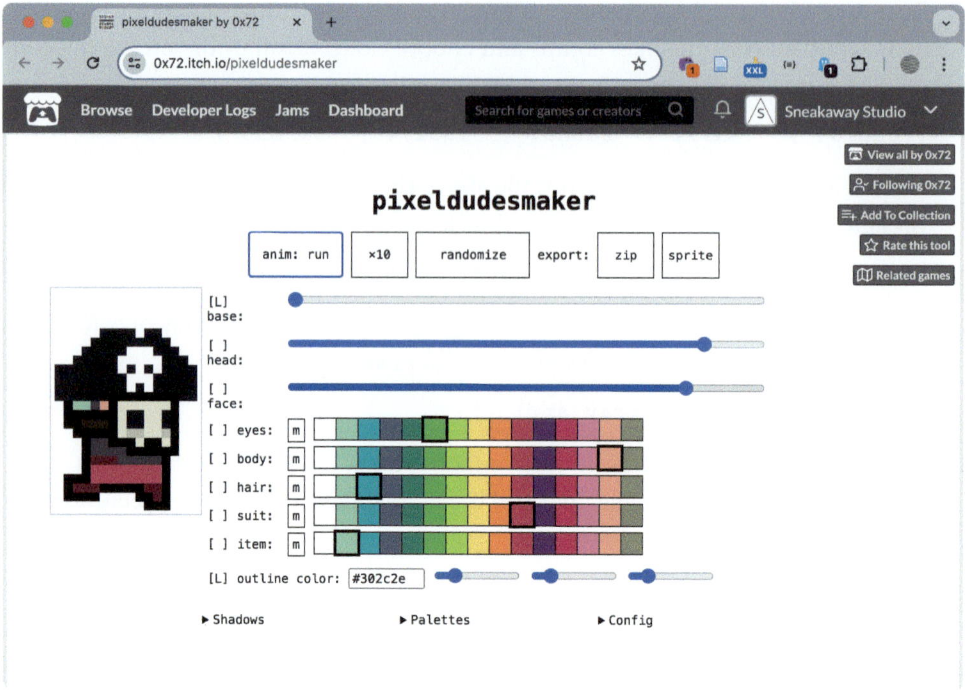

Figure 8.14
Pixeldudesmaker by 0x72 (2021), **0x72.itch.io/pixeldudesmaker** lets you modify your preferences after an initial completely random output. See other procedural generator interfaces on the chapter 8 wiki.

the *NSynth Sound Maker* by Yotam Mann, lets users create unusual new sound combinations by selecting instruments and animals from its interface.[31] The *Pixeldudesmaker* (figure 8.14) by 0x72 interface allows users to select combinations of attributes and colors that combine to create unique game character sprites of potentially millions of unique game character sprite sheets. Likewise, in this module, you'll add simple interface controls to encourage users to play and experiment with your Generative Arp project.

Exercise 8.3.3 Add Form Controls

The last part of our process involves adding controls to let users affect the outcomes. You'll add simple but operational controls using the `range` input.[32]

1. Add an HTML element for the inputs to the `<body>` above the `<svg>` element in **index.html**. Notice we are using a class called "controls" from the linked **arp.css** file.

```
<section class="controls"></section>
```

2. Add the input using the **range** type. It has an ID of **count** to match the **for** attribute assigned by its **label**, a **min**, **max**, and **value** that all correspond to any range and starting value you like, and a **step** attribute that controls the distance increments the slider can be dragged. If you test your work now, you can play with the slider in the lower left corner of the page, though the control hasn't yet been connected to the program that controls the visualization.

```
<section class="controls">
  <label for="count">count</label>
  <input type="range" id="count" min="1" max="200" value="8"
  step="1">
</section>
```

3. Add this code to the global section of **main.js**. It selects the input using its ID and adds a listener, handled by the **generate()** function.

```
let countEle = document.querySelector("#count");
countEle.addEventListener("input", generate);
```

4. Update the variable declaration inside the **generate()** function to match the code below.

```
let count = countEle.valueAsNumber || randomInt(6, 12);
```

You can see it adds a reference to the value of the **countEle** input, along with two || pipes, before the original **randomInt()** function call. We use **valueAsNumber** to ensure that the data type from the input will be a number.[33] The logical operator || (pipes) causes a short-circuit evaluation (see callout) to use the input value as long as it is acceptable, but defaults to the other method if there is an issue. You can read or translate the pipes to the word "or" as you read the code from left to right. Now that your **generate()** function is using data from the input, you can test your work.

Pro Tip: Short-Circuit Evaluation

Coders are lazy, or so it has been said, because they are always looking for tricks to make their work easier. With **short-circuit evaluation** this dictum becomes apparent. This method uses logical operators between multiple expressions, which are then evaluated from left to right. The value of the first **truthy** expression found (the one that is not a **falsy** value like **false**, **0**, **null**, **NaN**, **undefined**, or an empty string **""**) will then be returned, and the code skips evaluating the other expressions.

```
console.log (false || "" || "cat" || 0 || Math.random());
```

The first truthy value in the above expression, starting from the left, is "cat," so `Math.random()` will never be called. This method works just as well if you write it out as several `if/else if` statements, but the former saves a lot of typing! See the MDN Docs for more examples.[34]

5. In your HTML document, add a second `<input>` into the controls `<section>` to affect the scale of the polygons.

```
<label for="scale">scale</label>
<input type="range" id="scale" min=".05" max="5" step=".1"
value="1">
```

6. Add the selector and listener in the globals section of **main.js**.

```
let scaleEle = document.querySelector("#scale");
scaleEle.addEventListener("input", generate);
```

7. To apply the scale, multiply it by the width and height (**w** and **h**) values assigned in the parameters section of **main.js**. Update your code as follows. Preview your work, and you should now be able to control the number of polygons as well as their scale (see figure 8.4).

```
let w = randomInt(size * .8, size * 1.2) *
scaleEle.valueAsNumber;
let h = randomInt(size * .8, size * 1.2) *
scaleEle.valueAsNumber;
```

Check Your Work

This concludes the chapter exercises. We invite you to compare your work to the final outcome **criticalwebdesign.github.io#8-3** and code **criticalwebdesign.github.io#8-3-code** in the book repo. Don't forget to turn on GitHub Pages in your project and then stage and commit your work to make it live!

Author Note: Save Your Visualization as an .SVG File

If you want to save one of the visualizations you made, create a new SVG file (e.g., file.svg) in Codespaces. Then, inspect the source of your live Generative Arp HTML page and copy the `<svg>` element. Edit the text of your new SVG file and paste the element. You can drag these into Figma or Illustrator and continue to edit or even print them if you like.

Prompt 8.3 Add New Data to Your Project

It's impressive how using variables and functions keeps the code modular, which organizes it and makes the code easy to build on. *What would Jean Arp think?* Now that you have a handle on using loops, arrays, and SVGs to create a generative work, continue to experiment with the interface, parameters, and concepts of your project as you create a generative browser experience inspired by the history of art and interactivity. Think about **replayability** as you do to encourage users to return to and play with your work as they experience new outcomes.

Here are some potential components you could include in your idea and execution:

1. Randomness/chance—Consider reflecting on the tension between decisions/definitions created by the artist/author and the elements that are left to randomization/chance.
2. Color generation—Will color information be purely random, or influenced by other factors like time, interactivity, or other data?
3. Composition and form—What rules will you use in creating and positioning objects?
4. Sound/multimedia—How might sound or other media add to your ideas?
5. Rules—How will decisions you make be informed by the work you are inspired by? How might you put your project in conversation with art history? Think also about the discussion of fair use, notably with respect to the notion of transformation, in chapter 2.
6. Customization(s)—What interactivity might you add to allow the viewer to appreciate, modify, or play with the work? How might you encourage replayability as users return or revisit the page?

Regardless of your approach, your project should mimic or somehow find inspiration in these processes to reflect your own thinking on the subject.

9 Data Tracking

> Surveillance capitalism unilaterally claims human experience as free raw material for translation into behavioral data.
>
> —Shoshana Zuboff

Context

This chapter explores the various ways that web browsers allow access to user data, for better and for worse. We discuss how personal data is collected and analyzed in order to manipulate user behavior and how web design and development can (if we are not careful) reinforce tracking capabilities. Readers will use DevTools to examine and understand client-side data storage, then learn about incorporating data into their projects from remote APIs via asynchronous requests. To ensure that our instructions remain up to date, our solution to this chapter's prompt is published only on the wiki. Following the exercises, you will build a full-stack website consisting of a simple API and web front end that generates "bad" or easily hackable passwords in order to educate users about common mistakes.

About Personal Data

In common conversations about personal data, you might use or hear tech buzzwords like "privacy" or "cookies." However, concerns around these topics, as they so often do in general contexts, sometimes misrepresent issues as binary—polar opposites with only positive or negative impacts. For example, while most people wouldn't like their financial information shared with strangers, many have significantly different opinions about who can see photos of their pets. And, though everyone values privacy depending on the context, choices you make are also less black and white due to technical outcomes. If you don't accept cookies in your web browser, it may prevent websites from using them (among other methods) to track your behavior, but it also means the site won't "remember" your preferences or login status. As a result, you would have to enter your password on every new web page you visit to access your confidential information.

Inspiration

Terms and Conditions Apply was created by Wieden+Kennedy, Jon Plackett, Alex Bellos, and Adam Says. This critical game points to the absurdity of the language used to comply with terms and conditions online (see **termsandconditions.game**).

It's clear when you consider the amount of your data out in the world that while the type of information and context is important, everyone has different expectations of privacy. A person's status, for instance, as a child, a celebrity, or a politician, presents different expectations. Further, data privacy is different from **data security** because there are some types of information, like financial, health, and other information that should always be protected, regardless of someone's preferences for sharing cat photos.[1] These examples, as well as each individual's unique perspectives, show why privacy is a poor topic around which to frame these discussions, and why we proceed instead by looking at fundamental moral and legal entitlements that should apply to everyone.

About Your Data Rights

The word "surveillance" derives from the French "veiller" (to watch) and "sur" (above).[2] Yet, surveillance is usually depicted as the collection of data only and leaves out the other component. That is, "to watch from above" describes a position of power, an asymmetrical relationship that data collection reinforces and further tilts toward those with information gathering capabilities.

When the European Union (EU) was established, centuries of power asymmetries that included two world wars, the horrors of Nazism, and later, the surveillance and oppression from the East German Stasi, informed their drafting of documents governing the rights of citizens. The Charter of Fundamental Rights of the European Union, much like a constitution, lists the rights enjoyed by all EU citizens. This includes Article 7, "Everyone has the right of respect for [their] private and family life, home and communications," and Article 8, "Everyone has the right to the protection of personal data concerning him or her."[3]

Additional Materials and Resources

Explore links and other content related to this chapter: **criticalwebdesign.github.io#wiki-09**

In 2016 these rights were used to draft the General Data Protection Regulation (GDPR), the law that defines personal data and outlines data protections for EU citizens ("data subjects") against abusive and insecure data practices by companies, the state, and others who store or process their information ("data controllers"), both in and outside the EU. Unlike in the United States and other countries, these rights are enabled by default for citizens, so no one has to opt in to receive these protections or perform the work to opt out and exclude their data from immoral practices. Chapter 3 of the GDPR, "Rights of the Data Subject," explains eight rights, which we summarize here:

1. The Right to Information to let people inquire what data controllers collect and for what purpose
2. The Right of Access to know what personal data is processed, and how it is used
3. The Right to Rectification to change or modify data that is inaccurate
4. The Right to Erasure to tell a data controller to erase data they collected
5. The Right to Restriction of Processing to restrict analysis if it is inaccurate, unlawful, unwarranted
6. The Right to Data Portability to access and export your own data in a usable format
7. The Right to Object to processing, including for direct marketing purposes
8. The Right to Avoid Automated Decision-Making to avoid being subjected to legal decisions or profiling based solely on automated processing

The number of EU citizens affected by these laws caused most large companies who deal in data to change their practices and positively affected how user data is handled worldwide. As you can see, these rights address many of the issues alluded to by broad discussions of data privacy, yet they place responsibility firmly upon those who collect and profit from user data. The following story provides a concrete example for why these laws exist and why you should consider and fight for your fundamental data rights, even if you live in a place that doesn't guarantee them by law.

Gregg's Story

This is a story about "Gregg," a British man profiled in 2021 by *The New York Times*. Gregg was recovering from gambling addiction, having lost nearly $15,000 during a single nine-month betting binge, on top of $220,000 in other related debt from loans and mortgages. Gregg's favorite gambling app, Sky Bet, as it turns out, had collected troves of information on him, including "banking records, . . . location coordinates, and an intimate portrait of his habits wagering on slots and soccer matches."[4] As with their other users, Sky Bet continuously collected and processed Gregg's data, which identified him as a valuable customer to retain and lure back to the platform, using a predictive model for how much they could make from Gregg over twelve months, what some companies call a "winback" margin.[5] And they did, using email marketing and promotions promising big payouts to attempt to influence his activities and habits. Their behind-the-scenes data tracking that provided these and other insights, such as how often he opened and clicked through their marketing campaigns, only became known because Gregg hired a lawyer who used Britain's data protection laws to uncover the extent to which Sky Bet pursued him.

You may or may not be able to directly identify with Gregg's addiction, or you may know a friend or family member who can. You otherwise may find the actions of the company to be wrong only when you imagine what they did to Gregg performed in a time before the internet. Envision several human beings, employed to physically trail him down every street, into his work and home, scribbling furiously about the activities of a single person. They pass those notebooks over to another team of employees who analyze, categorize, and conclude how best to use the collected information to manipulate his behavior. Yet another group of employees use those recommendations to write copy, design, and print marketing graphics, and then join those following Gregg to jump in front of him, trying to distract, even obstruct him, from his current task with their imagery containing false promises of big money. While all of this occurs, another group notes his responses so as to add more ammunition to a constant barrage of behavioral targeting and manipulation that repeatedly collects and uses the growing set of information against him. It sounds insane, like an episode of *The Twilight Zone*, or its technologically informed descendent *Black Mirror*, but the components (figure 9.1) of this intense system of surveillance and manipulation are commonplace today. Further, they are enhanced by high-performance computers, instantaneous networked data, and billions of dollars of Silicon Valley tech funding, producing the most sophisticated surveillance apparatus known to humans.[6]

Regardless of how ridiculous and invasive this seems, in reality, without the speed of networked data, the slick interfaces of well-designed websites, and the underlying code that can collect and process the data, it wouldn't be possible to use surveillance to influence a person like this. Profiting from collecting data and selling the potential to change behavior, which Shoshana Zuboff describes as **surveillance capitalism**,[7] is today

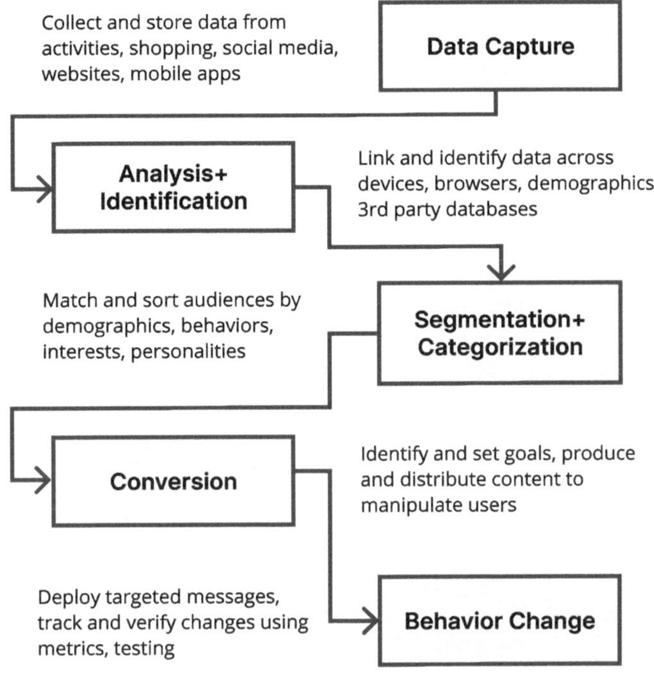

Figure 9.1
This flowchart shows how behavioral targeting starts with data capture and results in behavioral change.

not only automated and systematic but accepted as a common business practice and firmly entrenched into nearly all networked communications. Consider how indecent and lawless it would be for an organization to be allowed to perform these actions upon a single person. And how morally bankrupt and depraved the owners of these companies must be to direct this system of surveillance and control toward a person with an addiction. Instead of using it to identify and help Gregg, they rendered him powerless to fight his gambling addiction, without regard for how it wrecked his home, family, and life.

We relay Gregg's story in several contexts. First, the GDPR, which Gregg's lawyer used to reveal the level to which he was influenced, only protects EU citizens. While a handful of US states, including California, have put into place laws to protect user data, there will likely never be equivalent protections for US citizens thanks to lobbyist organizations deployed by Amazon, Apple, Facebook, Google, and Microsoft at the state and federal level.[8] Second, as we write this in early 2025, sports gambling continues to grow at an exponential pace. Thanks to a 2018 Supreme Court ruling, 38 of 50 US states now allow sports betting. Flutter Entertainment, which owns Sky Betting & Gaming, Fanduel, as well as other gaming apps, reported $9.72 billion in revenue in 2023 due to "rapid U.S. expansion."[9] The rise of gambling websites and apps, which prey on people's vulnerabilities, is already normalized to such a degree that even the most highly regarded professional athletes are endorsing them in advertisements. Third, the use of data, emotional appeals, and layers upon layers of behavioral psychology to change your purchases, behaviors, and even beliefs, via advertising, marketing, notifications, and so on, is also entrenched and continues to line the pockets of the wealthy and powerful. Finally, behavioral targeting is increasing in its technical complexity and reach, rendering users feeling powerless, coerced, and out of control of their personal information.[10,11]

Case Study: Owen Mundy, I Know Where Your Cat Lives

OM: Welcome to today's internet—you can buy anything, every website is tracking your every move, and anywhere you look you find videos and images of cats. *I Know Where Your Cat Lives* (**iknowwhereyourcatlives.com**) is a data visualization experiment that locates seven million public images of cats on a world map by the latitude and longitude coordinates users unknowingly uploaded in their metadata (figure 9.2). The photos were accessed via publicly available APIs provided by popular photo sharing websites, and then run through various clustering algorithms using a supercomputer to represent the enormity of the data source.

This project explores two uses of the internet: one that promotes sharing for the sociable and humorous appreciation of domesticated felines, and another where personal data is exploited by start-ups and international mega-corporations who are ushering in a new era of decreased privacy for all. *I Know Where Your Cat Lives* does not visualize all the cats on the net, only those that enable tracking where their owners have been.

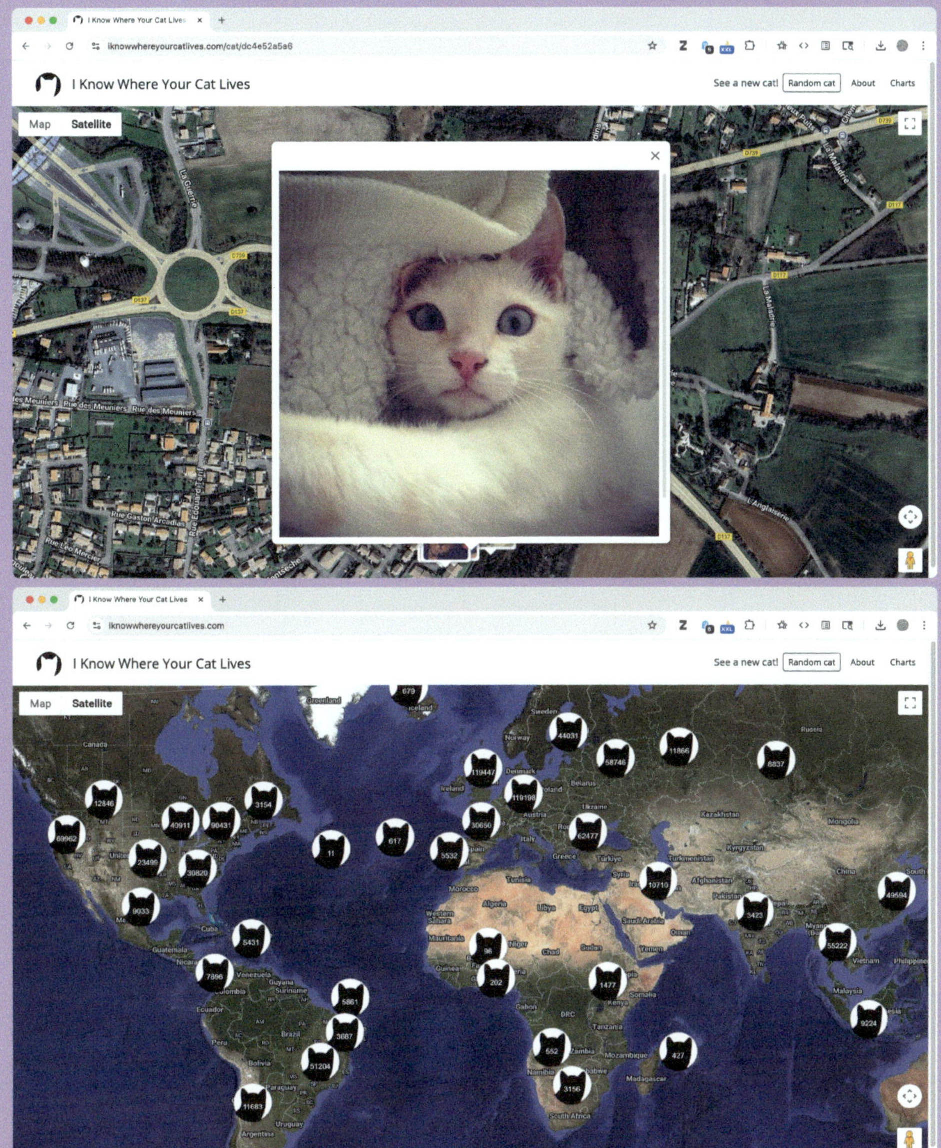

Figure 9.2
Owen Mundy, *I Know Where Your Cat Lives*, 2014.

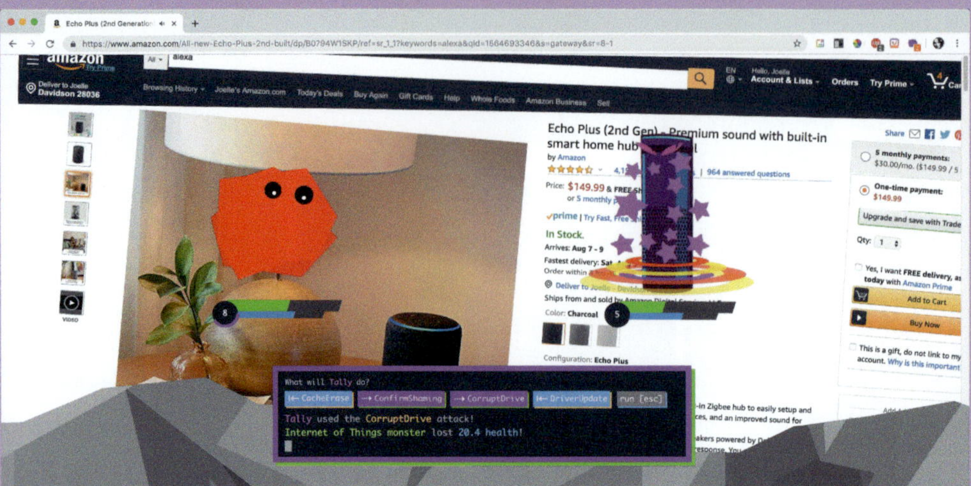

Figure 9.3
Joelle Dietrick and Owen Mundy, *Tally Saves the Internet*, **tallysavestheinternet.com** 2021.

My work often includes humor and references to popular culture in order to raise questions about how technology shifts power in unequal ways. A more recent example is my collaboration with Joelle Dietrick, *Tally Saves the Internet*, a browser extension that transforms the data advertisers collect into a multiplayer game.[12] Once installed, a friendly pink blob named Tally lives in the corner of your screen and warns you when companies translate your human experiences into free behavioral data. When Tally encounters "product monsters" (online trackers and their corresponding product marketing categories), you can capture them in a turn-based battle (e.g., "Pokémon style"), transforming the game into a progressive tracker blocker where you earn the right to be let alone through this playful experience (figure 9.3).

Prompt 9: What You'll Make
Create a Bad Password API

Regardless of the issue we've identified so far, we hope to enable and activate you to improve the situation, at least for yourself, by making the technical wizardry more accessible in our descriptions and exercises below. We will show you how to see what is being collected, processed, and used against you, and then show you how to create a *Bad Password API* that encourages others to increase their security and join with us to resist the surveillance of everyday life. Starting with the first module, you'll use DevTools to see how data is stored and transferred between clients and servers. In module 2 you will learn about JavaScript objects, JSON data, and the asynchronous functions in JS that can send and receive it. By the end of the chapter, you'll build a web page that can connect to and display data from our API.

View the results of our *Bad Password API* at **criticalwebdesign.github.io#9-3** (figure 9.4). You can see the final code at **criticalwebdesign.github.io#9-3-code**.

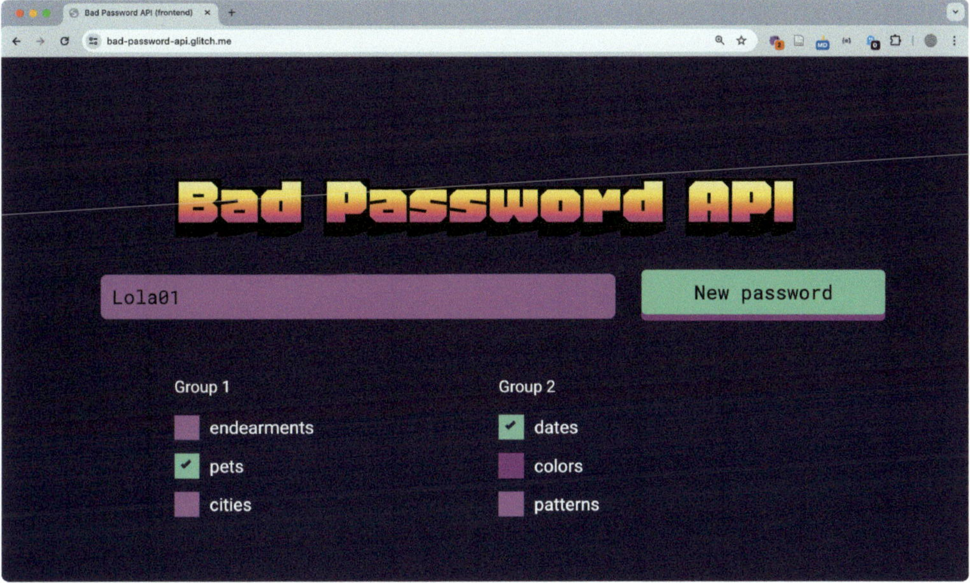

Figure 9.4
Upon completing exercises in module 9.3 you will build a Bad Password API.

Module 9.1 DevTools and Data

In this module we introduce an overview of the steps used to collect, analyze, and profit from user data, examining what is gathered via DevTools.

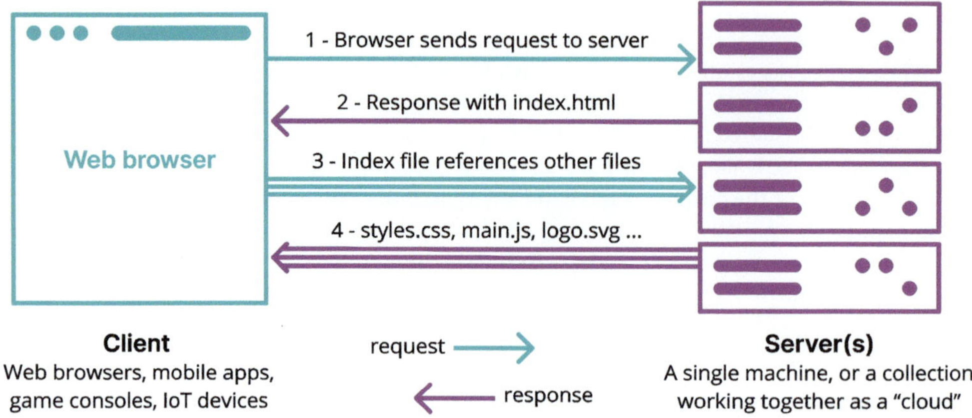

Figure 9.5
A diagram showing just a few of the many requests and responses between client and server when a page loads.

9.1.1 Data Capture

There are five general stages of most behavioral targeting systems. The processes and technologies involved and how they fit together, or the **tech stack**, necessarily begins with capturing and then matching data to individuals. One of the most common ways that user information is generated, and a primary source of web analytics tools, occurs thanks to how the internet inherently functions. For each web page you access online, each resource (every image, font, stylesheet, or script) in the page generates a new **request** from your browser (the client) to the server where the data is stored (figure 9.5). Every one of these requests includes a **request header** that contains meta information like the URL and your IP address. Each of those requests are then answered with a **response**, which returns the data requested (often cat pictures, but also CSS, JS, and other files), as well as other meta information in a **response header**. A summary of each request is saved in text files called **server logs**, which, in addition to data sent about you in the header, include the time, name, and response code of every file accessed, as well as errors and warnings that occur from those requests.

Activity: View Requests and Server Logs

View response and request headers inside DevTools to learn how data is captured for analytics.

1. Open any web page in Chrome. Then open DevTools and select the Network tab.

2. Reload the page and watch as the browser sends a request to the server and displays the results in an expanding list, including their filename, status, type, size, and time it took for them to arrive. While you see these in your browser, this data is also recorded in server logs, along with details about you. The first file in this list is the HTML page you requested, but all the resources in the page will be saved to these server logs.
3. You'll also notice the waterfall graphic at the top showing all the responses and how long each took from the request until they were received. Make sure "All" is checked in the filtering method or reload the page if you don't see them.
4. Select one of the files from the response list and examine the metadata that appears under the Headers tab on the right. The request headers include the URL, method, status code, and other information, while the response headers tell you the content type, server, and more.

As you can see from the previous activity, a lot of data is sent across the network with each file request. While access logs are recorded and stored on the server, **web analytics** tools such as Statcounter or Google Analytics collect data in the client and summarize it in web-based dashboards. Using charts and graphics, they represent both quantitative and qualitative data like the number of visitors, time of visit, or even the paths that visitors take through a website. This can help website creators ensure that a site is functional and that visitors can access intended content. Analytics tools also incorporate additional reference data to enhance site metrics, like reverse geolocating IP addresses to let site owners know where visitors are approximately located.

Analytics tools can provide all these insights because they operate through scripts embedded in web pages. This allows them to collect much more data about users than server logs, including any data that JavaScript can access, like the position of your cursor as you scan the page, how far you scroll, or even how long your mouse lingers over an advertisement. The `window.navigator` object (try it in the console) lets JavaScript access information about the state and identity of your browser, including the battery usage, memory, and geolocation of your laptop or device, the content saved in your clipboard, and even what you type.[13] The website **clickclickclick.click** playfully demonstrates just how much information can be concluded directly or through analyzing your data in the browser.

9.1.2 Analysis and Identification

Data captured from anonymous web traffic doesn't provide much context about users on its own, nor does it allow marketers to influence website visitors. As the sociologist and surveillance scholar David Lyon notes, "Identification is the starting point of surveillance."[14] This is why the next step in the behavioral targeting stack involves connecting users to their online activity. In addition to insights about their behavior, this provides the crucial method to identify and **retarget** users, transforming them from anonymous visitors to obeying consumers through surveillance-based advertising.

The process of retargeting (and similarly, remarketing) is the origin of the creeping feeling that everything you search online or say near your Alexa or other connected device is being recorded and used to inform the advertisements and recommendations you see. The predominance of free Google accounts means that their analytics tools have access to a lot of data on each user, including very private information, as well as interests, purchases, activity on other websites, and so much more.[15] For example, until 2017, Google used the content of private emails for ads,[16] a practice recently implemented by Microsoft.[17] Even if you aren't logged in, a data double is still created and evolves with each new data point collected (see the Incognito Mode callout). Still, it doesn't take much data to make very revealing assumptions about you by using statistical analysis and matching your activity to the behaviors of millions of other users. A study at the Psychometrics Centre of Cambridge University showed that with only five "likes" on Facebook they could "accurately predict a range of highly sensitive personal attributes including: sexual orientation, ethnicity, religious and political views, personality traits, intelligence, happiness, use of addictive substances, parental separation, age, and gender."[18]

Author Note: Incognito Mode

Incognito mode (aka private mode) is a common function that lets users browse the web in a new window without leaving a trace of their activity. An incognito window is similar to using a new temporary web browser, except it deletes your history and other data as soon as you close it. This means that when you surf the web, unless you log in, sites won't know who you are or have other information about your previous activity.

Still, there are misconceptions you should know about. While your activity in incognito mode won't be saved in your history when you close the window, it doesn't prevent those that control your network like your **ISP** (Internet Service Provider), school, or employer, from accessing your browser history.[19] While incognito mode is excellent for testing websites and apps that use cookies and other information for their functionality, it's clear that it isn't private or secure. Some browsers like **Ghostery Browser** (**ghostery.com**) can block trackers and cookies by default, but you would need to use a **VPN** (virtual private network) or the **Tor Browser** (**torproject.org**) to truly mask your online activity from your network.

Google Analytics is not the only third party listening in on websites you visit. If you see Facebook, X (Twitter), Youtube, or any other embedded widget, feature, or media on a page, then those services are watching your activity and connecting it to everything they know about you, even though you are surfing websites owned by others. Meta, who owns Facebook, WhatsApp, and Instagram, is a particularly abusive harvester of user information. With data-informed behavior manipulation being their primary revenue source, they persuade other companies to upload and link their customer databases to their users. A recent Consumer Report found that the Meta Ads Manager contained data submitted by 2,230 outside companies *on average for each user*, with some users identified by more than 7,000 companies.[20] In total, 186,892 companies uploaded data about their customers to the social network, which Facebook used to inform their own profiles on users.

In their book, *Supervision*, John Gilliom and Torin Monahan say we live in a surveillance society, where "virtually all significant social, institutional, or business activities in our society now involve the systematic monitoring, gathering, and analysis of information in order to make decisions, minimize risk, sort populations, and exercise power."[21] Note that all the services that profit on your data have access to much more than you share within each of those platforms, because they all engage with, purchase from, or even own **data brokers** (aka **data dealers**), companies who specialize in connecting you and your information across platforms, devices, and services. The information they sell can include your loyalty cards, your Instagram posts, your job history—anything and everything. In a critical turn, *Data Dealer*[22] is a web-based game created by Ivan Averintsev, Wolfie Christl, Pascale Osterwalder, and Ralf Traunsteiner that explored the myriad ways that such companies harvest and sell user information (figure 9.6, top). Ben Grosser's browser extensions modify the content users see on social media to question their influence. His Safebook extension[23] removes all content from Facebook, reminding users of the importance of their free labor to the company's bottom line (figure 9.6, bottom). Grosser's Facebook Demetricator extension[24] removes the metrics on posts that gamify interpersonal communication to drive engagement (and thus ad views). As with all browser extensions, these modifications are performed using JavaScript, but only in the browsers (clients) of users who install it.

Activity: Examine Cookies and Other Identifiers in DevTools

Use DevTools to see how trackers and other embedded scripts collect, store, and identify your data in the browser. Open this web example **criticalwebdesign.github.io#trackers** to explore how sites access your data, track your activity, and store your information through link tracking, cookies, browser fingerprinting, and tracking pixels.

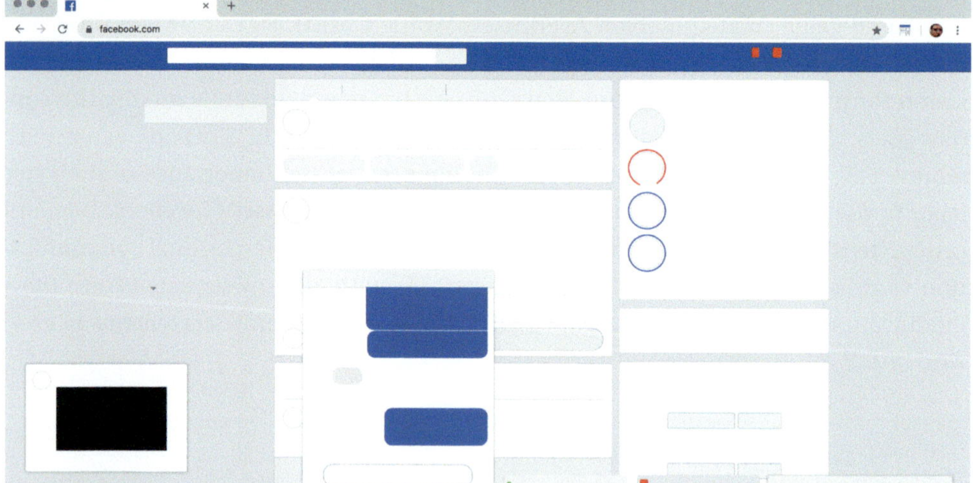

Figure 9.6

Top: Ivan Averintsev, Wolfie Christl, Pascale Osterwalder, and Ralf Traunsteiner, *Data Dealer,* screenshot. Bottom: Ben Grosser, *Safebook* extension (2019), screenshot.

9.1.3 Segmentation, Categorization and Conversion

So far we've discussed many ways that designers are asked by companies to access user data in the browser. Now we'll look at how all this data, connected to you in one way or another, is transformed into actionable attempts at behavioral manipulation.

While offering benefits, many analytics tools are unfortunately tightly integrated into advertising and behavioral targeting services. Google Analytics and Facebook's Ad Manager, for example, combine web traffic data with user demographics (e.g., age, gender, income, location) to allow advertisers to filter and sort users into **audiences** (a.k.a. groups, segments, et al., depending on the service) they can attempt to influence. When it comes to identifying audiences' interests, these services match users with various hierarchical collections of content, like Google "Verticals"[25] or the Internet Advertising Bureau's "Content Taxonomy."[26] These lists provide a common, albeit colorless and consumer-focused, language to describe the potential interests of the general public and sell their attention. Content taxonomies like these also influence the overabundance of recommended content and filter bubbles that seem to infect all social media feeds these days. The algorithms that determine what people see are, of course, hidden black boxes, as are the motivations and influences that censor or elevate specific content, as the debate around the Chinese ownership around TikTok has shown.

Advertising tools provided by these big corporations do not explicitly identify actual users—well, not anymore.[27] Instead they provide summaries of potential users to manipulate from which marketers may choose, much like one selects from product options on a shopping website. For example, you could create an audience containing environmentally conscious college athletes in North Carolina to influence them to sign up for your new edible water bottles. Or, since these ethically questionable tools are accessible by anyone, a dictator might build an audience of potential journalists critical of their regime to identify, threaten, and imprison them, by monitoring and tracing the network traffic, which they also control. While we wrote this originally about Egypt,[28] the state of press and information freedom worldwide continues to deteriorate.[29]

The next step in the stack, after segmentation and categorization, involves finding ways to match you to the goals of potential advertisers. When using these tools, advertisers have access to information telling them how well their ads and groups are performing. The most common metric for this is called **conversion rate**, which refers to how many visitors have *converted* from an anonymous visitor to one who has met a **conversion goal** set up by the advertiser. In the previous examples, purchasing the edible water bottle or getting a journalist to sign up for a mailing list would be achievable goals. The language of marketing blogs and websites around this portion of the process is often ethically questionable. It can make one sick to their stomach just to consider how someone can make their living asking questions like "How can we find the shortest path from user to value?" or by writing books titled *Using Computers to Change What We Think and Do*.[30] You can see much of this thinking when you consider the vast number of behavioral funnels guiding sales interactions that exist on the internet. The number of "goals" that might be included and A/B tested to see which methods are most effective through this behavioral manipulation scheme could include price fixing using dark patterns (as Amazon has done), advertisements that influence the swing district voters who are most likely to be persuaded to vote for Donald Trump through fear-mongering ad campaigns (as Cambridge Analytica did during the 2020 election), as well as a host of other unethical outcomes.

The final thought to consider within our survey of the surveillance society might be that Google, a company that provides the most popular search engine in the world, powerful web-based office software, as well as hundreds of other tools, services, and content, does so for "free." They do foremost, not because they are a technology company. Rather, the primary thing that Google sells, like Sky Bet, as well as Facebook, Youtube, and many others, is the data-informed potential for behavior modification, *in real time*.[31]

Advertising has been a primary source of revenue for newspapers and television since these mediums came into popularity. In the "good old days," ad purchasing was done based on little available data, like demographics from the ten-year census, but feedback about their effect came slowly. As with other technologies, these systems have evolved to be almost completely automated. Now, the speed of networked data makes the feedback immediate—for example, allowing advertisers to see which ad, message, or context resonates the most with which group of users. In addition to the increased velocity, the automation allows these processes to operate on a massive scale.

These stacks of automation technologies are perhaps most evident in the fundamental decentralized nature of the internet. For example, a large website has an average of seventy-five technologies running on it,[32] in addition to the many resources (images, stylesheets, scripts) required for each page. When you load a typical page with tracking technology the browser attempts to resolve all the required resources before rendering the information for the viewer. Among these requests are scripts from an array of trackers, marketing campaigns, and ad networks. As this *Ghostery Trackermap* network graph (figure 9.7) shows, the page sends data about the user (their interests, demographics, and other data that affects their potential to be influenced) to ad networks

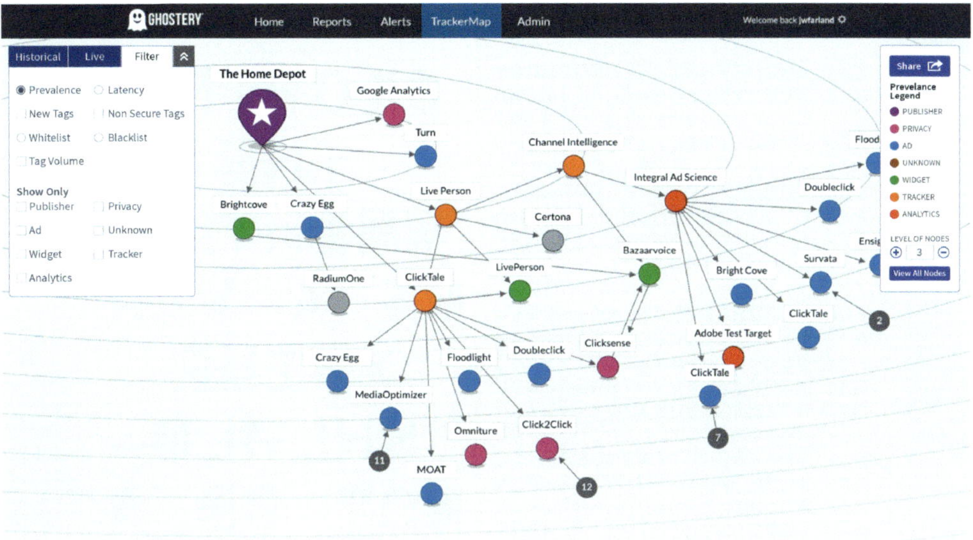

Figure 9.7

The *Ghostery Trackermap* is a directed network graph representing how embedded scripts transmit user data for ad auctions that determine which targeted messages are shown to each user. The Trackermap was originally created to identify and reduce latency and security issues, and has gone through many iterations, including this version by the designer Joey Kilrain, **kilrain.com**.

that then relay that data to potential advertisers. The advertiser who will pay the most to manipulate this user is ultimately selected using an **ad auction**, and the winning advertisement images and scripts are returned to the browser's request and loaded in the page. All of this happens so quickly that it finishes before the web page has loaded, revealing how automation and the increased speed of networked data have entrenched surveillance systems in every hidden millisecond of our browsing experience.

Inspiration: Typographic Activism

Two typographic projects that resist surveillance are *ZXX* by Sang Mun and Emil Kozole's *Project Seen* (figure 9.8). *ZXX*[33] (2012) was designed to increase privacy through thwarting optical character recognition (OCR) and automated machine intelligence methods. *Project Seen* (2015) is a typeface that points out content prone to surveillance by automatically striking through trigger words targeted by government agencies. Install the font or use the bookmarklet to explore it at **projectseen.com**.

"Seen"

is a project that deals with interception and filtering of our communication by the NSA, GCHQ and other security agencies. It is a typeface with a preloaded set of trigger words these agencies target when scanning through our online communication. The typeface can be installed and used as any other font, but once any of the trigger words is written, the font immediately crosses it out. This way it automatically highlights and points out the content prone to secret surveillance. Bookmarklet is an accessible tool that was developed to allow you to change any website's font to "Seen". Drag the link to your browser's bookmark and click it to reveal "spook words". In a broader way, the project explores linguistic systems through the analysis of everyday words and investigates the connection between language, data and surveillance.

Figure 9.8

Top: Sang Mun, *ZXX* (2012). Bottom: Emil Kozole, *Project Seen* (2015).

Prompt 9.1 Design: Iterate on a List of Bad Passwords

The *Bad Password API* you make in this chapter relies on and combines several lists of commonly used words and patterns that are easy to guess. Dojo.tech's study proves it is easy to automate software that can attempt to crack website security using these specific common categories.[34] Following Dojo's key findings, create an additional set of "bad passwords" (for instance, based on terms of endearment, pet names, or city names). Save your list. We will return to it when you compare it to the *Bad Password API* in prompt 9.3.

Module 9.2 JSON Data and APIs

The following introduction to **JSON (JavaScript object notation)** data, dynamic websites, and APIs, will prepare you to incorporate data from the internet in your projects.

9.2.1 JavaScript Objects

A JavaScript **object** is a hierarchical format for storing collections of **properties**. While an array stores a list of values identified by their index, object properties store and reference values using a **name** (also referred to as a **key**).[35] This code example shows how to create a new object (using curly braces) named "color" with a property named "id" set to the value "cyan" logged to the console using dot notation.

```
let color = {
  id: "cyan",
  hex: "00ffff"
}
console.log(color.id); //-> "cyan"
```

JavaScript objects can store any data type, including arrays, other objects, and even functions (referred to as **methods** when used in objects). This second version (below) of the color object contains new properties named "rgb" and "red." Calling the method stored in `red` returns the first index of the `rgb` array (the red channel) using a special keyword called `this` to refer to a property within the object itself.

```
let color = {
  id: "cyan",
  hex: "00ffff",
```

```
  rgb: [0,255,255],
  red: function () {
    return this.rgb[0]
  }
}
console.log(color.red()); //-> 0
```

Activity: Add New Methods

Try adding `green()` and `blue()` methods to this example on Codepen **criticalwebdesign.github.io#js-objects**

Pro Tip: JavaScript Prototype

Objects are commonly used to represent the properties and behaviors of entities in a programming model called **object-oriented programming (OOP)**. OOP languages use predefined classes and inheritance to derive behavior. For example, all objects of a car class will have wheels and headlights that turn on, which are inherited by its child classes that define more specific properties. JavaScript uses a **prototype** pattern to define objects. When you create a new variable in JavaScript, it creates a new copy of the object prototype, cloning all its functionality and data. If you log the `color` variable to the console, you can see the properties it received from the prototype. JavaScript's prototype shares many of the OOP's benefits. For example, JavaScript objects use **encapsulation** to group and identify similar information inside a single container (like formats for a color) and standardize access to their properties. See examples at **criticalwebdesign.github.io#wiki-09.**

A common use case for objects is grouping similar information into arrays to simplify storing, retrieving, and displaying data. Below, each index in an array called `colors` is logged to the console using a `forEach()` loop. On each loop the callback function accesses the object properties using a parameter called `item`, until it reaches the end.

```
let colors = [
  {id: "cyan", hex: "00ffff"},
  {id: "magenta", hex: "ff00ff"},
  {id: "yellow", hex: "ffff00"},
  {id: "black", hex: "000000"},
];
```

```
colors.forEach(function(item, i){
  console.log(`${item.id} = #${item.hex}`);
});
//-> "cyan = #00ffff"
//-> "magenta = #ff00ff"
//-> . . .
```

9.2.2 JSON Data

Data exchange formats help to standardize how data is stored and transmitted. **JSON** is a text-based data exchange format that follows the JavaScript object syntax we describe above. JSON is one of the most common formats used to organize or send data across the internet. The syntax is nearly identical to JavaScript objects, allowing the second version of our color object to be saved as a **.json** file (below) and imported into a program with three changes:

1. No functions: JSON data cannot include methods.
2. Syntax: Property names in JSON must be wrapped in double quotes.
3. Root character: Remove the variable definition so that the root character is either a curly brace or a square bracket (an array of JSON).

```
{
  "id": "cyan",
  "hex": "00ffff",
  "rgb": [0,255,255]
}
```

You can view these examples in the book's repo.[36]

Data exchange formats are generally either hierarchical, like JSON with its nested file structure, or tabular, where data values are arranged in rows and columns. **CSV (comma-separated values)** is a common tabular data exchange format, where each column of data is separated by a comma and every row by a line break. Like JSON, CSV (or tab-separated TSV) files can be opened and edited in VS Code or any spreadsheet application. The snippet below shows the `colors` array of JSON above as CSV data.

```
"id", "hex", "r", "g", "b"
"cyan", "00ffff", 0, 255, 255
"magenta", "ff00ff", 255, 0, 255
"yellow", "ffff00", 255, 255, 0
"black", "000000", 0, 0, 0
```

Best Practices: Data Conversion, Cleaning, and Validation

The following are considerations for using data of any type within a project:

1. **Data conversion** makes it easier to use data. There are many tools online like CSVJSON[37] to convert CSV to JSON (or other formats) by transforming the columns into an array of objects and storing each row using the column name as a key. Data conversion may also involve converting numbers stored as strings into actual number values (without the quotes) to save work performed by your program and increase performance.
2. **Data cleaning** involves identifying, removing, or correcting unreliable, inaccurate, or nonrelevant parts in a dataset. You can perform data cleaning by hand or with a program.[38] A simple method is to use the find/replace function in VS Code.
3. **Data validation** ensures your JSON files will be read correctly. Sometimes you can spot issues when VS Code suddenly shows inconsistent color formatting, but if you have a lot of data, a validator like **jsonlint.com** can be used to automatically check the syntax of your JSON code.

9.2.3 APIs

A common way you'll use JSON data is with **APIs (application program interfaces)**. APIs, sometimes called web services, can be found everywhere in today's networked culture. Any mobile app that shows live information is sending and receiving JSON data to an API behind the scenes. APIs are similar to search engines—when you enter a query, results are displayed on a page in HTML. An API works the same way, but for machines instead of users, returning the results in a machine-readable format like JSON to make the data easier to use in your code (see the callout on "Data Scraping").

Activity: Test an API

In this activity you'll learn to test APIs. There are hundreds of free APIs that offer a wealth of functionality and data for you to use in your projects. Some APIs require you to register and send requests along with a special key to prevent abuse, but there are plenty of **public APIs** you can use as well.[39]

1. We will use this free API that offers facts about cats. You should always refer to an API's documentation, in this case **catfact.ninja**, to learn about the **endpoints**, or specific URLs used to access particular information. Open the following link in a web browser and you should see a simple JSON document, organized by `key:value` relationships: **catfact.ninja/fact**.
2. Install the JSON Formatter extension for Chrome **criticalwebdesign.github.io#json-formatter** to make it easier to read JSON data in the browser, and reload the cat fact API (figure 9.9).

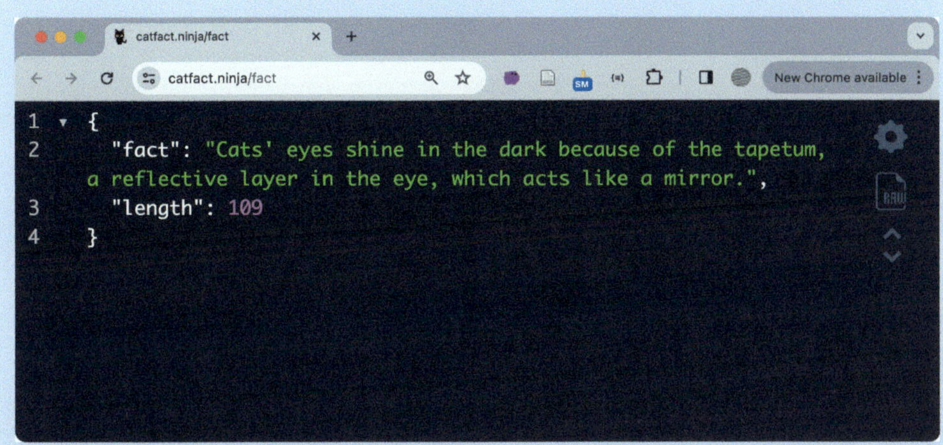

Figure 9.9
A cat fact in JSON formatted with JSON Formatter. *Fascinating.*

3. {JSON} Placeholder is a free "realistic" API for testing. For example, access the "users" endpoint to get a list of fake users: **jsonplaceholder.typicode.com/users.**
4. While basic API testing can be as simple as viewing a web page, sometimes you may need special tools to send data or authenticate. For the next API we'll use a tool called REQBIN to send information with the API request that lets you mimic a web form's POST request. The Real REST API **restful-api.dev** will use features endpoints that operate differently, depending on the HTTP verb you use in the request. Go to **reqbin.com** and add the following URL in the field—watch out for errant spaces at the end of the URL. Send the request with GET selected in the drop-down and you'll see a list of devices.
   `https://api.restful-api.dev/objects`
5. See the wiki for further testing with REQBIN, including one that uses POST method and a remote database.

Pro Tip: Data Scraping

Using free, preformatted JSON data from APIs is certainly handy. Companies publish APIs to encourage developers to build apps using their data, which increases their dependence on the service. However, APIs don't always provide all the data you may desire for a particular project. **Data scraping** is a method for gathering information by parsing specific elements directly from HTML. Most scraping methods fetch the HTML of a page and then remove HTML code to get only the desired content. For example, Tim Schwartz created a scraper[40] when he developed *Paris* (figure 9.10) to display the status of Google results for "paris." A good rule of thumb is: "If you can load a web page and inspect the contents by hand, then you can write a scraper to get that content." The ethics of scraping are hazy. While the practice usually violates the terms of use of most commercial websites, Google and other search engines do the exact same thing for profit, continuously crawling web pages to collect and display captured information. If your goals are centered on critical design practices, then you can likely claim fair use in defense of any scraping you do.

Figure 9.10
Tim Schwartz created *Paris* (2007), **timschwartz.org/paris**, by writing a data scraper that monitored news and search engines for "paris hilton" and "paris france" and displayed the results in real time.

9.2.4 Static and Dynamic Web Pages

Before we actually use data from other sources, we'll examine the concept of dynamic web pages. The layouts you created in prior chapters and published on GitHub Pages are referred to as **static web pages**. That is, their information does not change. Though you incorporated randomness and effects to update the interface, all the information in the page was contained only within the HTML, CSS, and JS documents you created. Thus, unless you manually update and upload the documents to the internet again, the live webpage does not include new content.

Opposite this, **dynamic web pages** are able to display new information that can change, whether it is updated by content posted by other users or automatically by software (figure 9.11). Dynamic web pages are all around us in online stores, news

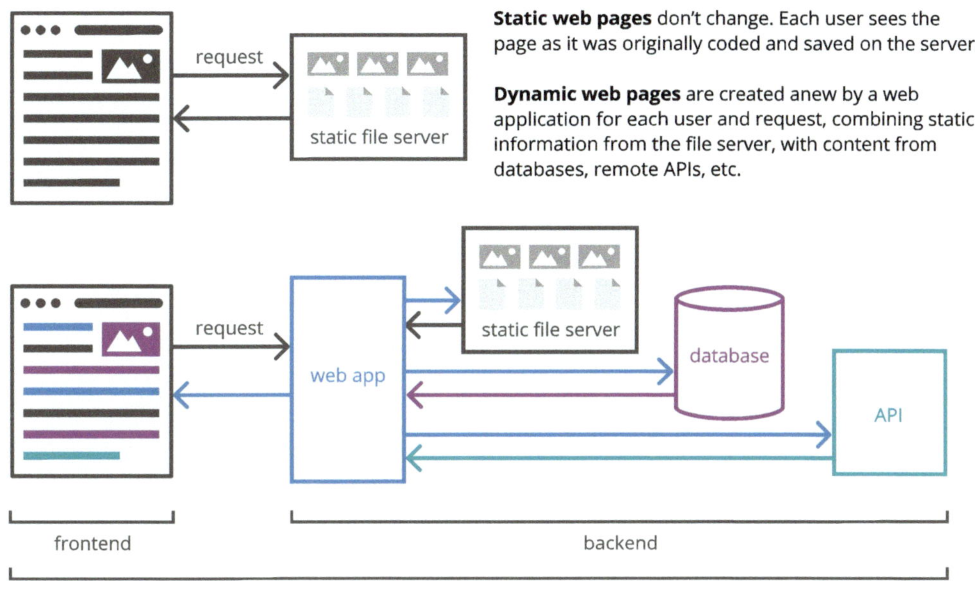

Figure 9.11
A diagram of a static vs. dynamic web page.

websites, social media platforms, and equally, in examples of critical web design. While nearly every software or dynamic website contains portions of static HTML and CSS used as templates, the content is populated in real time using live information that may change by the minute or even within seconds. Think about a weather app that shows the potential for rain by accessing the most recent satellite, temperature, and precipitation data layered over a map. If you refresh the app (usually a commercial site full of ads), it retrieves new, publicly available data from the **NOAA (National Oceanic and Atmospheric Administration)** to help, for example, Owen plan his bike ride and xtine know if the tennis courts will dry out. Likewise, Google and others use cookies stored on your device to identify, authenticate, and generate customized pages for each user.[41] Similarly, YouTube uses cookies to match records in their database and customizes the content you see, recommending only media you have not viewed previously. But not ads—Youtube will show you the same ad. Over, and over, and over, and over . . .

Creating a dynamic web page can be simple, or it can involve many moving and specialized components like databases, third-party authentication, and algorithms responsible for filtering content so that information appears constantly new and engaging. While static websites are relatively easy to build and cheap to host (or free on GitHub

Pages!), dynamic web pages involve more complexity and resources. Depending on the project, a dynamic website will rely on a **back end** that includes a web application running on the server, that can read and write data to a database, fetch several disparate pieces of information, and return dynamic web page content to the browser on the **front end**. There are many programming languages that can run on the server side to answer requests and manage data, like PHP, Python, or C#. Currently, the most popular back-end language is a version of JavaScript that operates directly on web servers called Node.js.[42] We will introduce Node.js in the next module.

Prompt 9.2 Code: Experiment with Other APIs

Continue experimenting with the APIs. Consider examples from this list of public APIs: **criticalwebdesign.github.io#public-apis.**

Module 9.3 Async JavaScript

Not surprisingly, strong passwords are an important but often forgotten component of data privacy. In fact, 83% of the most commonly used passwords can be cracked in less than a second.[43] It's no surprise that strong passwords include more characters, incorporate lowercase and uppercase letters, numbers, or symbols, and avoid common words and repeated phrases. And of course, using multifactor authentication is always a good practice in keeping data private. In this module, we show you how to use data from APIs in a static web page to playfully follow the theme of the chapter and create a "Bad Password API" that shows users *what not to do* when creating a password. On the wiki, we continue the prompt and show you how to create the entire full-stack application using Node.js.

9.3.1 Reducing Latency

Any time you load data over a network, you incur **latency**, a delay between when you make your request and the moment the response arrives. With zero latency, web pages feel speedy and the instant response is gratifying, while lag between user events can make a website clunky and frustrating. Latency increases with large files, poor server performance, and slow or overburdened networks. Even physical distance can increase download times,[44] which is why CDNs are commonly used to distribute site files (like Bootstrap) from servers at strategic locations around the world.[45] It may not be obvious with a fast connection, but you can confirm that there is a microsecond delay using the waterfall view of the DevTools Network tab (see the activity in 9.1).

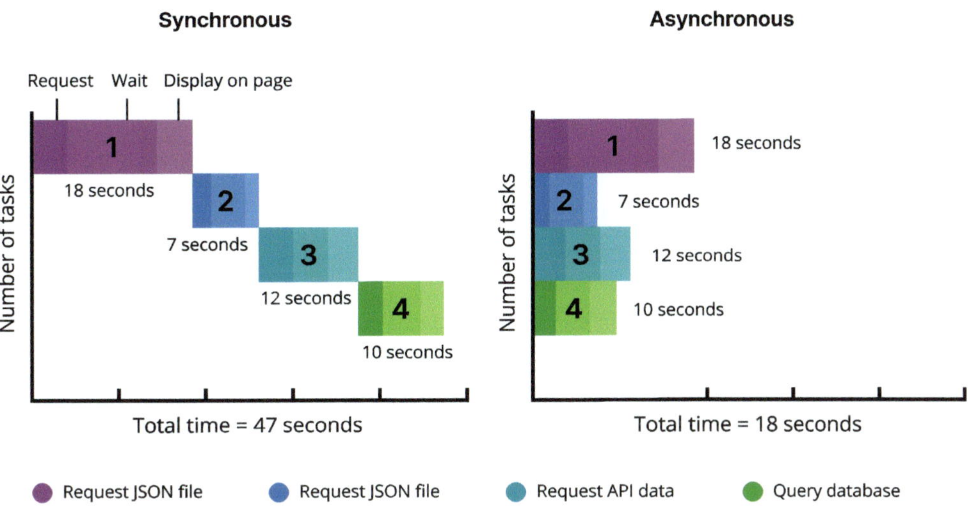

Figure 9.12
The performance benefits from using asynchronous code are visible on these side-by-side charts.

No one likes a slow web page. Whenever your page depends on data from other locations, you should plan for latency. If you use **synchronous** code that assumes each operation has completed before starting the next one, you will notice increased delays and even errors as the program tries to use content that hasn't finished loading. Using **asynchronous** (nonsequential) requests that run concurrently (figure 9.12) ensures that everything has loaded and results in pages that load faster and work better. Read on for some common solutions!

As you've seen, **callbacks** are anonymous functions that can handle asynchronous user events that occur any time during page interactions. For example, this callback function creates an alert in the browser. You don't know how much time will pass before a user clicks and initiates the listener, but when they do, your callback will handle it.

```
document.addEventListener("click", function(){
  alert("Hello from the callback function! ")
});
```

Best Practices: Avoid Callback Hell

Callbacks can be cumbersome when waiting on multiple contingent events. This example **criticalwebdesign.github.io#async-js** illustrates how nesting callbacks, a practice referred to as **callback hell**, can result in highly unmanageable code. It then shows methods to avoid the issue using JavaScript promises and `async/await`.

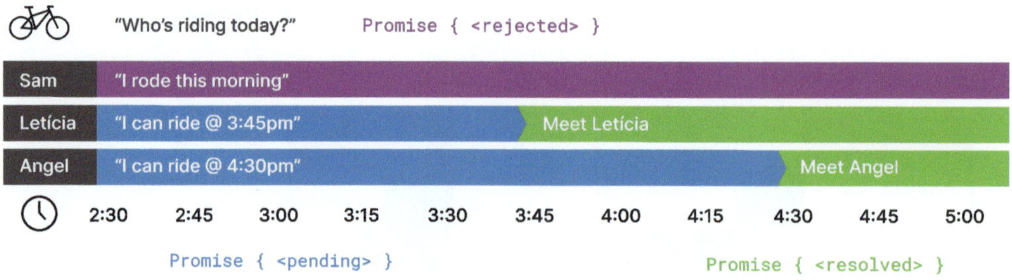

"Who's riding today?" Promise { <rejected> }

Sam "I rode this morning"

Letícia "I can ride @ 3:45pm" Meet Letícia

Angel "I can ride @ 4:30pm" Meet Angel

2:30 2:45 3:00 3:15 3:30 3:45 4:00 4:15 4:30 4:45 5:00

Promise { <pending> } Promise { <resolved> }

Figure 9.13
The workday is almost over and you want to go ride bikes with your friends. You reach out to see who is available (three requests) and wait for a reply. Of the three you ask, Sam cannot ride (promise rejected), Letícia can go at 3:45 p.m., and Angel can meet at 4:30 p.m. (two promises pending). You do other work while you wait, perhaps finishing the section of a chapter you are writing, and then head out to meet each friend who resolves their promise by arriving at the trailhead.

Promises are special objects in JavaScript that allow you to create asynchronous behavior. For example, JavaScript's `fetch()` function returns a promise while it "fetches" remote data. Once the request is complete, it will "fulfill" the promise, returning the data that was requested.[46] To wait for the response, use a **promise chain** that handles the eventual completion (or failure) of the asynchronous operation. A real-world example may help to illustrate this exchange (figure 9.13).

Exercise 9.3.1 Get Data from an API with Fetch

In this exercise you will use JavaScript's `fetch()` function and promises to get remote data from an API when your request for data is "fulfilled."

1. Open a new pen at **codepen.io** and add a fetch call to the cat fact API in the JavaScript section, and log it to the console. View the Codepen Console (press the bottom left button) to see the result message, `[object Promise]`, that lets you know it is attempting to make the request.

```
let result = fetch("https://catfact.ninja/fact")
console.log(result)
```

2. To use the data that is returned, you need to create a chain of functions that execute one by one. Change your JavaScript to the following fetch call to handle the API response.

```
fetch("https://catfact.ninja/fact")
  .then(response => response.json())
  .then(json => {
```

```
    console.log(json)
})
```

3. Examine the result in the console. In the first line of code, we called **`fetch()`** with the URL of the resource. Every line after (beginning with a dot) is part of the chain. The first **`.then()`** receives the result of **`fetch()`** using a variable called **`response`** (an arbitrary, but relevant name we used) and transforms it into a readable JavaScript object with **`.json()`**. The next **`.then()`** in the chain receives that result in a variable named **json** and logs it to the console, which you should see. Simply add whitespace inside the function to make Codepen run the request again. Note that functions with a single line can be written without the wrapping curly braces.
4. To make sure there are no issues, you can add a **`.catch()`** link in the chain, which will only run if there is an error. Hopefully you won't see any, but if you do, you can always try a different API or make sure a cat isn't sitting on your Wi-Fi router.

```
fetch("https://catfact.ninja/fact")
  .then(response => response.json())
  .then(json => {
    console.log(json)
  })
.catch(err => console.error("😿", err))
```

5. Change the URL in the **`fetch()`** function to the password generator in our chapter prompt and you'll see that this code can be easily reused to get all kinds of data!

```
fetch("https://bad-password-api.vercel.app/api/common")
```

Exercise 9.3.2 Display API Data

With an understanding of asynchronous concepts, we can add **`fetch()`** to the bad password API.

1. Create a new repo from our Bad Password API starter template at **github.com/criticalwebdesign/bad-password-api-starter** and name it "bad-password-api." Then go to **github.com/codespaces,** or your preferred code editor, and open your new repository following our steps in exercise 3.2.1.
2. Look inside your new project and see that **assets/js/main.js** already includes event listeners to call an **`updatePassword()`** function when either the page loads or an input is clicked. Notice also that this function uses an **`async`** keyword before the function declaration, which allows it to wait on events that take time. Update **`updatePassword()`** with the following code, add the Live Server extension, and preview your **index.html** page to see the data from the **/api** endpoint displayed in

the text field. Click the button to load new, common passwords! Notice that filtering results with the two groups of password types is currently not working—only common passwords appear. We'll fix this in the next step.

```
async function updatePassword() {
  let url = `https://bad-password-api.vercel.app/api/common`;
  await fetch(url)
    .then((response) => response.json())
    .then((json) => {
      password.value = json.message;
    });
}
```

3. Now that you are getting the most *common* bad passwords from the API into your web page, you can make use of the options under the form to let the user playfully recreate their own combinations. First, conduct a test in the browser by changing the **common** endpoint you used previously to a custom one. Paste the following URL into a new browser tab and then change the params value to other combinations (of endearments, pets, cities, dates, colors, or patterns) to see the new passwords (figure 9.14).
   `https://bad-password-api.vercel.app/api/custom?params=pets,dates`

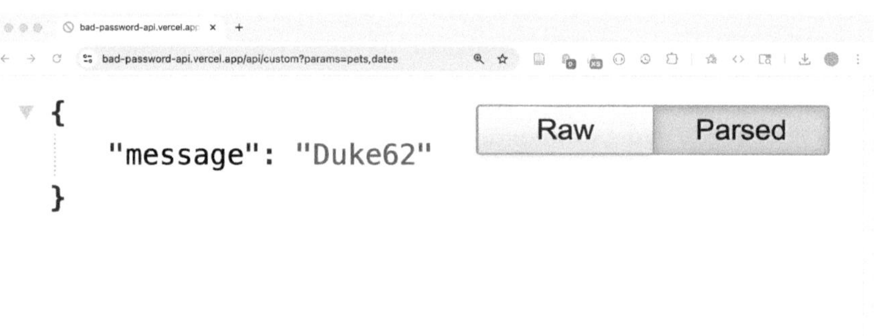

Figure 9.14
Our project returns JSON data from the API.

4. Send these custom parameters to the API when the user selects different options in the web page. Our design prompts users to check a radio button in two groups of common password types. Inside **main.js** we use a custom selector to see which parameter is chosen in each group. The selector looks for `<input>` elements with a

name attribute set to either **group1** or **group2** and stores either **true** (checked) or **false** in each variable. Add this code to the beginning of the **updatePassword()** function and check your console to see the result:

```
async function updatePassword() {
 let group1 = document.querySelector("input[name=group1]:checked");
 let group2 = document.querySelector("input[name=group2]:checked");
 console.log(group1, group2);
 let url = "https://bad-password-api.vercel.app/api/common";
```

5. Now you can send the choices to the API. Update the url variable to send the current checked value of the inputs as query parameters via the fetch request. Preview your project and revel in the awful passwords!

```
let url = `https://bad-password-api.vercel.app/api/custom?params=
${group1.value},${group2.value}`;
await fetch(url)
```

Check Your Work

This concludes the chapter exercises. We invite you to compare your work to the final outcome **criticalwebdesign.github.io#9-3** and code **criticalwebdesign.github.io#9-3-code** in the book repo. Don't forget to turn on GitHub Pages in your project and then stage and commit your work to make it live!

Prompt 9.3 Publish: Share Your Bad Passwords

Contrary to "best practices" of keeping passwords a secret, we invite you to share the *Bad Password API* broadly, as an act of service to your friends and family. Update the design to make the project your own. See the wiki for an additional module 9.4 to learn how to use Node.js to update the back end of the generator and publish it with Vercel.

Author Note: "If it needs a sign, it's a bad design."

We often find ourselves telling students, "Users don't read!" When we test final projects in class, if a project must be explained with a large textblock, we ask for a redesign.[47]

10 Design and Power

> [As designers] our job is to advocate for the people who aren't in the room. [...] We need to understand we have a greater responsibility to society than to the people who sign the checks.
> —Mike Monteiro

Context

Now that you have achieved a range of experiences and knowledge designing, coding, and publishing websites, we focus on potential positive uses of that power. In the Context, we discuss participation, engagement, and audience, while the modules will guide you to create a participatory work that empowers your audience using a database and web maps.

Power

We've already addressed many types of power in this book. For example, the affordances resulting from being included in (as opposed to excluded from) network structures (chapter 1); the prospects offered by open-source software and being able view the source of documents in the browser (chapter 2); the ability to direct users attention (chapter 4) and make information coherent through usable interfaces (chapter 5) while including and accommodating others' perspectives and limitations in the design process (chapter 7); the asymmetrical relationships enabled by corporate marketing (chapter 3) and a few of the ways that surveillance capitalism permeates and influences our daily lives (chapter 9); and likewise, the power that you have to confront such forces through critical web design (chapter 3), and when needed, to step away from distractions and disconnect from the noise of the internet (chapter 6) and AI-marketing speak (chapter 8).

This textbook strikes a balance between themes relevant to critical web design and foundational tools used to build for the web. As a result, we have only brushed the surface of the ways technologies for the internet fail to enable equitable situations for everyone involved. Wilneida Negrón described how hate crimes, harassment, and discrimination were increasing online in 2017, and that fake news, biased information, and propaganda would threaten democracy and free expression.[1] Nearly a decade later these concerns are still relevant. And it's unclear when or how this may change: Social media–constructed filter bubbles prevent opposing sides from sharing perspectives, and those same platforms continuously put increasing profit and power over users' privacy and desire to turn away from required ad views, as well as new forms of misinformation enabled by Silicon Valley's fervor for AI start-ups.[2]

It is also evident that design might be part of the problem. Design schools are often overly focused on commercial outcomes and place integrating students into the industry above emphasizing empathy and inclusive decision-making.[3] It's no surprise to hear designers admit that they often feel "responsible for making people feel terrible about themselves, only redeemable by buying this product or that service."[4] And Silicon Valley has no reason to change their emergent dominance, investing millions of dollars to lobby legislators and the public in order to secure their monopolies over users and markets.[5] In *Ruined by Design*, Mike Monteiro writes that issues like global warming, affronts to our privacy, and online safety happen primarily *because* these systems were designed to reward these acts. However, even among all these problems, there is cause for hope and positive thinking.

Optimism

Even with considerable downsides, technology can also enable and support big ideas among small groups of people who care. For example, there are a host of collectives and journalists dedicated to exposing and unpowering big tech. Tactical Tech is an organization that uses design and research to promote digital literacy through apps, experiences, interventions, and educational resources. Their Data Detox Kit can help "take control of your digital privacy, security, and wellbeing," among other practical outcomes.[6] Games for Change is a festival dedicated to empowering diverse voices and innovation around social issues through games.[7] The Markup creates journalism and web applications that challenge technology to serve the public good. One of our favorites, their Blacklight tool, is a real-time website privacy inspector that exposes tracking technologies like, well, a blacklight.[8] *LOW←TECH MAGAZINE* is an online publication that questions the value of technological progress, describes the potentials

Additional Materials and Resources

Explore links and other content related to this chapter: **criticalwebdesign.github.io#wiki-10**

of often-forgotten tech, and promotes sustainable energy practices.[9] Unlike the mind-numbing megawatts required for server farms and AI-focused data centers used by Amazon, Instagram, and TikTok, *LOW←TECH* focuses on efficiency in their design by removing advertising and using a static site generator (Hugo) to power their website with a single 50W solar panel[10] (figure 10.1). Even some Silicon Valley companies are exploring "calm technology" that can assist users without creating new notifications and distractions.[11]

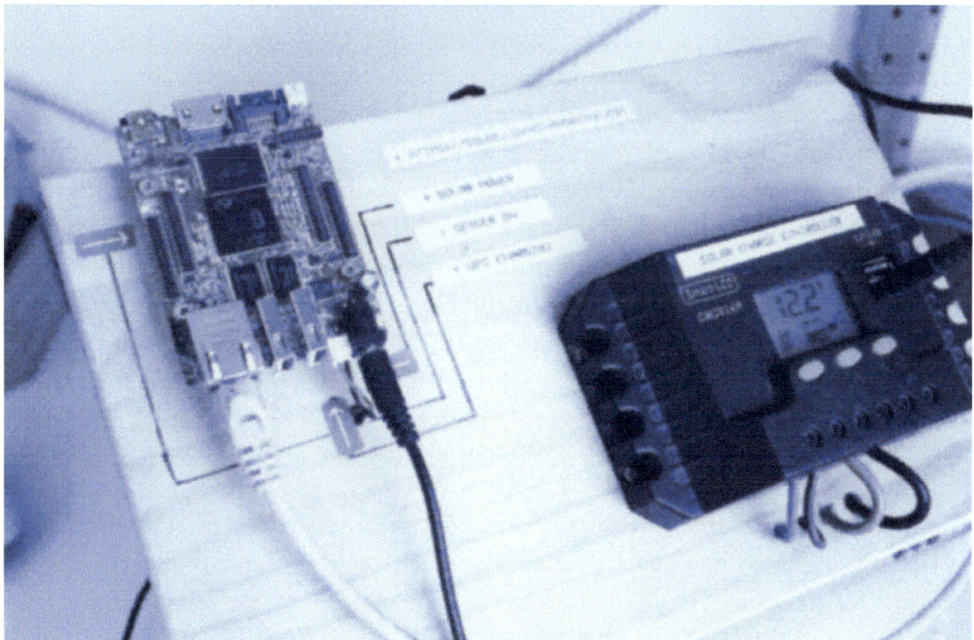

Figure 10.1
The first prototype of the solar powered server that runs the *LOW←TECH MAGAZINE* website **lowtechmagazine.com**. The solar charge controller (on the right) is powering the server (on the left). This image, like others on the site, is dithered to reduce the file size and make the server more efficient.

As authors, artists, and educators, our goals are aligned with these optimistic measures: We hope to encourage more thoughtful people to build and publish things that are not common; web pages and apps that ask important questions, that are weird, free to access, functional, and even fun.[12] We think that leaning into outcomes that perform utilities, something that traditionally separates design from art, is one way to move forward.

Participation

In chapter 1 we discuss the impact of the rise of the internet in relation to how the ability to link from a document to other resources—pages, content, or media—created a new inherently interactive media format. With links, buttons, mouse states, and page refreshes, for instance, the web is a place of predictable causality. Loosely, the user imagines the state of encounter to be: Click here and X happens. In this chapter, we encourage you to extend the interaction from an audience of one-person-clicking to a crowd of participants, actively engaging with your ideas, creating a whole that is greater than the sum of its individual parts, clicks, or interactions.

In his introduction to *The Art of Participation 1950s to Now*, Rudolf Frieling asks, "But is there an art of participation?"[13] In response, Frieling stresses how creating participatory works requires the audience to enter a situation without knowing what will become of the work or their engagement. Ultimately, this question of becoming is transferred to the people entangled in the work of art (or design). The back-and-forth act of communication and participation between the artist/designer's intention for their creation and the audience/participant's engagement *becomes* the experience. A work of participatory critical web design expands interaction from anticipated clicks to surprising encounters. Frieling notes, "Truly participatory art—that which goes beyond symbolic gestures—is a utopian ideal rather than an artistic or political reality."[14]

Participatory work that generates "utopian ideals" also shares a legacy with a genre of art called "socially engaged art" or art as "social practice." Tania Bruguera describes her work as "arte útil," a framework for artists to imagine "how one can use all the tools of art to change reality and how to incorporate themselves as artists and civic servants into that reality."[15] Pablo Helguera writes, "What characterizes socially engaged art is its dependence on social intercourse as a factor of its existence."[16] Socially engaged work is defined by its prioritization of process and transformation over objects; and with such a focus on imagining new and alternative realities, it aligns with participation within the context of critical web design. Several example projects and approaches within this context follow, organized loosely into connected themes.

Collective Information

- **GreatFire.org** is a site that brings "transparency to the Great Firewall of China."[17] Their GreatFire Analyzer tool makes visible and provides live reports on websites and apps blocked by the Chinese government using censorship, domain blocking, and deep packet inspection.[18]
- Brooke Singer and her team created **Toxic-Sites.us** to collect and reconfigure publicly available data into a more usable interface "to engage people in public information and encourage participation."[19]
- *Terms of Service; Didn't Read* **tosdr.org** grades websites and services on how well they respect users in their Terms of Service. The site contains a wealth of user-contributed stats on Facebook, Amazon, and others' nonobvious power grabs enabled in the agreements that everyone accepts but rarely reads.[20]

Shared Experiences

- Projects like Pip Shea's *Any Cast* transform a mundane activity (like agreeing to Terms of Use for free Wi-Fi) into a collectively generated stream of thoughts to create a whole truly greater than the sum of its parts.[21] A similar project (without Wi-Fi but still online today) is Alex Fuller's **onamountaintop.com**, which equally allows anyone to share a simple message outside of their bubble and without signing away one's privacy.[22]
- Dries Depoorter offers another humorous take on shared experience with a networked chat app that connects people around the world who have less than 5% battery left on their phones.[23]
- **Speedshow.net** was created by Aram Bartoll as a reusable model to transform internet cafés into one-night internet art exhibitions that others can extend or expand at any location.[24]

Participatory Service

- Miranda July created *Somebody* **somebodyapp.com**, an app and messaging service that was, in her words, "half-app, half-human."[25] The app connected participants in similar geographic areas, letting them send messages, or deliver them for others in person, as a social service (figure 10.2). The companion film she created offers the best description, representing it like a cross between *Uber* and *Craigslist*, where a stranger (or you) can transmit a message (an apology, an endearment, a breakup) in person that might be difficult to do yourself.
- **TheNicestPlace.net** offers hugs from its participants for a mediated audience. Informed by conceptual art practices, the website provides instructions so that others can join and make an impactful experience out of a collection of small acts.[26]

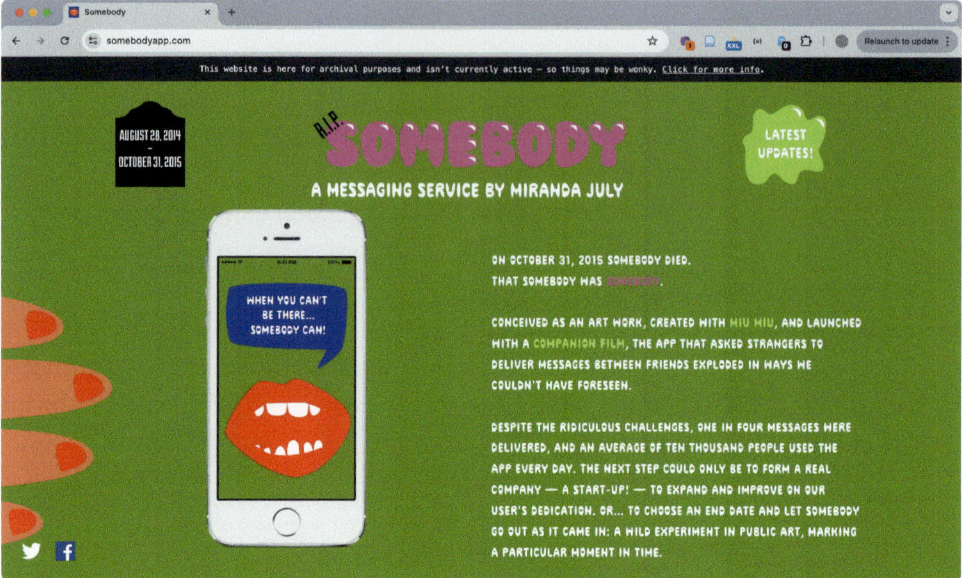

Figure 10.2

Somebody by Miranda July was a short-lived but imaginative reconfiguration of critical engagement and interpersonal communication. Source: **somebodyapp.com**.

Inspiration: Online Participation

See these and more examples at **criticalwebdesign.github.io#wiki-10**.

Case Study: We Feel Fine

We Feel Fine (2005), created by Jonathan Harris and Sepandar Kamvar, was an online project that visualized publicly available text (e.g., blogs, social media) that started with the phrase "I feel."[27] In their book, Harris and Kamvar write, "At its core, *We Feel Fine* is an artwork authored by everyone. It will grow and change as we grow and change, reflecting what's on our blogs, what's in our hearts, what's in our minds. We hope it makes the world seem a little smaller, and we hope it helps people see beauty in the everyday ups and downs of life."[28] Nearly twenty years later, this project continues to inspire us as a work that reimagines the world not as a melting pot of strangers but as a place made beautiful through the connection and volume of human feelings. While creating interactions between participants is a method for social engagement, the internet offers advantages that aren't bound by time or space. Saving information in databases, to be viewed later, and made meaningful through ways they might already be connected, such as location, empowers one to expand on the synthesis of participant experiences and create meaning from small interactions.

In the book that followed Kamvar and Harris's *We Feel Fine* online project, the authors pair studies of their database, including more than twelve million human feelings collected from personal blog entries from 2006 to 2009 (figure 10.3). They write, "It is a testament to the optimism of human nature that on that same night, as on every night since *We Feel Fine* started collecting data from blogs, hope was expressed more often than anxiety."[29]

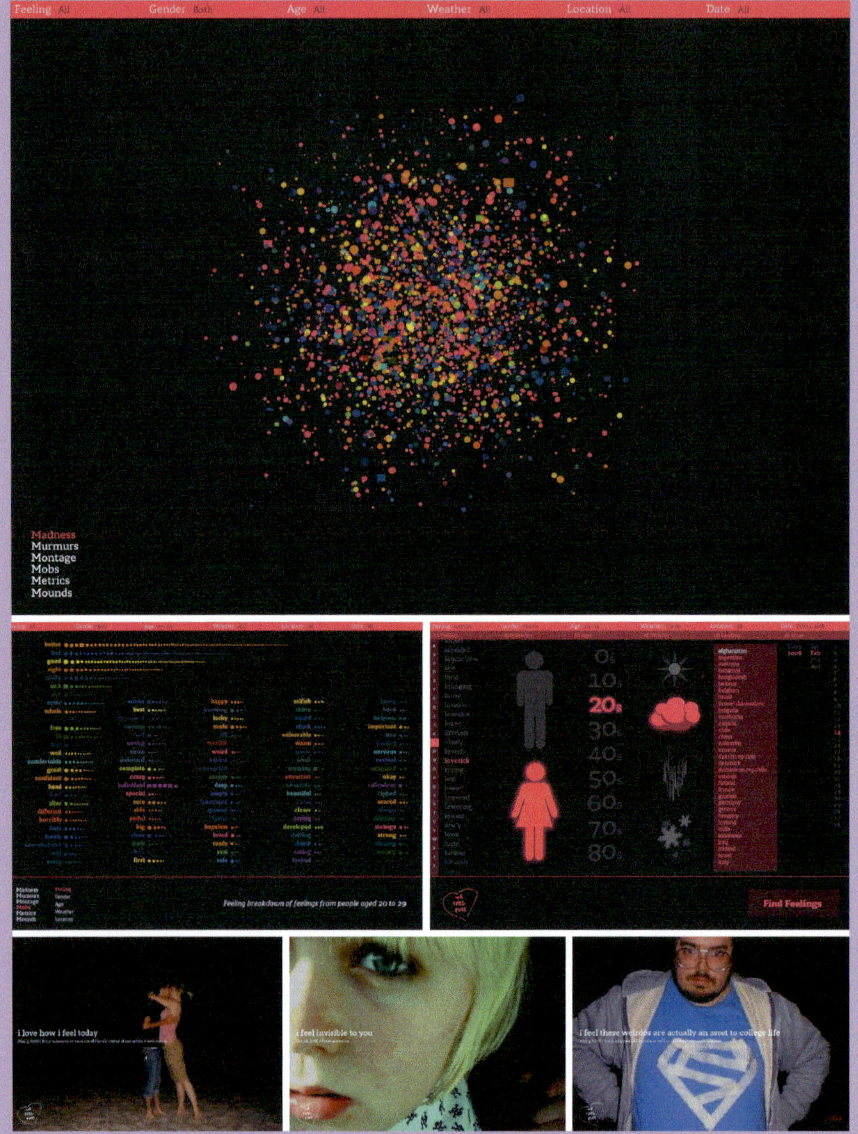

Figure 10.3
Jonathan Harris and Sep Kamvar, *We Feel Fine* (2006–2009). Top: "Madness," Middle: "Mobs Feeling Breakdown and Search Panel," Bottom: Collages made by participants. wefeelfine.org.

Prompt 10: What You'll Make
Harness the Power of Participants

Inspired by *We Feel Fine*, the modules in this chapter will lead you to build an interactive site that uses the web to harness the power of participant engagement. The technology Harris and Kamvar used (Java Applets) to create and publish the multifaceted interactive visualizations on **wefeelfine.org** are no longer supported by web browsers. This prompt is a modest homage to Harris and Kamvar's project. In module 1 you will read about how we planned and designed the prompt and use the structure to imagine your own version of this project. Module 2 is an introduction to Leaflet for making interactive maps. In module 3 you'll learn how databases store user contributions and then follow the full-stack tutorial on the wiki to visualize them on a map.

View the results of *Big Feelings* at **criticalwebdesign.github.io#10-3** (figure 10.4). You can see the final code at **criticalwebdesign.github.io#10-3-code.**

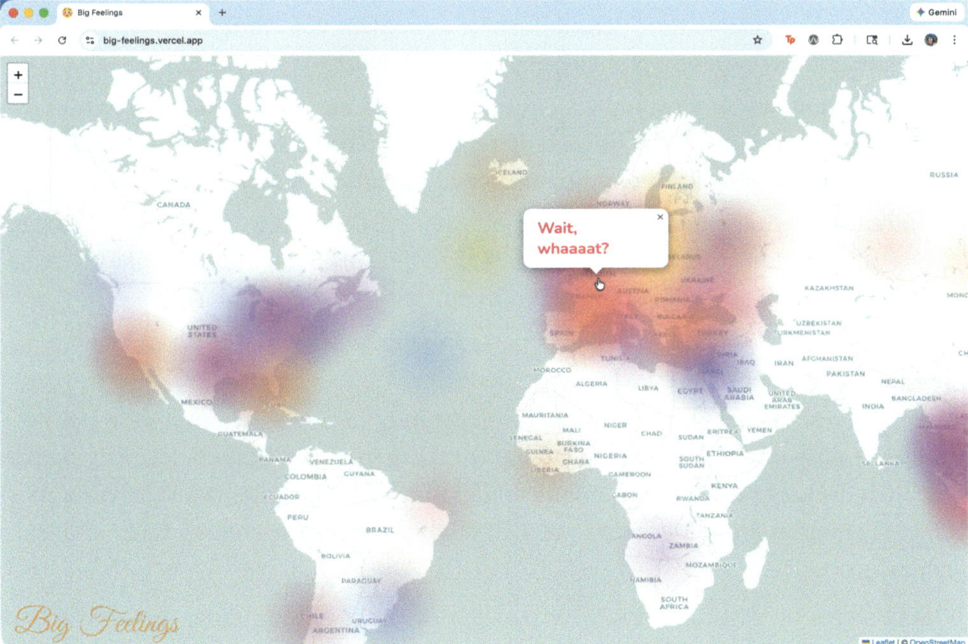

Figure 10.4
Upon completing exercises in module 10.3, *Big Feelings* will display user sentiment data on a map.

Module 10.1 Planning and Design

In this module we share our research and iterative process for creating the concept and design for *Big Feelings*, the project we created while generating prompts for this chapter. We will follow the structure of the "iterative design/prototype flowchart" we shared in module 5.3.

Exercise 10.1.1 Define Your Project Concept

We've shared multiple methods for conducting research and planning a project throughout this book. The prompts below outline a general strategy to consider when starting a project.

1. Identify potential topics to explore using brainstorming strategies (chapters 3 and 6). The scope of your project is important, as working with a theme or issue too specific can narrow your audience and one that is too broad may create the kind of "scope creep" that results in an unfocused message or simply a project too large to tackle in a reasonable time period. Is there a problem you want to solve? Or do you wish to address issues by problematizing your subject?
2. Write a summary of your topic(s) and research. Address why you are drawn to this topic and why it is important to explore. Identify the communities, resources, and issues involved. Include technology you will potentially use in your project.
3. Collect research (related texts) and inspiration (visuals and works of art and design) in a competition scan (chapter 5). Look through this book and the wiki for examples. Figure 10.5 includes examples from our research.

Exercise 10.1.2 Plan Your Project

We've also discussed various methods for generating ideas and planning for a project. While the planning phase involves visual thinking methods that could easily be part of a **pitch deck**, or proposal you might share to present your intentions, creating these is most beneficial for you because you will discover what you need to build and learn about the obstacles.

1. Brainstorm by writing about your concept or using experimental methods (chapter 6) that incorporate randomness within your themes.
2. Write a one-paragraph introduction to your concept and what you plan to make. Who will use this and why?
3. Create an initial attempt at a visual identity (e.g., a logo, word mark, style guide).

Figure 10.5

Top: *Queering the Map*, **queeringthemap.com** (2018), is a community-generated cartographic archive of queer experiences. Created by Lucas LaRochelle, the site catalogs, preserves, and locates the experiences of queer life, including encounters, collective action, and stories of coming out. Middle: *Exhausting a Crowd* (2015) **exhaustingacrowd.com** (2015) by Kyle McDonald is a web application that depicts detailed security camera footage upon which website visitors can add annotations synced with both the imagery and the time code of the video. The crowd-sourced text laid over the twelve hours of repeating footage from various sites offers curious commentary that perfectly balances the opposing forces of surveillance vs. privacy, looking vs. being seen, and control vs. pleasure that defines our information culture and public spaces. Bottom: *Pointer Pointer*, **pointerpointer.com** (2012) by **Studio Moniker** and **Studio Puckey** matches your mouse position to a random image of a person pointing, seemingly to that same location.

4. Create a diagram or flowchart to visualize the user experience, the flow of data, or wireframes with significant views in the interface such as introduction page, forms, results pages, and so on.
5. List technologies you will use. Pseudocode the main logic of your project. Include the unknown factors—parts of your idea that you don't yet know how to execute.

Exercise 10.1.3 Create a Prototype

The design and prototype for your project should begin and happen in unison. You might consider it to be a division of labor between your right and left brain, respectively. Although to be sure, you will find plenty of math and logic in the design process, and equally, much creative and imaginative thinking can help your code solutions. The best argument for working on these together is that first, they are both iterative processes that influence each other. What you learn from building the prototype—the working "proof of concept" for your project—will influence how you represent it in the design. The other important reason to keep them separate is that design is much easier in a layout program, where you can duplicate a frame to test changes quickly in new iterations (figure 10.6). Also, if you add a lot of CSS to your prototype, then that's extra code to troubleshoot when you really should be focused on functionality. Like figure 5.11 shows, you will eventually bring them together once they are both complete. Here are tips for developing a prototype:

1. Your prototype should contain the essential functions of your project.
2. Feel free to use any example template repository from the book to get started.
3. Save and refresh your work in the browser often to see your changes. Commit changes regularly.

Exercise 10.1.4 Design Your Project

Your design iterations should contain the main "views" of your project. Ideally, a landing page and other pages where users will spend a lot of time.

1. In addition to wireframes, it is good practice to start by creating a mood board showing how others have designed similar solutions.
2. Create your design iterations with Figma or another layout tool that is easy for you to use.
3. Consider using Figma's app prototyping tools that let you click, scroll, and experience a basic version of your project.[30]
4. Show your work! Do not delete previous versions of your designs so that you can see and compare your progress as you iterate and improve your designs.

5. Use *Owen's Design Process* (module 6.1) to create multiple iterations of each different page or view of your app. Look at relevant examples of good design to help you improve your own, then experiment and iterate!

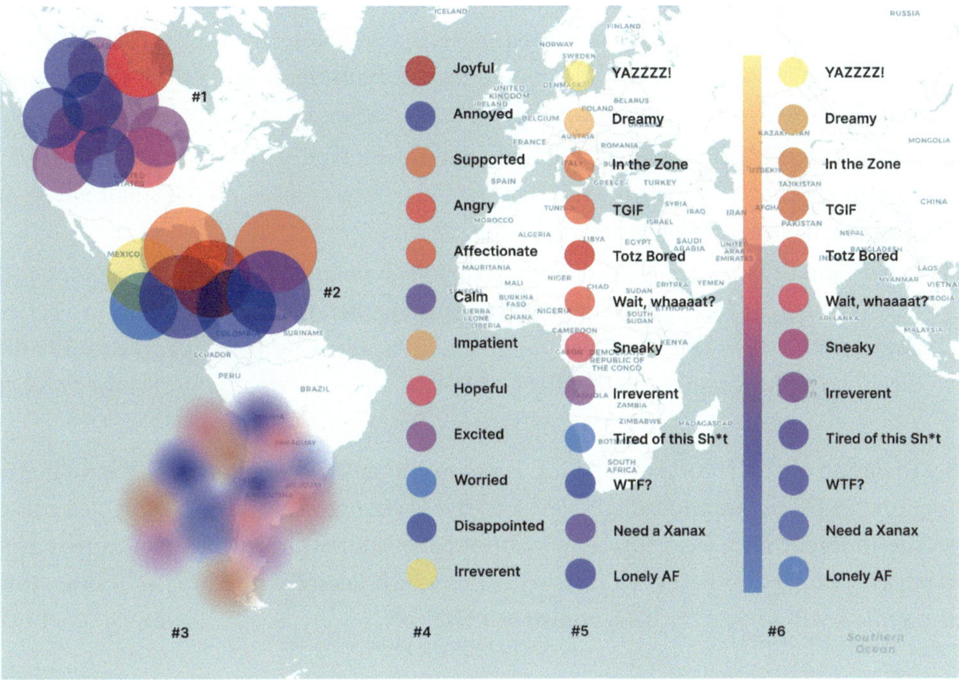

Figure 10.6
In our initial conversations about *Big Feelings* we imagined feelings as colorful bubbles on the map, and we wanted our map to feel mushy, like a bunch of feelings indefinitely overlapping each other. We experimented with color (1) and size (2), opacity, blending modes, and gradients (3) of the shapes on top of a map screenshot. Once we knew we wanted to represent a list of feelings with associated colors, we started with common sentiments and selected colors by hand (4). xtine created a new, more contemporary version of the mood languages and sorted them (5). Owen used a gradient in Figma within a mask of circles to make a continuous gradient to create consistent spacing between the color hues (6).

Multiple Audiences

In *Art as Social Practice: Technologies for Change*, Harrell Fletcher lists three audiences you should consider when you plan your work: creators of the work (designers/artists/cultural workers), people who participate in the work directly, and those who experience the work in mediated form.[31] We considered these audiences as we were designing the project you will build in this chapter, as well as its multiple configurations across devices, states, and interactions, including:

1. The "users" or the participants who interact with the map interface we envisioned and those "observers" who would experience the work without participating (over the shoulder or a screenshot).
2. Those who would add their own feelings to the database, or simply observe others' data; What motivations someone would have for communicating their experiences, and the potential to be given comfort by others doing the same.
3. The representation of data on the map, and how it would look (and change) across various zoom-levels. How the interface would be experienced on the small screen of a mobile device, or a large desktop display.
4. What kind of language would be simultaneously poignant and funny—serious and light—given the fact that we are writing this chapter and designing this project as parents. And how this language might be interpreted by participants at different locations, cultures, political leanings, as well as viewers who might find the work at a much later date.

To design a project for participation is not just to design the interaction but to imagine how its documentation might speak to the exchange years later. You are designing in the moment for a near future, which may feel somewhat predictable, as well as a faraway future that is harder to anticipate. It is worth taking extra time to consider how the project will unfold for these multiple audiences.

Prompt 10.1 Design: Consider Multiple Audiences

As you plan for your own projects, you should consider the perspectives of anyone who may encounter or participate in your project. Use our examples above to research, plan, design, and code a work full of surprises for others to experience. Consider making something that makes others feel like they belong; like they are not alone, but eternal, part of something bigger than the self. Imagine you are riding a bike adjacent to a large mountain. You pedal for hours, passing trees, structures, time, but the mountain is so large that it appears to still be in the same position, omnipresent, and forever. This is like our communal experience, as we participate in concert with others.

Module 10.2 Interactive Maps

In this module you'll learn to create web maps using JavaScript and Leaflet, then show information on a map layer with JSON data.

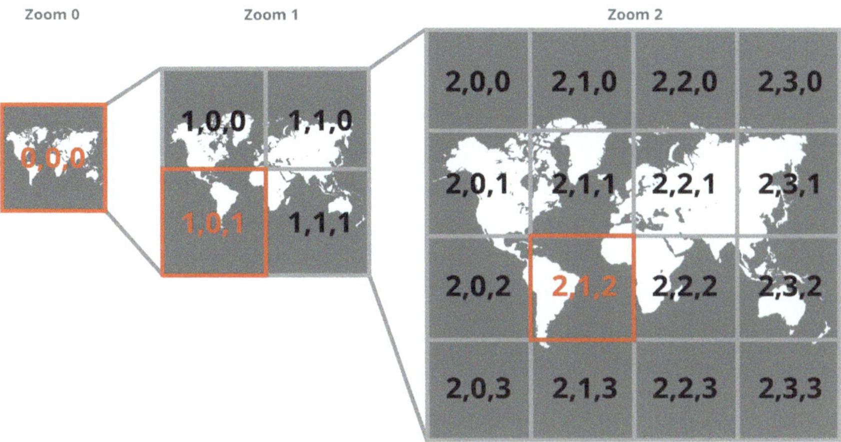

Figure 10.7

Three zoom levels in a map tileset. The labels in our graphic follow the z (zoom), x (longitude position), and y (latitude position) format of tileset templates. The orange square represents the viewport of the browser.

10.2.1 Web Maps

Interactive maps are everywhere. Whether embedded in a web page, a mobile app, or a screen in your car or a kiosk, the functionality is generally the same. Interactive maps load and display geographically aligned images as map layers and then provide context-specific controls for panning, zooming, selecting, and so on. Images in a web map consist of a **base layer** (the terrain) and **overlay layers** (e.g., roads, labels, or markers that can be clicked). The base layer of a web map is created from a **tileset**, a collection of raster (in the case of satellite photos) or vector images, displayed in a grid (figure 10.7). In addition to location, map tiles correspond to specific zoom levels. Zoom level 0 shows the full earth, while level 18 (in the case of Leaflet) shows details of a city.[32] Loading the base layer as tiles is efficient because the browser only needs to request those images visible in the viewport at that zoom level, until the user drags or zooms the map view to a new area and new tiles are loaded.

Exercise 10.2.1 Create a Map with Leaflet

There are several JavaScript frameworks that make it easy to create maps. This demo uses Leaflet, which is free, open source, and mobile friendly. In this exercise you will set up a new map view and change the base layer using Leaflet and Codepen.

1. Make a copy of our Leaflet Starter by pressing the **Fork** button in the lower right corner on Codepen at **criticalwebdesign.github.io#leaflet-starter** and examine the

basic Leaflet map. This Pen has the Leaflet CSS and JS code installed in the Pen Settings, as well as the following HTML element to display the map.

```
<div id="map"></div>
```

2. Analyze the JS code in the Pen. Importing the Leaflet JavaScript file instantly creates a new Leaflet object named `L`, which is used to access the library functionality. This initializes the map into a new variable and sets its default position and zoom level. Locations in Leaflet use an array with a **latitude** (position on the earth's y axis denoted by horizontal lines) and **longitude** (position on the x axis marked on vertical lines). Find your location using **latlong.net** and plug the two values into the array below (replacing ours) so that the map shows your location.

```
var map = L.map("map").setView([35.5, -80.85], 3);
```

3. When you initialize a map, you can set the **zoom** level (or view) to be low (close up) or high (far away). The number after the coordinates sets the zoom level from 0 to 18. Change the zoom level in `.setView` to see the effect.

```
var map = L.map("map").setView([35.5, -80.85], 9);
```

4. The map terrain is added using the `tileLayer()` function. Leaflet makes it easy to change the underlying map image by simply pointing to a different tileset server using the z/x/y template (zoom level/longitude/latitude), which automatically tracks and fetches the correct tiles for each location. This example code below sets the base layer to OpenStreetMap, but you can change it by selecting a different URL from a tileset provider.

```
L.tileLayer(`https://tile.openstreetmap.org/{z}/{x}/{y}.png`)
.addTo(map);
```

Explore the map tilesets at **criticalwebdesign.github.io#tiles**. There are many free tilesets you can use to change the color and feeling of your map. When you find one you like, press the **Info** button and copy and paste the tileset URL over the existing URL to see it in your map.

Author Note: Leaflet Help

If you select a base map and find it doesn't load quickly (or at all), it might be stored on a slow server. If you encounter technical issues, refer to the Leaflet Quickstart Guide, **leafletjs.com/examples/quick-start** for more information. We also link to several other free tile services in the wiki, **criticalwebdesign.github.io#wiki-10.**

5. With a base layer in place, you can now add overlays to the map. Add this code to create a new marker on the map at your position. Use **latlong.net** again to get

coordinates for a specific spot within your map view, and replace the latitude and longitude with your new location. If you add a marker not currently in your map view, you will need to zoom out or pan the map to find it. In the next exercise you'll continue adding markers to the map using GeoJSON data. Feel free to explore the leaflet documentation for more examples.

```
// set base layer tileset
L.tileLayer(`http://services.arcgisonline.com/arcgis/rest
/services/NatGeo_World_Map/MapServer/tile/{z}/{y}/{x}`)
.addTo(map);
var marker = L.marker([35.498116, -80.849124]).addTo(map);
```

Exercise 10.2.2 Create and Add GeoJSON to Leaflet

GeoJSON is a lightweight data format based on JSON with specific properties for representing geographic features (markers, shapes, or other visual information) and data linked to those features. In this exercise you'll create a GeoJSON file and add it to a Leaflet map.

1. Open **geojson.io** in a new tab in your web browser and keep your Codepen project (from above) open, as you'll return to it. Select a marker or drawing tool from the interface and click to add features to the map. As you draw, it will add data to the GeoJSON data on the right.
2. Add information to the map using a popup. Select a pin or other feature that you've added to the map. In the properties tab of the box that appears, you'll see a table with one row and two columns. Add a key to the left column to identify the value you add to the box on the right. Click save and the data will appear in the GeoJSON panel on the right. In figure 10.8 we added "name" as the key and "lefteye" as the value, but you can add anything you like. For example, you could mark or annotate places you know or want to go to or even add a URL for an image to display.
3. After you add a few features and data, select all the GeoJSON code in the panel on the right and copy it. Click back to the Codepen you created in the previous exercise and paste the GeoJSON data to the bottom of the script panel. Assign the GeoJSON object to a new variable called `geojsonFeature` and set it equal to the object you pasted. It will look something like this:

```
let geojsonFeature = {
  "type": "FeatureCollection",
  "features": [
  . . .
  ]
}
```

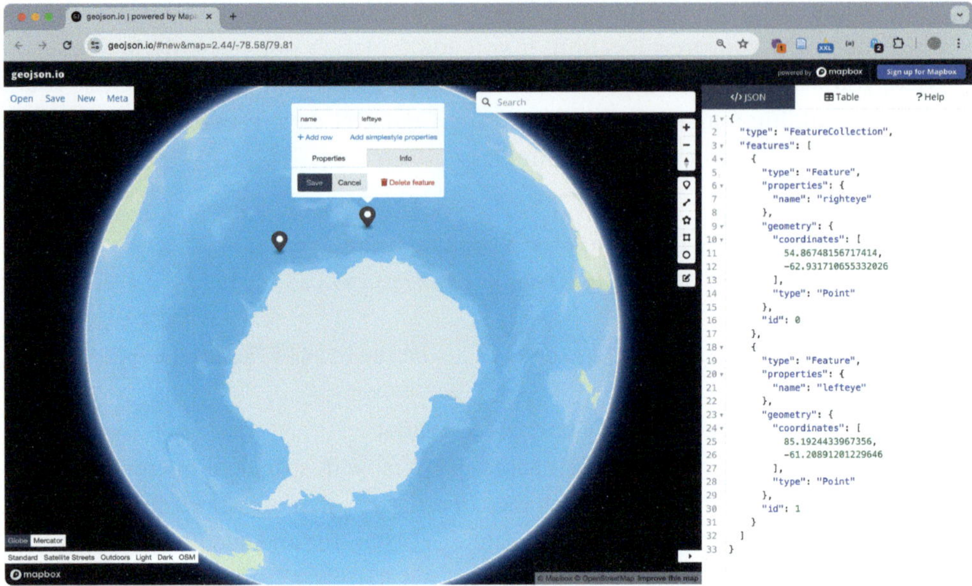

Figure 10.8
geojson.io is a user-friendly site for creating and formatting JSON map data.

4. Insert this code below the GeoJSON object to add the data to the map and browse the map to confirm your features were added.

```
L.geoJSON(geojsonFeature).addTo(map);
```

5. You can access and display the data for each feature you saved by implementing a callback function. Update your **geoJSON** function to match the below. This will call the function for each feature it adds. You can see it checks to make sure there is a **name** property and then binds a pop-up containing its value. Click on one of your features now and you will see a pop-up with that data. Our code assumes you have a property called "name." If not, alter our code to match the property identifier you used.

```
L.geoJSON(geojsonFeature, {
  onEachFeature: onEachFeature
}).addTo(map);
function onEachFeature(feature, layer) {
  if (feature.properties && feature.properties.name) {
    layer.bindPopup(feature.properties.name);
  }
}
```

6. Continue experimenting! If you want to see additional features in your marker pop-up, you can concatenate them using a **+** sign in the **bindPopup** method, like we did in the following code that displays a name and a color. (You will also need a **color** property for this to work!) You can see through this exercise how easily one can build a dataset to display information on a web map to create narratives, visualizations, or much more.[33]

```
function onEachFeature(feature, layer) {
  if (feature.properties && feature.properties.name
  && feature.properties.color) {
    layer.bindPopup(feature.properties.name + " "
    + feature.properties.color);
  }
}
```

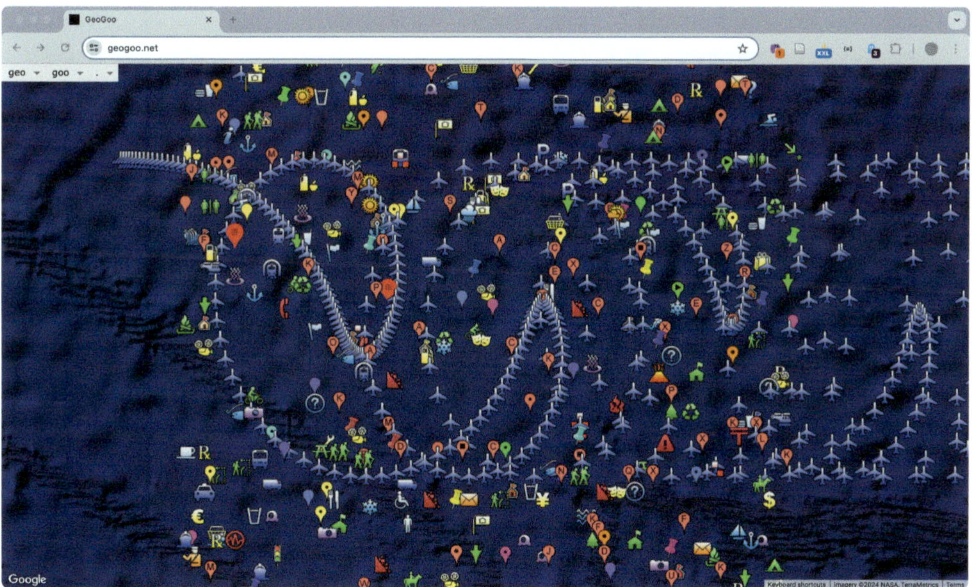

Figure 10.9
GeoGoo **geogoo.net** by Jodi (Joan Heemskerk and Dirk Paesmans) is a wonderfully chaotic series of animations using the default icons of the Google Maps API. Users can select from the drop-down options or simply refresh the page to load new iterations that visualize mathematical functions, symbols, or completely random designs across a variety of terrains and lunar surfaces. *While offline for a period, the site (thankfully) is live again.

Exercise 10.2.3 Add Leaflet Vector Markers

Now that you have a basic understanding of Leaflet, this exercise will show you how to create and display vector markers on a map. You'll be creating a work inspired by Jodi's *GeoGoo* project (figure 10.9).

1. Open the map you created in the first Leaflet exercise with Codepen. First, add this code to the bottom of the script panel to import a library called Faker.js,[34] which offers a wealth of fake but realistic data we can use to add shapes to the map.

```
import {faker} from "https://esm.sh/@faker-js/faker";
```

2. Like Leaflet, all the functionality of the library is available through this object. Add this code below the import statement to use Faker's location functions to select a new, random location and then add a marker to the map and update the map view to the new location.

```
let center = [faker.location.latitude(),
faker.location.longitude()];
var marker = L.marker(center).addTo(map);
map.setView(center, 8);
```

   You can see from the Leaflet documentation that there are a variety of vector layers one can add to the map. We'll start with the **circleMarker**, since that's the type used in the chapter prompt. You will add a **for** loop that creates a new random nearby location and uses it to add thirty circle markers to the map.

```
for (var i = 0; i < 30; i++) {
  let loc = faker.location.nearbyGPSCoordinate({
    origin: center, radius: 800
  });
  let circle = L.circleMarker(loc, {
    stroke: false,
    radius: 50,
    fillColor: "red",
    fillOpacity: 1
  }).addTo(map);
}
```

3. Now you can use other Faker.js functions from their documentation (see **fakerjs.dev**) to add variety to the shapes. Update your code by replacing the **radius**, **fillColor**, and **fillOpacity** values with the following Faker functions. Every time this page loads, it will select new locations and colors for the circles (figure 10.10).

```
let circle = L.circleMarker(loc, {
  stroke: false,
  radius: faker.number.int({min: 40, max: 100}),
  fillColor: faker.color.rgb(),
  fillOpacity: faker.number.float({min: 0.3,max: 0.7})
}).addTo(map);
```

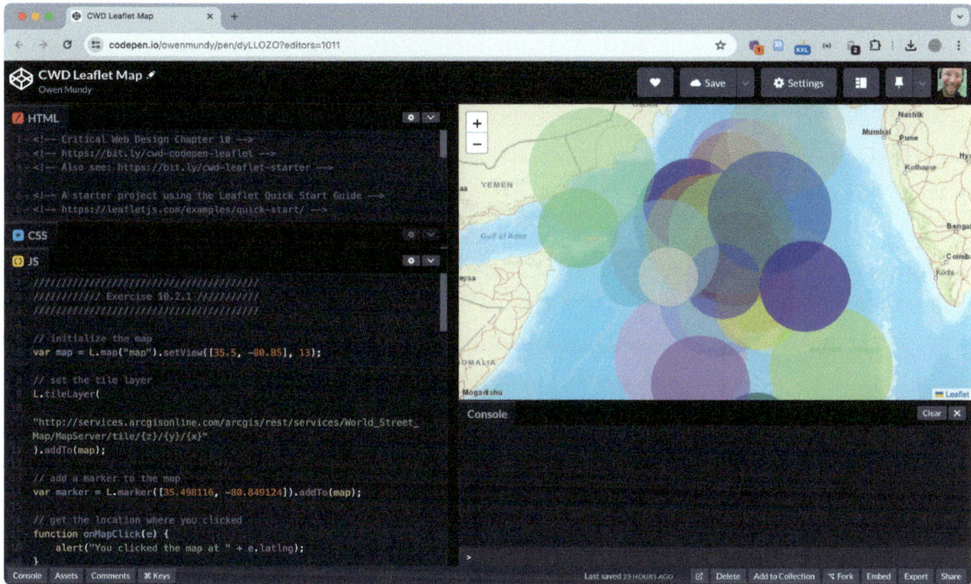

Figure 10.10

The result of exercises in module 10.2 is a map populated with fake data using two libraries, Leaflet (for the map) and Faker.js (for the data). See it online: **criticalwebdesign.github.io#leaflet**.

⚠ Watch Out!

Sometimes Leaflet's capitalization can be tricky. For example, the **LatLng** class is written in TitleCase, while the **L.latLng** method that converts a location to a **LatLng** is written in camelCase. Additionally, the documentation uses lowercase for the variable names. So both of the following examples will create a valid **LatLng** object.

```
let latlng = new LatLng([35.7, -82.2]);
let latlng = L.latLng([35.7, -82.2]);
```

Prompt 10.2 Code: Reimagine the Map Surface

Continue experimenting with Leaflet and Faker to reimagine the map surface!

Module 10.3 Data and Maps

In this module you will learn about features of databases, then, continuing the tutorial on the wiki, use Node.js with MongoDB database to let users store information to display on a map.

10.3.1 Data Persistence

Data persistence describes the practice of storing and using data beyond the life of a program or a web page. You encounter this every day when you save text to a file on your computer's hard drive and view it again later, an app remembers you have logged in because it saved a token inside a cookie, or when you post text or images on the internet for others to see. The technologies may change, but the concept does not—the software allows information to persist as part of its function, security, or customization. Using JavaScript in a web browser you can make information persist for users with a cookie or the Local Storage API. However, information saved in local storage is only accessible by that person—no one else can see it because the data exists only in that browser on that machine.

To make data contributed by individuals accessible to the whole world, you will need to run code on a web server with a server-side language like PHP or Node.js, or use a service that provides the same. While you could technically save information in a text file on the server and display it later, it is more efficient to use databases to create, read, update, and delete data (operations known as **CRUD**) in persistent storage. Generally, there are two types of databases. **Relational databases** like MySQL, PostgreSQL, and SQLite store information in tables using SQL (structured query language). They are intuitive like spreadsheets and reduce redundancy using references across tables (relations). **NoSQL databases** offer more flexible **schemas** (how databases structure information) and can be easier to use with JavaScript. NoSQL databases come in many flavors; for example, Mongo and Redis are called document databases because they use a structure similar to JSON files.[35]

Most databases require that you install special software to create, manage, and provide access to the information they contain. After you install database software on your computer or server, you would then connect to the service over the command line or use a library with Node.js to connect and run **queries** that create the database and execute commands.

10.3.2 Node.js and NPM

We've mentioned Node.js already a few times, and rightly so. With Node installed, you can run JavaScript on your computer or a web server and tap into unlimited functionality, build applications that can read and write to databases, create and manipulate files, communicate with other servers, and so much more. Node.js also includes the Node Package Manager (NPM), a tool that automatically installs and manages JavaScript libraries you can use in your projects.

Installing and running Node on your local machine is standard practice in professional web development, to not only test your full-stack applications on your machine but to automate and speed up your development. For example, you can use Grunt.js with Node to test, minify, and validate your project code every time you save a file. Node.js can also run scripts that set up and populate new projects or databases with components and data. We've included instructions in the wiki to install Node.js and work through the full-stack parts of chapters 9 and 10.

Publishing full-stack websites requires more resources because there is a back-end. We used Vercel in the book because it is a platform that provides scalable full-stack server capabilities that include a completely free tier. This means you can use Vercel to host static or dynamic websites using Node.js. However, platforms come and go (like Glitch, which we originally used for these last chapters!), so check the wiki for up-to-date instructions.

Exercise 10.3.1 Show Data on the Map

Since installing a database on a full-stack server is outside the scope of the printed textbook, we will use a prepared JSON file to visualize the "feelings" of our *Big Feelings* project on a Leaflet map. After you finish, we invite you to visit Module 10.4 in the chapter wiki to apply your new understanding of full-stack projects.

1. Create a new repo from our *Big Feelings* starter template at **github.com/criticalwebdesign/big-feelings-starter** and name it "big-feelings." Then go to **github.com/codespaces,** or your preferred code editor, and open your new repository following our steps in exercise 3.2.1.
2. You'll see the structure is similar to our *Bad Password API*, with all the back-end code hidden inside the **api/** folder, including the server files, which you can ignore

since we're only building the front-end project. Our work will take place inside **assets/js/main.js**—open it and add this code inside the function called `main()`. This calls the `fetchData()` function, which uses `fetch()` to connect to our version of the API. The `await` keyword makes sure the data arrives before logging the results. Preview your project in a new window and open the console and you should see an array containing all the data from the database.

```
let data = [];
async function main() {
  data = await fetchFeelings();
  console.log(data);
}
```

3. Update the map next. Add this code to the `main()` function.

```
async function main() {
  data = await fetchFeelings();
  console.log(data);
  await updateMap(data);
}
```

4. Open `map.js` and you will see it contains the basic Leaflet code you experimented with in 10.2. Find the `updateMap()` function and add this code to loop through the data it receives from the `main()` function. You should see the rows listed one by one in the Console.

```
function updateMap(data) {
  for (let i = 0; i < data.length; i++) {
    console.log(data[i]);
  }
}
```

5. Continue adding code to the `updateMap()` function. You first will remove any existing markers (to avoid adding them more than once) before looping through the data to create a new `circleMarker` using each row. The `createMarker()` function returns a reference to the marker that will be stored in the `markerLayer` array. Adding it to an array will make it easier to update or remove later on. Preview your work and you should now see the markers appear on the map (figure 10.4).

```
function updateMap(data) {
  removeMarkers();
```

```
  for (let i = 0; i < data.length; i++) {
    console.log(data[i]);
    markerLayer[i] = createMarker(data[i]);
  }
}
```

Check Your Work

This concludes the chapter exercises. We invite you to compare your work to the final outcome **criticalwebdesign.github.io#10-3** and code **criticalwebdesign.github.io#10-3-code** in the book repo. Don't forget to turn on GitHub Pages in your project and then stage and commit your work to make it live!

Prompt 10.3 Publish: Finalize Your Map

Continue adding customizations to your map. For example, you could use an `if` statement to filter only markers categorized as "TOTZ BORED." You could experiment with CSS blend modes. Or use the Leaflet documentation[36] to implement different types of pop-ups. Remember that the mapmaker has control, and the power you wield as the designer can be distributed among your participants.

See the wiki for Module 10.4! We created a full-stack tutorial that shows how to continue building the *Big Feelings* back end using Node.js and MongoDB, and then publish it with Vercel. We published it on the chapter 10 wiki to make sure we can keep it up to date.

Author Note: Join xtine's Virtual Punk Band!

The International Pussycats is a virtual post-punk band that transforms Do-It-Yourself efforts into a speculation on what happens if you Don't-Do-It-At-All. Together, we could be the world's largest punk band that never, not even once, performed. Join the band now! **criticalwebdesign.github.io#virtual-punk-band**

This project was made using some of the tools discussed in this chapter.

11 Distribution

> Before enlightenment, chop wood, carry water. After enlightenment, chop wood, carry water.
> —Zen Kōan

Context

Now that you have created your own works of critical web design, you might be wondering: What do I do with this? Where do I exhibit it? What do I do next if I want to work in the web industry? How can I continue learning, or where do I go to find a community of artists and designers? In this chapter, which we think of as a coda—a closing, "last class," or outro to the book, we will share some of our preferred spaces, both online and in the real world, where communities of practitioners engaged in critical web design thrive. Just as no two people will walk away from a book or a class with the same experiences, or even the same "take-aways," we understand that readers will have varying needs and interests that motivate their pursuits following the lessons we present. Below, we'll discuss venues for sharing and continued learning (11.1), tips and information about web servers (11.2), and advice for the labor market (11.3) and beyond.

Module 11.1 Continue Learning and Sharing

In an attempt at organization, we've listed CWD-related resources, organizations, and communities under broad headings.

11.1.1 Show and Tell

While we attempt to cover many of the grounds paved by our former students, we would be happy to hear from readers who climb new mountains and want to offer a view from the peak of their experience. You could, of course, post on your favorite social media using the hashtag #criticalwebdesign—but if you would like to share with other readers, you can post your work on the *Critical Web Design* book discussions forum.

Activity: Post to the CWD Discussion Page

1. Go to the Discussions on the book repo **criticalwebdesign.github.io#discussions.**
2. Click the **Show and tell** button from the list of Categories.
3. Click the **New discussion** button.
4. Add a short description and link to share original work you made while reading the book. We look forward to seeing what you've made!

11.1.2 Keep Playing

The following playgrounds and coding communities are terrific places to continue to play and experiment.

1. Take a look at projects from the community at Codepen Spark, **codepen.io**.
2. Participate in a game jam at Itch **itch.io** or the Interactive Fiction Database **ifdb.org**.
3. Take a free JavaScript course online with Codecademy, **codecademy.com**.
4. Search YouTube for *The Coding Train* series by Daniel Shiffman.[1]
5. Read a free JS book like Eloquent JavaScript, **eloquentjavascript.net**.
6. Join a hackathon like **bangbangcon.com** or **stupidhackathon.com**.
7. Read an article about design or art: **readings.design** or **monoskop.org**.

11.1.3 Keep Looking

A healthy part of any creative practice is to be aware of what else is going on. Whether you are finding work online or offline at museums, exhibitions, or festivals, there are many places to find inspiring and thought-provoking works.

- **whitney.org/artport**
- **anthology.rhizome.org**
- **docubase.mit.edu**

- **experiments.withgoogle.com**
- **arebyte.com**
- **singleservingsites.cool**
- **generative-unfoldings.mit.edu**
- **fckyeahnetart.tumblr.com/archive**
- **esoteric.codes**
- **arttab.xyz/web/explore**
- **wfgames.net**

Additional Materials and Resources

We covered a lot of concepts and technologies in this book but know that we've only touched on the methods and inspiring works you will want to explore further. In the *Critical Web Design Index*, **criticalwebdesign.github.io/index**, you will find projects like **thispersondoesnotexist.com** or **cowclicker.com**, which extend ideas on AI or data privacy from the chapters, or others that combine concepts into new outcomes, like **dronestre.am** by Josh Begley, which used data scraping to create an API about covert drone strikes. You will also see so many more that we would have loved to include, like **0100101110101101.org/dark-content** by Eva and Franco Mattes, which addresses labor and censorship on social media and, appropriately, can only be seen by visiting the dark web. Explore links and other content related to this chapter: **criticalwebdesign.github.io#wiki-11**.

11.1.4 Stay Connected

The following organizations have a legacy of bringing new digital and interactive works to viewers spanning net.art, speculative design, interactive stories, and other new media works.

- Ars Electronica **ars.electronica.art** (Austria) is an annual festival for art and technology.
- Electronic Literature Organization **eliterature.org** (international) is a conference and media arts festival for electronic literature and digital art.
- Eyebeam, **eyebeam.org** (NYC), is an art and technology center.
- HASTAC, **hastac.hcommons.org** (Humanities, Arts, Science, and Technology Alliance and Collaboratory, pronounced "haystack"), is an organization that supports scholars and hosts conferences that include panels, roundtables, discussions, and art exhibitions.
- ISEA, **isea-international.org** (international), is an academic technology symposium on electronic art.

- NEW INC, **www.newinc.org** (NYC and online), is an incubator for people working at the intersection of art, design, and technology.
- Rhizome, **rhizome.org** (NYC), supports new media art through exhibitions, scholarships, and preservation.
- The School for Poetic Computation, **sfpc.study** (NYC), supports experimental study in art, code, hardware, and critical theory.
- Akademie Schloss Solitude, **schloss-post.com/overview/web-residencies** (Germany), *Web Residencies* supports web-based practices.
- Transmediale, **transmediale.de/en** (Germany), is an annual technology festival.
- xCoAx, **xcoax.org**, is an annual international conference on "computation, communication, aesthetics & X" that includes panels and an art exhibition.

11.1.5 Explore Journals

- The HTML Review, **thehtml.review**, is an annual journal of literature made to exist on the web.
- The New River, **thenewriver.us**, is a journal promoting digital art and writing.
- Media-N, **iopn.library.illinois.edu/journals/median**, is the peer-reviewed, open-access journal of the College Art Association's New Media Caucus.
- The Journal for Artistic Research (JAR), **jar-online.net/en**, is an open-access journal that disseminates artistic research from all disciplines, but offers unique and creative methods for displaying digital media.
- Neural, **neural.it** (1993–), is a magazine about critical digital culture and media arts.
- Nettime, **nettime.org** (1995–), is a list-serv promoting the discussion of networked cultures, policies, and tactics.
- New Media Curating, **www.jiscmail.ac.uk/cgi-bin/webadmin?A0=new-media-curating** (2001–), is a list-serv intended for those involved in curating, exhibiting, archiving or interpreting new media.
- Taper, **taper.badquar.to**, is an online literary magazine for small computational pieces, published by Nick Montfort's small press, Bad Quarto **badquar.to**.

Module 11.2 Professional Practices

Here we offer advice for thinking about working in web design. Clearly, web development is an essential trade, and many practicing "artists" we know are also working in a related professional career. Some are in academia (like us), and a lucky few can support themselves only on commissions for their creative practice, but we surmise that most creative web designers and internet artists are working in a nine-to-five job or freelance (contract work) in web design or development. In academia and industry-facing positions, we appreciate the benefit of earning a living to hone your web design skills. Regardless of where you are headed at the moment, you will have to negotiate those relationships and resources (such as reliable hosting).

11.2.1 Servers and Hosting

As you further develop your practice, you may consider hosting your projects someplace other than GitHub Pages (GH). The primary considerations are: "What technology is required for your project?" and "What level of internet traffic do you expect?" For example, if you are hosting a static website and don't foresee traffic from thousands of visitors an hour, then GH is a trustworthy, free option. One can even register and use a custom domain name with GH to make it seem "official." You can also use Cloudflare's free CDN service to speed up your content delivery, which works great for a whole site, or just the static assets on a dynamic website.

Dynamic websites spark a different conversation. Shared hosting (multiple users on one server) used to be the standard method for hosting one or more sites. While shared hosting is still very affordable, the cost of domain names is rising, with the average annual registration fee being around $20 per domain. That, and the fact that there are now many free cloud-based platforms where one can host a dynamic website using a subdomain, makes free services like Vercel more convenient. Here is a short list of cloud platforms that use subdomains and have a free tier. Most of these don't include a web-based editor, so you have to push your code to their server using a Git repository.

- **vercel.com**
- **codesandbox.io**
- **stackblitz.com**
- **netlify.com**

Author Note: NLF,EO

Buyer beware, free services can come and go (ahem, Heroku.com, Glitch.com), mandating further revision and reposting. Nothing Lasts Forever, Especially Online (**NLF,EO**, yup, we just made that up).

11.2.2 Advice for the Labor Market

You may feel motivated to create a project at no cost to a friend or nonprofit organization simply for the opportunity to gain experience. And it is great practice talking with clients, outlining and articulating deliverable outcomes, delivering projects on time, and setting up billing contracts before taking your first freelance gig to high-paying strangers. But, one caveat we will offer is, "Don't sell yourself short!" While you might be able to create a project at no cost, the client shouldn't expect it to be fast or the highest quality. And don't be afraid to charge more if the client wants it to be perfect and "ready tomorrow." As the project **FastGood.Cheap** shows, often you can deliver on two of these ideas but not all three of them! Here are a few tips that we often pass along to our students as they enter the labor market.

1. **Pro Bono.** Don't work for free; work "pro bono." This Latin phrase translates to "for the public good." It means that you may be willing to work without receiving payment, or at a much lower rate, because you believe that the work you are creating services the public good. The website **shouldiworkforfree.com** offers a fun but honest take on how you may consider such opportunities. A great place to start testing the waters of working in a client-designer relationship is by volunteering for community groups to which you already belong.
2. **Contracts and Billing.** Whether you are working pro bono or charging a fee, use every opportunity to practice writing a contract of services and outlining your pricing. Use a design brief (chapter 7) to summarize the project expectations, resources, and commitments to answer any unknowns before they become a snag. You can zero out the cost, but it is good practice to deliver a billing statement. AIGA has terrific resources for freelance design contractors; see their website for contract templates and more.[2]
3. **Image Rights.** We wrote about fair use and copyleft in chapter 2. Commercial design practices, however, are more often concerned with copy*right* and ownership. If you work in the creative industries, you will become familiar with thinking about permissions and rights, for instance, for image reproductions, or you may be asked to sign a nondisclosure agreement. If you incorporate media into your designs that you did not create, you should at the very least attribute the media to its creator. In the case of professional media and services, you will likely incur a fee for permissions. Shepard Fairey's campaign design for Barack Obama makes an excellent case study for what happens if you fail to consider these issues.[3]

Module 11.3 How to Be Brave

We thought about ending this book with a list of resources for funding. To be honest, it would thrill us to know that someone read this book, worked through the exercises, and made something that was funded by an organization like Creative Capital, Mozilla Foundation, the National Endowment for the Humanities or the Arts (NEH/NEA)—all organizations for which we have both, separately, been applicants or even some level of finalists, and then been denied! It takes a lot of time to submit applications to these organizations and while it is a terrific learning exercise, especially for honing your writing skills, if there's one piece of advice we'd like to leave you with, it's this:

Just be brave and make the work. Don't worry about gatekeepers giving you permission or validating your ideas.

So how do you do this one, simple task? Start from the beginning. Create your next repo or start your next project, take a walk, sketch an idea, create a prototype, ideate, write the code, debug and publish it. When you share your work with at least one person, you are practicing being brave, seen, and validated.

> Remember, you can view the results *all* of the prompts in the book's repo **criticalwebdesign.github.io#repo**.

Notes

Introduction

1. Bret Victor, "A Brief Rant on the Future of Interaction Design," 2011. https://worrydream.com/ABriefRantOnTheFutureOfInteractionDesign/.

2. Ellen Lupton and Abbot Miller, "The New Primitives" in *Design Writing Research: Writings on Graphic Design* (Phaidon, 1999), 201.

3. Most cross-platform mobile apps are actually websites constructed using HTML, CSS, or JS and either wrapped by a "webview" or using a framework to tap into "native" mobile OS functionality.

4. Rachel Greene, *Internet Art* (Thames & Hudson, 2004), 13.

5. Julian Stallabrass, *Internet Art: The Online Clash of Culture and Commerce* (Tate, 2003), 12.

6. Loes Bogers and Letizia Chiappini, "Introduction" in *The Critical Makers Reader: (Un)learning Technology*, edited by Lowes Bogers and Letizia Chiappini (Institute of Network Cultures, 2019), 11.

7. Bogers and Chiappini, "Introduction," 11.

8. Anthony Dunne and Fiona Raby, *Speculative Everything: Design, Fiction, and Social Dreaming* (MIT Press, 2013), 43.

9. Dunne and Raby, *Speculative Everything*, 159.

10. Dunne and Raby, *Speculative Everything*, 161.

11. Michael Bierut, *Seventy-Nine Short Essays on Design* (Princeton Architectural Press, 2007), 13.

12. Bierut, *Seventy-Nine Short Essays*, 13

13. Michel Foucault quoted in "Disciplines of Design: Writing with Foucault," in *Design Writing Research: Writings on Graphic Design* by Ellen Lupton and Abbott Miller (Phaidon, 1999), 66.

14. Wikimedia Foundation, "User Agent Breakdowns," accessed July 2, 2023, https://analytics.wikimedia.org/dashboards/browsers/#all-sites-by-browser.

15. Chris Anderson, *The Long Tail: Why the Future of Business Is Selling Less of More* (Hachette Books, 2008).

16. Statcounter GlobalStats, "Browser Market Share Worldwide," accessed February 20, 2023, https://gs.statcounter.com/browser-market-share.

17. Mozilla, "The History of Web Browsers," accessed July 1, 2023, https://www.mozilla.org/en-US/firefox/browsers/browser-history/.

Chapter 1

1. Bruce Sterling, "A Short History of the Internet," *The Magazine of Fantasy and Science Fiction* (February 1993), 7–12. https://www.internetsociety.org/internet/history-internet/short-history-of-the-internet/.

2. Sterling, *Short History*.

3. Steven Levy, *Hackers: Heroes of the Computer Revolution* (O'Reilly Media, 2010).

4. Eltjo Buringh and Jan Luiten Van Zanden, "Charting the 'Rise of the West': Manuscripts and Printed Books in Europe, A Long-Term Perspective from the Sixth Through Eighteenth Centuries," *Journal of Economic History* 69, no. 02 (June 2009): 409. https://doi.org/10.1017/S0022050709000837.

5. Gary Wolf, "The Curse of Xanadu," *Wired Magazine*, June 1, 1995, https://www.wired.com/1995/06/xanadu/.

6. "P," Can I use . . . , accessed August 31, 2023, https://caniuse.com/?search=p.

7. "The W3C Markup Validation Service," accessed August 31, 2023, https://validator.w3.org/.

8. "<p>: The Paragraph Element," MDN_Webdocs, accessed June 13, 2023, https://developer.mozilla.org/en-US/docs/Web/HTML/Element/p.

9. "HTML Standard," accessed August 31, 2023, https://html.spec.whatwg.org/multipage/.

10. MDN_Webdocs, "Void Element," accessed June 8, 2023, https://developer.mozilla.org/en-US/docs/Glossary/Void_element.

11. Here we acknowledge Glitch.com, a simple online code editor and platform that allowed for full-stack and database-driven projects. We originally wrote chapters 9 and 10 using this tool, only to learn of its demise one week before submitting our final draft!

12. MDN_Webdocs, "HTML Elements Reference," accessed April 9, 2024, https://developer.mozilla.org/en-US/docs/Web/HTML/Element.

13. "IP Address," in Wikipedia, accessed October 14, 2023, https://en.wikipedia.org/w/index.php?title=IP_address&oldid=1180158006.

14. "Domain Name System," *Wikipedia*, March 22, 2024, https://en.wikipedia.org/wiki/Domain_Name_System.

Chapter 2

1. Explore a nearly complete archive of the *Whole Earth Catalog* at wholeearth.info, created by Barry Threw, Jon Gacnik, and Mindy Seu.

2. The TED Talk "Free Software, Free Society: Richard Stallman at TEDxGeneva 2014" delivers a concise introduction to Stallman and his ideas: https://www.tedxgeneva.net/talks/richard-stallman-free-software-free-society/.

3. Steven Levy, *Hackers: Heroes of the Computer Revolution* (O'Reilly Media, 2010).

4. Roland Greene, "From Dante to the Post-Concrete: An Interview with Augusto de Campos," Summer 1992, *UBU Web*, accessed January 24, 2023, https://www.ubu.com/papers/greene02.html.

5. Kenneth Goldsmith, "From (Command) Line to (Iconic) Constellation," *UBU Web*, accessed January 24, 2023, https://www.ubu.com/papers/goldsmith_command.html.

6. Paul Ford, "What Is Code? If You Don't Know, You Need to Read This," *Bloomberg.Com*, accessed September 2, 2023. http://www.bloomberg.com/graphics/2015-paul-ford-what-is-code/.

7. Mark Tribe, "Intermedia Art: An Ornithology of Net Art," Tate Online, accessed September 2, 2023. https://www.tate.org.uk/intermediaart/entry15274.shtm.

8. Usability.gov, "Usability Evaluation Basics," accessed October 8, 2013, https://www.usability.gov/what-and-why/usability-evaluation.html.

9. MDN_Webdocs, "Lang," accessed March 11, 2024, https://developer.mozilla.org/en-US/docs/Web/HTML/Global_attributes/lang.

10. "UTF-8," *Wikipedia*, accessed September 1, 2023, https://en.wikipedia.org/wiki/UTF-8.

11. "List of ISO 639–1 Codes," *Wikipedia*, accessed September 1, 2023, https://en.wikipedia.org/wiki/List_of_ISO_639-1_codes.

12. "Boilerplate Code," *Wikipedia*, accessed June 10, 2024, https://en.wikipedia.org/wiki/Boilerplate_code#HTML.

13. MDN_Webdocs, "<div>," April 10, 2025, https://developer.mozilla.org/en-US/docs/Web/HTML/Reference/Elements/div.

14. MDN_Webdocs, "The Box Model," accessed July 17, 2023, https://developer.mozilla.org/en-US/docs/Learn/CSS/Building_blocks/The_box_model.

15. MDN_Webdocs, "<span>," accessed April 17, 2025. https://developer.mozilla.org/en-US/docs/Web/HTML/Reference/Elements/span.

16. "Expressions and Operators," MDN_Webdocs, accessed August 12, 2023, https://developer.mozilla.org/en-US/docs/Web/JavaScript/Guide/Expressions_and_Operators.

17. MDN_Webdocs, "Expressions and Operators," August 12, 2023, https://developer.mozilla.org/en-US/docs/Web/JavaScript/Guide/Expressions_and_operators.

18. MDN_Webdocs, "Console," accessed August 2, 2023, https://developer.mozilla.org/en-US/docs/Web/API/console.

Chapter 3

1. Anthony Dunne and Fiona Raby, *Speculative Everything: Design, Fiction, and Social Dreaming* (MIT Press, 2013), 34.

2. "Spoofs," *Adbusters*, accessed September 19, 2023, https://www.adbusters.org/spoof-ads.

3. Robert N. Proctor, "The History of the Discovery of the Cigarette–Lung Cancer Link: Evidentiary Traditions, Corporate Denial, Global Toll," *BMJ Journals*, May 2011, http://dx.doi.org/10.1136/tobaccocontrol-2011-050338.

4. Marilyn DeLaure and Moritz Fink, eds., *Culture Jamming: Activism and The Art of Cultural Resistance* (New York University Press, 2017), 25.

5. Mark Dery, "Culture Jamming: Hacking, Slashing, and Sniping in the Empire of Signs," (Open Magazine Pamphlet Series, 1993), accessed February 8, 2023, https://www.markdery.com/books/culture-jamming-hacking-slashing-and-sniping-in-the-empire-of-signs-2/.

6. Carl DiSalvo, *Adversarial Design* (MIT Press), 115.

7. See https://vimeo.com/129322969.

8. Julian Bleecker, "Design Fiction: A Short Essay on Design, Science, Fact and Fiction," Near Future Laboratory, 2009.

9. Grant H. Kester, "Conversation Pieces: The Role of Dialogue in Socially-Engaged Art," in *Theory in Contemporary Art since 1985*, edited by Simon Leung and Zoya Kocur, 1st ed. (Wiley, 2012), 153–164.

10. "Binky: Your New Favorite App," accessed September 14, 2023, https://www.binky.rocks/.

11. Ian Bogost, "The App That Does Nothing," *The Atlantic* (June 9, 2017), https://www.theatlantic.com/technology/archive/2017/06/the-app-that-does-nothing/529764/.

12. Bogost, "The App That Does Nothing."

13. Kim Severson, "The Little Coffee Shop Around the Corner," *The New York Times*, May 4, 2005, https://www.nytimes.com/2005/05/04/dining/the-little-coffee-shop-around-the-corner.html.

14. S. Umit Kucuk, "Consumer Exit, Voice, and 'Power' on the Internet," *Journal of Research for Consumers* (vol. 15, 2008), p. 5, accessed on January 2, 2024, https://jrconsumers.com/academic_articles/issue_15/exit-voice-power-academic2.pdf.

15. See the Wayback Machine for prior designs, such as https://web.archive.org/web/20090710005225/http://www.delocator.net/.

16. I am grateful for the generosity in developing and maintaining the site over the decades made by Vasna Sdeung, who created the databases used in the first iteration, followed by maintenance,

upkeep, and redesign by Kyle Cummings, Jim Bursch, and Tom Brickman. I started this project with Finishing School, before I left the school. They were instrumental in getting the work in the public eye at the San Francisco Art Institute's Walter and McBean Gallery, April 1, 2005.

17. Copyright.gov, "U.S. Copyright Office Fair Use Index," last updated August 2025, https://www.copyright.gov/fair-use/.

18. Paula Scher, "Great Design Is Serious, Not Solemn," TED Talk, 2008, https://www.ted.com/talks/paula_scher_great_design_is_serious_not_solemn.

19. Jonathan Barnbrook et al., "First Things First Manifesto 2000," (printed on the cover) *Emigre #51* (American Web), 1999.

20. Frictionless, "Ben & Jerry's Brand Guide," accessed September 13, 2023, https://frictionlesshq.com/brand-guide/ben-jerrys/.

21. B Corp, "About B Corp Certification," accessed September 2, 2023, https://www.bcorporation.net/en-us/certification.

22. For example, Gap released a 1993 advertising campaign that included a manipulated image of Jack Kerouac wearing Gap khaki pants, see https://www.openculture.com/2013/02/kerouac_wore_khakis.html; Nike released a commercial featuring the subversive Beat writer William S. Burroughs, see https://www.youtube.com/watch?v=HvLTu8Xfhf4; the streetwear brand Supreme borrows from Barbara Kruger's typographic style, see https://www.grapheine.com/en/history-of-graphic-design/barbara-kruger-supreme-who-is-hijacking-whom; and Apple recreated a work by Christian Marclay, instead of licensing it from the artist for their iPhone release video, see https://www.nytimes.com/2008/07/13/arts/design/13fine.html.

23. Figma.com, accessed July 19, 2023, https://www.figma.com/figma-vs-adobe-xd/.

24. We also recognize that by the time this book is published, Figma will have likely changed. Thus, we recommend reviewing the onboarding videos and tutorials.

25. Ellen Lupton, *Thinking with Type.*

26. "SVG: Scalable Vector Graphics," MDN_Webdocs, March 6, 2023, https://developer.mozilla.org/en-US/docs/Web/SVG.

27. MDN: The Web Open Font Format (WOFF), https://developer.mozilla.org/en-US/docs/Web/Guide/WOFF.

28. Marijn Haverbeke, *Eloquent Javascript 4th Edition*, accessed May 30, 2024, https://eloquentjavascript.net/02_program_structure.html.

29. The function querySelector() will only select one element on a page. In this case, if there is more than one <h2> it will only select the first one. Later you will use querySelectorAll() to select and reference an array of elements on the page.

30. MDN_Webdocs. "This," September 25, 2023, https://developer.mozilla.org/en-US/docs/Web/JavaScript/Reference/Operators/this.

Chapter 4

1. Jakob Nielsen, "Thinking Aloud: The #1 Usability Tool," Nielsen Norman Group, accessed September 19, 2023, https://www.nngroup.com/articles/thinking-aloud-the-1-usability-tool/.

2. Apple Inc., "Design," Apple Developer, accessed September 19, 2023, https://developer.apple.com/design/.

3. Apple Developer Documentation, "Layout," accessed September 19, 2023, https://developer.apple.com/design/human-interface-guidelines/layout.

4. Apple Developer, "Apple Design Resources: iOS 17 and iPadOS 17," accessed August 17, 2023, https://developer.apple.com/design/resources/.

5. NASA Graphics Standards Manual 1976, accessed May 30, 2024, https://standardsmanual.com/products/nasa-graphics-standards-manual.

6. Apple Developer Documentation, "Charts," accessed September 19, 2023, https://developer.apple.com/design/human-interface-guidelines/charts.

7. William Lidwell, Kritina Holden, and Jill Butler, *Universal Principles of Design, Revised and Updated: 125 Ways to Enhance Usability, Influence Perception, Increase Appeal, Make Better Design Decisions, and Teach Through Design* (Rockport Publishers, 2010), 24.

8. Lidwell, Holden, and Butler, *Universal Principles of Design.*

9. Bootstrap, "Breakpoints," accessed September 5, 2023, https://getbootstrap.com/docs/5.3/layout/breakpoints/.

10. Websites that publish technology analysis like https://trends.builtwith.com/websitelist/Bootstrap-Basic and https://www.wappalyzer.com/technologies/ui-frameworks/bootstrap/ are also good sources.

11. https://pudding.cool/.

12. Jennifer Ding with Jan Diehm and Michelle McGhee, "Can Data Die? Why One of the Internet's Oldest Images Lives On Without Its Subjects Consent," The Pudding, 2021, https://pudding.cool/2021/10/lenna/.

13. Michelle McGhee with Russell Goldenberg and Jan Diehm, "Who's in the Crossword?" The Pudding, 2020, https://pudding.cool/2020/11/crossword/.

14. The Pudding and The Smithsonian National Portrait Gallery, "Votes for Women: A Portrait of Persistence, 2019–2020," video and interactive companion, see https://pudding.cool/projects/votes-for-women/ and https://npg.si.edu/exhibition/votes-for-women.

15. Jan Diehm with data work by Kelsey Campbell and illustrations by Lace Garcia, "I Kissed a Girl to Call Me By Your Name: A Story About Hearing Yourself Represented with Same-Gender Lyrics for the First Time," The Pudding, 2021, https://pudding.cool/2021/06/same-gender-lyrics/.

16. Jared Wilber, "The Good, the Rad, and the Gnarly: An Exploration into the Music of Skateboarding," The Pudding, 2018, https://pudding.cool/2018/06/skate-music/.

17. "Can Data Die?," https://pudding.cool/2021/10/lenna/.

18. Bootstrap, "Buttons," https://getbootstrap.com/docs/5.3/components/buttons/.

19. Bootstrap, "Versions," https://getbootstrap.com/docs/versions/.

20. CSS-Tricks, "CSS Custom Properties Guide," https://css-tricks.com/a-complete-guide-to-custom-properties/.

21. Sass, "Sass Basics," accessed April 10, 2024, https://sass-lang.com/guide/.

22. Bootstrap, "Color Contrast," https://getbootstrap.com/docs/5.3/customize/sass/#color-contrast.

23. Bootstrap's color modes, https://getbootstrap.com/docs/5.3/customize/color-modes/, are likely to be improved upon in future iterations.

24. Lev Manovich, *The Language of New Media* (MIT Press, 2002), 65.

25. W3C, "CSS Values and Units: 5.2. Absolute Lengths," https://drafts.csswg.org/css-values-3/#absolute-lengths.

26. W3C, "CSS Values and Units: 5.1. Relative Lengths," https://drafts.csswg.org/css-values-3/#relative-lengths.

27. Bootstrap, "Typography," accessed September 3, 2023, https://getbootstrap.com/docs/5.3/content/typography/.

28. Bootstrap, "Typography."

29. Bootstrap, "Containers," accessed April 24, 2025, https://getbootstrap.com/docs/5.3/layout/containers/.

30. Bootstrap, "Spacing," accessed September 5, 2023, https://getbootstrap.com/docs/5.3/utilities/spacing/.

Chapter 5

1. Steve Krug, *Don't Make Me Think: A Common Sense Approach to Web Usability*, 2nd ed. (New Riders, 2006), 1.

2. Krug, *Don't Make Me Think*.

3. Learn more about Hugh Dubberly at https://aigasf.org/hugh-dubberly/.

4. Rikke Friis Dam and Teo Yu Siang, "The History of Design Thinking," The Interaction Design Foundation, May 20, 2022, https://www.interaction-design.org/literature/article/design-thinking-get-a-quick-overview-of-the-history.

5. Steven McCarthy, "Design Thinking? Thank an Engineer," *Dialectic* 3, no. 1 (January 11, 2022), https://doi.org/10.3998/dialectic.14932326.0003.102.

6. Hugh Dubberly, "How Do You Design? A Compendium of Models," 2005, http://www.dubberly.com/articles/how-do-you-design.html.

7. Stanford d.school, *Design thinking bootleg*, Hassno Plattner Institute of Design (Stanford University), https://dschool.stanford.edu/resources/design-thinking-bootleg.

8. Sarah Gibbons, "Design Thinking 101," Nielsen Norman Group, 2016, https://www.nngroup.com/articles/design-thinking/.

9. Alexei Shulgin and Ianina Prudenko, "Art Footprint Manifesto," http://artfootprint.xyz/.

10. https://userinyerface.com/.

11. John Brooke, "SUS: A Quick and Dirty Usability Scale," *Usability Evaluation in Industry* (1995), 189, accessed June 28, 2023, https://www.researchgate.net/publication/228593520_SUS_A_quick_and_dirty_usability_scale.

12. See moz.com/top500, accessed May 30, 2025.

13. Marieke McCloskey, "Task Scenarios for Usability Testing," Nielsen Norman Group, accessed August 27, 2023, https://www.nngroup.com/articles/task-scenarios-usability-testing/.

14. Kara Pernice, "Talking with Users in a Usability Test," Nielsen Norman Group, accessed February 21, 2024, https://www.nngroup.com/articles/talking-to-users/.

15. "Stack Overflow Developer Survey 2023," Stack Overflow, accessed August 25, 2023, https://survey.stackoverflow.co/2023/#most-popular-technologies-language.

16. MDN_Webdocs, "JavaScript Data Types and Data Structures," accessed September 29, 2023, https://developer.mozilla.org/en-US/docs/Web/JavaScript/Data_structures.

17. "Number," MDN_Webdocs, accessed August 21, 2023, https://developer.mozilla.org/en-US/docs/Web/JavaScript/Reference/Global_Objects/Number.

18. "Typeof," MDN_Webdocs, accessed April 5, 2023, https://developer.mozilla.org/en-US/docs/Web/JavaScript/Reference/Operators/typeof.

19. "Comparison Operators," MDN_Webdocs, accessed April 5, 2023, https://developer.mozilla.org/en-US/docs/Web/JavaScript/Guide/Expressions_and_operators#comparison_operators.

20. "Equality (==)," MDN_Webdocs, accessed April 5, 2023, https://developer.mozilla.org/en-US/docs/Web/JavaScript/Reference/Operators/Equality.

21. "Inequality (!=)," MDN_Webdocs, accessed April 5, 2023, https://developer.mozilla.org/en-US/docs/Web/JavaScript/Reference/Operators/Inequality.

22. "Strict equality (===)," MDN_Webdocs, accessed April 5, 2023, https://developer.mozilla.org/en-US/docs/Web/JavaScript/Reference/Operators/Strict_equality.

23. "Event: preventDefault() Method," MDN_Webdocs, accessed July 20, 2023, https://developer.mozilla.org/en-US/docs/Web/API/Event/preventDefault.

24. Jeff Sauro, "Measuring Usability with the System Usability Scale (SUS)," accessed February 3, 2011, https://measuringu.com/sus/.

25. "HTML Attribute: Required," MDN_Webdocs, accessed April 13, 2023, https://developer.mozilla.org/en-US/docs/Web/HTML/Attributes/required.

26. "<label>: The Label Element," MDN_Webdocs, accessed May 19, 2023, https://developer.mozilla.org/en-US/docs/Web/HTML/Element/label.

27. Bootstrap, "Form Controls," accessed August 29, 2023, https://getbootstrap.com/docs/5.3/forms/form-control/.

Chapter 6

1. Jeffrey Keedy, "The Rules of Typography According to Crackpots / Experts," Eye Magazine, Winter 1993, https://www.eyemagazine.com/feature/article/the-rules-of-typography-according-to-crackpotsexp.

2. Eye Magazine, "First Things First Manifesto 2000," accessed September 13, 2023, https://www.eyemagazine.com/feature/article/first-things-first-manifesto-2000.

3. Ellen Lupton and Abbott Miller, *Design Writing Research: Writing on Graphic Design* (Phaidon, 1999), 5.

4. Roland Barthes, *Image Music Text* (Fantana 1977), 142–148.

5. Barthes, *Image Music Text*, 9. This is a reference to "semiotics," the study of signs, symbols, and interpretations.

6. Barthes, *Image Music Text*, 9.

7. Andy Beckett, "A User's Guide to Artspeak," *The Guardian*, January 27, 2013, https://www.theguardian.com/artanddesign/2013/jan/27/users-guide-international-art-english.

8. CanopyCanopyCanopy, "International Art English," accessed September 15, 2023, https://canopycanopycanopy.com/contents/international_art_english.

9. MIT Press, "Throwback Thursday Featuring Muriel Cooper," November 13, 2014, https://mitpress.mit.edu/university-press-week-throwback-thursday-featuring-muriel-cooper/.

10. Nolwenn Maudet, "Muriel Cooper, Information Landscapes," Back Office, accessed September 15, 2023, http://www.revue-backoffice.com/en/issues/01-making-do-making-with/nolwenn-maudet-muriel-cooper-information-landscapes.

11. Jeffrey Keedy, "OK Identity," Instagram, March 11, 2016, https://www.instagram.com/p/BC0kF9VsE5G/.

12. See David Carson on Instagram, https://www.instagram.com/davidcarsondesigner/.

13. See Herdimas Anggara's portfolio website, accessed May 21, 2025, https://ritual.engineer/.

14. See: https://art.yale.edu, https://rhizome.org, and https://canopycanopycanopy.com.

15. Angelica Frey, "The Era of Rebellious Web Design Is Here," AIGA Eye on Design, May 16, 2022, https://eyeondesign.aiga.org/the-era-of-nonchalant-web-design-is-here/. See: https://scarymommy.com, https://nylon.com, and https://www.elitedaily.com as examples.

16. Kate Compton, *Tracery Zine*, accessed May 22, 2025, https://www.galaxykate.com/pdfs/galaxykate-zine-tracery.pdf.

17. See Colombia University's online resource for Asian history and culture: http://afe.easia.columbia.edu/at/basho/hbb04.html.

18. Masterpiece-of-Japanese-Culture.com, accessed June 3, 2024, https://www.masterpiece-of-japanese-culture.com/literatures-and-poems/famous-haiku-poems-matsuo-basho.

19. Frank Chimero, *The Shape of Design*, 2012, online, accessed June 3, 2024, https://shapeofdesignbook.com/.

20. John Coltrane, "Giant Steps," YouTube video, accessed May 21, 2025, https://www.youtube.com/watch?v=30FTr6G53VU.

21. Coltrane, "Giant Steps," 38.

22. Mailchimp, "Competitor Analysis: What It Is and How to Conduct One," accessed September 15, 2023, https://mailchimp.com/resources/what-is-competitor-analysis/.

23. Erik Messaki, "How to Perform Competitive Analysis in Web Design," Medium, September 27, 2021, https://uxplanet.org/how-to-perform-competitive-analysis-in-web-design-a-step-by-step-guide-90d8f50fcd3f.

24. Sarah Cantrell, "Systematic Reviews: Types of Reviews," Duke University, accessed September 15, 2023, https://guides.mclibrary.duke.edu/sysreview/types.

25. Milanote, "How To Make A Moodboard: 2023 Step-By-Step Guide," accessed September 15, 2023. https://milanote.com/guide/create-better-moodboards.

26. Aldous Huxley, *The Art of Seeing* (Montana Books, 1975), 104.

27. Mike Bostock, "Design Is a Search Problem," YouTube video, https://youtu.be/fThhbt23SGM.

28. Bostock, "Design Is a Search Problem."

29. Caitland Conley, "How to Convert Videos into GIFs," Vimeo.com (blog), updated May 1, 2025, https://vimeo.com/blog/post/how-to-turn-your-videos-into-gifs/.

30. Bootstrap, "Grid System," accessed September 26, 2023, https://getbootstrap.com/docs/5.3/layout/grid/.

31. MDN_Webdocs, "Introduction to CSS Layout," accessed July 17, 2023, https://developer.mozilla.org/en-US/docs/Learn/CSS/CSS_layout/Introduction.

32. MDN_Webdocs, "Overflow," accessed August 16, 2023, https://developer.mozilla.org/en-US/docs/Web/CSS/overflow.

33. MDN_Webdocs, "Flex," July 17, 2023, https://developer.mozilla.org/en-US/docs/Web/CSS/flex_value.

34. MDN_Webdocs, "Background," July 18, 2023, https://developer.mozilla.org/en-US/docs/Web/CSS/background.

35. MDN_Webdocs, "Rotate()," accessed August 23, 2023, https://developer.mozilla.org/en-US/docs/Web/CSS/transform-function/rotate.

36. MDN_Webdocs, "Template Literals," accessed September 12, 2023, https://developer.mozilla.org/en-US/docs/Web/JavaScript/Reference/Template_literals.

37. Joelle Dietrick, Gretta Louw, and Owen Mundy, "Browser Blowup: Explode Web Pages Containing Third-Party Trackers," *Signal Culture Cookbook*, vol. 2, edited by Jason Bernagozzi (2019), github.com/sneakaway-studio/explode-the-web.

Chapter 7

1. Aral Balkan and Laura Kalbag, "Ethical Design Manifesto," ind.ie. accessed September 27, 2023, https://ind.ie/ethical-design/.

2. The Universal Declaration of Human Rights (UDHR) upholds the rights and freedoms of all human beings, including their right to "freedom of thought" (Article 18), https://www.un.org/en/about-us/universal-declaration-of-human-rights.

3. Chadia Abras, Diane Maloney-Krichmar, and Jenny Preece, "User-Centered Design," in *Berkshire Encyclopedia of Human-Computer Interaction*, edited by William Sims Bainbridge (Berkshire Publishing Group, 2004), 2:445–456.

4. Constantine Stephanidis, "Design for All," in *The Encyclopedia of Human-Computer Interaction*, 2nd ed., accessed May 25, 2023, https://www.interaction-design.org/literature/book/the-encyclopedia-of-human-computer-interaction-2nd-ed/design-4-all.

5. Don Norman, *The Design of Everyday Things: Revised and Expanded Edition* (Basic Books, 2013), 14.

6. Section508.gov, "Universal Design: What Is It?" accessed October 10, 2023, https://www.section508.gov/blog/Universal-Design-What-is-it/.

7. Centre for Excellence in Universal Design, "The 7 Principles," accessed October 10, 2023, https://universaldesign.ie/what-is-universal-design/the-7-principles/.

8. Access Press Staff, "Curb cuts and ramps cleared way for better accessibility," *Access Press,* November 1, 2023, https://accesspress.org/curb-cuts-and-ramps-cleared-way-for-better-accessibility/.

9. Centre for Excellence in Universal Design, "What Is Universal Design," accessed October 11, 2023, https://universaldesign.ie/what-is-universal-design/.

10. fcc.gov, "Section 508 of the Rehabilitation Act," accessed October 11, 2023, https://www.fcc.gov/general/section-508-rehabilitation-act.

11. Figma, "4-Accessibility & Inclusively—Learn with Figma," Figma, accessed August 26, 2021, https://www.figma.com/resources/learn-design/inclusion/.

12. Accessibility and inclusion are popular areas of focus across the "web design" canon. Books such as O'Reilly's *Accessibility Handbook: Making 508 Compliant Sites* by Katie Cunningham and M. Regine Gilbert's *Inclusive Design for a Digital World: Designing with Accessibility in Mind* on Apress's Design Thinking series are important resources for learning to implement accessible and inclusive web design standards. We encourage readers to dive deeply into this topic.

13. One early example was the first search result for "Miserable Failure" showing the biography for President George W. Bush after the invasion of Iraq under false pretenses. See Tim Chartier, *Math Bytes: Google Bombs, Chocolate-Covered Pi, and Other Cool Bits in Computing* (Princeton University Press, 2014), 123.

14. W3C, "Accessibility," accessed October 9, 2023, https://www.w3.org/mission/accessibility/.

15. For more on the history and context of inclusive design, see Cyndi Wiley, "Nothing About Us Without Us . . . Including Pizza: The Practice of Designing with Accessibility in Mind," accessed June 3, 2024, https://educators.aiga.org/nothing-about-us-without-us-including-pizza-the-practice-of-designing-with-accessibility-in-mind/.

16. Colin J. Neill, Philip A. Laplante, and Joanna F. DeFranco, *Antipatterns: Managing Software Organizations and People*, Applied Software Engineering Series, 2nd ed. (CRC Press, 2011).

17. Sarah Kahn, "The World of UX Anti-Patterns," May 8, 2013, https://webdesign.tutsplus.com/the-world-of-ux-anti-patterns--webdesign-12198a.

18. Harry Brignull, "Types of Deceptive Patterns," deceptive.design, accessed October 12, 2023, https://www.deceptive.design/types.

19. Brignull, "Types of Deceptive Patterns."

20. Brignull, "Types of Deceptive Patterns."

21. Marina Vujnovic, "Hypercapitalism," *Wiley-Blackwell Encyclopedia of Globalization*, 2017, https://onlinelibrary.wiley.com/doi/10.1002/9780470670590.wbeog278.pub2.

22. Caroline Sinders, "How Companies Use Dark Patterns to Keep You Subscribed," The Pudding, accessed October 17, 2023, https://pudding.cool/2023/05/dark-patterns.

23. Harry Brignull, "Dark Patterns: Deception vs. Honesty in UI Design," AListApart.com, November 1, 2011, https://alistapart.com/article/dark-patterns-deception-vs.-honesty-in-ui-design/#section2.

24. Charles Arthur, "Facebook Emotion Study Breached Ethical Guidelines, Researchers Say," The Guardian, June 30, 2014, sec. Technology, https://www.theguardian.com/technology/2014/jun/30/facebook-emotion-study-breached-ethical-guidelines-researchers-say.

25. See UI Patterns, "Design Patterns," https://ui-patterns.com/patterns.

26. UXPA International, "UXPA Code of Professional Conduct," accessed October 9, 2023, https://uxpa.org/uxpa-code-of-professional-conduct/.

27. Also see the use of this phrase in Google's original (now deprecated) motto, when its founders believed that "advertising funded search engines [would] be inherently biased towards the advertisers and away from the needs of the consumers," https://research.google/pubs/pub334/.

28. M. D. Mulvenna, J. Boger, and R. B. Bond, "Ethical by Design: A Manifesto," *Proceedings of European Conference on Cognitive Ergonomics* (Umeå, Sweden, September 19–22, 2017), https://doi.org/10.1145/3121283.3121300.

29. The A11Y Project, "How-to: Use Title Attributes," April 22, 2013, https://a11yproject.com/posts/title-attributes/.

30. Apple Developer, "Human Interface Guidelines: Accessibility," accessed October 15, 2023, https://developer.apple.com/design/human-interface-guidelines/accessibility.

31. WCAG 2.1 at a Glance, accessed May 29, 2023, https://www.w3.org/WAI/standards-guidelines/wcag/glance/.

32. Background on WCAG 2, accessed May 28, 2025, https://www.w3.org/TR/WCAG21/#background-on-wcag-2.

33. W3C Web Accessibility Initiative (WAI), "Web Accessibility Perspectives—Compilation of 10 Topics/Videos," YouTube video, accessed May 24, 2023, https://www.youtube.com/watch?v=3f31oufqFSM.

34. W3C, "Web Accessibility Evaluation Tools List," accessed October 19, 2023, https://www.w3.org/WAI/ER/tools/.

35. Eren Ilknur, "Web Accessibility—Common ARIA Mistakes to Avoid," FreeCodeCamp, January 13, 2023, https://www.freecodecamp.org/news/web-accessibility-common-aria-mistakes-to-avoid/; "Bad ARIA Practices," Accessibility Developer Guide, accessed May 27, 2023, https://www.accessibility-developer-guide.com/knowledge/aria/bad-practices/.

36. MDN_Webdocs, "ARIA," August 16, 2023, https://developer.mozilla.org/en-US/docs/Web/Accessibility/ARIA.

37. MDN_Webdocs, "ARIA: Article Role," April 16, 2023, https://developer.mozilla.org/en-US/docs/Web/Accessibility/ARIA/Roles/article_role.

38. Centers for Disease Control and Prevention, "Fast Facts About Vision Loss," accessed May 29, 2023, https://www.cdc.gov/vision-health/data-research/vision-loss-facts.

39. National Eye Institute, "Types of Color Vision Deficiency," accessed November 3, 2023, https://www.nei.nih.gov/learn-about-eye-health/eye-conditions-and-diseases/color-blindness/types-color-vision-deficiency.

40. Chrome for Developers, "What's New in DevTools (Chrome 83)," March 10, 2020, https://developer.chrome.com/blog/new-in-devtools-83/.

41. Christopher Alexander, Sara Ishikawa, Murray Silverstein, and Center for Environmental Structure, *A Pattern Language: Towns, Buildings, Construction* (Oxford University Press, 1977).

42. Toptal Engineering Blog, "The Comprehensive Guide to JavaScript Design Patterns," accessed November 10, 2023, https://www.toptal.com/javascript/comprehensive-guide-javascript-design-patterns.

43. Datylon, "Icon Array," accessed October 22, 2023, https://www.datylon.com/resources/chart-library/icon-array.

44. UI Patterns, "Cards Design Pattern," accessed October 19, 2023, https://ui-patterns.com/patterns/cards.

45. Bootstrap, "Cards," accessed October 19, 2023, https://getbootstrap.com/docs/5.3/components/card/.

46. UI Patterns, "Progressive Disclosure Design Pattern," accessed October 22, 2023, https://ui-patterns.com/patterns/ProgressiveDisclosure.

47. The A11Y Project, "Checklist," accessed December 15, 2023, https://a11yproject.com/checklist/.

48. The A11Y Project, accessed November 9, 2023, https://www.a11yproject.com/about/.

49. MDN_Webdocs, "Keyboard-Navigable JavaScript Widgets," accessed November 21, 2023, https://developer.mozilla.org/en-US/docs/Web/Accessibility/Keyboard-navigable_JavaScript_widgets.

50. MDN_Webdocs, "Dataset Property," accessed September 8, 2023, https://developer.mozilla.org/en-US/docs/Web/API/HTMLElement/dataset.

Chapter 8

1. Jean Arp, *Untitled (Collage with Squares Arranged according to the Law of Chance)*, Museum of Modern Art, accessed May 25, 2025, https://www.moma.org/collection/works/37013.

2. We found the "ice cream machine" analogy that distinguishes these three methods informative: Sai Sreekar Chebiyyam, "Computational vs Parametric vs Generative Design," Novatr, accessed January 16, 2024, https://www.novatr.com/blog/computational-parametric-generative-design.

3. ArchDaily, "How Architecture Firms Are Using Generative Design Today," accessed August 4, 2021, https://www.archdaily.com/965973/how-architecture-firms-are-using-generative-design-today.

4. Jan Robert Leegte and Superposition, *Web*, 2023, https://opensea.io/collection/web-2023.

5. Mads Haahr, "Introduction to Randomness and Random Numbers," random.org, accessed January 12, 2024, https://www.random.org/randomness/.

6. "Ethics of Artificial Intelligence," UNESCO, accessed April 9, 2024, https://www.unesco.org/en/artificial-intelligence/recommendation-ethics.

7. Amy Alexander, "Deep Hysteria," Medium, https://medium.com/@amyjalexander/deep-hysteria-46ff1650f502.

8. See also "Dead Internet Theory," Wikipedia, https://en.wikipedia.org/wiki/Dead_Internet_theory.

9. Noam, Chomsky, Ian Roberts, and Jeffrey Watumull, "The False Promise of ChatGPT," *New York Times*, accessed March 8, 2023, https://www.nytimes.com/2023/03/08/opinion/noam-chomsky-chatgpt-ai.html.

10. Heydon Pickering, "What's The Deal with Large Language Models?" accessed April 9, 2024, https://briefs.video/videos/whats-the-deal-with-large-language-models.

11. Carolyn Lazard, *A Recipe for Disaster*, accessed 20 February 2024, https://vimeo.com/267429320.

12. Lauren Lee McCarthy, "LAUREN," https://lauren-mccarthy.com/LAUREN.

13. Lauren Lee McCarthy, "Voice in My Head," https://lauren-mccarthy.com/Voice-In-My-Head.

14. See this work on the Internet Archive, accessed May 27, 2025, https://archive.org/details/1970LillianSchwartzPixillation.

15. Mark Amerika, "AN INTERVIEW WITH FRIEDER NAKE," RightClickSave, accessed August 8, 2022, https://www.rightclicksave.com/article/an-interview-with-frieder-nake

16. Casey Reas, "923 EMPTY ROOMS #874," *ArtTab*, https://arttab.xyz/?id=114.

17. See Nanette Wylde, "Storyland," https://collection.eliterature.org/1/works/wylde__storyland.html.

18. See https://github.com/ruffle-rs/ruffle.

19. Electronic Literature Archive, Volume 1, https://collection.eliterature.org/1/index.html.

20. Allison Parrish, "The Nonsense Laboratory," Experiments with Google, https://experiments.withgoogle.com/nonsense-laboratory.

21. See Allison Parrish, Pincelate on GitHub, https://github.com/aparrish/pincelate.

22. "Development of *No Man's Sky*," Wikipedia, accessed September 16, 2023, https://en.wikipedia.org/wiki/Development_of_No_Man%27s_Sky.

23. See Siobhan Roberts, "John Horton Conway: The World's Most Charismatic Mathematician," The Guardian, July 23, 2015, https://www.theguardian.com/science/2015/jul/23/john-horton-conway-the-most-charismatic-mathematician-in-the-world.

24. Their names are often used interchangeably, but note that frameworks are considered to be more "opinionated," so you are required to use it a specific way, working within their code structure. Libraries, however, are more flexible, letting you choose when or how you adopt their functionality.

25. MDN_Webdocs, "Math.Random()—JavaScript | MDN," accessed August 24, 2023, https://developer.mozilla.org/en-US/docs/Web/JavaScript/Reference/Global_Objects/Math/random.

26. MDN_Webdocs, "Math.Random()."

27. JSDevJournal, "Functional Programming with JavaScript: A Deep Dive," HackerNoon, accessed January 18, 2024, https://hackernoon.com/functional-programming-with-javascript-a-deep-dive.

28. See https://github.com/criticalwebdesign/book/tree/main/assets/js/functions.js.

29. Eric Elliott, "What Is Functional Programming?" JavaScript Scene, August 24, 2021, https://medium.com/javascript-scene/master-the-javascript-interview-what-is-functional-programming-7f218c68b3a0.

30. See criticalwebdesign.github.io#8-2-code.

31. See Yotam Mann, NSynth Sound Maker, 2017, accessed May 28, 2025, https://experiments.withgoogle.com/sound-maker.

32. MDN_Webdocs, "<input Type="range">," accessed January 8, 2024, https://developer.mozilla.org/en-US/docs/Web/HTML/Element/input/range.

33. A caveat to **valueAsNumber** is that it will return zero if you don't add a default value to the input. Can I use . . . , "HTMLInputElement API: valueAsNumber," accessed January 26, 2024, https://caniuse.com/mdn-api_htmlinputelement_valueasnumber.

34. MDN_Webdocs, "Logical OR (||)," accessed September 25, 2023, https://developer.mozilla.org/en-US/docs/Web/JavaScript/Reference/Operators/Logical_OR.

Chapter 9

1. David McCandless, Tom Evans, and Paul Barton, "World's Biggest Data Breaches & Hacks," Information is Beautiful, accessed April 23, 2024, https://informationisbeautiful.net/visualizations/worlds-biggest-data-breaches-hacks/.

2. Merriam-Webster, Definition of "Surveillance," accessed February 18, 2024, https://www.merriam-webster.com/dictionary/surveillance.

3. Charter of Fundamental Rights of the European Union, 2000, accessed June 11, 2024, https://www.europarl.europa.eu/charter/pdf/text_en.pdf.

4. Adam Satariano, "What a Gambling App Knows About You," *New York Times*, 2021, https://www.nytimes.com/2021/03/24/technology/gambling-apps-tracking.html.

5. Wolfie Christl, "Digital Profiling in the Online Gambling Industry," 2022, https://crackedlabs.org/en/gambling-data.

6. Owen Mundy wrote about this more than a decade ago in "The Unconscious Performance of Identity: A Review of Johannes P. Osterhoff's 'Google,'" Rhizome.org, August 22, 2012, https://rhizome.org/editorial/2012/aug/22/unconscious-performance-identity-review-johannes-p/.

7. Shoshana Zuboff, *The Age of Surveillance Capitalism: The Fight for a Human Future at the New Frontier of Power* (PublicAffairs, 2019).

8. Todd Feathers and Alfred Ng, "Tech Industry Groups Are Watering Down Attempts at Privacy Regulation, One State at a Time—The Markup," May 26, 2022, https://themarkup.org/privacy/2022/05/26/tech-industry-groups-are-watering-down-attempts-at-privacy-regulation-one-state-at-a-time.

9. Stephen Chapman, "Sky Bet Owner Reports 27% Growth," *Prolific North* (blog), March 2, 2023, https://www.prolificnorth.co.uk/news/sky-bet-owner-reports-27-growth/.

10. Mark Andrejevic, "The Big Data Divide," *International Journal of Communication* 8 (2014): 1673–1689, http://ijoc.org/index.php/ijoc/article/view/2161.

11. Anders Albrechtslund, "Online Social Networking as Participatory Surveillance," *First Monday* 13, no. 1–8 (2008), http://firstmonday.org/ojs/index.php/fm/article/view/2142/1949/.

12. Owen Mundy and Joelle Dietrick, *Tally Saves the Internet*, accessed May 30, 2025, https://tallysavestheinternet.com.

13. MDN_Webdocs, "Navigator—Web APIs," accessed January 9, 2024, https://developer.mozilla.org/en-US/docs/Web/API/Navigator.

14. David Lyon, *Identifying Citizens: ID Cards as Surveillance* (Polity, 2009), 4.

15. Security.org, "The Data Big Tech Companies Have on You," accessed February 8, 2024, https://www.security.org/resources/data-tech-companies-have/.

16. Nick Statt, "Google Will Stop Scanning Your Gmail Messages to Sell Targeted Ads," The Verge, June 23, 2017, https://www.theverge.com/2017/6/23/15862492/google-gmail-advertising-targeting-privacy-cloud-business.

17. Edward Komenda, "Outlook Is Microsoft's New Data Collection Service," Proton, January 5, 2024, https://proton.me/blog/outlook-is-microsofts-new-data-collection-service.

18. Michael Kosinski, David Stillwell, and Thore Graepel, "Private Traits and Attributes Are Predictable from Digital Records of Human Behavior," *Proceedings of the National Academy of Sciences* 110, no. 15 (March 11, 2013): 5802–5805, https://doi.org/10.1073/pnas.1218772110.

19. Mozilla, "Incognito Browser: What It Really Means," accessed February 27, 2024, https://www.mozilla.org/en-US/firefox/browsers/incognito-browser/.

20. Don Marti, Lin Fengyang, Matthew Schwartz, and Fahs Ginny, "Who Shares Your Information with Facebook: Sampling the Surveillance Economy in 2023," Consumer Reports, 2024, https://innovation.consumerreports.org/wp-content/uploads/2024/01/CR_Who-Shares-Your-Information-With-Facebook.pdf.

21. John Gilliom and Torin Monahan, *Supervision: An Introduction to the Surveillance Society* (University of Chicago Press, 2013).

22. Ivan Averintsev, Wolfie Christl, Pascale Osterwalder, and Ralf Traunsteiner, *Data Dealer*, accessed May 31, 2025, https://datadealer.com/play/.

23. Ben Grosser, "Safebook," 2019, https://bengrosser.com/projects/safebook/.

24. Ben Grosser, Facebook Demetricator, 2012–2022, https://bengrosser.com/projects/facebook-demetricator/.

25. Google Ads, "Verticals," accessed April 18, 2024, https://developers.google.com/google-ads/api/data/verticals.

26. "InteractiveAdvertisingBureau/Taxonomies" (2023; repr., IAB Tech Lab, March 29, 2024), https://github.com/InteractiveAdvertisingBureau/Taxonomies.

27. Brian Swichkow, "The Ultimate Retaliation: How I Pranked My Roommate with Eerily Targeted Facebook Ads," Ghost Influence, September 6, 2014, http://mysocialsherpa.com/the-ultimate-retaliation-pranking-my-roommate-with-targeted-facebook-ads/.

28. See "Egypt: Freedom on the Net 2020 Country Report," Freedom House, accessed April 18, 2024, https://freedomhouse.org/country/egypt/freedom-net/2020.

29. Reporters Without Borders, "Index," September 29, 2023, https://rsf.org/en/index.

30. Dr. B. J. Fogg, "Fogg Behavior Model," https://behaviormodel.org/.

31. Kylie Jarrett, "A Database of Intention?" In *Society of the Query Reader: Reflections on Web Search*, edited by René König and Miriam Rasch, INC Reader #9 (Institute of Network Cultures, 2014), accessed June 11, 2024, https://networkcultures.org/query/reader/articles-for-download-society-of-the-query-reader/.

32. Ed Liguori, "What Is Tracker Map," Crownpeak, accessed June 11, 2024, https://community.crownpeak.com/t5/Tag-Auditor-and-Trackermap/What-is-Trackermap/ta-p/690.

33. Sang Mun, *ZXX*, Walker, "Making Democracy Legible: A Defiant Typeface," June 10, 2013, https://walkerart.org/magazine/sang-mun-defiant-typeface-nsa-privacy.

34. Dojo, "The Most Hacked Passwords List 2023," accessed May 28, 2024, https://dojo.tech/card-machine/most-hacked-passwords-study/.

35. "Working with Objects," MDN_Webdocs, September 25, 2023, https://developer.mozilla.org/en-US/docs/Web/JavaScript/Guide/Working_with_objects.

36. View these examples at http://criticalwebdesign.github.io#data-examples.

37. See http://csvjson.com/csv2json.

38. Tableau, "Guide to Data Cleaning: Definition, Benefits, Components, and How to Clean Your Data," accessed March 18, 2024, https://www.tableau.com/learn/articles/what-is-data-cleaning.

39. See https://github.com/public-apis/public-apis.

40. Tim Schwartz, "Paris," 2007, https://www.timschwartz.org/paris/.

41. Google.com, "How Google Uses Cookies," Privacies and Terms, accessed April 24, 2023, https://policies.google.com/technologies/cookies?hl=en-US.

42. "Stack Overflow Developer Survey 2024," Stack Overflow, accessed May 29, 2025, https://survey.stackoverflow.co/2024/technology#2-programming-scripting-and-markup-languages.

43. Nordpass, "Most Common Passwords List," accessed September 19, 2025, https://nordpass.com/most-common-passwords-list/.

44. Kevin Slavin, "How Algorithms Shape Our World," accessed March 20, 2024, https://www.ted.com/talks/kevin_slavin_how_algorithms_shape_our_world.

45. Cloudflare, "What Is a Content Delivery Network (CDN)?" accessed March 20, 2024, https://www.cloudflare.com/learning/cdn/what-is-a-cdn/.

46. MDN_Webdocs, "Promise," accessed November 29, 2023, https://developer.mozilla.org/en-US/docs/Web/JavaScript/Reference/Global_Objects/Promise.

47. See Lena V. Groeger, "If It Needs a Sign, It's Probably Bad Design More Words Won't Solve Your Design Problem," ProPublica, September 21, 2016, https://www.propublica.org/article/if-it-needs-a-sign-its-probably-bad-design.

Chapter 10

1. Wilneida Negrón, "10 Tech Issues That Will Impact Social Justice in 2017," *Ford Foundation*, 2017, 1–5. https://www.fordfoundation.org/ideas/equals-change-blog/posts/10-tech-issues-that-will-impact-social-justice-in-2017/.

2. Seth Flaxman, Sharad Goel, and Justin M. Rao, "Filter Bubbles, Echo Chambers, and Online News Consumption," *Public Opinion Quarterly* 80, no. S1 (2016): 298–320. https://doi.org/10.1093/poq/nfw006.

3. George Aye, "Design Education's Big Gap: Understanding the Role of Power," *Medium*, 2017, 1–13. https://medium.com/greater-good-studio/design-educations-big-gap-understanding-the-role-of-power-1ee1756b7f08.

4. Nathan Shedroff, *Design Is the Problem: The Future of Design Must Be Sustainable* (Rosenfeld Media, 2009), xxxv.

5. Rob Larson, *Bit Tyrants: The Political Economy of Silicon Valley* (Haymarket Books, 2020), https://www.haymarketbooks.org/books/1447-bit-tyrants.

6. See http://www.tacticaltech.org and their project, datadetoxkit.org, accessed May 30, 2025.

7. See http://www.gamesforchange.org, accessed May 30, 2025.

8. See http://www.themarkup.org/series/blacklight, accessed May 30, 2025.

9. See http://www.lowtechmagazine.com, accessed May 30, 2025.

10. Decker, Kris De, Marie Otsuka, and Roel Roscam Abbing, "How to Build a Low-Tech Website?" LOW←TECH MAGAZINE, September 24, 2018, https://solar.lowtechmagazine.com/2018/09/how-to-build-a-low-tech-website/.

11. Liz Stinson, "Calm Technology Is Staging a Comeback—Can Good Design Make It Stick?" Eye on Design, February 10, 2020, https://eyeondesign.aiga.org/calm-technology-is-staging-a-comeback-can-good-design-make-it-stick/.

12. Kyle Chayka, "Why the Internet Isn't Fun Anymore," *The New Yorker*, October 9, 2023, https://www.newyorker.com/culture/infinite-scroll/why-the-internet-isnt-fun-anymore.

13. Rudolf Frieling, "Introduction," *The Art of Participation 1950 to Now*, edited by Rudolf Frieling, Boris Groys, Robert Atkins, and Lev Manovich (SF Moma, Thames & Hudson, 1998), 12.

14. Frieling, "Introduction," 12.

15. Art 21, "Interview: Defining an Artist: Tania Bruguera," accessed May 31, 2025, https://art21.org/read/tania-bruguera-defining-an-artist/.

16. Pablo Helguera, *Education for Socially Engaged Art: A Materials and Techniques Handbook* (Jorge Pinto Books, 2011), 2.

17. GreatFire.org; for instance, search the *New York Times* website in the search bar at the top of the page.

18. See https://en.greatfire.org/analyzer, accessed May 30, 2025.

19. See https://www.toxicsites.us, accessed May 30, 2025.

20. See https://tosdr.org, accessed May 30, 2025.

21. Pip Shea, accessed June 11, 2024, https://dev.themaninblue.com/anycast/.

22. Alex Fuller, *On a Mountain Top*, accessed May 30, 2025, https://www.alexfuller.com/On-a-Mountain-Top.

23. Dries Depoorter and David Suprenant, *Die with Me*, accessed May 30, 2025, https://diewithme.online/.

24. Aram Bartoll, *Speed Show*, accessed June 11, 2024, http://speedshow.net/.

25. Miranda July et al., *Somebody*, accessed June 11, 2024, https://somebodyapp.com/.

26. *The Nicest Place*, accessed June 11, 2024, https://thenicestplace.net/.

27. Jonathan Harris and Sepandar Kamvar, *We Feel Fine*, accessed May 30, 2025, http://wefeelfine.org.

28. Sep Kamvar and Jonathan Harris, *We Feel Fine: An Almanac of Human Emotion* (Scribner, 2009), 151.

29. Kamvar and Harris, *We Feel Fine*, 151.

30. Designlab. "Figma 101: Design an App Screen," accessed May 1, 2024, https://designlab.com/figma-101-course/design-an-app-screen.

31. Harrell Fletcher, "Introduction" in Section II Windows and Mirrors, xtine burrough and Judy Walgren, editors, *Art as Social Practice: Technologies for Change* (Routledge), 75–77.

32. "Zoom Levels," Leaflet, accessed April 28, 2024, https://leafletjs.com/examples/zoom-levels/.

33. Aaron Sankin and Leon Yin, "Slow Internet? Find Out What Side of the Digital Divide You're On," The Markup, May 11, 2023, https://themarkup.org/build-your-own-dataset/2023/05/11/slow-internet-find-out-what-side-of-the-digital-divide-youre-on.

34. See https://fakerjs.dev/.

35. MongoDB, "Relational Vs. Non-Relational Databases," accessed April 26, 2024, https://www.mongodb.com/resources/compare/relational-vs-non-relational-databases.

36. See https://leafletjs.com/reference.html#popup.

Chapter 11

1. At the time of writing, this series is here: https://www.youtube.com/channel/UCvjgXvBlbQiydffZU7m1_aw.

2. AIGA, "Business and Freelance Resources," accessed April 16, 2024, https://www.aiga.org/resources/business-freelance-resources.

3. David Ng, "Shepard Fairey Admits to Wrongdoing in Associated Press Lawsuit," *Los Angeles Times*, October 16, 2009, https://www.latimes.com/archives/blogs/culture-monster-blog/story/2009-10-16/shepard-fairey-admits-to-wrongdoing-in-associated-press-lawsuit.

Index

Publisher contact:
The MIT Press
Massachusetts Institute of Technology
77 Massachusetts Avenue, Cambridge, MA 02139
mitpress.mit.edu

EU Authorised Representative:
Easy Access System Europe, Mustamäe tee 50,
10621 Tallinn, Estonia
gpsr.requests@easproject.com

Printed by Integrated Books International,
United States of America